HISTORY AND HUMANITIES

Wilbur S. Shepperson

HISTORY AND HUMANITIES

ESSAYS IN HONOR OF
WILBUR S. SHEPPERSON

EDITED BY FRANCIS X. HARTIGAN

UNIVERSITY OF NEVADA PRESS
RENO AND LAS VEGAS

Publication of this book was made possible by a generous grant from
the University of Nevada-Reno Foundation.

The paper used in this book meets the
requirements of American National Standard
for Information Sciences—Permanence of
Paper for Printed Library Materials, ANSI
z39.48-1984. Binding materials were chosen
for strength and durability.

Library of Congress Cataloging-in-Publication Data

History and humanities: essays in honor of Wilbur S. Shepperson /
   edited by Francis X. Hartigan.
     p.   cm.
   "Publications by Wilbur S. Shepperson": p.
   ISBN 0-87417-148-2 (alk. paper)
   1. Nevada   History.   2. West (U.S.)   History   3 Europe—History
4. Humanities.   5. Shepperson, Wilbur S. (Wilbur Stanley)
I. Shepperson, Wilbur S. (Wilbur Stanley)   II. Hartigan, Francis X.
F841.5.H57 1989
978—dc19   88-30724
                                                         CIP

University of Nevada Press, Reno, Nevada 89557 USA
Copyright © 1989 University of Nevada Press
All rights reserved
Designed by Dave Comstock
Printed in the United States of America
Frontispiece photo by John Running

CONTENTS

FOREWORD

A _festschrift_—a written celebration—is a customary practice when scholars wish to honor one of their number. Yet few scholars earn the wealth of respect from their colleagues to warrant a _festschrift_. _History and Humanities_ honors a scholar who has won the respect and admiration of his colleagues by the breadth and depth of his interests. Wilbur S. Shepperson is the most significant historical scholar in the state of Nevada and the most significant historian to emerge from the University of Nevada, Reno, since its inception in 1874.

Shepperson has served his discipline in this state since 1951 when he arrived here as an assistant professor after receiving his Doctor of Philosophy degree in history from Western Reserve University. From the beginning Shepperson dedicated himself to his profession and its enhancement. He concentrated his scholarship on immigration, especially from Britain to the United States, and his first book was _British Emigration to North America_, which Basil Blackwell published in Oxford in 1957. Pursuit of his interest in immigration history has made him an expert in the history of Europe, America, and Nevada. Beginning with doctoral studies in British history, Shepperson's immigration studies brought him into intimate contact with American history and eventually with Nevada history. In his long career at UNR he has taught in each of these three fields, but the majority of his teaching effort has gone into British and European history. Shepperson's excellent scholarship is recognized by the outstanding presses which have published his books and articles and by the many scholars who have used his work. He has won recognition in other ways as well; for example, he was awarded a Fulbright Fellowship to teach at the University of Liverpool. In addition to many prizes and awards Shepperson's scholarship received its greatest recognition when he was awarded in 1987 the department of history's first endowed chair, the Grace A. Griffen Chair in History.

In addition to scholarship Shepperson has distinguished himself by his service to the profession. He has been active in professional associations such as the Organization of American Historians' committee for the promotion of history. He has been chairman and member of the board of trustees of the Nevada Historical Society, and he has taken a major role in the development of the *Nevada Historical Society Quarterly*. Shepperson was responsible for the establishment of a southern Nevada office of the historical society in 1976. He is active in Phi Alpha Theta, the national honorary history society, and has served on the advisory board of that organization's journal, *The Historian*. He promoted historical studies at the University of Nevada Press, especially the Nevada Studies in History and Political Science series. He has served as chairman of the history department for more than half his time at UNR.

His service to the profession of history has brought him into the wider area of the humanities. Through the University of Nevada Press and the Nevada Historical Society Shepperson has helped develop and strengthen humanities in Nevada. His achievements led him to be named by the governor to the Nevada Humanities Committee. This state-based committee, under the National Endowment for the Humanities, was begun under his leadership, and he has served it often as chairman and as a member since its inception. Few institutions have done more to foster humanities in Nevada than the Nevada Humanities Committee, and much of its success is attributable to Wilbur Shepperson. It was his recommendation and his hard work that led to the creation of *Halcyon: A Journal of the Humanities*, which has provided for the dissemination of ideas about the humanities since 1978.

Outstanding scholarship, advancement of history and the humanities, and successful management of humanistic programs are among the reasons why his colleagues have come together to honor Wilbur Shepperson. In doing so we have attempted to do justice to the diversity of his achievements by offering to him our work in the history of Nevada and the West, European history, and the humanities. But even this diverse offering fails to equal the great range of Shepperson's work. As is the case in his own historical work, an immigration strand runs through the historical sections: exploring a new environment, violence among immigrant groups, a pioneering Chinese woman, town making, sense of place, British imperialism in Africa. The other contributions treat Nevada and the humanities: Nevada and the atomic age, a gambling lexicon, images of medicine, literary analysis, toleration, and the university ideal.

We scholars from across the state offer these articles to one who has aided our careers by his example and his support. Behind the historian and humanist there is the man himself: a master of "getting things done," a man who encourages, guides, and helps his colleagues, a man who is impatient with petty bureaucratic trifling, a man who believes that a sense of humor is one of life's necessities, and, above all, a man who has earned more from his colleagues than respect because he has won their esteem. On the occasion of his seventieth birthday we wish to say thank you and to express our admiration for the man we affectionately call "Shep."

Francis X. Hartigan

ACKNOWLEDGMENTS

Any undertaking of this size is necessarily the work of many people and it is not possible to thank each by name. I want nevertheless to express my personal gratitude to everyone who assisted me in ways great and in ways small, for without such assistance this *festschrift* would not be possible.

Thanks are due to my colleagues in the history department at the University of Nevada, Reno, and to its secretary, Margaret Supencheck, who conspired with me to keep knowledge of this project away from the honoree. I want to thank especially Michael J. Brodhead, Jerome E. Edwards, John G. Folkes, Martha L. Hildreth, Jim Hulse, and Elizabeth Raymond. Elizabeth gave additional assistance in the difficult task of keeping this project a secret by providing selections from her collection of World War II security posters. One poster always on duty in the history department reminded conspirators that "a slip of the lip can sink a ship." Other UNR colleagues whose assistance is appreciated are Phillip C. Boardman, Robert E. Diamond, and Ann Ronald.

Special thanks goes to Judith Winzeler, executive director of the Nevada Humanities Committee, who, as an original conspirator, provided advice and encouragement from the beginning. Peter L. Bandurraga, director of the Nevada Historical Society, provided useful information and encouragement.

Our colleagues at the University of Nevada, Las Vegas, were especially helpful. The contributing authors from UNLV were always more prompt in meeting deadlines than their northern counterparts. If power is as power is perceived, then perhaps the editor seemed more powerful from the distance of several hundred miles than on his own campus. Perhaps, though, the diligent work of Joseph A. Fry, historian and associate dean, College of Arts and Letters, explains the success the editor enjoyed with UNLV contributors. Andy's help in the early stages of the project was particularly important, and he kept the secret. The support of Tom Wright, dean of the College of Arts and Letters, and John Unrue, vice-president for academic affairs, gave additional strength to the editor.

The administration at UNR also helped keep the secret. Paul Page and William P. Wallace, deans of the College of Arts and Science, thought that a *festschrift* for Wilbur Shepperson was an excellent idea. The university president, Joseph N. Crowley, deserves special thanks because of his moral and financial support for the project. His assistance allowed an idea to become a reality.

The staff at the University of Nevada Press has cooperated with the project from the beginning. It too kept the secret despite the fact that Shep is on the press board. Among those deserving special mention are Cameron Sutherland for her production assistance, Nicholas Cady for his kindly insistence that the editor get the job done, and John Stetter, the former director of the press, for his encouragement and healthy skepticism that we could keep this project secret. Thanks to him and many others, we have.

NEVADA
AND THE WEST

CONTRIBUTIONS OF MEDICAL OFFICERS OF THE REGULAR ARMY TO NATURAL HISTORY IN THE PRE–CIVIL WAR ERA

MICHAEL J. BRODHEAD

In 1942 there appeared a work entitled *Ornithologists of the United States Army Medical Corps* by Edgar Erskine Hume.[1] It is a useful, indeed essential work for anyone studying the history of natural science in America. Yet it has created a false impression wholly unintended by its author: several historians, having consulted it, concluded that within the nineteenth-century army the pursuit of natural history was confined largely to medical officers and that they concentrated primarily on the study of birds.

Actually, however, personnel representing all branches and ranks of the army contributed mightily to the expansion of knowledge of North American flora and fauna throughout the past century. The tradition of the American military naturalist began with those astute observers of nature, Capt. Meriwether Lewis of the First Infantry and Lt. William Clark of the Regiment of Artillerists.[2] The present writer has identified nearly two hundred other "naturalists in blue." Their scientific endeavors ranged from casual observation and collecting of plants and animals to more sophisticated efforts. Not a few of them published major scientific articles and books.[3]

Although medical officers by no means monopolized these activities, army surgeons, especially considering their relatively small numbers, played a conspicuous part. Given the scientific nature of their calling and the long hours of leisure often available to them, this is not surprising. Nor is it surprising that Donald

Jackson's novel of early nineteenth-century western exploration has an army surgeon–naturalist, Rafael Bailey, as its main character.[4] We will examine the period from 1820 to 1860, and note some of the more significant army surgeon–naturalists and their accomplishments.

Like most other army naturalists, the surgeons usually did their scientific work in frontier areas. After the Lewis and Clark expedition, the next army explorations to make noteworthy contributions to natural history were those of Bvt. Maj. Stephen H. Long of the Topographical Engineers. The scientists who accompanied him to the Rocky Mountains in 1819 and 1820 were civilians, among them Dr. Edwin James. James, the expedition's botanist and geologist, wrote the most valuable report on the journey. Subsequently he was appointed assistant surgeon in the army. Shortly after receiving his commission he was assigned as surgeon, botanist, and geologist to Long's expedition to the St. Peter's River in 1823, but he missed the Long party at the designated meeting place. Throughout his military career (1823–1833) and later, James wrote scientific articles, chiefly on Indians and geology.[5]

Indisputably, the towering figure in American botany in the first half of the nineteenth century was John Torrey. An often overlooked fact was that he served as an assistant surgeon in the regular army from 1824 to 1828. During this time he was acting professor of chemistry, mineralogy, and geology at the United States Military Academy. While at West Point he published articles in the *American Journal of Science and Arts* and the *Annals of the Lyceum of Natural History of New York;* among them were notices of the botanical results of the Long expeditions and the Cass expedition to the Great Lakes (1820). After leaving the army he enlarged his already considerable reputation by preparing (sometimes in collaboration with his protégé, Asa Gray) the botanical reports for the military exploring expeditions of the 1840s and 1850s, such as those of John C. Frémont, William H. Emory, Lorenzo Sitgreaves, Randolph B. Marcy, Joseph C. Ives, and the Pacific railroad survey parties.[6]

After Torrey, the next army surgeon to achieve recognition in natural history was Melines Conkling Leavenworth. He received his medical education at Yale, graduating in 1817.[7] Prior to his appointment to the regular service he was a civilian (contract) surgeon for the army from 1831 to 1833. In this capacity he collected plants in Alabama, publishing some of his results in the *American Journal of Science and Arts*.[8] Following the receipt of his commission as an assistant surgeon in 1833 he continued botanizing in the southern states and territories, including Florida, Louisiana, Texas, Georgia, Tennessee, and what is now Oklahoma.[9]

He regularly sent his dried specimens, along with "copious notes," to Torrey, who named a genus of cruciferous plants (*Leavenworthia*) for him. The notes, said an obituary writer, were of more use than the specimens, because the latter "were seldom neatly preserved." The same writer observed that "the pages of [Torrey's] *Flora of North America*, upon which [Leavenworth's] name so often occurs, testify to his zeal and success as a botanical explorer and pioneer."[10]

He resigned his commission in 1840. Torrey's suggestion that Leavenworth be employed as surgeon and naturalist for Frémont's expedition of 1843–1844 was never acted upon.[11] He saw military service again, in the Civil War, as an assistant surgeon with the Twelfth Connecticut Infantry: "no sooner had he landed with his regiment on the southern coast than he zealously began to collect the plants he met with, and note their peculiarities." He died near New Orleans in 1862.[12]

Leavenworth's pioneering efforts in natural science in the Old Southwest were matched in the Old Northwest by Zina Pitcher, who became an assistant surgeon in the army immediately after graduating from Middlebury College, Vermont, in 1822.[13] While stationed at Fort Brady, in Michigan's Upper Peninsula, he collected numerous "reptiles and other zoological objects" and, in 1829, presented them to the Lyceum of Natural History of New York, of which he was a corresponding member.[14] Later that year, from Fort Gratiot, Michigan, he sent to the lyceum "a valuable collection of mammals" which included a badger, plains pocket gopher, meadow jumping mouse, and, "for the first time found within the limits of the United States," a northern flying squirrel.[15]

From 1831 to 1834 Pitcher was stationed at Fort Gibson, Indian Territory. In this vicinity, and perhaps as far south as the Red River, he collected extensively, mostly fossils and plants. He sent several of the latter to Torrey, who honored Pitcher in the naming of species believed to be new to science; for example, *Falcata pitcheri*, Pitcher's hog peanut.[16]

Pitcher attained the rank of major and surgeon in 1832, became president of the Army Medical Board in 1835, and resigned from the service the next year. He returned to the army briefly in 1839 but soon resumed his practice in Detroit. Pitcher played a major role in establishing the medical department of the University of Michigan and was a regent of the university for many years.[17]

The appointment of Spencer F. Baird as assistant secretary of the recently established Smithsonian Institution in 1850 ushered in a golden age for the military naturalist. Baird (a protégé of Audubon's and the son-in-law of the army's inspector general) was enormously successful in using the army to swell the Smithsonian's natural history collections. The most conspicuous example of War Department–Smithsonian cooperation in the antebellum period came with the expeditions to survey routes for a transcontinental railroad. Baird persuaded the army to attach naturalists to the various Pacific railroad survey parties that traversed the Trans-Mississippi West in the 1850s. Almost all of them were civilians and many were contract surgeons.[18]

An important exception to the civilian status of the naturalists of the railroad surveys was George Suckley.[19] In 1853, two years after graduating from the College of Physicians and Surgeons, Suckley was attached to the northernmost of the surveys, which was under the command of Isaac Ingalls Stevens. In June, Suckley (in the capacity of contract surgeon and naturalist to the main party) set out with Stevens and others from St. Paul. En route, Stevens divided his party into smaller units to explore specific areas in detail. One party, consisting of Suckley and three others, canoed from Bitterroot Valley to Fort Vancouver, Washington Territory. During his travels Suckley was commissioned an assistant surgeon in the regular army.

By the end of his journey, Suckley had amassed what Stevens described as "very handsome" collections in natural history.[20] Suckley collaborated with James Graham Cooper, a contract surgeon, in compiling the natural history reports of the Stevens explorations. They appear in volume 12 of the Pacific railroad surveys' *Reports*.[21] The portions written principally or wholly by Suckley were those on mammals, geology, water birds, and fishes. Volume 1 included his medical report and his account of the canoe trip.[22]

Upon completion of his duties with the survey, Suckley was assigned to Fort Dalles, Oregon Territory. While attached to an expedition to eastern Oregon against the Snake Indians he collected specimens along the way. From July to December 1855, he was on leave of absence in the East. At Philadelphia he spent many pleasant and rewarding hours with John Cassin, Joseph Leidy, John L. Le Conte, and other luminaries of the prestigious Academy of Natural Sciences, of which he was a corresponding member. He also made good use of the academy's library. From Philadelphia he traveled to Washington, where he visited Baird at the Smithsonian.[23]

Suckley arrived at his new duty station, Fort Steilacoom, Washington Territory, in January 1856. There he remained and collected specimens until his resignation from the army in October. Soon thereafter there appeared in a medical journal his "Report on the Fauna and Medical Topography of Washington Territory."[24]

The Civil War brought Suckley back into uniform. He attained the position of medical director of the Department of Virginia and the brevet rank of colonel. At the end of the war he resigned and in 1869 he died in New York City. Hume has noted that "Suckley has been more or less overlooked by American ornithological historians . . . though references to him are numerous in the writings of ornithologists of his day."[25]

Noteworthy as the achievements in natural history of the Pacific railroad surveys were, at least equally noteworthy were the collections made in the same period by surgeons, other officers, and enlisted men stationed at America's scattered army posts, particularly in the West. Being a part-time field naturalist was a marvelous way to relieve the tedium of frontier garrison life, as well as a cheaper and healthier means than whiskey for chasing away boredom. Some of these individual collecting activities are noted in volumes of the railroad surveys' *Reports*. But they are more fully apparent in the "List of Donations" found in the annual reports of the Smithsonian in the 1850s. Although the donations came from all corners of the nation and from other countries, and from civilians as well as military personnel, the officers and men of the regular army, most of whom were stationed in the West, were especially well situated for gathering and sending plants and animals to the Smithsonian. The names of soldiers on these lists are conspicuous and their donations are conspicuous for their size and importance. Since the possibilities were great for acquiring species new to science in the relatively virgin lands beyond the Mississippi, packages received from the western posts were doubly welcome at the Smithsonian.

One of the most able of the surgeon-naturalists in Baird's network was Thomas Charlton Henry, a graduate of Philadelphia's Jefferson Medical College.[26] From 1851 to 1853 he worked as a contract surgeon while awaiting a commission as an assistant surgeon, serving chiefly at Forts Fillmore and Webster, New Mexico. Upon obtaining the appointment in the regulars, he was transferred to Fort Thorn, New Mexico. The *Philadelphia Inquirer* printed a letter from Henry telling of his journey to the Southwest. The editorial introduction described him as "a member of the Academy of Natural Sciences of this city, and an enthusiastic naturalist." Henry's letter told of his being bitten by a not-quite-dead rattlesnake and of working long into the night preparing skins of birds ("new, many of them") shot en route. In another newspaper piece Henry discussed the game animals of New Mexico, including the grizzly bear, whose reputation for ferocity, he believed, was quite undeserved.[27]

From 1853 until 1857 Henry was stationed at various New Mexico forts. His most significant service to science while there was largely in the field of ornithology. Capt. John Pope of the Topographical Engineers acquired "the very extensive series of birds gathered by Dr. T. C. Henry" and added them to his own southwestern collection, which was soon deposited with Baird, who used it extensively in the ornithological volume of the Pacific railroad surveys' *Reports*.[28] In the later 1850s three ornithological articles by Henry appeared in the *Proceedings* of the Academy of Natural Sciences of Philadelphia.[29] One of them contained a description of a bird new to science, the crissal thrasher, discovered by Henry at Fort Thorn.

Henry also supplied written descriptions of other southwestern avifauna which were quoted in his friend John Cassin's work, *Illustrations of the Birds of California, Texas, Oregon, British and Russian America* (1856). Cassin praised Henry as "a zealous and talented young naturalist" and named what is now a subspecies of the common nighthawk (*Chordeiles minor henryi*) in recognition of Henry's "exertion in the investigation of the natural productions of New Mexico . . . and the formation of large collections in various departments, which attest to his zeal and attachment to zoölogical science."[30]

Sickness forced Henry to leave the army in 1859. His health did not deter him from serving as a surgeon of volunteers during the Civil War. A sunstroke suffered during the war hastened his death, which came in 1877. A year later Elliott Coues lauded this "zealous naturalist, whose untimely recall from this world's duties cut short a career which opened in full promise of usefulness and honor."[31]

Another graduate of Jefferson Medical College was a New Yorker, Edward Perry Vollum.[32] He would likewise make his mark as a naturalist in the army. Vollum served as post surgeon at Fort Belknap, Texas, from where in 1856 he sent plants to the Smithsonian. After a tour of duty at Fort Hamilton, New York, he was sent west again, this time to Fort Umpqua, Oregon, where he dispatched to Baird "fishes and other animals, and specimens of the 'rock oyster'" and a "box of zoological specimens in alcohol, skins of animals, and birds' eggs."[33] He spent the remainder of the decade at the post at Alcatraz Island and Fort Crook, California. In the Smithsonian's report for 1860, Baird wrote that Vollum's specimens, along with those from other military men stationed on the West Coast, had "proved of scientific interest in determining the geographical distribution and variation of the species of California animals, many of the facts elicited being quite unexpected."[34] In the pages of the same report there appeared Vollum's "Notes on the Wingless Grasshoppers of Shasta and Fall River Valleys, California."[35]

With the outbreak of the Civil War Vollum was transferred to the East. In 1863 he became medical inspector of the Army of the Potomac. By 1866 he was in Galveston, Texas. Although his postwar correspondence with Baird discussed collecting possibilities in Texas, his days as an active field naturalist seem to have been over. Colonel Vollum became the army's chief medical purveyor in 1890.

Another surgeon who added to the literature of natural history in the pre–Civil War era was John Frazier Head, a native of Massachusetts.[36] His army career began during the Mexican

War, but in Minnesota rather than the scene of the conflict. His collections and observations at Fort Ripley resulted in an article for the Smithsonian's report for 1854, "Some Remarks on the Natural History of the Country about Fort Ripley, Minnesota."[37] During the next several years, Head saw duty in many parts of the nation, including West Point, where he was the military academy's chief medical officer during the Civil War. Later, in 1878, there appeared his only other known published contribution to natural history, a brief note on the breeding habits of the American woodcock.[38] He retired from the army in 1885 with the rank of colonel.

Head's report on the natural history of the Fort Ripley vicinity was actually extracted from an 1856 publication of the Surgeon General's Office, a volume entitled *Statistical Report on Sickness and Mortality in the Army.*[39] In gathering the material for the volume, Surgeon General Thomas Lawson had issued a circular to the medical officers requesting information on each fort's or camp's "medical topography," a term which embraced descriptions of the "geographical position of the post, the physical aspect of the surrounding country; the geological formations; its flora [and] fauna (the animals, trees, and plants belonging to it)."[40]

Regarding the flora and fauna found in the vicinity of their posts, many of the reporting surgeons spoke in general terms of "hawks," "sparrows," "rabbits," "salmon," and "oak trees." But several others displayed a wide knowledge of natural science, often employing the Latin binomials and precise common names of the plants and animals they recorded. This more sophisticated group included, among others, the following assistant surgeons: Joseph K. Barnes (later surgeon general, 1864–1882), reporting from Forts Scott and Riley, Kansas; Jonathan Letterman, Fort Meade, Florida; Rodney Glisan (author of *Journal of Army Life*), Fort Arbuckle, Indian Territory; and John Fox Hammond, Post at Socorro, New Mexico, and Fort Reading, California. Especially full botanical lists are found in the reports of Drs. S. Wylie Crawford, Fort McKavett, Texas, and William S. King, Post of Monterey, California.[41] Indeed, most of the above-mentioned surgeons showed more awareness of trees, shrubs, flowers, and grasses than of the fauna—a fact that is not surprising given the close relationship between botany and materia medica.

In 1860 the surgeon general published another *Statistical Report*.[42] The 1860 work is less rich in natural history, but a few of the surgeons reporting therein are entitled to be added to the roll of military naturalists. Among them is John Moore, whose report from Camp Scott, in present-day Wyoming, contains speculation on the disappearance of the buffalo in that area, which, wrote Moore, was occurring prior to the coming of the white man.[43] Surgeon Roberts Bartholow, reporting from Utah Territory, concluded that the most remarkable animal in those parts was *homo sapiens* and then offered his professional views on the practice of polygamy.[44] Another contributor to the 1860 volume, Bernard John Dowling Irwin, deserves mention, not only for his full commentary on the plant and animal life of Fort Buchanan, New Mexico (now Arizona), but also for the fact that he was then training a young enlisted man in the arts of collecting, identifying, and preparing specimens. The soldier, Charles E. Bendire, became a commanding figure in ornithology later in the century.[45]

Of course several of those contributing to the statistical reports of 1856 and 1860 were adding to the Bairdian horde of specimens in Washington. So too was Assistant Surgeon William A. Hammond, of Fort Riley.[46] Hammond (later surgeon general, 1862–1864) was performing an even greater service to science by teaching an enlisted man how to collect and prepare faunal specimens. Pvt. (later Hospital Steward) John (János) Xántus developed into an accomplished field naturalist, and in 1856 was elected a life member of the Academy of Natural Sciences of Philadelphia. After returning to his native Hungary, he became director of the Zoological Gardens of Budapest and later administered the ethnographic division of the National Museum.[47] In 1858 Xántus named a new bird after his mentor. Hammond's flycatcher (*Empidonax hammondii*) is but one of several examples of the honoring of army medical men in biological nomenclature. Yet such commemorating does not give full recognition to this intrepid band who did so much to enlarge botanical and zoological knowledge in the years before the Civil War.

The war suspended nearly all natural history activity by surgeons and other military men. Afterward, a new generation of military naturalists renewed this work. The postwar group also contained several medical officers. Indeed, surgeons Elliott

Coues, Edgar A. Mearns, Robert W. Shufeldt, and Valery Havard were not only among the most distinguished army scientists of the time but major figures in American natural history in the later nineteenth century.

NOTES

Note: This essay was originally delivered as a paper at the annual meeting of the American Military Institute, held at Bethesda, Maryland, April 5, 1986.

1. Edgar Erskine Hume, *Ornithologists of the United States Army Medical Corps* (Baltimore: Johns Hopkins University Press, 1942).

2. Paul Russell Cutright, *Lewis and Clark: Pioneering Naturalists* (Urbana: University of Illinois Press, 1969); William H. Goetzmann, *Army Exploration in the American West, 1803–1863* (New Haven: Yale University Press, 1959).

3. Michael J. Brodhead, "The Military Naturalist: A Lewis and Clark Heritage," *We Proceeded On* 9 (November 1983): 6–10.

4. Donald Jackson, *Valley Men: A Speculative Account of the Arkansas Expedition of 1807* (New Haven and New York: Ticknor and Fields, 1983).

5. Max Meisel, *A Bibliography of American Natural History: The Pioneer Century, 1769–1865*, 3 vols. (Brooklyn: Premier Publishing Co., 1926), vol. 2, 420, vol. 3, 604; Edwin James, comp., *An Account of an Expedition from Pittsburgh to the Rocky Mountains, under the Command of Major Stephen H. Long, from the notes of Major Long, Mr. T. Say, and other Gentlemen of the Exploring Party* (Barre, Mass.: Imprint Society, 1972), xxxiv.

6. The fullest account of Torrey's life is Andrew Denny Rodgers, *John Torrey: A Story of North American Botany* (Princeton, N.J.: Princeton University Press, 1942).

7. Rogers McVaugh, "The Travels and Botanical Collections of Dr. Melines Conkling Leavenworth," *Field and Laboratory* 15 (1947): 57–70; Francis B. Heitman, *Historical Register and Dictionary of the United States Army, from Its Organization, September 29, 1789, to March 2, 1903*, 2 vols. (Washington, D.C.: U.S. Government Printing Office, 1903), vol. 1, 622.

8. Melines Conkling Leavenworth, "Notices of Four New Species Collected in Alabama," *American Journal of Science and Arts* 7 (November 1823): 61–63; idem, "List of the Rarer Plants Found in Alabama," ibid. 9 (January 1825): 74.

9. Leavenworth, "Description and History of a New Plant, *Tullia pycnanthemoides*," *American Journal of Science and Arts* 20 (July 1831): 343–47; Eli Ives, William Tully, and Leavenworth, "Catalogue of the Phaenogamous Plants and the Ferns, Found within Five Miles of Yale College," in Ebenezer Baldwin, *Annals of Yale College* (New Haven, Conn.: H. Howe, 1831), 264–302; Leavenworth, "On Several New Plants," *American Journal of Science and Arts* 49 (July 1845): 126–31; Susan Delano

McKelvey, *Botanical Exploration of the Trans-Mississippi West, 1790–1850* (Jamaica Plain, Mass.: Arnold Arboretum of Harvard University, 1955), 386, 559–63, 584, 1057.

10. *American Journal of Science and Arts,* 2d ser. 35 (May 1863): 451.

11. Donald Jackson and Mary Lee Spence, eds., *The Expeditions of John Charles Frémont,* 3 vols. (Urbana: University of Illinois Press, 1970–1984), vol. 1, 130, 131n; McKelvey, *Botanical Exploration,* 767.

12. *American Journal of Science and Arts,* 2d ser. 35 (March 1863): 306; ibid. (May 1863): 451.

13. *Appleton's Cyclopaedia of American Biography,* vol. 5, 31; Heitman, *Historical Register,* vol. 1, 794; McKelvey, *Botanical Exploration,* 443–48.

14. *American Journal of Science and Arts* 16 (1829): 356.

15. Ibid. 18 (1830): 194.

16. McKelvey, *Botanical Exploration,* 282, 386, 443–47.

17. Ibid., 443.

18. William Healey Dall, *Spencer Fullerton Baird: A Biography* (Philadelphia: J. B. Lippincott, 1915), 209–10; William A. Deiss, "Spencer F. Baird and His Collectors," *Journal of the Society for the Bibliography of Natural History* 9 (April 1980): 635–45.

19. The fullest account of Suckley's life is in Hume, *Ornithologists of the U.S. Army Medical Corps,* chap. 28.

20. *Reports on Explorations and Surveys, to Ascertain the Most Practicable and Economical Routes for a Railroad to the Pacific Ocean,* 12 vols. (Washington, D.C.: Beverly Tucker, 1859), vol. 12, part 1, 36. Hereafter the volumes in this series will be cited as *Reports.*

21. Ibid., parts 2 and 3. A commercial edition of the Cooper-Suckley report was entitled *The Natural History of Washington Territory* (New York: Baillière Bros., 1859).

22. *Reports,* vol. 1, 177–79, 291–301.

23. Dall, *Baird,* 328; *Proceedings of the Academy of Natural Sciences of Philadelphia* 7 (1854–1855): 454.

24. Suckley, "Report on the Fauna and Medical Topography of Washington Territory," *Transactions of the American Medical Association* 10 (1857): 181–217.

25. Hume, *Ornithologists,* 429.

26. Unless otherwise noted, the facts of Henry's career were found in ibid., chap. 14.

27. Ibid., 210, 211.

28. *Reports,* vol. 9, xiv.

29. Thomas Charlton Henry, "Notes Derived from Observations Made on the Birds of New Mexico during the Years 1853 and 1854," *Proceedings of the Academy of Natural Sciences of Philadelphia* 7 (1855): 306–17; idem, "Descriptions of New Birds from Fort Thorn, New Mexico," ibid. 10 (1858): 117–18; idem, "Catalogue of the Birds of New Mexico as Compiled from Notes and Observations Made while in that Territory during a Residence of Six Years," ibid. 11 (1859): 104–9.

30. Quoted in Hume, *Ornithologists*, 220.

31. Elliott Coues, *Birds of the Colorado Valley: A Repository of Scientific and Popular Information Concerning North American Ornithology* (Washington, D.C.: U.S. Government Printing Office, 1878), 74.

32. The main source for the leading facts of Vollum's life is Hume, *Ornithologists*, chap. 30.

33. *Annual Report of the Smithsonian Institution*, 1858, 62; ibid., 1859, 77.

34. Ibid., 1860, 68–69.

35. Ibid., 422–25.

36. Details of Head's military career are found in George W. Cullum, *Biographical Register of the Officers and Graduates of the U.S. Military Academy*, 2d ed., 2 vols. (New York: D. Van Nostrand, 1868), vol. 1, 66.

37. *Annual Report of the Smithsonian Institution*, 1854, 291–93.

38. John Frazier Head, "Breeding of the Woodcock in Georgia," *Bulletin of the Nuttall Ornithological Club* 3 (July 1878): 151.

39. Richard H. Coolidge, comp., *Statistical Report on Sickness and Mortality in the Army of the United States, compiled from the Records of the Surgeon General's Office; embracing a Period of Sixteen Years, from January, 1839, to January, 1855* (Washington, D.C.: A. O. P. Nicholson, 1856).

40. Ibid., 3–4.

41. See also Hume, *Ornithologists*, chaps. 5, 11, 19 for biographical data on Crawford, Hammond, and King.

42. Richard H. Coolidge, comp., *Statistical Report on Sickness and Mortality in the Army of the United States, compiled from the Records of the Surgeon General's Office; embracing a Period of Five Years, from January, 1855, to January, 1860* (Washington, D.C.: George W. Bowman, 1860).

43. Ibid., 295.

44. Ibid., 301.

45. Hume, *Ornithologists*, chap. 15; Bendire, *Life Histories of North American Birds, with Special Reference to Their Breeding Habits and Eggs*, 2 vols. (Washington, D.C.: U.S. Government Printing Office, 1892 and 1895), vol. 1, 83; Edgar Alexander Mearns, *Mammals of the Mexican Boundary of the United States: A Descriptive Catalogue of the Species of Mammals Occurring in That Region; with a General Summary of the Natural History, and a List of Trees*. Bulletin of the United States National Museum no. 56 (Washington, D.C.: U.S. Government Printing Office, 1907), 109.

46. Hume, *Ornithologists*, chap. 12.

47. Henry Miller Madden, *Xántus: Hungarian Naturalist in the Pioneer West* (Palo Alto, Calif.: Books of the West, 1949); Ann Zwinger, *John Xántus: The Fort Tejon Letter, 1857–1859* (Tucson: University of Arizona Press, 1986); John N. Xántus, *Letters from North America*, trans. and ed. Theodore Schoenman and Helen Benedek Schoenman (Detroit: Wayne State University Press, 1975); idem, *Travels in Southern California*, trans, and ed. Theodore Schoenman and Helen Benedek Schoenman (Detroit: Wayne State University Press, 1976).

BY THE KNIFE: TONOPAH'S GREGOVICH-MIRCOVICH MURDER CASE

PHILLIP I. EARL

Until the publication of Wilbur S. Shepperson's *Restless Strangers: Nevada's Immigrants and Their Interpreters,*[1] the literature of the state's history was almost totally devoid of ethnic themes, although the social, political, and economic contributions of individuals of foreign birth had previously been noted in a number of standard works. The principal theme introduced by Shepperson was the concept of ethnic conflict—intense rivalry between various foreign-born groups seeking a place in this rough land, or violent confrontation between individuals.[2] Among the immigrant groups which have been the object of scholarly attention since the release of Shepperson's pioneering study are Nevada's South Slavs, principally the Serbians, Croatians, Slovenians, and Montenegrans, who settled in the copper camps of White Pine County shortly after the turn of the century or flocked to the booming mining camps of central Nevada that developed in the wake of Jim Butler's discovery of rich silver outcroppings on the west flank of the San Antonio Range in May 1900.[3]

A large number of Dalmatian Croatians had settled in California before the Mexican War. The Gold Rush attracted thousands of additional Slavs to the West Coast in the 1850s, and immigrants from the Adriatic were well represented in the silver rush to Nevada's Comstock Lode in 1860. Thereafter, they migrated on to Aurora, Unionville, Austin, Eureka, Treasure City, Pioche, and other mining camps throughout the state. The Slavic populations of the copper camps—McGill, Ruth, Kimberly, and Veteran—and the silver metropolis of Tonopah were of more recent origin, however, mirroring the "New Immigration" of large numbers of southern and eastern Europeans who came to fill the need for a cheap, stable labor force in the mines operated by the corporations, which took over the new western enterprises within a few years of their initial development.[4]

Sizable Slavic communities were thus established in Nevada. Tonopah's Slavs—mostly Serbs from the Dalmatian Coast, Hercegovina, and Montenegro—formed a close-knit social group, but were otherwise integrated into the everyday life of the town. Those of McGill and Ruth, however, Serbs and Croatians, resided in segregated sections of their communities, isolated in a small Slavic world. Orthodox Serbian Catholics living side by side with Roman Catholic Croats in McGill sometimes allowed their religious differences and nationalistic hatreds to boil over into conflict, but the troubles between Tonopah's Slavs were more a matter of family feuds, individual disputes, saloon fights, and drunken brawls, which gained them a bad reputation among the larger native population and lent impetus to the latent xenophobia which periodically surfaced in the local press.[5]

The Slavic custom of settling disagreements by the knife became an accepted aspect of life in the mining camps since the victims were usually members of the Slavic community themselves, but the murder of Tonopah businessman John Gregovich by a Montenegran miner, Andrija Mircovich, in May 1912 brought the citizens up short, revealing the true depths of Slavic hatreds and the ends to which certain of them would go to right a perceived wrong.

A native of Castellastoa, Austria-Hungary, Gregovich was one of Nevada's Slavic pioneers, having settled in Tybo in 1872, where he developed several mining properties and engaged in the smelting business. In 1884, he established a mercantile business in Eureka. Elected to the county commission in 1886, he served two terms before moving up to the office of county treasurer in 1890. Gregovich stood for the Nevada State Senate in 1894, representing Eureka County in the seventeenth and eighteenth sessions in Carson City. Disposing of his Eureka interests in 1903, he relocated in Tonopah, where he established another business and became one of the community's leading citizens.[6] His killer, on the other hand, was a recent immigrant. Thirty-three years of age, Mircovich was barely literate in the Serbian dialect of his section of Montenegro and spoke little English.[7]

There was an element of destiny in the circumstances which brought the respected Tonopah merchant and the young miner together at the Tonopah depot that fateful morning of May 14, 1912. Fifteen months earlier, February 23, 1911, Mircovich's cousin Christopher was among seventeen miners who lost their lives in a fire at the Tonopah Belmont Mine. Since he was single at the time and died without a will, his estate was placed in the hands of Nye County Public Administrator Arthur H. Keenan on February 28. Andrija Mircovich had meanwhile contacted another Tonopah merchant, George D. Banovich, seeking his assistance in getting a settlement. Banovich advised him to circumvent Keenan and contact an attorney to look into the possibility of securing a power of attorney from his cousin's brother and sister, Vasso and Maria Mircovich of Triest. Together, they went to the office of attorney P. E. Keeler. A power of attorney was subsequently drawn up and sent to Europe through the consul for Austria-Hungary in San Francisco, but Mircovich soon learned that he himself would not be able to act as administrator of his cousin's estate because he was not a citizen, although he had filed his first papers. Attorney James A. Sanders, Nye County's district attorney, to whom he had submitted the document, suggested that he contact Gregovich, the administrator for two other Serbs who had died in the fire. Mircovich reluctantly agreed and the two met with Gregovich on May 10, 1911. After examining the legal papers, Gregovich told Mircovich that he would take on the responsibility, but Mircovich suddenly became upset, cursing both Sanders and Gregovich as well as the laws which prevented him from handling the matter on his own. Sanders again explained that the law, not he or Gregovich, dictated the manner in which estates were to be settled and Mircovich said that he understood.[8]

On May 16, Sanders filed a petition with Robert C. Pohl, clerk of the Fifth Judicial District, requesting that the letters of administration issued to Public Administrator Keenan be revoked and that John Gregovich be named in his place. Pohl forwarded the document to the office of District Judge Peter J. Sommers. At a hearing held on June 22, Sommers examined the power of at-

torney and appointed Gregovich as administrator. The merchant
filed a $100 bond the next day and letters of administration were
issued on June 27. At that time, Christopher Mircovich's estate
totaled $520, the amount of cash found in his room after his
death. Gregovich gave Mircovich a check in the amount of $50
on July 17, holding the remainder until a $2,000 settlement came
in from the Tonopah Belmont Company on July 22. On that day,
Gregovich issued a check on the Tonopah Banking Corporation
for $1,742.50 in favor of Vasso and Maria Mircovich. He also
paid Sanders $200 for his services and took care of various legal
and administrative fees. On August 12, a check in the amount of
$507.32 arrived from the U.S. Postal Service for money orders
being held at Bishop, California, in Christopher Mircovich's
name at the time of the fire, leaving a balance in the estate of
$966.25 according to a statement filed by Gregovich on Novem-
ber 14, 1911, when he petitioned Judge Sommers to be released
as administrator.[9]

In the records of the public administrator in Tonopah, there is
no indication of the reasons for Gregovich's failure to disburse
the remainder of the funds, but Andrija Mircovich felt that he
had been cheated and vowed to himself and others that he
would set the matter right in some fashion. Subsequent testimony at Mircovich's trial indicated that he had uttered threats
on Gregovich's life several times and had once been forcibly
ejected from the man's place of business when he tried to con-
front him personally.[10]

May 14, 1912 dawned clear and sunny. John Gregovich had
gone down to the Tonopah and Goldfield depot that morning to
collect a grocery bill from a Serbian miner whom he had learned
was about to leave town. As it happened, Mircovich had decided to walk out to the cemetery north of town. As he neared
the depot, he noticed the train coming in from the north and decided to walk over to see who was arriving. Noticing Gregovich
standing on the platform, he strode toward him through the
crowd and began to pull a knife from beneath his coat. The
attack on Gregovich took place with such suddenness that even
those at the scene later gave slightly varying accounts of what
took place. Gregovich was standing on the edge of the dock
talking with Dr. J. R. Masterson. Just as the physician turned
and began to walk back toward the telegraph office, he noticed

Mircovich approaching Gregovich on the man's left and slightly to the rear. As he reached the elderly merchant, Mircovich muttered a curse in Serbian, then said, "I will get you, you old son-of-a-bitch" in English. He then pulled the knife, took a sideways swipe at his intended victim, and buried the blade halfway to the haft in the body cavity between the fifth and sixth ribs on the left side. Withdrawing it, he struck again, but hit a rib. Gregovich then turned to his left, cursing and attempting to grapple with his assailant, but Mircovich turned to his right and plunged the knife into the man's left kidney. Quickly withdrawing the blade, he got an underhanded grip and ripped Gregovich in the right groin area. Suddenly realizing what had happened, Gregovich blurted out, "My God, I am cut! I am dying! Take me to a hospital!" Another bystander, William C. Harding, cried out, "He's cutting that man" just as Gregovich staggered backward. Steve Sabovich, standing nearby, then grabbed Mircovich's right arm, pressing on his wrist and forcing him to drop the knife. Just at that moment, Deputy Sheriff William Walker ran from the Pullman car where he had been standing. "That's him," someone said, pointing to Mircovich, and Walker grabbed him by the shoulders. "What do you think you are doing?" the deputy said, but he got no reply. Mircovich stood as though transfixed, glowering at his portly victim, now lying on the platform. Dr. Masterson had initially tried to walk Gregovich over to the delivery express auto, but he had fainted. The physician and three other men had then started to carry him, but Masterson noticed blood coming out of the groin area so they laid him down on a lap robe someone had brought over. Tearing away Gregovich's trousers, Masterson saw blood beginning to spurt from an artery. Taking a hemostat from his bag, he inserted his finger deep in the knife wound and clamped off the artery. He then commandeered an automobile to take Gregovich to the Miners' Hospital.[11]

Deputy Walker had meanwhile gotten the knife from Sabovich and called for an automobile to take Mircovich to the Nye County Jail. During the short trip uptown, he asked his prisoner if the knife belonged to him. Mircovich nodded that it did and told the deputy that Gregovich had taken money from him. Walker knew nothing of this and Mircovich was locked up a few minutes later. When Sheriff Ed Malley came in, he talked to Mircovich in his cell. Without informing him that anything he said could be used against him when he went to trial, Malley asked him why he had attacked Gregovich. Mircovich replied only that the man had stolen some money from him. "I wanted to make John Gregovich die," he was later quoted by Malley as having said.[12]

At the hospital, Dr. Masterson and Dr. Edward S. Grigsby were making heroic efforts to save Gregovich's life. They determined that one of the chest wounds had punctured the left lung, making breathing extremely difficult, but considered the severing of the femoral artery in the groin area to be the only wound which was life threatening. Before operating, Dr. Masterson ordered a hypodermic of strychnine administered as a stimulant to the heart and central nervous system. They also considered a blood transfusion and called in Dr. Percy D. McLeod and Dr. Gilmour M. Roberts to assist, but Gregovich was in deep shock by that time and the physicians were unable to stabilize him. Some four hours after the incident at the depot, at 1:00 P.M., Gregovich died.[13]

At a coroner's inquest the next morning, those who had been present at the depot testified as to what they recalled of the events surrounding the stabbing. With some minor discrepancies, they left no doubt that Mircovich had been responsible for the act, a view reflected in the verdict. At a grand jury hearing in the court of District Judge Mark Averill the next day, Dr. Masterson again testified, as did Deputy Walker, Steve Sabovich, William C. Harding, J. C. Peck, and Miles McCormick. An indictment was returned that day and Averill appointed attorney George B. Thatcher as counsel for Mircovich. After the reading of the indictment, Thatcher asked for a postponement to allow him time to study the case and consult with his client. Averill then recessed the proceedings until 7:30 P.M. Back before the judge at that time, Thatcher pleaded Mircovich not guilty. The plea was accepted and Averill set June 4 as the trial date.[14]

John Gregovich's funeral was being held at the family home at Brougher and Summit the day the grand jury met. Businesses closed, the Tonopah Musicians Union postponed a dance scheduled for that evening, and floral wreaths spilled out of the house and across the front lawn. George B. Gallup, rector of St. Mark's Episcopal Church, presided over the services. Speaking to family members and a few dozen friends crowded into the parlor, he recounted the many accomplishments of the deceased in the course of his long life but could hardly restrain himself when the reality of Gregovich's passing crossed his mind, referring to him as having been "ruthlessly torn away from his devoted family and wide circle of friends by the heartless cruelty of a cowardly assassin." Noting the strong feelings of the community over the murder, he concluded that "a lack of righteous indignation at deeds of violence betrays a depraved conscience." [15] Burial was to be in Reno, and a dozen uniformed members of the Odd Fellows led the line of march to the depot the next morning. The ladies of the Rebeccas followed the flag-draped casket, and Tonopah's volunteer firemen brought up the rear. District Attorney Sanders, J. H. Holmes, and March Androvich, a cousin, accompanied the family on the journey north. [16]

On Sunday, May 18, Reverend Gallup spoke on "The Teachings of the Church on Capital Punishment" at evening services. Across town, Reverend Herman L. Burnham of the Presbyterian church devoted his sermon to the subject of "Human Life: Shall It Be Destroyed or Protected?" As spokesmen for a higher morality, the clergymen perhaps had mixed feelings about their innermost thoughts on Gregovich's death and might well have attempted to communicate a sense of their own ambivalence to their respective congregations, but editor W. W. Booth of the *Tonopah Bonanza* spoke out without reservation. In a May 20 editorial on a Boston poisoning case in which an insanity plea had become a part of the proceedings, he criticized both the psychologists who conceived such a defense and the attorneys who had the temerity to make use of it in seeking the acquittal of their clients. With the Gregovich murder fresh in his mind, and perhaps anticipating an insanity defense on the part of attorney Thatcher, he contended that society must protect itself. "The law says that a man who knows the nature of the act he commits and that it is contrary to law is guilty, when he commits an overt act, no matter whether he thinks it is right or wrong," he wrote. "The fanatic who believes in offering a human sacrifice is guilty of murder if he puts his belief in practice because he knows the nature of death and that the law forbids killing." [17]

Since the Gregovich slaying was a capital offense, Judge Averill set no bail, and Mircovich languished in jail for the next several weeks. Notices were sent out to prospective jurors on May 22, but Thatcher was not on hand June 4 when court convened for the purpose of impaneling a jury. On June 1, he had left for the Democratic State Convention in Fallon. After attending the gathering, he went on to Reno. Neither Averill nor District Attorney Sanders had been informed that Thatcher would be out of town, but the judge proceeded anyway, appointing attorney Patrick M. Bowler to act in Thatcher's stead for the initial jury phase of the proceedings. Bowler was only passingly familiar with the case but agreed to take over with the stipulation that he could withdraw when Thatcher returned. Averill agreed and jury selection began. During the first phase, Averill excused thirty-two veniremen because their jobs in the mines required their continual presence or because they were to be away on business for the trial period. One man was allowed to step down because of his age and the condition of his health, two were railroaders who had discussed the killing in some detail with their fellows, and one was released because of his position as an officer with the Manhattan volunteer fire department. Following the reading of the names of those men who were to be examined further, Bowler entered an objection to the manner in which the jurors were summoned and to the excuses accepted by Judge Averill, contending that neither was in conformity with state statutes. To force him to proceed under these circumstances, he said, would deprive his client of a fair and impartial trial. He cited neither statutory provisions nor case law to back up his assertion, however, and Averill denied the challenge. Sanders and Bowler then proceeded with jury selection. Each prospective juror was questioned carefully as to his views on capital punishment, those who were emphatically opposed being released immediately. They were also interrogated in regard to their feelings about "Bohunks" and their understanding of the difference between a grand jury and a trial jury. To a man, they denied having any prejudices against the defendant because of his nationality, but several indicated a belief that an indictment was an indication of guilt. When questioned about their knowledge of the case, several said they knew of the circumstances of Gregovich's murder and had formed a firm opinion as to Mircovich's guilt. Both attorneys inquired as to how the men came to know of the killing, from witnesses, press accounts, or street talk, and whether or not they could consider the evidence in an impartial manner.

They were also asked if they knew either Mircovich or Gregovich and, if so, under what circumstances. Several had dealt with Gregovich in his store and three knew him personally, but none were acquainted with the defendant. Those who were acquainted with Gregovich in any way were dismissed at that point. At 5:00 P.M., Averill recessed, three jurors—John Murray, a Tonopah miner; William F. Kelley, also of Tonopah, a carpenter; and Willard Moran, a Round Mountain miner—having been passed by both attorneys.[18]

Thatcher was still absent when court reconvened the next morning, June 5, so Bowler continued. Several prospective jurors who had talked to witnesses of the killing were dismissed, as were those who seemed to have formed unshakable opinions on Mircovich's guilt, but Bowler's questioning of several of those called indicated that he considered a guilty verdict to be a foregone conclusion. He thus took a new tack later in the day, querying several men as to whether or not mitigating circumstances could induce them to consider incarceration of the defendant rather than the inflicting of the death penalty should he be found guilty. Those who indicated by their responses that they could entertain such a notion were dismissed for cause by District Attorney Sanders, however, and only William Cress of Manhattan was taken that day.[19]

Tonopah's delegates to the Fallon convention arrived back in town at 9:30 A.M. the next morning, but Thatcher did not appear in court until just before 11:00. Bowler examined the first seven prospective jurors called, and he and Sanders agreed upon two of them, Frank C. Humphrey of Manhattan and J. A. Mayette, of Berlin. At that point, Thatcher took over and a seventh juror, A. J. Joyner, a Tonopah merchant, was accepted. Another four men were then examined, exhausting the venire. Both attorneys indicated a desire to proceed with jury selection as soon as possible, but neither could agree upon the number of new prospective jurors the sheriff should summon. Sanders suggested fifteen, but Thatcher urged Averill to call thirty-five. The judge considered the matter and signed an order for twenty-five before declaring court to be in recess until Saturday, June 8.[20]

The new jurors were on hand when court reconvened, most of them from Manhattan and Round Mountain. H. H. Richardson, a Manhattan hotelman, was the first taken that morning, followed by P. H. Gove, Round Mountain; A. H. Deahl, Manhattan; M. L. Caffrey, Tonopah; and L. A. Fisher, operator of a Manhattan freight and transfer business. Both attorneys accepted the jury as the afternoon session opened, and Sanders made his opening statement after the reading of the indictment, recounting the series of events which preceded the killing, Mircovich's threats against Gregovich, and the episode at the depot on May 14. He told the jurors that he intended to prove that the slaying was "willful, deliberate and premeditated" and that he would be asking them to fix the punishment at death if they should find the defendant guilty. Court then adjourned until Monday, June 10.[21]

Called as the first witness for the prosecution, Dr. Masterson described his meeting with Gregovich at the depot and the stabbing. He also told of his efforts to save the life of the deceased. Thatcher objected to some of the details of the treatment at the hospital, telling Averill that all that was necessary was for the prosecution to show that Gregovich was dead. On cross-examination, he got the physician to admit that he had talked over the murder with other witnesses. He also questioned Masterson closely on what he saw at the depot and brought out some slight inconsistencies with respect to his previous testimony at the coroner's inquest and before the grand jury. J. E. Peck, station agent, recalled for the jury what he saw that morning, as did William Harding, both adding a few details to previous testimony. Neither man was cross-examined. Deputy William C. Walker then took the stand, contributing little to previous accounts of the slaying other than identifying the knife. Thatcher objected to all questions about what Mircovich said to Walker, claiming that his client had not been informed of his right to remain silent, but Averill overruled him on every point. In the afternoon session, Steve Sabovich identified the knife and told the court of how he took it from Mircovich and gave it to Walker. The weapon was then offered in evidence. Expressman Miles McCormick gave a few more details, as did another witness, William Van Patten. Walker was then recalled by Sanders to testify as to whether he had offered any inducements or made any threats to Mircovich in order to get a statement from him. He denied that there were any. Judge Averill then asked about the supposed statements, one that Gregovich owed him money and a second identifying the knife, and the lawman again said that he had done nothing to elicit them. Dr. Edward S. Grigsby followed with testimony on the nature of Gregovich's wounds and the cause of death. With the calling of Nick Kosich, Sanders and Thatcher opened up the question of Mircovich's motives. Kosich told the jurors that Mircovich had come to him for assistance in getting an attorney to help him collect moneys owed to him by Gregovich. He called attorney Frank Pittman, he said, but Mircovich did not follow up. Kosich also said that Mircovich told him that one of Gregovich's employees had thrown him out of the man's store when he tried to talk to him about the supposed debt. In Thatcher's cross-examination, it was revealed that Mircovich had tried to start a fight with Gregovich on that occasion. Nikola Chiatovich, the clerk who had confronted Mircovich, confirmed Kosich's testimony. Tom Kulichea was then called by the prosecution to relate a conversation in Goldfield in which Mircovich threatened to kill both Gregovich and Sanders.[22]

Thatcher began the afternoon session by calling Kulichea back for cross-examination, eliciting the fact that he felt badly for not having informed either man of the threat. On redirect, Sanders tried to pin down the date of the conversation, January or February 1912, and revealed that Kulichea had told him of the threat after the killing. Constable Charles G. Smith was then put on the stand to relate the circumstances of his being asked by Gregovich to keep Mircovich away from his place of business. Lowell Daniels, county clerk, followed Smith to the stand, and Sanders introduced into evidence the letter of administration for the estate of Christopher Mircovich issued to A. H. Keenan on February 28, 1911, a petition for revocation of the document on June 20, the order canceling the document and empowering Gregovich to administer the estate, and Gregovich's bond certificate dated June 27, 1911. Thatcher objected to the introduction of the papers, claiming that they showed neither premeditation nor malice on the part of his client, but he was overruled. Sanders then introduced Gregovich's petition to be released as an administrator and had Daniels read it aloud. He also asked for an accounting of the funds Gregovich turned over, but Daniels did not have it in hand. Sheriff Ed Malley was next sworn in. He told the jury that Mircovich had indeed made a voluntary confession while in the county jail. Thatcher interrupted to raise the objection that Mircovich had not been informed of his right to remain silent, but he was overruled. Malley then related a conversation at the jail in which Mircovich denied that he had come from Goldfield to kill Gregovich, but he had seen the train coming in that morning when he was on his way to the cemetery and had spotted Gregovich on the platform as he walked by, and he had made the decision then and there to kill the man. Malley also said that he had asked Mircovich if he was a member of the Black Hand. He denied it, Malley said, but, in response to another question, admitted that he was an "anarchist." Thatcher had no comment on this latter testimony, even though the interrogation Malley described was something more than a casual conversation. Deputy Sheriff Charles Slavin followed Malley to testify that he had heard part of the conversation. He denied that any threats were made to induce Mircovich to talk, but Thatcher objected to his being placed on the stand because Sanders had not notified him that the deputy was to be a witness. Averill agreed but did not ask the jurors to ignore Slavin's testimony. He then recessed until Wednesday, June 12, informing the attorneys, the defendant, and the jurors that Governor Tasker L. Oddie had declared June 11 to be a legal holiday in memory of Senator George S. Nixon, who had died on June 5.[23]

When the trial resumed, arguments on the part of both Thatcher and Sanders were surprisingly brief. James Dacovich was called to testify to a conversation between Mircovich and Gregovich to which he had been a witness. He said that Gregovich told Mircovich that the matter of the money in his cousin's estate was in the hands of the court. He also backed up previous testimony to the effect that Mircovich had threatened and cursed Gregovich in his presence before Nick Chiatovich intervened. Thatcher asked what language they were speaking and Dacovich replied, "Slavonian." George Banovich followed with an account of his assistance to Mircovich in getting an attorney to assist him in securing a power of attorney to enable him to handle his cousin's estate himself. He also related a scene at Sanders's office in which Mircovich cursed both the court and the district attorney when he learned that he could not act as administrator himself. He also said that he had heard Mircovich speak badly of Gregovich at a saloon frequented by the men of Tonopah's Serbian community, but Thatcher objected on the grounds that "abusive language" did not necessarily constitute a "threat." Judge Averill said that it was difficult for him to make the distinction that Thatcher saw, so he overruled him. During cross-examination, Thatcher elicited further details of Banovich's part in the matter of the power of attorney and tried to bring forth testimony to the effect that his witness, Gregovich, and Sanders were somehow involved in a collusive scheme to take the money which rightly belonged to Mircovich. C. E. Wood, a railroad conductor who was an eyewitness to the murder, provided a few more details before Mrs. John Gregovich was called to identify a letter from Mircovich found in her late husband's papers, but Thatcher objected and she was excused. Sanders's last witness, Steve Pavlovich, the interpreter in court, was then sworn. Sanders asked him to identify the letter. He replied that he was not familiar with Mircovich's signature, but the attorney tried to submit the document in evidence anyway. Averill asked Sanders if the signature had been confirmed as that of the defendant. Sanders hesitated before admitting that it had not, but maintained that it was similar to that on another document known to have been signed by Mircovich. The judge replied that the signature could have been forged easily enough and Thatcher objected that he had no translation. Pavlovich said that a rendering of the letter into English might take several days. The judge and the attorneys discussed the matter of a recess to allow time for the translation, but no decision was made to do so. Sanders then handed Mircovich's knife to the jury foreman, requesting that he pass it along to the others for their inspection. He rested the state's case at that point, with the exception of the translation of the letter. A recess was then called until 1:30 that afternoon.[24]

In an emotional summation when court reconvened, Sanders stated flatly that the evidence against Mircovich had "forged a chain of guilt" which impelled him to ask for the death penalty. Should the jurors not see it that way, he said, "then I say to you that you are twelve men who do not believe in that law of man handed down to us from God, that who sheddeth man's blood, the same shall be required from him." Citing further evidence to show premeditation on Mircovich's part, he asked the jurors whether they had the "manhood" to help him "defend the law of my country and its liberty-loving people." If they did not, he said, "we might just as well dynamite this old courthouse. We might just as well take his Honor off the bench and say we have no law in Nye County." He then launched into a philosophical justification of capital punishment, citing countries and states which had abolished it and later brought it back. "If you cannot pronounce, by your verdict, the death penalty upon this defendant," he intoned, "I say let's resurrect old Casey that killed Mrs. Bishop in Goldfield and let him live again." He then spoke to the jurors of their duty to uphold the law, asking them "how long it will be before anarchists take possession of this country" if good men shirked their duties. Sanders had only Malley's testimony to uphold the contention that Mircovich held anarchist views, but he continued that line of reasoning, referring to Presidents John Garfield and William McKinley as both having been murdered in a crowd, just as Mircovich killed Gregovich, by anarchists.[25]

Court observers expected Thatcher to put Mircovich on the stand in an attempt to establish an insanity defense, but he rested immediately after Sanders's summation. Judge Averill then instructed the jury, defining murder, malice, intent, and the concept of reasonable doubt. The jurors selected Frank Humphrey as foreman and got the case at 4:30. Fifty-two minutes later, at 5:22, Humphrey called the bailiff and he in turn informed Judge Averill that a verdict had been reached. With Mircovich standing before him, he ordered Deputy Clerk Daniels to read the verdict, guilty of murder in the first degree, for which Mircovich should suffer death. Mircovich hung his head as the court interpreter relayed the clerk's words but made no outward display of emotion. Averill had the jury polled and all twelve indicated their agreement. Thanking the jurors, he dismissed them and set June 15 as the date for pronouncing formal sentence.[26]

A *Bonanza* newsman talked to several jurors a few minutes later and learned that the question of Mircovich's guilt was never an issue during their deliberations. Only two ballots were taken, he was told, the first resulting in eleven votes for the death penalty and one for life imprisonment, and a second in which there was unanimous agreement on death. At least two jurors faulted Thatcher for not calling Mircovich to the stand since they felt that there were mitigating circumstances, but, upon questioning by the reporter, they admitted that there was little he could have done to get an acquittal. Editor Booth agreed, commenting that the proceedings had been as fair and impartial as possible under the circumstances. He commended Judge Averill for refusing to countenance delays over technical points and viewed the case as an indication that a "new era" had dawned in Nye County criminal proceedings.[27]

On Friday, June 14, Thatcher appeared before Judge Averill with a request that he be allowed to step down from the case in favor of attorney J. E. McNamara. Neither Sanders nor Mircovich objected, so the judge ordered that the substitution be made. The next morning, he pronounced sentence on Mircovich, setting August 23 as the execution date. Under a revision of the Nevada Penal Code enacted by the 1911 legislature, Mircovich was given the choice of either being executed by a firing squad or hanged. When interpreter Pavlovich relayed the judge's question, Mircovich unhesitatingly replied that he preferred to be shot. Attorney McNamara then made a motion for a new trial on the grounds that Averill had misdirected the jury in matters of law and had erred in deciding questions of law during the course of the trial. He also asserted that the verdict of the jury was contrary to the law and the evidence and charged District Attorney Sanders with misconduct in his closing summation. Averill denied the motion and McNamara requested a transcript of the trial proceedings.[28]

After Mircovich was returned to his cell, a reporter was allowed in to interview him. In broken English, he indicated that he still believed that Banovich and Gregovich had conspired to take the money from his cousin's estate which he believed to be rightfully his. He also said that he had never spoken to Tom Kulichea—had never seen the man before he appeared on the stand at his trial. When asked why he preferred to go before a firing squad instead of facing the noose, he replied that "death from shooting was quicker" in his judgment, "but I don't care. I am ready to go anytime. The administrator business made me crazy. For a long time I did not know what I was doing."[29]

On June 17, Sheriff Malley accompanied Mircovich to the depot to catch the train to Carson City. A small crowd had gathered to witness their departure and one of Mircovich's friends assured him that he would be treated well at the Carson City in-

stitution. "Yes," he responded in English, "they will treat me to
a shower of cold lead." During the trip north, Mircovich became
nauseated and begged Malley to intercede with Warden George
Cowing to have him executed at once. Malley explained that his
attorney was planning to take his case to the Nevada Supreme
Court, but Mircovich appeared not to comprehend the appeals
process and made the same plea to Cowing when they arrived at
the prison that evening. Cowing did not bother to explain that
there would soon be an appeal pending but put Mircovich in
solitary confinement and assigned a guard to his cell as a death
watch in case he attempted suicide.[30]

Mircovich's execution by a firing squad was to be the first
under the 1911 statute, and rumors were soon circulating to the
effect that the guards at the prison who would be responsible
for carrying it out considered shooting "cold-blooded murder."
A Reno newsman picked up the story and it soon hit the wire
services with a Reno dateline. Over the next several weeks,
Warden Cowing and Washoe County Sheriff Charles P. Farrell
received several hundred letters from men willing to do the job
if the state could not otherwise see that it was carried out by
prison personnel. Typical of the communications was the following, which was published in the *Carson City News* on September 5:

> 188 Talbot Street,
> Brierly Hill,
> Birmingham,
> England
> August 23, 1912

Dear Sir;

Having read of the difficulty in Nevada to obtain men to
carry out the new execution orders, I would like to know if
Englishmen would suit you; if so, could you forward me full
particulars of wages etc. If suitable, I would undertake your
problem. I am married, age 28, height about 5 ft., 10 inches.
Have worked in Venezuela, South America, from where I can
supply characters, also from England if desired. Can forward
photograph if necessary. Thanking you in anticipation of an
early reply.

> Yours Sincerely,
> Thomas William Gillrooker[31]

The editor of the *News* was appalled by the realization that there were men who could consider the taking of a human life in the same light as a simple business proposition. "Think of a man wanting to come all the way from England to Nevada to murder a man for a few dollars," he wrote, "and then speaking about being able to send characters. The character of a man like this should smell unto the high heavens." Sheriff Farrell was also upset, telling a reporter that he was tempted to reply to a query from a Pennsylvania man that "the price is 92 1/2 cents and he must pay his way to Reno and return." Warden Cowing would only comment that the story was "a rank fake from end to end" and said that his guards would do their duty when the time came. He also denied rumors that he was trying to convince Mircovich to agree to be hanged.[32]

The Mircovich case also drew a response from those opposed to capital punishment under any circumstances. On August 24, the *Bonanza* carried a letter from one Ben P. Mitchell, who observed that in spite of "great advancements in science and philosophy, humanity is still controlled by emotions, sentiment, rather than reason." Referring to Mircovich's case, he contended that "in thirsting for the blood of man, we are also murderers." On a poetic note, he asked, "Justice and reason, where art thou? Will humanity never rise above that primitive idea of an eye for an eye, a tooth for a tooth?"[33]

Attorney McNamara filed an appeal for a new trial with the clerk of the Nevada Supreme Court on August 14 but neglected to ask for a stay of execution. Attorney General Cleveland Baker, being told that the execution would have to be carried out if not formally stayed, filed the proper document on Mircovich's behalf two days later, however, and the case passed out of the news until it came before the court in March 1913. George Thatcher had meanwhile taken over as attorney general, replacing Baker, who had died on December 5, 1912, and there was also a change in the wardenship of the prison when George Cowing resigned on January 10. To replace him, Governor Oddie named former governor Denver Dickerson.[34]

Before his resignation, Cowing had ordered a piece of custom equipment designed to ease the qualms of those guards detailed to carry out the execution. Manufactured by an eastern ordnance company, the "shooting gallery," or "execution machine," as it came to be called, consisted of a steel framework hut with three small ports in the front from which the muzzles of three .30–30 Savage rifles would protrude. The weapons, equipped with Maxim silencers, were to be aimed at a steel backdrop, in front of which the doomed man would be strapped to a chair bolted to a platform. The rifles were to be pre-aimed and fired by a coiled spring mechanism set off by the simultaneous cutting of three strings, only one of which would fire the two weapons loaded with real bullets. The hut was louvered in such a way that none of the guards would be able to see the victim die. Following the delivery of the device on February 1, prison officials kept it crated up, but an inmate doing carpentry work in the yard discovered it. It was then unpacked and set up. Weighing 1,000 pounds, it was reported to be similar to devices used in other states.[35]

Three men were on death row at that time, and two of them, Mircovich and Nimrod Urie, had chosen to die by the bullet. Urie's execution was scheduled for March 7, but the Board of Pardons granted a clemency plea that last day, commuting his sentence to life imprisonment.[36]

Over in the legislature, Assemblyman F. J. Kinghorn, Republican of Mineral County, had introduced a bill on February 27 providing for execution by electrocution. In a short speech that day, he said that he considered hanging to be a "relic of barbarity" and that shooting was "not much better." Electrocution, on the other hand, was less trouble for prison officials and for the guards who had to perform the gruesome task, he said. Requesting an appropriation of $1,000 to purchase the necessary equipment, he told his colleagues that an electric chair would save the state money and would be "a move along modernism." The bill coursed the legislative mill in short order, passing the lower house on March 6 by a vote of 39 to 7 and the Senate on March 20 by a unanimous vote, 20 to 0. Governor Oddie vetoed the measure on March 31, however, informing the lawmakers that he considered it to be "unconstitutional."[37]

While Kinghorn's bill was under consideration, the Supreme Court was taking up Mircovich's appeal for a new trial. In his brief, McNamara contended that Sanders's mention of the Casey murder case influenced and biased the jurors against his client, as did his reference to Mircovich as an "anarchist." He also pleaded that Sanders's use of a "street opinion" by Tom Kulichea that "the county should be spared the expense of a trial" was "improper" and "prejudicial." As to Mircovich's rights, he maintained that his client had not been informed of his right to remain silent when he was questioned about the knife. McNamara also brought up the matter of premeditation, an element in the first-degree conviction, stating flatly that the evidence indicated that Mircovich was on his way to the cemetery that day. Writing for the court, Chief Justice George F. Talbot cited an opinion written by Attorney General Baker before his death which denied that Mircovich's confession was obtained by either "threats" or "promises of benefit" but, rather, was voluntary. Baker also defended Sanders's summation as "proper comment on the matters in evidence in the case." If there were some improprieties, Baker concluded, attorney Thatcher should have extended an objection at the time. Talbot then took on McNamara's brief point by point. On the matter of the interviews conducted by Walker and Malley, he wrote that the evidence indicated that Mircovich's statements were made voluntarily. He also pointed out that Nevada had no statute barring the admission of a confession made by a defendant in custody unless he had been previously warned that anything he said could be used by the prosecution in his trial. Concerning the conversation about the knife, a valid objection could be raised were there not "direct and undisputed evidence" otherwise that was not of a circumstantial nature. Talbot considered the fact that evidence was introduced regarding Mircovich's identification of the knife a "harmless error" because the ownership of the weapon was conclusively established by other witnesses whose testimony was not contradicted. Regarding Sanders's reference to the Casey murder case, Talbot held that it was not "beyond the bounds of legitimate argument," nor was his characterization of Mircovich as an "anarchist," since evidence had been adduced that the defendant had himself so stated. He also upheld Sanders's use of Tom Kulichea's statements since they were originally brought out in Thatcher's cross-examination. The Court thus affirmed the original verdict in the case and denied the motion for a new trial. Justice Frank H. Norcross concurred, commenting only that Sanders's final summation "in some particulars . . . is not to be commended" but did not, taken as a whole, "violate the substantial rights of the defendant." Justice Patrick A. McCarran, having joined the

Court after the argument and submission of the case, did not participate in the opinion.[38]

The decision was made public on March 15, but an order directing Judge Averill to set a new execution date was delayed in the office of the clerk of the court until April 16. Once the directive was received by County Clerk Pohl in Tonopah, Averill studied the opinion, vacated the original execution date, and announced on April 23 that the new date was to be May 14. The Board of Pardons had meanwhile convened on April 15, but the members were not able to consider McNamara's application for a commutation of Mircovich's death sentence because of the delay in forwarding the papers.[39]

In the interim period, Andrija Mircovich had taken it upon himself to make a plea. Sitting in his cell on April 10, he penned a letter to the Board of Pardons in the Serbian dialect used in his native Montenegro. Criticizing the newsmen who had covered the killing and his subsequent trial, he claimed that he had not been treated fairly and had been denied his right to have his side of the story told. He now wanted to testify, he wrote, and have witnesses called, but he did not insist upon his innocence.[40]

He gave the letter to a guard, Austin Jackson, but the prison employee was not able to read the cramped missive, so he forwarded it to Ross Lewers, acting president of the University of Nevada, to be translated. Preparations for the execution were meanwhile going forward. On Thursday, May 8, the guards brought Mircovich out to the prison yard, seated him in front of the execution machine, and preset the rifle sights on a small piece of cardboard the size of a heart which they had pinned to his shirt. After he was led away, they positioned the cardboard to the chairback. They then fired the weapons to test their aim, one bullet piercing the exact center of the heart and the other hitting it a fraction of an inch away. Warden Dickerson had been sending out invitations to the execution, but reports persisted that the guards still had little stomach for the manner in which it was to be carried out. To resolve the dilemma, the warden had the guards put their names in a hat to allow him to choose three men at random. He also rigged up a screen between the exit from death row and the rear entrance to the execution machine so the spectators could not see the men who were to carry out Mircovich's sentence as they came out and left afterward.[41]

The prison chaplain, Reverend Lloyd B. Thomas of Carson City's St. Peter's Episcopal Church, had come to know Mircovich in the eleven months since he had arrived from Tonopah. On the morning of May 13, he appealed to a hastily convened meeting of the Board of Pardons for a commutation of the condemned man's sentence to life imprisonment, but to no avail. He then asked Governor Oddie, a member of the board, for a grant of executive clemency but was again turned down. When Dickerson informed Mircovich of the decision later in the afternoon, he condemned Judge Averill and again stated his belief that Gregovich and Banovich had taken his money. The warden admonished the guard assigned to death row to watch him should he attempt to take his own life, but Mircovich did little more than pace up and down in his cell muttering in his native language.[42]

Mircovich slept fitfully that night, awakening at 5:00 A.M. and dressing before he ate breakfast. Reverend Thomas visited him in his cell at 7:30, but he refused to receive the sacraments or the last rites of the Episcopal church. At one point, he said that he could not do so because he was Greek Orthodox, but he later stated that it would be "too much trouble." Several reporters had been allowed on death row that morning, but Mircovich was in no mood for an interview. He again cursed Judge Averill and said that he had been justified in taking Gregovich's life and should not have been convicted of first-degree murder. When a newsman from the *Carson Appeal* asked him what punishment he felt might be more fitting, he replied that he thought two years behind bars would be sufficient. At 10:45, the three guards walked out from death row and took their places behind the rifles. The twelve spectators then joined five guards in the roped-off enclosure from which they were to witness the execution. Warden Dickerson released Mircovich from his cell at that point in the proceedings. As Mircovich stepped out into the corridor, Dickerson asked him if he wanted a copy of the execution warrant read to him. He seemed confused for a moment, but finally replied in English, "I no understand very well, maybe so." As the warden read the document, Mircovich stood stroking his light moustache, his dark eyes riveted on the man's face. A guard then escorted him to the exit leading from the corridor and Dickerson asked him if he wanted a black cap or a blindfold. "No, I want to see," he replied. The warden then shook hands

with him and said, "God be with you and good-bye." As Mircovich grasped his hand, he said, "I much obligated to you. You be
good man to me." Shaking hands with the reporters, he said,
"You please excuse me." As they walked out into the prison
yard, John Muller, the captain of the guard, said, "Now die like
a soldier and show the people you are brave." "I die like soldier," Mircovich responded. Out in the yard, he glanced at the
spectators, stooped under the rope, walked unaided to the
chair, seated himself, and stretched out his arms to be strapped
in. One guard seemed to be using excessive force, so Dickerson
stepped forward and told him in a low voice to be a bit more
gentle. As the guards completed their work, Mircovich put his
head back and stared at the fleecy clouds overhead. He then
glanced at the spectators before momentarily turning his gaze
on the muzzles of the rifles. When Dr. Donald McLean, the
prison physician, came forward to pin a paper heart over his
heart, Captain Muller told him to hold his head up. He straight-
ened up, his eyes squinting as he glared intently forward, a solemn look on his face. Dickerson paused a moment, awaiting
word that the rifles had been properly sighted, then gave the
signal to proceed. "Make ready! Take aim!" Muller intoned,
"One, two, three, fire!" The muffled rifles cracked as one.
Mircovich's head fell on his chest as the bullets tore through his
heart, then jerked backward and lolled from side to side before
he sank back in the chair like a man wearied and seeking an
easier position. A moment later, Dickerson announced that the
execution had taken place according to the law. The spectators
were escorted out at that point in the proceedings and the guards
walked out behind the screen. The other guards unstrapped the
body and carried it to an adjoining room where Dr. McLean conducted a brief examination. He said that Mircovich had died instantly, the movements of the head being due to a muscular
reaction.[43]

At 2:00 P.M., Reverend Thomas conducted an informal grave-
side service at the prison cemetery. The grave had originally
been dug for Patrick Coak, who had died in the prison hospital
on February 10, 1912, but whose body had been claimed by
his relatives before burial. The prisoners had cleaned it out
in March for Nimrod Urie, but it became the final resting place

for Mircovich when the Board of Pardons saved the Humboldt County murderer at the last minute. Mircovich's body also occupied the rough pine coffin which the carpentry crew had made for Urie. As the Reverend Thomas read the burial service of the Episcopal church, several guards and half a dozen convicts stood with heads bowed. A choir consisting of the warden's wife, Thomas, and two other guards then sang two hymns before the convicts filled in the grave and placed a wooden marker at the head. A few hours later, Reverend Thomas entered Mircovich's name in the Parish Register, although he had refused to the last to accept an offer of salvation.[44]

Governor Oddie, Chief Justice Talbot, and Justice Norcross were in Reno that morning to attend graduation exercises at the university. Oddie spoke briefly as he presented military commissions to graduating cadets and President Lewers delivered a short address when he gave out the diplomas. A reception for the graduates and their families was held later in the day. When Lewers returned home a few hours later, he picked up the afternoon *Reno Evening Gazette*. On the front page, along with an account of the graduation, was the story of Mircovich's execution. It then occurred to him that the letter from Austin Jackson and Mircovich's untranslated communication to the Board of Pardons remained on his desk. He had given the letter to Chris Novacovich, a Reno merchant, earlier and had been told that it was a request to be allowed to appear before the Board of Pardons, but he had neither had the letter translated nor had he gotten back to Jackson. After dinner, he sat down at his typewriter and pecked out an apologetic note explaining why he had not responded sooner. Enclosing the communication with Mircovich's untranslated letter, he mailed it the next morning. When Jackson received the letter, he turned it over to the file clerk to become a part of Mircovich's records.[45]

W. W. Booth of the *Tonopah Bonanza* briefly noted the execution in his column of May 15, commenting that Mircovich had been offered "every opportunity to establish his innocence" before the people finally had recourse to "the old Mosaic belief of an eye for an eye and a tooth for a tooth." In conclusion, he sought to ease whatever remorse might be troubling those who had had to carry out the execution. "The law is plain," he wrote, "and the responsibility of the execution of Mircovich rests upon no man's head."[46]

In his report to the 1915 legislature, Dickerson penned a brief account of the Mircovich execution and expressed the opinion that "executions by shooting are a trifle less barbarous than by hanging and have the further merit of eliminating many of the possibilities of bungling," but he was deeply troubled personally. In an editorial on the death penalty which appeared in the *Nevada Democrat* on January 15, 1915, he criticized editors and other public spokesmen "who throw fits of protest whenever the suggestion is made that capital punishment be abolished." He maintained that the possibility of death was seldom a deterrent to murder when a man was caught up in the passion of the moment, when "mind and hand are acting with lightning like rapidity." Dickerson remained as warden until replaced by Rufus B. Hendricks on December 5, 1916. He later took a federal appointment as an inspector with the U.S. Bureau of Prisons. When the administration in Washington changed in 1921, he spent some time in New York City working as a boxing promoter with Tex Rickard before returning to Nevada. After serving as inspector of pharmacies for the Nevada State Health Department, he was once again appointed warden of the Nevada State Prison on December 23, 1923. As irony would have it, he was called upon to preside over the lethal gas execution of Gee Jon two months later, February 8, 1924, a first for Nevada as well as the nation. That experience served to reinforce his feelings against capital punishment, and he was writing an article opposing the practice for a national penal journal at the time of his death in November 1925.[47]

The execution machine was never used again. J. Frank Trammer, Nimrod Urie's partner in the 1911 Imlay murder for which both had been sentenced to die, had his sentence commuted to life imprisonment by the Board of Pardons on November 2, 1916. Two years later, September 16, 1918, he died of natural causes. Nimrod Urie, whose coffin and grave were occupied by the body of Andrija Mircovich, was admitted to parole on December 30, 1922. Eleven months later, November 22, 1923, he was released. The execution machine had been moved to a back storage area near the old rock quarry by that time and was forgotten after Nevada went to lethal gas executions in 1924. In July 1942, the old relic was included in some fifty tons of metal collected at the prison in the course of a wartime scrap drive. Two of the rifles were maintained in the prison armory until 1977. They were discovered during an inventory in June of that year and were donated to the Nevada State Museum by Warden Charles Wolfe.[48]

In summary, the defense of Andrija Mircovich by George Thatcher was a daunting undertaking, given the nature of the evidence, the many eyewitnesses, and the prevailing sentiment of the community, but it does appear that there were indeed errors made by the prosecution which should have been given more serious consideration by Chief Justice Talbot when the case reached the Supreme Court. Mircovich did not understand, nor was he told, that he had the right to remain silent about the case, an error that modern-day jurists would consider more carefully. A more astute defense attorney would have cited the intimidating circumstances of Mircovich's initial incarceration in the Nye County Jail as a justification for excluding the remarks about the knife and his admission of guilt to Sheriff Malley, but Talbot was correct in his position that there was sufficient evidence otherwise to substantiate the fact that Mircovich had taken John Gregovich's life. Had Thatcher called Mircovich to testify, he may have been able to more forcefully make a point about the mitigating circumstances of the case. Had he called a psychiatrist, if such existed in Tonopah at that time, Mircovich's state of mind at the time of the slaying might have become a factor in his defense and could possibly have led the jury to return a verdict of something less than first-degree murder or to impose a life sentence rather than the death sentence.

In a sense, in addition to a murder case, we also have a clash of cultures, a situation in which a man acted according to his own cultural imperatives, those he had grown up with in his native Montenegro, but was prosecuted by a system which did not recognize his right to circumvent the law in seeking redress of grievances. This matter goes entirely beyond the issues of the case, such as they were at the time it was tried, but is worthy of examination in regard to other instances of ethnic violence in Nevada's history.

NOTES

1. Wilbur S. Shepperson, *Restless Strangers: Nevada's Immigrants and Their Interpreters* (Reno: University of Nevada Press, 1970).

2. Ibid., 1–9, passim.

3. Lenore Marie Kosso, "Jugoslavs in Nevada," M.A. thesis, University of Nevada, Reno, 1975.

4. George T. Prpic, *South Slav Immigration in America* (Boston: Twayne Publishers, 1978), 56–65; Russell R. Elliott, *Nevada's Twentieth Century Mining Boom: Tonopah, Goldfield, Ely* (Reno: University of Nevada Press, 1966), 254–58, passim; Kosso, "Jugoslavs in Nevada," 24–47, 48–56.

5. Elliott, *Mining Boom*, 228–31; Lenore M. Kosso, "Yugoslavs in Nevada," part 1, *Nevada Historical Society Quarterly* 28, no. 2 (Summer 1985): 71–74.

6. Sam P. Davis, ed., *The History of Nevada*, vol. 2 (Reno: Elms Publishing Co., 1913), 1197–98.

7. Nevada State Prison File no. 1479, Andrija Mircovich, Nevada Division of Archives and Records, Carson City, Nevada.

8. Sally S. Zanjani, "The Fire in the Tonopah Belmont Mine," *Journal of the West* 20, no. 2: 82–89; *Tonopah Daily Bonanza*, February 23, 1911, 1:2–5; February 24, 1911, 1:1–6; March 4, 1911, 4:3–6; March 7, 1911, 1:3–4; March 29, 1911, 1:1–2, passim; *Tonopah Miner*, March 11, 1911, 2: 1–6, 8:3; *State of Nevada* vs. *Andrija Mircovich*, Fifth Judicial District, Nye County, Nevada, Testimony of George D. Banovich, June 12, 1912, 416–39.

9. In the Matter of the Estate of Christopher Mircovich, Deceased, Records of the Office of Public Administrator, Nye County Courthouse, Tonopah, Nevada.

10. Conversation with Myrtle Tate Myles, Reno, Nevada, August 4, 1973; *State* vs. *Mircovich*, Testimony of Tom C. Kulichea, 337–98; Testimony of Nikola Chiatovich, 383–86; Testimony of Nick Kosich, 378–420.

11. *Tonopah Daily Bonanza*, May 14, 1912, 4:1; *Tonopah Miner*, May 18, 1912, 4:2; *State* vs. *Mircovich*, Testimony of Sheriff Ed Malley, June 10, 1912, 408–11; In the Matter of the Inquest over the Body of John Gregovich, May 15, 1912, Records of the Office of Coroner, Tonopah Township, Tonopah, Nevada, Testimony of J. R. Masterson, William C. Harding, William R. Walker, Steve Sabovich, and William Marsh.

12. *Tonopah Daily Bonanza*, May 14, 1912, 1:1–6; *State* vs. *Mircovich*, Testimony of Sheriff Ed Malley, June 10, 1912, 408–11.

13. *State* vs. *Mircovich*, Testimony of J. R. Masterson and Dr. Edward S. Grigsby, 336–55, 376–77; Death Certificate of John Gregovich, Division of Vital Statistics, Nevada State Department of Health, Carson City, Nevada.

14. *Tonopah Daily Bonanza*, May 15, 1912, 1:1, 5–6; May 17, 1912, 1:1; *Tonopah Miner*, May 18, 1912, 4:2; Gregovich Inquest; *State* vs. *Mircovich*, Indictment of Andrija Mircovich.

15. *Tonopah Daily Bonanza,* May 16, 1912, 1:5, 4:1, 3; May 17, 1912, 1:3–4.

16. Ibid., May 16, 1912, 4:1, 3; May 17, 1912, 1:4.

17. Ibid., May 18, 1912, 4:2; May 20, 1912, 2:1–3.

18. Ibid., June 3, 1912, 3:6; June 4, 1912, 4:2; June 5, 1912, 1:3, 4:4; June 6, 1912, 1:2–4, 4:1, 4; June 8, 1912, 1:3, 4:1; *State* vs. *Mircovich,* Jury Selection, 1–111.

19. *State* vs. *Mircovich,* Jury Selection, 113–85.

20. *Tonopah Daily Bonanza,* June 6, 1912, 4:1; *State* vs. *Mircovich,* Jury Selection, 185–241.

21. *Tonopah Daily Bonanza,* June 6, 1912, 1:2–4, 4:4; June 8, 1912, 1:3; *State* vs. *Mircovich,* Jury Selection, 242–337; Indictment of Andrija Mircovich, 328–29; Opening Statement of District Attorney Sanders, 330–35.

22. *State* vs. *Mircovich,* Testimony of Dr. J. R. Masterson, 336–55; Testimony of J. E. Peck, 356–57; Testimony of William Harding, 352–60; Testimony of William R. Walker, 361–66; Testimony of Steve Sabovich, 366–68; Testimony of Miles McCormack and William Van Patten, 366–68; Testimony of Dr. Edward S. Grigsby, 376–77; Testimony of Nick Kosich, 378–82; Testimony of Nikola Chiatovich, 383–86; Testimony of Tom G. Kuliacha, 387–89; cf. *Tonopah Daily Bonanza,* June 10, 1912, 4:5.

23. *State* vs. *Mircovich,* Testimony of Tom G. Kulichea, 390–97; Testimony of Charles G. Smith, 398–400; Testimony of Lowell Daniels, 401–7; Testimony of Sheriff Ed Malley, 408–10; Testimony of Charles Slavin, 411–13; cf. *Tonopah Daily Bonanza,* June 10, 1912, 4:5.

24. *State* vs. *Mircovich,* Testimony of James Dacevich, 414–16; Testimony of George D. Banovich, 416–39; Testimony of C. E. Wood, 439–42; Testimony of Mrs. John Gregovich, 442–43; Testimony of Steve Pavlovich, 442–46; cf. *Tonopah Daily Bonanza,* June 12, 1912, 4:4.

25. *State* vs. *Mircovich,* District Attorney Sanders's Arguments for the State, 448–63.

26. *Tonopah Daily Bonanza,* June 12, 1912, 4:4; June 13, 1912, 1:5–6, 2:1–2; June 15, 1912, 1:1–2, 4:1; *State* vs. *Mircovich,* Charge to the Jury, 58–72; Verdict, 73.

27. *Tonopah Daily Bonanza,* June 13, 1912, 1:5–6, 2:1–2.

28. *State* vs. *Mircovich,* Request for Substitution of Attorney, 49; Judgment, 74–75; Motion for a New Trial, 79; *Tonopah Daily Bonanza,* June 15, 1912, 1:1–2.

29. *Tonopah Daily Bonanza,* June 15, 1912, 1:1–2.

30. Ibid., June 17, 1912, 1:3; June 19, 1912, 3:1; June 20, 1912, 3:3.

31. *Reno Evening Gazette,* August 12, 1912, 1:1, 3:5; *Tonopah Daily Bonanza,* August 13, 1912, 1:2; August 14, 1912, 1:3–4; August 18, 1912, 2:1; August 22, 1912, 2:3; *Carson City News,* August 14, 1912, 1:3–4; August 18, 1912, 2:1; September 5, 1912, 2:1.

32. *Carson City News,* September 5, 1912, 2:1; *Reno Evening Gazette,* August 21, 1912, 5:2; *Tonopah Daily Bonanza,* August 12, 1912, 1:3; Au-

gust 13, 1912, 1:2; August 22, 1912, 2:3; August 24, 1912, 5:3; *Carson City Daily Appeal*, August 13, 1912, 1:3–4.

33. *Tonopah Daily Bonanza*, August 24, 1912, 5:3.

34. Ibid., August 15, 1912, 1:6; *Carson City Daily Appeal*, December 5, 1912, 1:1–3; December 6, 1912, 1:3–4; January 7, 1913, 1:1; March 10, 1913, 1:3; March 15, 1913, 1:4.

35. *Tonopah Daily Bonanza*, February 18, 1913, 8:3; *Carson City News*, February 14, 1913, 1:5–6, 4:4.

36. *Carson City News*, February 14, 1913, 1:5–6, 4:4; *Carson City Daily Appeal*, March 3, 1913, 1:5; March 6, 1913, 1:2–3; March 7, 1913, 1:1–2; April 1, 1913, 1:5.

37. *Journal of the Assembly*, 26th Session, 177, 185, 221, 223, 399; *Journal of the Senate*, 26th Session, 168, 170, 181, 202, 303, 304, 307; *Carson City Daily Appeal*, March 3, 1913, 1:5; April 1, 1913, 1:5.

38. *State of Nevada, Respondant*, vs. *Andrija Mircovich, Appellant*, Case no. 2032, *Report of Cases Determined in the Supreme Court of the State of Nevada*, vol. 35 (1913), 485–93; *Carson City Daily Appeal*, March 15, 1913, 1:1; *Tonopah Daily Bonanza*, March 18, 1913, 1:2–3.

39. *Tonopah Daily Bonanza*, March 18, 1913, 1:2–3; April 10, 1913, 1:4; April 15, 1913, 2:3; April 16, 1913, 1:1; April 23, 1913, 1:6; *Carson City Daily Appeal*, April 15, 1913, 1:1; April 16, 1913, 1:4; April 17, 1913, 1:3.

40. Andrija Mircovich to Board of Pardons, April 10, 1913, Nevada State Prison File no. 1479, Nevada Division of Archives and Records, Carson City, Nevada, trans. Mary Nicklanovich Hart; Personal correspondence, Mary Nicklanovich Hart, April 16, 1976.

41. Ross Lewers to Austin Jackson, May 14, 1913, Nevada State Prison File no. 1479, Nevada Division of Archives and Records, Carson City, Nevada; *Tonopah Daily Bonanza*, May 12, 1913, 1:6–7; *Nevada State Journal*, May 14, 1913, 1:4.

42. *Nevada State Journal*, May 14, 1913, 1:4; *Carson City News*, May 15, 1913, 1:4–5, 4:5; *Carson City Daily Appeal*, May 14, 1913, 1:4.

43. *Reno Evening Gazette*, May 14, 1913, 1:1, 3–4; *Carson City Daily Appeal*, May 14, 1913, 1:1–4; *Carson City News*, May 15, 1913, 1:4–5, 4:5; *Nevada State Journal*, May 15, 1913, 4:2.

44. *Biennial Report of the Warden of the Nevada State Prison* (1911–1912), 32; *Carson City News*, May 15, 1913, 1:4–5; *Parish Register*, St. Peter's Episcopal Church, Carson City, Nevada, vol. 3, 220, Archives of the Nevada Historical Society, Reno, Nevada.

45. *Reno Evening Gazette*, May 14, 1913, 1:1, 7, 2:2–4; Ross Lewers to Austin Jackson, May 14, 1913, Mircovich File.

46. *Tonopah Daily Bonanza*, May 15, 1913, 2:1–2.

47. *Biennial Report of the Warden of the Nevada State Prison* (1913–1914), 8; *Nevada Democrat*, January 15, 1915, 4:1; *Reno Evening Gazette*, December 5, 1916, 1:2–3; November 30, 1925, 1:8, 2:2; *Fallon Standard*, April 6, 1921, 3:5; August 17, 1921, 1:3; *Carson City News*, December 18,

1923, 1:3–4; Loren B. Chan, "Example for the Nation: Nevada's Execution of Gee Jon," *Nevada Historical Society Quarterly* 18, no. 2 (Summer 1975): 91–106; Telephone conversation with Noreen Dickerson Buck, daughter of Denver Dickerson, Reno, Nevada, October 16, 1978.

48. *Reno Evening Gazette,* November 3, 1916, 6:1; September 18, 1918, 8:3–4; *Humboldt Star,* January 3, 1923, 1:4; Nevada State Prison File no. 1402, Nimrod Urie, Nevada Division of Archives and Records, Carson City, Nevada; *Carson City Daily Appeal,* July 28, 1942, 1:2; *Carson City Chronicle,* August 7, 1942, 1:6; *Biennial Report of the Warden of the Nevada State Prison* (1940–1942), 4–5; Interview with former Nevada State Prison Warden Jack Fogliani, Jacks Valley, Nevada, May 7, 1977; *Nevada Appeal,* June 17, 1977, 1:1–3.

GUE GIM WAH: PIONEERING CHINESE AMERICAN WOMAN OF NEVADA

SUE FAWN CHUNG

Unlike many of the restless strangers to Nevada,[1] Gue Gim Wah came to a small, rural mining community in 1916 and stayed. She was not a sojourner, "a stranger who spends many years of his lifetime in a foreign country without being assimilated by it," or, in other words, a temporary resident who came to earn money but would eventually move back to his or her homeland for permanent settlement.[2] She is representative of a small minority of Chinese who found the offerings of Nevada attractive and, despite several opportunities to change her home, chose to remain in Nevada. She is also characteristic of many Chinese Americans who, by the turn of the twentieth century, began to express their desires for assimilation.[3] Since assimilation requires changes in values, a change in the reference group, and acceptance by the majority society, the process for the Chinese was slow.[4] It was especially difficult for them because their heritage came from the oldest continuous civilization in the world and they often clung to their group identity in the face of American hostility and discrimination. Nevertheless, a segment of the Chinese in the United States, usually born around the turn of the century, made great strides in the assimilation process and were firmly committed to the United States as their permanent homeland. The process was aided by the growing acceptance of Chinese Americans in the twentieth century, in sharp contrast to the discrimination and anti-Chinese movements of the late nineteenth century.

The story of Gue Gim Wah symbolizes the struggles, contributions, and achievements of many Chinese in Nevada as well as elsewhere in the United States. She reaffirmed her commitment to her adopted homeland several times in her lifetime. This was especially unusual for a woman, who, by nature of her gender and role in life, is usually the cultural preserver. What were the factors contributing to her assimilation and success? In this paper I hope to answer these questions. Her success did not go unrecognized. On October 31, 1980, in celebration of Nevada's 116 years of statehood, Gue Gim Wah served as the grand marshal for the Nevada Day Parade in the state capital, Carson City. Proudly she rode in an open car with her lifelong friend and neighbor Mary Thomas, who was also from the small mining town of Prince, Nevada, and with her Hong Kong–born granddaughter Wei Ling Chow and her husband, Stanley Chow.[5] She was the first person of Asian ancestry and the second woman to be so honored by the state.

This study of her life is based primarily upon oral interviews conducted separately by myself and Mrs. Elizabeth Patrick, newspaper and magazine articles on Gue Gim Wah, and a survey of the local Lincoln County newspapers.[6] The first part, "Background," is a reconstructed history and uses works on Chinese American history to supplement the sketchy information provided by Mrs. Wah. The second and third sections, "Tom Fook Wah" and "Gue Gim Wah in Nevada," rely heavily upon the oral interviews, newspapers, and magazines. The fourth part, "Conclusion," is an analysis of her life in terms of general Chinese American history and the questions of biculturalism and assimilation.

BACKGROUND

When Gue Gim was born in 1900 in Lin Lun Li, a village probably in the Hoiping (present-day Kaiping) district of Guangdong province, not far from Hong Kong and Guangzhou (Canton), her father, Ng Louie Der (or Der Ng Louie in Chinese), had his main home and business in San Francisco, California. Der, like many other young Chinese men in traditionally Chinese emigrant communities like Hoiping in the late nineteenth century, had been lured to Gum Shan (literally, the "Golden Mountains," the Chinese name for California) by the promise of wealth. There were many reasons for this massive Chinese exodus.[7] The

Manchu Qing Dynasty (1644–1911) was on the decline. The people of South China had experienced two foreign wars and an internal rebellion, all of which eventually resulted in high taxation, widespread unemployment, and general discontent. Land-ownership, a valued commodity in agricultural China for centuries, became increasingly concentrated in the hands of a few, so many peasants left their homes because of the high rents and marginal or subsistence level of living. Millions of Chinese from Guangdong province and the surrounding areas emigrated overseas between 1840 and 1900 in the hopes of improving their financial situation so that they could return home and thereafter live a comfortable life. The majority of the Chinese went to Southeast Asia. However, news of the discovery of gold in California in 1849 brought hundreds of Chinese to the United States in search of instant wealth.[8] Later, labor brokers for the railroads, agriculturalists, and other businesses in the United States also promised great wealth to the Chinese and freely distributed alluring circulars, such as the one translated here, in the greater Canton area: "Americans are very rich people. They want the Chinaman to come and make him very welcome. There you will have great pay, large houses, and food and clothing of the finest description. . . . It is a nice country, without mandarins [officials]. . . . All are alike; big man no larger than little man. There are a great many Chinamen there now, and it will not be a strange country. . . . Money is in great plenty and to spare in America."[9]

In an effort to escape the worsening economic and agricultural conditions in Guangdong, Der left his native land of Hoiping sometime around 1870 or 1880 in search of this great land of opportunities. Since he eventually became a merchant in Chinatown, it is probable that a relative had attained some degree of success in San Francisco and urged him to make the trip. In 1861 about 2,000 (4 percent) of the 50,000 Chinese in the United States were classified as merchants, and by 1868 San Francisco's Chinese merchants had been able to expand their businesses so that they sold goods to Chinese miners and others throughout the western United States.[10] One of the common ways to finance these businesses was through the traditional rotating credit systems carried overseas by the Chinese in the form of a *hui* (often called a *piu wui* in Cantonese).[11] By the late nineteenth century, the extended Der family in San Francisco's Chinatown, probably with the help of their *hui*, began to specialize in the hardware and candy store businesses. Their prosperity was increased when a mercantile feud broke out in San Francisco in the 1890s among the Sam Yup ("Three Counties"), which had dominated the business scene in Chinatown, and the Sze Yup ("Four Counties," which include Hoiping), which gained supremacy after the feud.[12] According to Gue Gim Wah, by 1912 her father had his own store, which was probably a hardware and candy store, and was a prosperous member of the Chinatown mercantile community.

Like many of the early Chinese immigrants, Der was married before he left China. In keeping with tradition, his wife remained in the home or village of his parents so that she could serve them during his absence.[13] This system kept the Chinese emigrant bound to his homeland. Whenever he could afford it, Ng Louie Der returned to China to see his wife and parents. His wife bore him five children, including three boys and little Gue Gim, during the intervening years.[14] Because her mother died when she was eight, Gue Gim went to live first with her recently married older brother and then with an aunt and uncle in their little village not far from Hong Kong. Meanwhile, her father married a woman living in Canton and started a second family.

By 1912 Der decided that he wanted to bring his family to San Francisco, thus ending his "mutilated family" system.[15] In addition, it was becoming increasingly risky to travel back and forth to China with the increasing amount of anti-Chinese legislation designed to discourage Chinese immigration to the United States. For example, the Scott Act of 1888, which prohibited Chinese laborers from entering the United States, prevented some 20,000 laborers, who had gone back to China for a visit and had reentry permits, from returning even though they had property and family here.[16] One never knew what anti-Chinese agitators would try. The 1893 McCreary Amendment to the 1892 Geary Act had increased restrictions on Chinese businessmen, and threats of greater restrictions loomed on the horizon.[17] By the turn of the century, more families were living in San Francisco's Chinatown. As a result, Chinatown was becoming less and less like the bachelor society that had been dominant in the late nineteenth century. A 1900 U.S. Supreme Court decision allowed

Chinese merchants to bring their wives and minor children into this country.[18] Many Chinese merchants had probably taken this opportunity to move their families to the United States. While he was still able to get them into the United States, Der decided to take four of his children and his second wife back with him to live in San Francisco.

In 1912 the Der family sailed to California by way of Hong Kong and Honolulu. According to Gue Gim, she was very sick from the pills that were given "to kill the worms inside." [19] From the late 1800s until the early 1920s, the Chinese immigrants had to be examined for hookworm infestation in addition to the generally required physical examination.[20] By taking the pills, she hoped to pass the examination at Angel Island, but she had a difficult passage because of them. She had been anxious to go to the United States because she had heard the tales of immense wealth and luxurious living. However, her initial experience was far from pleasant.

When the Der family reached San Francisco, they were sent by boat to Angel Island for questioning. Most of the 175,000 Chinese who entered the United States between 1910 and 1940 were interviewed by U.S. immigration officials with the aid of interpreters at the island. Gue Gim, who knew no English, was the first person on the boat to be summoned by the officials. Her fears were quieted somewhat when her stepmother was the next person summoned. Although she had been questioned for only two days, she was kept "locked up like [in] a jail" for five days on the island. She was lucky. Many Chinese had been and would be detained for longer periods, even months. The walls of the detention building were covered with poems written in Chinese, such as the following:

> I had always admired America as a land of leisure.
> Immediately I had raised funds and started my voyage.
> For over a month I experienced fully the winds and waves.
> Now on arrival I am subject to the ordeal of imprisonment.
> I see Oakland close by and yet I cannot land.
> I wish to return to China and again be a farmer.
> My belly is full of discontent and I found it difficult to sleep.
> Therefore I write these few lines to express my thoughts.[21]

There had been only three Chinese families aboard ship and Gue Gim had become acquainted with them, so when they all reached Angel Island they felt a common bond. The women were segregated from the men in relatively barren rooms. Gue Gim was very curious about the women from India who also shared their quarters. This was her introduction to a totally different culture.

The interviews by the officials were long and tedious and included the recognition of photographs of her father and uncle which had been taken when they were younger. Her brothers' interviews were easier because their father knew English and could assist them. Der also had a Caucasian friend (probably an attorney or layman familiar with the immigration system) who advised them throughout the interrogations. After extensive questioning, they were given a "physical" examination. Fortunately for the Der children, they all resembled their father. According to Gue Gim, although she was very slender, she had her father's face and the boys had his portly figure. None of them could be considered "paper children"; that is, children who claimed to be related to a Chinese already residing in the United States for the purposes of immigration.[22] From Angel Island, the Der family proceeded to San Francisco's Chinatown.

Gue Gim's four-year stay in San Francisco was not as pleasant as she had hoped. Years later Gue Gim would recall, "I no like San Francisco. Dirty city. Horses make manure on street. Always smell. [I like] Hong Kong better. No horses. Use rickshaw, no dirty up streets."[23] Nevertheless, San Francisco's Chinatown had a familiar atmosphere with its typical Chinese stores, Chinese signs, smells of Chinese cooking, and the ever-present sound of Cantonese, spoken everywhere in this ten-block-square ghetto.[24] The housing conditions were extremely crowded. One- or two-room apartments for an entire family were common during the early twentieth century. Gue Gim's father, like many other businessmen, had converted the back part of his store into a home for his family. This kind of living arrangement was observed by California historian Hubert Howe Bancroft, who wrote that the wives of Chinese merchants lived in quarters behind their husbands' stores wherein "the furniture . . . is of the simplest, and more limited than at the store establishment save an extra plant or so. Indeed the wife is kept so secluded that all show may be dispensed with."[25] Chinese wives and female children of the upper class had little contact with the outside world.

The young Mrs. Der was kept busy by the ever-increasing size of the Der family, and Gue Gim, being the oldest female child, undoubtedly had to help at home.

Gue Gim had two approved activities outside her home: Chinese language school and church. At the age of twelve, she was supposed to attend the public English language Oriental School (later called Commodore Stockton School) in Chinatown, but the school was overcrowded and housed in a two-story temporary building.[26] The Oriental School also placed recently arrived students in classes with younger native-born Chinese children. Gue Gim might have felt awkward in such a situation. Her father chose to send her to a private Chinese language school. Chinese language schools had been organized as early as 1884 and often supplemented the public school education. Since one could live one's entire life in Chinatown without speaking English, Ng Louie Der probably felt it was unnecessary for his daughter to learn English. Moreover, many of the well-to-do Chinese men preferred traditional Chinese wives, so a knowledge of English would not be important to them. Nevertheless, Gue Gim was exposed to the children of Chinatown and many of them were beginning to adopt American ideas and American ways.

Gue Gim's other outside activity played a more important role in her acculturation process. For many years during the late nineteenth and early twentieth centuries, the Christian missions, especially the Presbyterian and Methodist ones, proudly pointed out that they were the only American institutions that were open and friendly toward the Chinese immigrants.[27] Often the missionaries would help the wives and children accommodate or acculturate into American life through Sunday schools, English language classes, social gatherings, and other activities.

Shortly after his arrival in the United States, Der had joined the Methodist Episcopal church. A Christian identity established the trustworthiness of the Chinese merchants, especially among those who had to work with the majority society.[28] It would not be surprising if he had become acquainted with the famous Reverend Otis Gibson, who headed the Methodist Mission in San Francisco's Chinatown in the 1870s and 1880s and wrote a work in defense of the Chinese immigrants entitled *The Chinese in America* in 1877.[29] Perhaps he also knew the notable

Walter N. Fong (Fong Kum Ngon), who first arrived in the United States in 1881, studied at Stanford University, became a Methodist minister, and was appointed professor of Chinese language and literature at the University of California, Berkeley.[30] In 1910, when Angel Island opened, Methodist women would volunteer to help out the new Chinese immigrants, especially the women, during their detention period. These kinds of activities probably persuaded Der that his children should be Christians, so when Gue Gim was born, she was baptized in a canal in China shortly after her birth, thus fulfilling her father's religious desires. When the family arrived in San Francisco, all of the members attended the Powell Street Methodist Episcopal Church in San Francisco's Chinatown.[31] The church also operated a church school and Gue Gim might have been a student there. This was a major step in the integration of the family into the major society.

The image of the "heathen Chinee" was not applicable to Gue Gim and her family.[32] The fact that she had a religious, Christian upbringing would make her more acceptable to the majority society when she moved to Prince, Nevada. There she joined the Episcopal church in nearby Pioche because the town did not have a Methodist Episcopal church. Even in her eighties, she attended church as regularly as possible and was active in church affairs and activities.

TOM FOOK WAH

Gue Gim's entire life changed radically one day in 1915 when she met Tom Fook Wah. Tom was born in the mining town of Marysville, California, in 1871.[33] During the first year of his life, both of Tom's parents died. Shortly thereafter, his aunt and uncle took him to their native village in Hoiping (Kaiping), Guangdong, where he met Gue Gim's father. When Tom reached the age of twenty-one, his uncle decided to take him back to the United States. Tom's aunt chose to remain in China probably because she did not like the harsh conditions of rural California. In 1892 Tom reached the shores of California, but he had a difficult time proving that he was not a "paper son." Immigration officials were very suspicious of this "honorable deception" practice of the Chinese and worked hard to enforce the 1882, 1888, and 1892 anti-Chinese immigration laws.[34] According to Gue Gim, after long interrogation sessions in the wooden shed at the

Pacific Mail Steamship Company wharf on the San Francisco waterfront, Tom was "re-admitted" to the country, but his Marysville birth was not acknowledged and he was regarded as a "foreign-born" Chinese. Moreover, United States immigration officials, not always realizing that the Chinese gave their family name first as an indication of their pride in their family line, reversed his name and gave him the first name of Tom, instead of Fook Wah, and the last name of Wah, instead of Tom. This was a common problem for Chinese immigrants until the mid-twentieth century.

Tom accompanied his uncle back to Marysville and worked there as a cook for an American family, who taught him some spoken and perhaps even some written English. This made Tom more comfortable in the larger community and helped him accommodate to American ways. The training in Western cooking was going to be invaluable for him because he would find his ultimate career as a cook. Many other Chinese cooks shared this experience with him. His next job was as a farmhand in the Sacramento Valley. Among his many tasks was the clearing of land for hops cultivation. By 1882, the California Chinese made up 50 to 75 percent of the agricultural labor force in California, so it was not surprising that Tom found his way into this type of occupation.[35] However, Tom became restless and decided to seek better job opportunities. He heard about the new wealth provided by the Arizona copper mines, so he left California and headed for Yuma and Tucson. He found that he could make a better, though modest, living through his cooking talent, so he opened up a small restaurant in Yuma for the copper miners. For many other Chinese in America, the restaurant business was "the first choice of the self-employed Chinese."[36] When the restaurant burned down and he found himself broke, he moved on. This mobility of young, restless Chinese men was typical of this period.

Tom heard about a new mining boom centered in Nevada, so he decided to try his luck there. The discovery of gold in California in 1849 had lured some 2,716 Chinese to the gold fields of California between 1849 and 1851.[37] The possibility of instant wealth through mining was still a dream that preoccupied the hearts and minds of many Chinese immigrants. Tom no doubt also shared in this dream. What he did not know was that Nevada was primarily a hard rock, not a placer, mining state. Hard rock mining required a considerable investment in equipment and manpower, so mining companies, rather than individuals, generally controlled the hard rock mining sites. Chinese miners favored the more independent placer mining, so even during the peak years of Nevada's mining operations there were few Chinese miners. For example, in 1870, out of the state's 42,491 people, only 3,152 were Chinese, and of these, only 240 (7 percent) were miners, partly as a result of anti-Chinese legislation and of the nature of hard rock mining.[38] Thus the Chinese in Nevada frequently found employment in positions such as cooks, boarding house managers, owners or managers of general stores, laundrymen, gambling house operators, produce growers or peddlers, and railroad workers rather than as miners. But Tom did not know this as he headed for Goldfield, Nevada.

Tom faced some difficult situations in Nevada. Until 1910, the Chinese made up the second largest minority group in Nevada. Anti-Asian sentiment prevailed in many boomtowns. When, around 1909, Tom boarded the train for Goldfield, he did not know that the townsfolk had passed a number of anti-Chinese laws, including one prohibiting the Chinese from disembarking from the train in their town.[39] When Tom discovered this, he was forced to stay on the train until he reached the small mining community of Ely. There he opened up a small restaurant, but anti-Chinese sentiment quickly arose and the miners, using a common tactic throughout Nevada, decided to boycott the restaurant. This forced Tom to leave Ely and head south again. He finally settled down in Caliente to work as a cook for the railroad company, but he disliked the job because there was no icebox to keep the food cold and the weather was too hot. Then one day a man from Salt Lake City, Utah, stopped at Tom's restaurant, told him about the future opening of the nearby Prince Mine, and persuaded him to apply for the position of cook there.

Mining company officials often searched for good cooks in Nevada. They knew that one way to keep the itinerant miners on the mine site was to offer good food. Chinese cooks had an excellent reputation since the first mining booms in Nevada and most of the Chinese in the Comstock Lode area in the 1870s and 1880s had been cooks or boarding house managers.[40] These cooks made familiar American dishes since most Americans

TABLE 1.
1900 NEVADA CENSUS BULLETIN*

Population of Nevada			42,335
Natives			32,242
Males	25,603		
Females	16,732		
Foreign-born			10,093
Chinese		1,352	
Males	1,283		
Females	69		

*Census taking was very inaccurate at this time in Nevada. This report was published in the *Lincoln County Record*, August 30, 1901.

were ill at ease with Chinese dishes prior to World War I. In 1902 the *New York Times* expressed the general American attitude toward Chinese cuisine by remarking, on the occasion of a Chinese banquet given for American politicians, that the coroner was the only person fit to pronounce judgment on the dishes that had been served. Tom had acquired a reputation of being a good cook, so he took the chance and went to Prince, the new mining community located ten miles south of Pioche.

Tom probably took the Union Pacific, a line that had been completed by 1905, to Pioche, then went by foot or wagon to Prince, which was being built by the Prince Consolidated Mining Company.[41] He never dreamed in 1911 that this isolated desert community was going to be his home. He would no longer be a restless stranger. Since the kitchen and boarding house were not finished when he got to Prince, he started by working as a general handyman. He made some new friends, including Louie Lim, who was nicknamed "Monkey Wrench." Another Chinese worker was known to the local populace as "China Ed." China Ed had lived in Lincoln County since the 1870s and had operated restaurants in both Pioche and Delamar before becoming a cook at the Bullionville boarding house of the Prince Mines.[42] Tom became known as "Chinaman Tom." The Prince Mine began to prosper, and by 1912 some eighty men constructed a private railroad to Pioche so that ore could then be transported by the Union Pacific.[43] This brought more miners into the area, and Tom Wah's boarding house became the center of social activities for miners in Prince. World War I brought great prosperity into the area for the miners.

Tom had gained some status in the community, but when the isolation became too much to bear and when work permitted, he probably went into Pioche. Pioche was named after the reputed millionaire F. L. Pioche, a native of France who went to California with the Argonauts.[44] Gold had been discovered there in 1863 by the Pauite Indians, who brought it to the Mormon missionary William Hamblin of Santa Clara, Utah. In 1867 Pioche sent his assistant, Charles Hoffman, to the area to stake his claim. By 1870 the little post office called Pioche was established in the depression of the northern slope of a 6,000-foot mountain range. Soon it became the county seat of Lincoln County. Between 1863 and 1872 some $40 million was produced from crude mining. The population soared to 14,000, but by 1871 the mining boom began to wane. By 1875 there were only 2,753 people living in Pioche. New life was given to the town around 1892 when the railroad was built between Salt Lake City, Utah, and Los Angeles, California.

A Chinatown gradually developed in Pioche. This was typical of many western rural mining communities. By 1872 the Chinatown population was estimated at two hundred.[45] Although most of the Chinese in the area were males, Gue Gim heard rumors that there were also some twenty to thirty "red light girls" to serve the Chinese and white male population. Chinatown was located on lower Main Street on the hillside below the courthouse and was bounded on the west by Pioche Street and on the east by Main Street. There were several gambling houses that served the Caucasian as well as Chinese population, a joss house (temple) that was the focal point of Chinese New Year celebrations even into the early 1900s, several restaurants and hand laundries, and at least one general store.[46] These were the essential features of Chinatowns throughout Nevada and the western United States.

The residents and miners of the Pioche area apparently liked the meals prepared by the Chinese. At the turn of the century, two Chinese restaurants were so popular that the Chinese owners advertised regularly in the local newspaper.[47] Woo Tom's Restaurant and China Dick's Restaurant (later called Hang Chung's), both on Main Street, featured their "3 meals for $1" special and pointed out their specialty of pies and other baked goods. The local newspaper editor regarded China Dick, who had been in business in Lincoln County for a number of years, as "a first-class restaurant man."[48] The most notable Chinese restaurant owner in Pioche was Yee Wah Ling, or "China Charlie," who lived in Pioche from 1881 until his death in 1931 at the age of eighty-four.[49] When he died, he left his New Pioche Cafe to his son, Yee Wing, whom he had brought from Canton in 1916 at the age of eighteen.[50] Yee Wing, a Christian, had a wife, two daughters, and a son in China. When he died in 1934 at the age of forty-four, the local newspaper commented, "It is said of [Yee] Wing that no one left his place hungry. If they did not have the money with which to pay, all were given a meal and sent on their way rejoicing."[51] According to Gue Gim, they had been friends, and when Yee Wing died he left some of his Chinese treasures to her.[52]

These long-time Chinese residents of Lincoln County, such as China Dick, China Charlie, and Tom Fook Wah, felt at home in this area. Unlike many of the mining communities of the western United States, the residents of Pioche and suburbs such as Prince were fairly tolerant of the Chinese. The reasons for this tolerance were similar to those that existed in certain other parts of the western United States.[53] First and foremost, the Chinese in the Pioche area occupied an important economic niche in the community by performing menial but necessary low-paying jobs. They had a good reputation for reliable hard work, were not fond of liquor as some other minority groups were, and provided needed services such as restaurants, laundries, and entertainment centers. For these reasons, the mining companies that controlled hard rock mining often encouraged the Chinese to settle in their communities whenever possible. These mining companies also could regulate the economic role of the Chinese since they provided the specific jobs in a relatively stable, controlled community.[54] The frontier spirit prevailed in this mountainous desert area that was subject to heavy snows in the winter and severe flooding in the spring. The economy of the region had great boom and bust periods. As a result, most of the people were transients and Pioche had the reputation of being a "wild" place until the Mormon influence and a more stable community became established in the 1930s. Few people could endure these hardships and those who did, regardless of their race or sex, were regarded as valuable "old-timers" by the local populace. Another factor in this tolerance was the fact that the Chinese formed only a small percentage of the total population in Lincoln County, which, at the turn of the century, was the largest county in the state in terms of area.[55] Moreover, the Chinese population continued to dwindle in the area. Finally, in an area where the Chinese made up such a minority of the population, they were forced to adjust to the majority population. This accommodation or acculturation in a frontier community made them more acceptable to the rest of the population. This atmosphere of relative friendliness and tolerance contributed to the long-time residency of the Chinese in Lincoln County's Pioche and neighboring towns.

Tom began to settle down and by 1915 felt that it was time to find a wife. His decision was partially based upon the growing prosperity of the Prince Mine. During World War I, the mine was thriving with a continuous increase in its production and its employment of some four hundred miners who needed to be housed and fed.[56] Tom was the manager of the mine-owned boarding house and restaurant. His social hall was the center of social activities in Prince.[57] He had several Chinese assistants and together they prepared the meals for the executive dining room and the mess hall. One day in 1914 or 1915, the mine owners told him there was a large vein of silver running under the kitchen, so Tom was forced to move all of his equipment.[58] During the move, the wagon loaded with meat grinders, chairs, pots, cleavers, and other equipment accidentally knocked Tom down. His leg was injured. Distrustful of Western medicine, Tom sent a telegram to the famous San Francisco herbalist, Ong Ting Shew.[59] According to Gue Gim, Ong sent another herbalist, Dr. Chan Ting How, to treat Tom's leg. Chinese herbalists had been practicing since the 1850s in the United States and were popular not only among the Chinese but also among the Caucasian population. In Nevada in 1870 there were eighteen Chinese doctors and by 1880 the number had increased to twenty-two.[60] In the 1870s and 1880s Pioche even had its own Chinese doctor, who was considered part of the social elite of the town.[61] But in the early twentieth century, Tom had to wait for four days until Dr. Chan could arrive from San Francisco and treat his injury.

TABLE 2.
LINCOLN COUNTY: CHINESE POPULATION*

	Nevada		Lincoln County	
Year	All People	Chinese	All People	Chinese
1890	47,355	2,833		34
1900	42,335	1,352		72
1910	81,875	927		32
1920	77,407	689	2,287	18
1930	91,058	483	3,601	7
1940	110,247	286	4,130	1
1950	160,083	281	3,837	3
1960	285,278	572	2,431	3
1970	488,738	955	2,557	2
1980	800,493	2,979	3,732	5

*U.S. Bureau of the Census, *General Population Characteristics: Nevada* (title varies), (Washington, D.C., 1900–1980).

As Dr. Chan treated Tom, he urged him to get married so that he would have someone to take care of him.

Tom probably was persuaded that the time had come for marriage, but the problem was where he would find a wife. There were very few Chinese women in the United States—a ratio of twenty-six males to one female at this time—and an even smaller number lived in Nevada. Tom probably heard about the alternatives that some Chinese men had taken. In 1904, the local press reported that a Chinese male had married an Indian squaw.[62] In that same year, Joe Sing, an American citizen who voted several times and lived in nearby Eureka, wanted to marry a Caucasian girl, but this was denied due to an 1861 state law that specifically prohibited interracial marriages of "whites with Indians, Chinese, mulattos, and Negroes."[63] Tom did not wish to follow these precedents. He was traditional enough to want a Chinese bride, but the problem was how to find one.

Just before the heavy winter snowfalls of 1915, Tom decided to take a vacation and see the Panama Exhibition with a brief stop in San Francisco. While visiting his friend, Ng Louie Der and perhaps buying some supplies from him, he noticed Gue Gim going in and out of the store. Here was his

TABLE 3.
CHINESE POPULATION BY SEX*

	United States		Nevada	
Year	Males	Females	Males	Females
1870	58,633	4,566	2,817	306
1880	100,686	4,779	5,102	306
1890	103,620	3,868	2,749	84
1900	85,341	4,522	1,283	69
1910	66,856	4,675	876	51
1920	53,891	7,748	630	59

*U.S. Bureau of the Census, *Ninth Census* through *Fourteenth Census* (Washington, D.C., 1872–1921).

solution! He asked Der for her hand in marriage and Der, realizing that the time of marriage had come for Gue Gim and that Tom was a good prospect, agreed. Most well-to-do young Chinese men in the United States returned to China to find a bride because of the greater selection and the myth that a girl who married a Chinese American would have a rich and luxurious life.[64] However, Tom was already forty-three and with his leg injury did not care to travel back to China to find a bride. He wanted to marry Gue Gim right away, but because Gue Gim's stepmother was pregnant and needed her help, the marriage was postponed until January or October, 1916.[65]

At the age of fifteen, Gue Gim was not enthusiastic about the prospects of marrying a man twenty-eight years older than she was. However, like millions of Chinese daughters before her, she obeyed her father's directive. Marriage to older men was not uncommon in Chinese society. They had a traditional Chinese wedding, as was the custom in San Francisco's Chinatown. Since her stepmother was Buddhist and her father was Christian, Gue Gim had two religious ceremonies during the wedding, which was held in the hotel where Tom usually stayed. It was customary for the groom to plan the celebration and pay the expenses. According to Gue Gim, she wore a long Chinese dress that was made specially for the occasion, bid farewell to her stepmother at home, and was escorted by two females (probably the go-betweens) to

Tom's hotel. This symbolically marked her separation from her own family. When she reached the hotel, she was greeted by firecrackers. "This scared me," she recalled. During the ceremony, in the tradition of their native village, she fanned her husband three times in order to show her union with him and he drank three small cups of rice wine to finalize their marriage bonds. In Western fashion, rice was thrown as they left the hotel. They went to her parents' home to meet the relatives and later that day, attended a huge traditional wedding banquet.

GUE GIM WAH IN NEVADA

The newlyweds went to Prince, Nevada, and a new chapter in Gue Gim's life began. Upon hearing news of the marriage, the mine supervisor and his wife decided to hold a social gathering to welcome Tom's bride. (The last notable Chinese marriage had occurred in November, 1877, when Charlie Beene, one of Pioche's most prominent Chinese merchants, married Sen Choy, who had come directly from China.[66] That marriage was celebrated by some of the most prominent citizens in town, including the local newspaper editor.) Gue Gim, dressed in her traditional Chinese long gown, attended her first American social gathering. Tom realized that she had to have some contact with the American community, despite any fears that she might have about "blue-eyed" people, so he taught her her first English sentence, "You come again," so that she could encourage members of the community to visit them.

Gue Gim realized that learning English would be important in her new world. Since she was just sixteen, she was very shy. She maintained the practice she had learned from her stepmother and other women in Chinatown of staying secluded at home. This later gave rise to the rumor that Tom kept his wife chained to the front porch in order to keep her at home, but Gue Gim vehemently denied the rumor. When she went to visit her parents for a few months shortly after her move to Nevada, she learned a few more words of English from a teacher there. Since the early twentieth century, progressive groups in San Francisco's Chinatown had been advocating the education of women, who consequently would make better wives, mothers, and citizens.[67] Gue Gim apparently was influenced by this trend. One of the mine owners, aware of her desire, offered to make arrangements for her to attend the Prince School. With Tom's encouragement, she went.

The experience was going to be a major cultural adjustment for her, and it had an impact upon her new classmates. There were approximately thirteen students in the one-room schoolhouse that held classes from the first to eighth grades. The children were enthusiastic about their new classmate and helped her with her English, often by acting out stories so she could understand what was going on. They made her feel welcome. During the recess, the teacher would give her individual instructions in English. Eventually, the children wanted to know more about her background, so the teacher devised a special program called "A Trip to Asia" in November 1917, and parents and friends attended the special event.[68] The program and activities were actually part of a larger trend in the United States that strove toward greater world understanding as a part of the World War I experience and the "melting pot" belief that all immigrants would eventually merge with the greater society.[69] During this period, there was a great Americanization drive and, unknowingly, Gue Gim Wah was caught up in the movement. Her positive educational experience at the Prince School would change her outlook on life.

Gue Gim learned English, broadened her horizons, and made new friends at school, which began at 9 A.M and ended at 4 P.M. She was the oldest student. Because she was able to learn quickly, she passed through the eight grades within a few years. During her student days she became good friends with Mary Thomas, daughter of Leonard G. Thomas, superintendent of the Combined Metals Reduction Company of the Prince Mine, and a lifelong friendship blossomed between the two girls. Mr. Thomas became a benefactor of the Wahs as the years passed. When Elizabeth Gemmill's father purchased the Prince Consolidated Mining Company, eight-year-old Elizabeth and twenty-four-year-old Gue Gim began their lifelong friendship at the school.

During this time, between 1916 and 1927, the fortunes of the Prince Mine and the Wahs rose and fell. Tom's boarding house was noted as the community's social center and Tom became a well-known figure. However, after the end of World War I, the number of miners in the area decreased drastically. Just as things were looking bleak, a new mine site was opened near Prince. The site, named for J. A. Caselton, who directed the National Lead Company's participation in the operations of the Combined Metals Reduction Company, was in operation by the early 1920s and shipped its ore to a mill at Bauer, Utah.[70] Then, in 1925, the Prince Mine reported a new, large strike in silver and lead and by 1926 there were sixty men on the mine's payroll.[71] Tom Fook Wah was busier than ever until tragedy struck. A fire broke out in the boarding house in 1927 and the Wahs were ruined. Gue Gim said, "Those [were] good days. We make much money, but [like many Chinese Americans], Tom no believe in banks. He keep money in house. One day [there was] a fire. Tom, he throws bags of money out, but [they] catch fire . . . and wind blow money back into fire. All burn up. We start over." At first, Tom did not know where to turn. Then he decided to try to collect some of his inheritance from his father's estate and liquidate some of his investments in South China. This meant a trip to China.

The return to the country of her birth was to be a novel and memorable experience for Gue Gim. When she arrived in Hong Kong, she was surprised at how "big and crowded" it was, especially in comparison to her quiet life in the high desert country. Gue Gim enrolled in a teacher's training school in order to continue her education while Tom tried to straighten out his business affairs. They had planned to return within the year, but Tom fell ill and got an official extension for his stay away from the United States for another year. Gue Gim's extension, however, was not approved and this was going to cause them some legal problems. The Immigration Law of 1924 excluded all aliens ineligible for citizenship, such as Asians and Chinese-born wives of American citizens.[72] Gue Gim knew enough about American ways to realize that she needed help, so she contacted her father in San Francisco and he, in turn, hired an attorney who persuaded the American consulate in Hong Kong to grant her permission to reenter the United States in 1929. When the Prince-Caselton-Pioche communities heard about the Wahs' plight, they also came to the rescue by sending an affidavit expressing their desire for the Wahs' return to their area.

Meanwhile, during their stay in China, Tom and Gue Gim became parents. One day they encountered an impoverished fam-

ily. The parents and grandmother of a two-year-old boy persuaded the childless Wahs that the Wahs were in a better position
to raise the boy than they were. The boy had been suffering
from starvation and other illnesses. Gue Gim was at first reluctant, but Tom was ecstatic. Perhaps this was Tom's chance to
have an heir to carry on his family line. The Wahs persuaded the
parents to accept some money for the child and they named him
Tan Kong Sing (Tan is the original spelling of Tom Fook Wah's
last name). Some of the joys and heartbreaks of parenthood
were now theirs.

The Wahs did not realize that they were going to face some
insurmountable problems. When they tried to obtain permission from the U.S. government to bring their adopted son home,
they encountered all kinds of legal difficulties. Although the
state of Nevada might have recognized the adoption as legitimate with the passage of a law in 1921 allowing an "adult Mongolian" to adopt a Mongolian child, American government officials did not regard the adoption as legitimate.[73] A 1906 request
of an American woman who wanted to adopt a Chinese child
and bring her into the United States was denied and the decision was reaffirmed in a 1914 case extending the situation to include adopted children of Chinese Americans.[74] Brokenhearted,
the Wahs were forced to leave the child in Hong Kong with
Tom's relatives, who promised to raise him. Tom never saw
Kong Sing again, but the Wahs regularly sent him money. After
World War II, when the Chinese exclusion acts had been repealed and more lenient immigration laws toward Chinese had
been passed, Gue Gim tried numerous ways and times to bring
her son to the United States. She even appealed to U.S. senators
and other government officials, but she was not successful. In
1971 she gave up her campaign to bring him home and went to
visit him instead. By that time, he had married and was the father of two boys and two girls. Eventually, Gue Gim was able to
bring one of her granddaughters, Wei Ling, home and in the
1970s Wei Ling graduated from Lincoln County High School, received a scholarship to attend a small private college in Utah,
graduated from college, and married Stanley Chow of San Francisco in 1979.

In 1929 the Wahs began their return trip home. They were sad
because they had to leave their adopted son behind, but they re-

alized that the economic possibilities in China were more limited than the prospects in Prince. Tom's good friend, "Monkey Wrench," Louie Lim, had kept the boarding house business going while the Wahs were in China. Monkey Wrench probably informed Tom that the mineral production for 1928 had recovered from the decline that had begun in 1921 and picked up briefly. Perhaps he even knew about Nevada Governor Fred Balzar's optimism about Nevada's economic future based on the 1928 mining figures.[75] This optimism was shared by many until the October 1929 stock market crash, which was not felt in Nevada until 1930, when mineral production dropped by almost half.[76] Tom probably anticipated better things as he left Hong Kong for San Francisco.

The Wahs had to pass through Angel Island once again. The conditions and treatment of the Chinese had become so bad there that several riots were recorded.[77] Since they already had worked out their reentry technicalities in Hong Kong, they probably passed through the procedure relatively quickly.

Tom decided to leave Gue Gim in San Francisco with her relatives while he returned to Prince to reestablish himself and obtain a permanent home for them. They were short on funds, so Gue Gim went to work for the first time. Like many unskilled women of her generation, she found a job in one of the over thirty garment factories located in Chinatown.[78] She worked on men's and children's overalls and did finishing work. She recalled with pride that her supervisor often praised her for the fine quality of her workmanship. However, being in Chinatown alone without Tom was strange to her and she longed to return to Prince.

When Tom arrived in Prince, things were not as good as he had hoped. In February of 1930, the Combined Metals Reduction Company was still the biggest producer of zinc in Nevada and also produced silver and lead, but the Depression was beginning to have an impact.[79] The mine at Caselton was doing better than the mine at Prince, so Tom decided to relocate and raised $400 to rent a building that eventually became known as Wah's Cafe. Perhaps he noticed the growing Mormon influence in the area and saw that the miners and locals were no longer as transient as they had once been. Even Pioche, noted for its tough and rowdy character since the 1870s, was more peaceful in the

1930s. These were hard times and those who stayed seemed to pull together and be of one spirit.

Tom needed Gue Gim's help, so he sent for her. In an effort to save on costs, he asked her, for the first time, to help with the cooking and serving in his boarding house restaurant. This was her introduction to a career that would span another fifty-plus years. In the midst of their economic woes, their old friend Yee Wah Ling of Pioche died at the age of eighty-four in December 1931.[80] Yee Wah Ling had lived in Pioche for fifty years and owned property there.[81] According to the local press, he was so wealthy that he reputedly loaned out $10,000 to various people. His death, the Depression, and Tom's declining health created a gloomy atmosphere for the Wahs. By 1933, Tom's injured leg began to bother him so much that a trip to San Francisco for treatment was deemed to be urgent, but they did not have sufficient funds. When Leonard G. Thomas, superintendent of the mines, heard about Tom's plight, he appealed to the community for funds. The community responded and in August the Wahs left for San Francisco. Unfortunately, it was too late and Tom died of cancer at the age of seventy-one on August 17, 1933.[82] Like his friend Yee Wah Ling, his remains were sent back to China for burial. This had been a common practice among the Chinese from the mid-nineteenth to mid-twentieth centuries.[83] Gue Gim stayed with her relatives for a few weeks and then returned to Prince to settle her affairs. She recalled of this period, "I cried all the time." She did not know what the future held for her.

Her friends in the Prince-Caselton-Pioche area welcomed her back. Leonard Thomas arranged for her to live in his guesthouse and guaranteed her a little income if she cared for his elderly aunt. He also told her that an $8 million plant was in the planning stage and if it materialized there would be boarding house and cooking work. The character of the mine workers would not be as rough as before because E. H. Snyder, president of the Combined Metals Reduction Company, had appointed Henry Coleman, a bishop in the Mormon church, as one of the superintendents in the hope that more Mormons, who were family-oriented and therefore more stable, would work in the mines. Many of the old-time miners did not want to work with the Mormon "farm boys," so they left the area.[84] The situation seemed right. Gue Gim decided to stay in Prince, where she was more comfortable, despite continuing pleas from her relatives to return to San Francisco's Chinatown.

Mining production in the Caselton-Prince area began to revive. One of the reasons was Nevada's U.S. senator Key Pittman's agitation for a silver purchase program, resulting in the 1934 Silver Purchase Act.[85] This spurred silver production. At the same time, because Pittman had tied his silver program to the China Market (China was on the silver standard) since his 1931 trip to China, he also created a positive and friendly attitude toward China and the Chinese in his home state.[86] Another reason was the reopening of the Prince Mine, which, in 1935, had been leased for a year by William H. Pitts and W. M. Christian of Pioche from the International Smelter Corporation and National Lead Interest and the Gemmill estate.[87] This all meant work and money for Gue Gim Wah.

Prosperity seemed to return once again. 1936 was a good year for Nevada's mining companies as the silver, lead, zinc, gold, and copper production totaled almost $29 million.[88] Most of the lead, zinc, and some silver came from this area in Lincoln County. The Prince Mine was the only producer of large quantities of oxidized manganese minerals in the Pioche area.[89] Another boost to the local economy was the advent of electrical power from Hoover Dam (then called Boulder Dam).[90] By 1941 the Prince Mine was rehabilitated so that it could utilize this new source of energy and had modernized its operational system so that it was similar to the operations at nearby Caselton.[91] However, the biggest stimulus to the economy was the gearing up of the mines for and during World War II.

The mines in the Pioche area were once again active. According to Gue Gim, the government paid high wages despite the fact that the price of metals was still low simply because the government needed the lead and zinc for the construction of military equipment. Since mining was not considered defense work, there was a great mining manpower shortage until the government came up with the plan of exempting military men from active duty if they had mining experience or were willing to work in the mines. David L. Gemmill, then president and manager of the Combined Metals Reduction Company at Prince, interviewed the "soldier miners," as Gue Gim called them, and brought the total manpower to about two hundred for the mines.[92] Some of the men were former coal miners from Pennsylvania while others came from Utah and California. All of them were fed by Gue Gim Wah and her staff between 1942 and 1945.

The war years were busy ones for Gue Gim. At first she concentrated her activities in Prince, but when the Caselton Mine also needed a cook because the cook who had been hired by the government left after six months, she worked for both mines. The operations at Caselton were much larger than those at Prince. By April 1943, some forty dwelling houses (four units per house with four rooms each) and seventy dormitories, two of which housed 140 single men alone, were built by the National Housing Authority.[93] Gue Gim paid one dollar per month for the rental of the building used for the restaurant in Caselton. The fee included oil, water, gas, and electricity. She did not get this position without some difficulty. For example, the government required that the snow be shoveled from the area around the restaurant. Gue Gim knew she did not have the strength to do this and was about to decline the job as cook when Leonard Thomas volunteered the mine workers for the task. Another problem she faced was how to get help. She advertised that she would pay the fare for interested parties to come to Prince and, after much effort, she finally found some assistants. One of her greatest helpers at this time was Ong Wing, who had worked in the kitchens in nearby Ely, White Pine County, Nevada, and Sacramento, California. Ong Wing even introduced her to Chinese cooking for the American palate. Food rationing during World War II had led to creative cooking and the beginning of the popularity of Chinese cooking in American homes. Now Gue Gim had learned the secrets and she combined this knowledge with her natural gifts for cooking in order to attract new customers to her restaurant. After the war, she would attract many southern Nevadans to Wah's Cafe with her Chinese cuisine. Another Chinese helper, Kelly, who was also from Ely, taught her how to drive a car so that he could go home on a regular basis. This expanded her little world so that she could travel freely to Pioche and other neighboring communities after the war.

Gue Gim worked long hours during these war years. Although the mines operated three shifts a day, she worked it out so that she provided only sack lunches and thus did not have to get up at 2 A.M. to feed one of the shifts their lunch. She had to worry about supplies, which were difficult to obtain. Meat was easy because the nearby Mormon farmers in Panaca and Caliente could supply this. Sugar was the hardest item to acquire. The miners had to give her their food stamps so that she could buy the necessary items and this entailed a lot of bookkeeping and handling. She was so busy that she occasionally would fall asleep in a chair while she was working at the Caselton restaurant. As a result of this, the Caselton mine owners built a small addition to the boarding house–restaurant for her to live in. In the 1980s, she spent most of her time in the Caselton restaurant, called Wah's Cafe, and only occasionally visited her home in Prince in the daytime.

Herbert Hoover, one of the Caselton mine owners, became a great fan of hers. During the war years, Hoover visited the mines to get firsthand information on the mining situation. One day he told the miners, "You fellows are eating better food than anyone else in this country." [94] He knew this because he often ate Gue Gim's cooking and it was rumored that whenever he was in the general vicinity, he would charter a special airplane to take him to Wah's Cafe. He had renewed his interest in mining between 1933 and 1937 and invested in several mines, including the Caselton Mine, in order to keep busy after he lost his bid for reelection as president of the United States. During his visits, he would tell her about his experiences in China from 1898 to 1901 and about his interest in the translation of Chinese mining laws. [95] Jokingly, he even told her about one of his first lessons in diplomacy, which he learned in China. Gue Gim recalled, "He [was] an] engineer. He told me [he] went to China. All the railroad ties [were] stolen in one night. He offered reward of fifty cents to bring back ties. By next morning, all ties brought back." He even discussed his inventions with her and was especially proud of his uniform light bulb base. This impressed Gue Gim because she hated the fact that the different watt light bulbs had different size bases. When one of his visits fell on his birthday, she made him and Mrs. Hoover a special dinner and a huge birthday cake. Gue Gim found Hoover to be a very warm person. He loved to compliment her on her cooking and was fond of her silver-dollar pancakes, filet mignon, prime rib, steaks, and tasty desserts, such as her apple pie.[96] When the Hoover Memorial Library in Iowa was dedicated in the 1960s, Gue Gim was among the honored guests.

The prosperity in the area attracted other Chinese chefs. The Silver Cafe in Pioche featured Chinese and American food and opened from 6 A.M. until 1 A.M.[97] One of the Silver Cafe's chefs, Hong Young, decided to open his own restaurant, the Young Cafe, in September 1943.[98] Hong Young had lived in Ely, Nevada, since 1917 and his three boys were born and raised there. His oldest son was in the U.S. Army and the other two boys moved from Ely to help their father in his new venture. As early as 1849, the Chinese had been involved in the restaurant business in the United States because it did not require a large amount of capital, yet it offered the Chinese a proprietary status and was a symbol of success.[99] The restaurants in Pioche, like Gue Gim's facilities, probably did well during these few years.

However, after the war ended, the miners returned to their homes in other states. A few miners stayed, but by this time the bachelor character of the miners had changed. Miners now had families and would drive home for dinner. Only a small number of miners participated in the package offering of room and board at Wah's. Occasionally, Gue Gim's income was augmented by a special program, such as one conducted by the Bureau of Land Management one summer, but otherwise the Caselton-Prince area had a ghost town atmosphere.

The isolation and desolation created a few problems for Gue Gim. Her home in Prince and Wah's Cafe in Caselton were robbed several times when she was away. One of the most memorable and frightening experiences occurred one day after the war had ended. A young man with a rifle suddenly appeared at her front door and shouted that he wanted to get revenge for all the Americans killed by the Japanese at Pearl Harbor. In her charming, quiet, ladylike manner, Gue Gim calmed down the intruder, explained that she was Chinese and therefore an ally during the war, offered him a cup of coffee and a piece of delicious pie, and listened to his outbursts of anger. When the young man finally left Wah's Cafe, he was in better spirits.

Gue Gim faced hard times in the 1950s and 1960s. By 1957 the economy of the Pioche area, which was dependent upon mining, declined sharply due to the government's policy of allowing a large inflow of low-priced foreign metals into the country.[100] By 1962 there was a standstill in the mining industry and the only miners in the area were fifty men who were doing mostly exploratory work. Gue Gim had to find customers elsewhere. Fortunately, her reputation as an excellent chef spread throughout Nevada and residents from as far away as Las Vegas, 175 miles south of Pioche, made reservations to dine at the exclusive ghost town restaurant. At one time, some of her local supporters put up a sign pointing out where Wah's Cafe was from the main road, but in 1966 the sign blew down during a big windstorm and Gue Gim never bothered nor wanted to put it back up. Since that time, one had to know where to turn on the road in order to find the restaurant.

Wah's Cafe continued to serve American and Chinese food. In order to enhance the foods which she purchased from regular visits to the grocery stores in Pioche, Cedar City (Utah), and Las Vegas, she grew her own vegetables and herbs in her Prince garden. At times she even raised her own chickens and pigs. For her Chinese meals, she ordered special ingredients from San Francisco's mail order Chinese grocery stores. Since help was limited and difficult to find and keep, she usually prepared and served the meal, then took her time cleaning up and washing the dishes. Her fame began to spread. On November 25, 1971, Charles Hillenger published a story about her ghost town restaurant in the *Los Angeles Times*. This gave her regional fame and prompted Jason Rubinsteen to write about her in the May/June 1980 issue of *Nevada: The Magazine of the Real West*. The interest was continued by Elizabeth Patrick, who published a story about her in the *Las Vegas Review-Journal*, "The Nevadan," on May 7, 1982. By this time, she was in her eighties and decided that advanced reservations were needed before she would cook. She also limited her open days to three days a week. By late 1985, she essentially retired from a profession that she had begun over half a century earlier. On June 15, 1988, she died in her home in Prince and was buried in nearby Pioche.

CONCLUSION

Gue Gim Wah's experiences were not unlike those of many Chinese American women of her generation. She was firmly com-

mitted to the traditional Chinese heritage of her birth as a result
of her early life in China, her early education, her upbringing in
the Der family household, and her experiences in San Francisco's Chinatown. However, once she moved to San Francisco
and then Prince, her life changed and she began to accommodate to American society as a result of her Methodist church activities, her contact with American-born Chinese children in
Chinatown, her marriage to Tom Fook Wah, who had made
some adjustments to American society, her acceptance by the
Prince community after her marriage, and her education at the
Prince School. Unlike Chinese immigrant women of her generation who lived in urban Chinatowns, she had to interact with
the white community. She was more successful than the average
Chinese immigrant women who lived in rural areas because of
her education in Prince and the acceptance of her and her husband by the white community.[101] By the 1920s, she was a typical
"marginal man," a person who lives in two worlds at the same
time and assumes the role of a cosmopolitan and a stranger.[102]
Her return trip to China and additional education in China reinforced her traditional values but probably also made her realize that she did not feel comfortable in that world. She already
had made her commitment to an American life-style. Therefore,
she and her husband returned to the Prince-Caselton area.

In the 1930s she began the process of assimilation. Assimilation requires both a positive orientation toward, and an identification with, the majority community and an acceptance by that
community, with changes in values on both sides.[103] Like many
Chinese American women of the Depression years, she worked
with her husband in order to supplement his income and learned
that survival came through hard work.[104] When he died, she decided to make her home in the Prince-Caselton area despite the
pleas of her relatives to return to San Francisco and settle there.
The Thomas family undoubtedly helped in making her feel welcome and useful during the years after Tom's death. Although
there were some in the community who did not like her, she felt
that most of the people accepted and wanted her there. The war
years, though filled with hard work and trying times, completed
the process and she was now at ease in her American environment. Around this time, she introduced Chinese cuisine to her
menu and the community accepted this as a novel dining experi-

ence which eventually made her famous in southern Nevada and then in the southwestern region. Even in the 1980s, her relatives in San Francisco tried to persuade her to leave her isolated and ghost town–like community, but Gue Gim Wah had thrived for so many years in the Prince-Caselton area that she had no desire to leave. Wah's Cafe, with its huge American kitchen and dining room decorated with Chinese and American objects, was a physical example of the combination of the two cultures which influenced Gue Gim's life. She was a pioneering Chinese American woman of Nevada, and upon her death she was hailed as "Pioche's most famous resident." [105]

NOTES

1. Wilbur S. Shepperson, *Restless Strangers: Nevada's Immigrants and Their Interpreters* (Reno: University of Nevada Press, 1970).

2. Paul C. P. Siu, "The Sojourner," *American Journal of Sociology*, 58, no. 1 (July 1952): 34–44 and Gunther Barth, *Bitter Strength: A History of the Chinese in the United States, 1850–1870* (Cambridge, Mass.: Harvard University Press, 1964), who focuses upon the theme of the Chinese sojourners.

3. Sue Fawn Chung, "The Chinese American Citizens Alliance: An Effort in Assimilation, 1895–1965," in *Chinese America: History and Perspectives, 1988* (San Francisco, Calif.: Chinese Historical Society of America, 1988), 30–57.

4. The differences between acculturation and assimilation have been summed up by Raymond H. C. Teske, Jr., and Bardin H. Nelson, "Acculturation and Assimilation: A Clarification," *American Ethnologist* 1, no. 2 (May 1974): 351–68. See also Stanley L. M. Fong, "Assimilation of Chinese in America: Changes in Orientation and Social Perception," *American Journal of Sociology* 71, no. 3 (November 1965): 265–73. A different position is taken by Ling-chi Wang, "Post-war Development in the Chinese American Community," in Genny Lim, ed., *The Chinese American Experience* (San Francisco, Calif.: Chinese Historical Society of America and the Chinese Culture Foundation of San Francisco, 1981), 267–73.

5. *Lincoln County Record* (hereafter cited as *LCR*), November 6, 1980. Her selection was announced in the local newspaper on September 17, 1980.

6. I was introduced to Mrs. Wah in 1979 by Gail and Donna Andress of Las Vegas and interviewed her in May 1980 and March 1984 in Cantonese and English with the assistance of Jane Chung and Bill Leaf. My own interviews were greatly augmented by the work of Elizabeth N. Patrick, who interviewed Mrs. Wah and her friend Elizabeth ("Betty")

Gemmill Frizzell for six hours in December 1981 and deposited the tapes in UNLV's Special Collections. See also Elizabeth Patrick, "Missy Wah of Prince: American from China," *Las Vegas Review-Journal*, "The Nevadan," March 7, 1982; Charles Hillenger, "Ghost Town Cafe," *Los Angeles Times*, November 25, 1971, 2:1, 8, which gave her regional attention, and Jason Rubinsteen, "A Taste of China," *Nevada* 40, no. 3 (May/June 1980): 36–37. The local newspapers include the *LCR*, *Pioche Record*, *Pioche Daily Record*, and *Pioche Weekly Record*.

7. This has been explored by many scholars, most notably Barth, *Bitter Strength*; Jack Chen, *The Chinese of America* (San Francisco, Calif.: Harper and Row, 1980); June Mei, "Socioeconomic Origins of Emigration: Guangdong to California, 1850–1882," in Lucie Cheng and Edna Bonacich, eds., *Labor Immigration under Capitalism* (Berkeley, Calif.: University of California Press, 1984), 219–47; Mary R. Coolidge, *Chinese Immigration* (New York: Henry Holt and Company, 1909); Ta Chen, *Emigrant Communities in South China* (New York: Institute of Pacific Relations, 1940); Kil Young Zo, *Chinese Emigration into the United States, 1850–1880* (New York: Arno Press, 1971); and Shih-shan Henry Tsai, *The Chinese Experience in America* (Bloomington: University of Indiana Press, 1986), chap. 1.

8. See Barth, *Bitter Strength*; Rose Hum Lee, *The Chinese in the United States of America* (Hong Kong: Hong Kong University Press, 1960); Betty Lee Sung, *Mountain of Gold: The Story of the Chinese in America* (New York: Macmillan, 1967) for more details.

9. This particular circular may not be genuine, but the contents reflect the types of handbills and rumors that circulated in the Canton area during the mid-nineteenth century. From Alexander McLeod, *Pigtails & Gold Dust* (Caldwell, Idaho: Caxton Press, 1947), 23.

10. Undated newspaper clipping, ca. 1861, *Bancroft Scraps: Chinese Clippings*, v. 6, 1 and Linda Pomerantz, "The Chinese Bourgeoisie and the Anti-Chinese Movement in the United States, 1850–1905," *Amerasia Journal* 11, no. 1 (Spring/Summer 1984): 3–4.

11. Although this has not been studied in depth in the United States, the operation of the *hui* has been studied among the Chinese in New Guinea. See David Y. H. Wu, "To Kill Three Birds with One Stone: The Rotating Credit Associations of the Papua New Guinea Chinese," *American Ethnologist* 1, no. 3 (August 1974): 565–84.

12. The four counties are: Toishan/Xinning, Hoiping/Kaiping, Sunwui/Xinhui, and Yungping/Enping (traditional spelling/pinyin spelling). See Mei, "Socioeconomic Origins," 389.

13. Stanford M. Lyman, *The Asian in North America* (Santa Barbara, Calif.: Clio Press, 1970), 49–51; California Historical Society of Southern California, *Linking Our Lives: Chinese American Women of Los Angeles* (Los Angeles, Calif.: Chinese Historical Society of Southern California, 1984), 1–9; and Judy Yung, *Chinese Women of America: A Pictorial History* (Seattle, Wash.: Chinese Culture Foundation of San Francisco, 1986).

14. One child probably died early in life. Mrs. Wah did not specify its sex.

15. A term used to show that the father resided apart from the family in the home country. See Sung, *Mountain of Gold*, 155–56. See also Lyman, *The Asian*, 67–75.

16. Sung, *Mountain of Gold*, 54.

17. See R. D. McKenzie, *Oriental Exclusion: The Effect of American Immigration Laws, Regulations, and Judicial Decisions upon the Chinese and Japanese on the American Pacific Coast* (Chicago, Ill.: University of Chicago Press, 1927); Elmer C. Sandmeyer, *The Anti-Chinese Movement in California* (Urbana: University of Illinois Press, 1939); Tien-lu Li, *Congressional Policy of Chinese Immigration or Legislation Relating to Chinese Immigration to the United States* (South Nashville, Tenn.: Methodist Episcopal Church, 1916); Shien Woo Kung, *Chinese in American Life, Some Aspects of Their History, Status, Problems, and Contributions* (Seattle, Wash.: University of Washington Press, 1962).

18. *United States* vs. *Mrs. Cue Lim* (1900); Tsai, *Chinese Experience*, 102.

19. Elizabeth Patrick, oral interview of Gue Gim Wah, UNLV Special Collections.

20. For an intimate look at the Angel Island experience, see Him Mark Lai, "The Chinese Experience at Angel Island," *East West* (San Francisco), February 11, 18, 25, 1976, 10:7–9. See also Him Mark Lai, Genny Lim, and Judy Yung, *Island, Poetry and History of Chinese Immigrants on Angel Island 1910–1940* (San Francisco, Calif.: San Francisco Study Center, 1980). Gue Gim's personal experiences during this period are based on her interview with Patrick, "Missy Wah."

21. Translated by Mary Lee Young in Connie Young Yu, "Rediscovered Voices," *Amerasia*, 42, no. 2 (1977): 123.

22. The phenomenon of "paper sons" has been described in Sung, *Mountain of Gold*, chap. 7.

23. Rubinsteen, "Taste of China," 36.

24. Helen Cather, *History of San Francisco's Chinatown* (San Francisco, Calif.: R and E Associates, 1974); Thomas W. Chinn, ed., *A History of the Chinese in California, A Syllabus* (San Francisco, Calif.: Chinese Historical Society of America, 1969); Laverne Mau Dicker, *The Chinese in San Francisco* (New York: Dove Publications, 1979); and Charles C. Dobie, *San Francisco's Chinatown* (New York: Appleton, 1936).

25. Hubert Howe Bancroft, "Mongolianism in America," in *Essays and Miscellany* (San Francisco, Calif.: San Francisco History Co., 1890), 327–28.

26. For a detailed study of education in San Francisco's Chinatown, see Victor Low, *The Unimpressible Race: A Century of Educational Struggle by the Chinese in San Francisco* (San Francisco, Calif.: East/West Publishing Co., 1982).

27. Stanford Morris Lyman, *Chinese Americans* (New York: Random House, 1974), 46–48.

28. See foreword by Stanford Morris Lyman in Robert Seto Quan, *Lotus among the Magnolias: The Mississippi Chinese* (Jackson: University Press of Mississippi, 1982), xii.

29. Otis Gibson, *The Chinese in America* (Cincinnati, Ohio: Hitchcock and Walden, 1877).

30. Shih-shan Henry Tsai, *China and the Overseas Chinese in the United States, 1868–1911* (Fayetteville: University of Arkansas Press, 1983), 138, n. 41, and Him Mark Lai, "Chinese American Studies: A Historical Survey," in *Chinese America: History and Perspectives, 1988* (San Francisco, Calif.: Chinese Historical Society of America, 1988), 13.

31. For more information on the church, see David K. Lee, "Brief History of the Chinese Methodist Church in San Francisco," in pamphlet entitled *United Methodist Church* (n.p., n.d.), 7–9, Bancroft Library.

32. See Robert McClellan, *The Heathen Chinese: A Study of American Attitudes Toward China, 1890–1905* (Columbus: Ohio State University Press, 1971) and Stuart C. Miller, *The Unwelcomed Immigrant: The American Image of the Chinese, 1785–1882* (Berkeley, Calif.: University of California Press, 1969).

33. There was no record of this. Marysville was the third largest Chinese enclave in California during this period. An excellent study of this area is Sucheng Chan, "Chinese Livelihood in Rural California: The Impact of Economic Change, 1860–1880," *Pacific Historical Review* 53, no. 3 (August 1984): 273–308.

34. For more details on the anti-Chinese immigration laws, see Tienlu Li, *Congressional Policy;* McKenzie, *Oriental Exclusion;* and William L. Tung, "The Legal Status of the Chinese in America," in Paul K. T. Sih and Leonard B. Allen, eds., *The Chinese in America* (New York: St. John's University, 1976), 3–16.

35. Him Mark Lai et al., *The Chinese of America: 1785–1980* (San Francisco, Calif.: Chinese Culture Foundation of San Francisco, 1980), 26.

36. Chinben See, "Chinese Americans in the San Francisco Bay Area: A Survey Study," in Yuan-li Wu, ed., *The Economic Condition of Chinese Americans* (Chicago, Ill.: Pacific/Asian American Mental Health Research Center, 1980), 155.

37. See Ping Chiu, *Chinese Labor in California, 1850–1880* (Madison: University of Wisconsin, 1963); Pauline Minke, *Chinese in the Mother Lode, 1850–1870* (San Francisco, Calif.: R and E Associates, 1974); and McLeod, *Pigtails.*

38. See Richard E. Lingenfelter, *The Hardrock Miners: A History of the Mining Labor Movement in the American West, 1863–1893* (Berkeley: University of California Press, 1974), 107–27.

39. Loren B. Chan, "The Chinese in Nevada: An Historical Survey, 1856–1970," *Nevada Historical Society Quarterly* 25, no. 4 (Winter 1982): 282.

40. For a general background on the Chinese in Nevada, see Gary P. Be Dunnah, *History of the Chinese in Nevada, 1855–1904* (San Francisco, Calif.: R and E Associates, 1973; publication of 1966 master's thesis in

history, University of Nevada, Reno). For occupational statistics, see Gregg Lee Carter, "Social Demography of the Chinese in Nevada: 1870–1880," *Nevada Historical Society Quarterly* 18, no. 3 (Summer 1975): 77–78, 83.

41. Russell R. Elliott, *History of Nevada* (Lincoln: University of Nebraska Press, 1973), 110. On the construction of the railroad line, see *LCR*, October 23, 1903.

42. Obituary, *Pioche Weekly Record* (hereafter cited as *PWR*), December 8, 1916.

43. Lloyd K. Long, "Pioche, Nevada and Early Mining Developments in Eastern Nevada," M.A. thesis, University of Nevada, Las Vegas, August 1975.

44. Kathryn Hastings, "History of Pioche," *Pioche Record*, November 19, 1936, gives an account of the town.

45. Chan, "Chinese in Nevada," 288–91, discusses Pioche and Lincoln County. See also Diana Gail Brown, "Chinese Sojourn in Lincoln County, Nevada, 1870–1950," proseminar paper, University of Nevada, Las Vegas, 1983, Special Collections.

46. *LCR*, February 14, 1902, describes the New Year's celebration.

47. See, for example, *LCR*, February 1, 1901, September 4, 1903.

48. *LCR*, September 4, 1903.

49. See obituary, *LCR*, January 8, 1932; see also *Pioche Record*, November 1, 1924.

50. See obituary, *Pioche Record*, July 5, 1934.

51. Ibid.

52. She does not refer to him by name but talks about a well-known Chinese restaurant owner in Pioche who died in the 1930s.

53. George M. Blackburn and Sherman L. Ricards, "The Chinese of Virginia City, Nevada: 1870," *Amerasia* 7, no. 1 (1980): 68, see these same conditions.

54. This was seen in Virginia City. See ibid., 68.

55. This was proudly pointed out in the local newspaper, *LCR*, October 5, 1900.

56. Reports of mine production were published regularly in the local newspaper, *Pioche Record*.

57. Long, "Pioche," and Ralph J. Roske and Marta Planzo, *An Overview of the History of Lincoln County* (Las Vegas, Nev., 1978).

58. This account differs from Mrs. Gimmell's account. She stated that Tom's kitchen was a firetrap, so the owners wanted to tear it down, resulting in the need for the move.

59. Dr. Ong Ting Shew advertised his services in the *Chinese Defender* (San Francisco) 1, no. 1 (August 1910).

60. Herbalists were often classified as doctors by Nevada census takers. See Carter, "Social Demography," 89.

61. For more on Dr. Wing, see *PWR*, March 12, 1874, August 30, 1887.

62. *LCR*, March 25, 1904.

63. Approved November 28, 1861, *Nevada Statutes, 1861–1885,*

#4760–4763. The Japanese were exempt from this law, so that Japanese immigrants of the early twentieth century married Caucasian women in Nevada. This law was not repealed until 1959. In 1967 the Supreme Court ruled the miscegenation laws in other states (there had been fourteen state laws on this) were unconstitutional. The account of Joe Sing was reported in the *LCR*, May 13, 1904.

64. Lyman, "Marriage," 67–71.

65. During her interview with Patrick, she indicated a January date, but in my interview she mentioned October. She may have been confusing the meeting date and the marriage date.

66. *PWR*, December 1, 1877. A follow-up story appeared a week later, on December 8, 1877, when Beene had another man, who claimed that Sen Choy was his intended bride, arrested and jailed. In those days, arranged marriages, even across the Pacific, were common.

67. Judy Yung, "The Social Awakening of Chinese American Women as Reported in *Chung Sai Yat Po*, 1900–1911," in *Chinese America: History and Perspectives, 1988* (San Francisco, Calif.: Chinese Historical Society of America, 1988), 88–91.

68. *Pioche Record*, December 7, 1917.

69. For more details on this subject, see Milton M. Gordon, "Assimilation in America: Theory and Reality," *Daedalus* 90 (Spring 1961): 263–85. Arguing against the melting-pot myth is Henry Pratt Fairchild, *The Melting-Pot Mistake* (Boston, Mass.: Little, Brown and Company, 1926) and Wang, "Post-war Development."

70. Roske and Plantz, *Overview*.

71. *Pioche Record*, June 6, 1925, and *LCR*, January 21, 1926.

72. See Mears, McKenzie, *Oriental Exclusion*, and Tung, "Legal Status," for more details.

73. *Nevada Statutes, 1921*, chap. 91, section 1, eliminated the prohibition against Mongolian adoptions in an 1885 law.

74. U.S. Government, *Foreign Relations of the United States,*1906, vol. 1, 288–290, and 1914, 3–4.

75. Elliott, *History*, 273.

76. Ibid., 274.

77. See, for example, *San Francisco Chronicle* headline story, "Troops Quell Angel Island Chinese Riot," July 2, 1925.

78. For more information on the garment factories, see Cather, *History*, 54.

79. *LCR*, February 6, 1930.

80. Ibid., January 8, 1932.

81. His land ownership was noted in the *Goldfield Chronicle*, April 4, 1908. Unlike in California, any Chinese could own land in Nevada as long as he intended to make Nevada his home. As early as 1871 a deed was recorded in the Lincoln County records of Ah Chin's ownership of land.

82. *Pioche Record*, August 10, 1933, August 24, 1933, carried the story.

83. Chen, *Chinese of America*, 20, 51.

84. Patrick, "Missy Wah."

85. Arthur Sewall, "Key Pittman and the Quest for the China Market, 1933–1940," *Pacific Historical Review* 44, no. 3 (August 1975): 351–71; Elliott, *History*, 292; and the *LCR*, especially 1931–1934.

86. This is obvious from the news coverage. See, for example, *LCR*, August 20, 1931.

87. *Pioche Record*, October 17, 1935.

88. Ibid., February 4, 18, 1937.

89. Ibid., July 15, 1943.

90. Ibid., August 19, 1937.

91. Ibid., July 15, 1943, story on David Gemmill, president of the Prince Mine.

92. *LCR*, September 17, 1980, interview of Gue Gim Wah.

93. *Pioche Record*, February 25, April 29, 1943.

94. *LCR*, September 17, 1980, interview of Mrs. Wah.

95. See, for example, Joan Hoff Wilson, *Herbert Hoover: Forgotten Progressive* (Boston, Mass.: Little, Brown and Co., 1975), 12, 22; George H. Nash, *The Life of Herbert Hoover: The Engineer, 1874–1914* (New York: W. W. Norton, 1983), chaps. 7–11; and Eugene Lyons, *Herbert Hoover: A Biography* (Garden City, N.Y.: Doubleday and Co., 1964), chap. 5, "Adventure in China," 44–55. Two other notable studies on Hoover are Edgar Eugene Robinson and Vaugh Davis Bornet, *Herbert Hoover: President of the United States*, (Stanford, Calif.: Hoover Institution Press, 1975) and Gary Dean Best, *Herbert Hoover: The Postpresidential Years, 1933–1964*, 2 vols. (Stanford, Calif.: Hoover Institution Press, 1983).

96. Rubinsteen, "Taste of China," assumed that Hoover went to Wah's Cafe for Chinese food, but Mrs. Wah told me that he liked her American cuisine.

97. *Pioche Record*, September 16, 1943.

98. Ibid., September 9, 1943.

99. Rose Hum Lee, *Chinese in the United States*, 261.

100. The economic picture of Lincoln County is summarized by Chan Young Bang, *A Survey into the Economic Development of Lincoln County, Nevada* (Las Vegas, Nev., 1969).

101. Yung, *Chinese Women*, 24–30.

102. For a discussion of Robert E. Park's theory in relationship to the Chinese, see Lyman, *The Asian*, 18–23, and Park's original writings, *Race and Culture*, ed. Everett Cherrington Hughes et al. (Glencoe, Ill.: The Free Press, 1950).

103. Teske and Nelson, "Acculturation," 358–65.

104. Yung, *Chinese Women*, 40–43.

105. *Las Vegas Sun*, June 18, 1988.

TOWN MAKING ON THE SOUTHERN NEVADA FRONTIER: LAS VEGAS, 1905–1925

EUGENE P. MOEHRING

Planted beside a lush oasis and surrounded by miles of rolling desert, Las Vegas was a thriving town of two thousand people within weeks of its settlement in May 1905. Five years later, despite the calamitous Panic of 1907 and several track washouts, nearly a thousand people still called Las Vegas home. To a large extent, the town's 1910 population fit the classic model fashioned by Wilbur Shepperson in his study of Nevada's immigrants.[1] Indeed, almost 20 percent of the town's residents were foreign-born, with the majority coming from Europe, Canada, Mexico, and Japan. Though dozens of immigrants toiled as maids, common laborers, and railroad men, many also owned substantial businesses and helped shape the town's development. The Germans, for instance, were led by Jake Beckley, a merchant, and his brother Will, a clothier. Both played an active role in the city's chamber of commerce. Edward Horstman operated a restaurant, Moritz Richter sold cigars, Anthony Schweibig wholesaled meats, and Adolf Levy owned a popular grocery store. Canadian residents were also prominent: Jesse Rolicheau operated a shoe store, Joseph Laravy a blacksmith shop, and Ella Mason a hotel, while Sam Gay served as Clark County's popular sheriff. In fact, virtually every nationality was represented on the census and property rolls. Together, they teamed with hundreds of second-generation Americans to lay the foundation for Las Vegas's later success.[2]

Their accomplishment was substantial. Town making on the Nevada frontier had always been a formidable challenge, as the state's immense number of ghost towns would suggest. To be sure, the process involved more than the mere physical construction of buildings. This was especially the case in Las Vegas. Though long a way station for weary travelers plying the Old Mormon Trail, the town of Las Vegas was literally invented by Senator William Clark in 1902 when he purchased two thousand acres of Helen Stewart's ranch for a division point on his proposed railroad connecting Los Angeles with Salt Lake City. Immediately following the two-day auction and sale of lots in May 1905, several thousand people, including many from the McWilliams Townsite west of the tracks (today the Westside), began erecting tents, houses, and stores upon their lots. But, while the invention of Las Vegas was accomplished by a few strokes of Senator Clark's pen and a flurry of land sales, town making itself was a much longer process. Three events were crucial: establishing local government and municipal services, achieving a sense of community, and reducing the town's dependence upon the railroad.

Though preoccupied with the construction of homes and businesses in the weeks immediately following the auction, Las Vegans also recognized the need to organize a government. With the approval of Lincoln County commissioners, residents chose an informal town board in August 1905 to oversee the provision of municipal services. However, the political emphasis switched rapidly to county government. Even before Las Vegas's creation, the economic balance of power in sprawling Lincoln County had begun shifting away from the once prosperous mining districts of Pioche and Delamar southward to new boom areas like Searchlight, fifty-five miles south of the new Las Vegas townsite. By 1905, growing resentment over the 350-mile round trip to the county seat at Pioche had already encouraged Searchlight leaders to try and move the center of government to their town. The action spawned a similar effort by Las Vegans to snare the prize for their community. As early as 1906, the new railroad town began exerting an influence in county affairs. Clearly, southern growth was the underlying force behind this intracounty power struggle. The spark, however, was the lingering controversy over the huge debt incurred by a generation of irresponsible county commissioners. By 1905 the debt, consisting largely of unpaid bonds for the 1872 Lincoln County courthouse, exceeded $600,000—an outrageous figure by any standard. Seizing upon the scandal and determined to wrest control of the government from their counterparts in Pioche, twenty-five Las Vegas business and professional men helped organize the Consolidated Political League of Lincoln County in July 1906. Working with activists in Searchlight, Overton, and other communities, the group promoted a slate of candidates representing southern county interests. Backed by this support, Las Vegas forwarding agent Ed W. Clark was elected county treasurer in November 1906.

Over the next two years tensions rose to fever pitch as northern and southern newspapers vied for the lucrative county advertising trade. Similar competition marked the effort by local banks to secure county revenues. Indeed, a major issue in the 1908 county treasurer's campaign between Clark and Panaca businessman Henry Lee was the former's use of Las Vegas's First State Bank as the depository for county funds. All these events strengthened the resolve of local businessmen to capture control of the county seat. The initiative failed, however, as the stubborn opposition of Pioche interests eventually forced Clark and his allies to switch strategies and instead seek formation of a new county. To this end, townsmen formed a "county division" committee in 1908. Members included Ed W. Clark, hotelman John F. Miller, railroad employee Harley Harmon, newspaperman Charles ("Pop") Squires, and land developer Peter Buol, among others. The story is an involved one, has been told before, and will not be repeated here. In short, thanks to a concerted effort by the Lincoln County Division Club at the county Democratic and Republican party conventions in 1908, platforms and candidates favoring county division were approved. Subsequent legislation in 1909 at Carson City mandated the creation of Clark County on July 1, 1909.[3]

Following the incorporation of Clark County, the next logical move was the incorporation of Las Vegas. The action was necessary to insulate the town partially from the whims of county control while also providing the community with bonding powers and other municipal privileges needed to operate a growing city. Anxious to project a modern, "progressive" image, the Las Vegas Promotion Society (and later the chamber of commerce) wisely pushed for a "commission" form of government—Nevada's first. To this end, Clark County's delegation to the 1911 session of the state legislature secured an incorporation bill providing Las Vegas with a mayor and four commissioners. Signed by Governor Tasker Oddie on March 17, 1911, the incorporation law was contingent upon local voter approval. That came at a June 1 referendum in which voters elected land developer Peter Buol mayor and lumber merchant Ed Von Tobel and three others to the city commission.[4]

While it took six years to set the new city and county governments in place, the development of newspapers was almost immediate. In March 1905, almost two months before the platting of Senator Clark's townsite, James Brown and Frank Reber began the *Las Vegas Times*, a four-page weekly printed in the so-called Original Las Vegas Townsite (today the Westside), a booming tent town west of the newly opened railroad tracks. Six days later, W. W. Wallace introduced the *Las Vegas Advance*, which was followed a week later by the *Las Vegas Age*, published by T. G. Nicklin and managed by the venerable Charles C. ("Corky") Corkhill. Only the *Age* survived the town's infancy and adolescence, thanks largely to the energy and determination of Charles ("Pop") Squires, who purchased it in 1907. Together with the *Clark County Review* (today the *Las Vegas Review-Journal*), begun by Corkhill in 1909, Las Vegans were served by two quality newspapers for many years.[5]

Basic community services also came rapidly. Law enforcement was a special concern in an infant community where few people knew one another and social control had yet to be institutionalized. During the first year, townsmen occasionally acted as a vigilante force to combat burglaries, street fights, arson, and other serious crimes. Like many Nevada frontier towns remote from the county seat, Las Vegas could not rely on the sheriff. In fact, lack of support from the Lincoln County sheriff's office ultimately contributed to the local movement for county division. To appease residents, the sheriff in 1908 finally appointed popular Canadian Sam Gay as deputy for the Las Vegas District. Gay, a former bouncer at Goldfield's Northern Club and the ever popular Arizona Club, had been elected Las Vegas constable in 1907. A year later, when Clark County was formed, voters chose newspaperman Charles ("Corky") Corkhill as sheriff and Gay as under sheriff. The choice was a bad one; tension between the two strong-willed men was inevitable. Finally in 1909, after several stormy encounters, Corkhill fired Gay for removing prisoners from their sweltering cells downtown and chaining them to the shady cottonwoods at the Old Stewart Ranch. Gay, in turn, won a measure of revenge in 1910 by defeating Corkhill for sheriff in a close election. For the next twenty years, Sam Gay's firm hand guided the city and county through a stormy youth marked by street fights, holdups, arson, murder, and labor turbulence.[6]

Unfortunately, the town's fire protection was somewhat less effective, especially in the early years. As tents yielded to frame buildings in the months after the May auction, fires posed an immediate threat. In June 1905 a major fire in the Original Las Vegas Townsite prompted demands for creation of a fire department. Noting that local firefighters "had no system whatsoever to check the ravages of the seething flames," the *Las Vegas Times* warned that "with the increase of tinder-box buildings, . . . the danger of a swift . . . fire will be increased and the residents will ever be in the shadow of such a danger." To minimize the peril, townsmen organized a volunteer "hose company" to fight a substantial number of blazes resulting from the frontier community's forced dependence upon kerosene lamps and liquified gas.[7]

While the need for more police helped boost the movement for county division, improvement of the so-called fire department strengthened the campaign for incorporation. As the referendum on incorporation drew near in spring 1911, boosters like *Las Vegas Age* publisher Charles Squires used any event to promote the cause. Fires were particularly helpful because they exposed the weakness of town board government. As fate would have it, just seven days before the crucial election flames destroyed a Las Vegas landmark, the Overland Hotel. It was conceivable that, had a northwest wind been blowing that night, the entire business district would have been lost. As it was, low water pressure hampered efforts to douse the stubborn flames. Squires therefore used the occasion to refute the arguments of those who insisted that incorporation would raise taxes. Contending that formal city government would improve all municipal services and therefore raise taxable property values, Squires predicted that "each of us [will] pay no more money for taxes than we are paying now." In the end, incorporation triumphed and fire protection improved, especially after 1917, when the city purchased its first fire truck. For a while longer, though, service was spotty. Small fires were handled by the town's occasional hose company while larger blazes continued to require an all-hands response. Finally in 1924, a measure of institutionalization was achieved when fifteen men formed a permanent volunteer company which began operating from an alley behind the Apache Hotel with a 1907 pickup truck and a 1917 REO Speedwagon.[8]

In addition to police and fire protection, education was a major priority in an infant community eager to retain its large family element. Unlike Nevada's mining camps, its railroad towns counted a large number of children from the first days of settlement. Even before the May 1905 auction, Lincoln County commissioners appointed the first Las Vegas school trustees in anticipation of a large class of students from the already existing McWilliams Townsite. Shortly after the May auction, settlers chose a three-member school board and approved a $1,500 levy for a three-room schoolhouse. To save time, the board instead purchased the old Salt Lake Hotel building and moved the four-room structure to Second and Lewis. Classes began in fall 1905 with enrollment approaching one hundred pupils. However, the Panic of 1907 and its lingering effects upon railroad traffic and ore shipments cut the fall 1909 enrollment to just eighty-five students. They were taught by a modest faculty comprised of "Professor" P. B. Martin, the principal, and three female teachers in charge of the high school, grammar, and primary students, respectively. Initially, pupils were assessed $5 per month to cover their teacher's salary. While the latter was hardly a drain upon the community's funds, the need for a modern school building mandated a substantial bond issue. Las Vegans recognized that such an expenditure was needed to symbolize the town's commitment to education. As one editor noted, a modern school was "not only an economic necessity, but should [also] appeal to the community as a matter of pride and patriotism." Several months later in August 1908 voters approved bonds for a $30,000 high school. This time board officials sought a larger site capable of accommodating future expansion.

In its typically paternalistic fashion, Senator Clark's railroad offered a two-block site (bounded by Bridger, Clark, Fourth, and

Fifth Streets) for a $10 fee. Construction began in 1910. Blue-prints called for a two-story, fourteen-classroom, mission-style building. In September 1911, the new Clark County High School opened its doors to 111 elementary students and a seventeen-member high school class (the first high school graduation was 1913). "Senior students" occupied the second floor until their numbers swelled to the point where a new facility was needed. Residents built the city's first high school in 1918. Within two years, however, even more construction was necessary as soaring enrollments forced School Superintendent A. S. Henderson to ask the board for a new branch school across the railroad tracks to service Westside students. This facility on D Street opened in 1921 and solved the enrollment problem until the late 1920s, when news of Boulder Dam began inundating the town with thousands of newcomers.[9]

Aside from providing basic municipal services, Las Vegans also struggled to build a utility and street infrastructure. Within weeks of the town's settlement, the Las Vegas Land and Water Company (the railroad's land subsidiary) began constructing a water line from the Big Springs west of town past the railroad tracks into Clark's Townsite, where a network of redwood pipes distributed water to every lot. For the next few years the Las Vegas Land and Water Company was largely autonomous. Most residents, grateful for service of any kind, offered little opposition to the paternalistic company. This laissez-faire atmosphere continued until November 1909, when the newly created Board of Clark County Commissioners granted the company a franchise and established a schedule of water rates.

As early as fall 1905, the company's water supply was inadequate, prompting a search for new sources. On November 11, 1905, Peter Buol, W. R. Thomas, M. S. Beal, Las Vegas Land and Water Company agent Walter Bracken, and others formed the Vegas Artesian Water Syndicate for the purpose of "boring for artesian water in the Las Vegas Valley." Their efforts were rewarded a short time later. In 1908, forwarding merchants Ed Clark and C. C. Ronnow hit a major well on their ranch seven miles south of town. A year later, Ed Von Tobel and Jake Beckley drilled a large well on their ranch in Paradise Valley. Over the next few decades, the existence of substantial aquifers under the Las Vegas Valley would prove essential to the city's growth.

Since the railroad did not hold title to most of Las Vegas's new subdivisions beyond the original townsite, the carrier had little incentive to enlarge its mains and improve its water service. Even businesses in town soon found the supply inadequate. As early as 1909, the Hotel Nevada (later the Sal Sagev) at Fremont and Main planned to augment its supply by digging a well on its property. To support suburban expansion, developers like Peter Buol and Capt. James Ladd drilled wells in the various "additions" and then offered to pipe water to unserviced subdivisions. In May 1914, for example, city commissioners permitted James Ladd to lay water mains in the streets and alleys of the Ladd and Fairview additions for "irrigating and domestic purposes." These private efforts were essential because the railroad's supply never kept pace with urban development. Hot summers were particularly troublesome when the demand for water and ice overwhelmed the utility's capacities. Typical was the dry summer of 1919, when businessmen, homeowners, and even the chamber of commerce complained in vain to railroad authorities about chronically low water pressure in city pipes and fire hydrants.[10]

Like water, electric power was also vital to safety. As early as 1905, residents were troubled by the fire hazard posed by the use of kerosene and gasoline lamps. Finally, after a disastrous conflagration at the Trocadero Theatre in 1906, banker John S. Park, Charles Squires, and three other businessmen vowed to end the local menace by forming the Consolidated Power and Telephone Company. In 1906, after negotiating a deal to utilize a spare generator in the Armour Company ice plant, Squires and his associates secured redwood poles from a nearby lumberyard and several thousand feet of heavy copper wire. Within weeks, local men began stringing wire from the ice plant across Main to First Street and thence northward along an alley to Stewart. Eventually, the company extended its network to most of Clark's Townsite, and Las Vegans began exchanging their gasoline lamps for thirty-two-candlepower carbons.

The euphoria was short-lived. Within a year, demand outstripped supply and the heavy copper wire could not deliver enough current to all of the town's customers. Lamp brightness declined markedly due to the power drain, forcing the utility to purchase "Old Betsy," a new ninety-horsepower, single-cylinder engine (with two flywheels over six feet in diameter) capable of

generating 2,300 watts. Subsequent improvements included re-
placement of the network's heavy copper street lines with more
efficient, thinner wire. Still, service was inadequate. Power was
only available at night for lighting and cooking; gas powered the
town by day. Although capacity was nearly doubled in 1912
with the purchase of a second generator, full service came in
1915 when Consolidated Power contracted to buy all the town's
electricity from the railroad's newly constructed powerhouse.
This arrangement served the town's needs until 1937, when
Hoover Dam took over. The only exception occurred during the
national railroad strike of 1922, when the Union Pacific shut
down the local powerhouse, forcing the union town into an un-
wanted dependency upon kerosene lamps for light and ice for
refrigeration.[11]

Besides water and electric power, Las Vegans also needed a
sewer system to diminish the health menace posed by kitchen
and cesspool wastes left baking in the summer heat. For the first
few decades of the city's existence, women and children left
town each summer before the prevailing "fevers" could afflict
the population. Physicians like Dr. Roy Martin as well as other
civic leaders knew that the desert city would have to remove its
wastes more efficiently if it hoped to project a modern image. In
spring 1909, a group of prominent businessmen from the Las
Vegas Promotion Society formed a "sanitary committee" to
lobby the railroad for help. In response, the company donated
the expertise of its engineering department, which, in turn, submitted its recommendations to the committee that fall. Plans
called for a $40,000 bond issue to finance mains servicing every
lot in Clark's Townsite along with a treatment plant, consisting
of ten septic tanks northeast of downtown on the Old Stewart
Ranch. Following approval, officials scheduled a bond election
for November 8. The town's newspapers closed ranks in support
of the question. Typical was a column by Corkhill, who, after
reminding voters that because of the town's "innumerable cess-
pools and toilet vaults, it is only good fortune that has prevented
a serious epidemic," urged approval for the sewer bond issue.
Corkhill's efforts and those of Squires were rewarded a few days
later when residents endorsed the bond issue as another gesture
of support for their community's improvement program.[12]

Although utilities, waste removal, and municipal services

were all vital, perhaps no activity was more welcomed than the paving of the townsite's streets. In June 1905 citizens rejoiced at news that the Las Vegas Land and Water Company had let bids for the oiling, grading, and guttering of seven miles of Las Vegas streets. Promoters like Squires knew that if Las Vegas was to become a "most desirable point" for homes and businesses, it would have to eliminate "the great waves of dust that rear skywards from the cutting of roadways in and around the city by heavy freighting teams." Fortunately, the work moved rapidly and was largely completed by 1906.

In addition to street paving, residents also recognized the importance of county and state highway construction to Las Vegas's growth and accessibility. Thus in August 1905, Las Vegans welcomed the new toll road to Bullfrog which shortened the heavily traveled route to just ninety-eight miles, cutting the stagecoach ride from twenty-two to seventeen hours. At the same time, the opening of the new forty-eight-mile route to Indian Springs reduced the wagon ride to just a few hours. Not surprisingly, C. O. Whittemore, Las Vegas Land and Water Company president and now president of Senator Clark's new auto stage company, hailed the completion of these projects as the key to "win-[ning] the victory for Las Vegas over all Nevada points for quick and efficient service into . . . Goldfield."

In the long run, roads to Salt Lake and Los Angeles would be even more crucial to the city's future. Under pressure from the local chamber of commerce, Clark County commissioners voted in January 1914 to "authorize" an auto road from St. Thomas, Utah, through Moapa, Las Vegas, and Jean to the California line. Thanks to some limited county and federal funding, work on the thoroughfare soon got underway. By May 1915, the local press reported that the highway linking Las Vegas and Los Angeles was progressing. Both townsmen and potential investors understood the project's value: once completed, the road would cut a hundred miles off the existing route (through the Owens River Valley). Moreover, since the route bypassed high mountain passes and long stretches of barren desert, its reliability and safety would combine to make it the major link between southern California and the main transcontinental truck route through Salt Lake.[13]

At the same time, the town's aggressive business community,

symbolized by the chamber of commerce, was busy promoting roads to other destinations as well. Throughout 1913, work progressed on a highway to the booming zinc-lead camps at Goodsprings in the mountains southwest of Las Vegas. Upon the road's completion in March 1914, a procession of Las Vegas's leading businessmen formed a Sunday morning "auto pilgrimage" to mark the occasion. Then in 1916, another major connection—this time with the southeast—was established when a group of investors inaugurated "auto stageline service" (via the El Dorado ferry across the Colorado) between Las Vegas and Kingman, Arizona. Just a year earlier, local developer E. W. Griffith had contributed a new dimension to Las Vegas's recreational economy when he opened an auto road through Kyle Canyon to his resort northwest of town at Mt. Charleston. Ensuing years would see his facility attract a steady stream of tourists and local residents anxious to escape summer's heat. Prospects of continuing the road farther north beyond Goldfield and even Tonopah brightened in 1919, following the termination of service on Senator Clark's Las Vegas & Tonopah Railroad. In a farsighted move, the Las Vegas Chamber of Commerce acted quickly to initiate the process for constructing a modern auto link between Las Vegas and Reno. In February 1919, the group urged Clark and Nye county commissioners to purchase the railroad's bridges along the route to guarantee their presence once highway paving began.

The major project, however, remained the auto link with Los Angeles and Utah. Grading work dragged along during the war years into the 1920s, slowed by a lack of highway funds. Then in 1922 the U.S. Bureau of Public Roads offered to pay 87 percent of the cost of paving Fremont, First, and Main streets with durable concrete as part of the highway's route through the city. In response, twenty-seven prominent citizens urged support for the $50,000 bond issue to give the city's main business street a more substantial appearance. Following voter approval, highway officials paved Fremont in 1925 and largely completed work on the road north of the city to the Arizona line. Widening, grading, and paving southward toward San Bernardino continued for the next five years. The highway was completely finished by the New Deal in the early 1930s.[14]

While government, municipal services, and infrastructure

were all vital to Las Vegas, town making also involved the formation of social networks. Even though residents spent most of 1905 building homes and establishing businesses, time was reserved for social gatherings. To be sure, there was no lack of picnics, meetings, and get-togethers. One of the earliest was a July 1905 social held at the "dance pavilion" by the community's lone Presbyterian "missionary." In a column promoting the event, the *Las Vegas Times* recognized that "in places where all are strangers to each other . . . something must be done to get people to know each other." Baseball games contributed further to developing a sense of community. While later years witnessed regional contests between Las Vegas players and opponents from Needles, Tonopah, and other railroad centers, that first year saw games played between such local teams as the Rancheros and the Uptowners. These contests, along with a growing number of other sports and social activities, kept idle time to a minimum. Gradually, certain events became annual affairs. Beginning in 1908, the town's Hose Company No. 1 sponsored a Labor Day "fireman's ball," which featured a number of events, including a hose race by the local company. By 1915, the town's annual Labor Day carnival boasted horse races, hard rock drilling contests, wrestling matches, burro and foot races, children's games, an "open air dance," and an auto race down Fremont Street from the railroad station to Kiel Ranch. All of these events combined to diminish the sense of isolation and knit the community closer together.

As the town matured, the number of organizations multiplied and the town's social calendar bulged with activities. A typical week in July 1912 saw the Methodist ladies hold an "ice cream social" at the First State Bank building, followed a few days later by a "grand ball" at James Ladd's recently opened "resort" off Fremont Street. In fact, on any given Saturday night a good portion of the town's adult population could be found at Ladd's. Though small, Las Vegas hardly wanted for nighttime entertainment. Supplementing the dance bands at Ladd's were the Majestic Theatre (opened in 1912), which featured first-run movies, and the Isis Theatre next to the town's Opera House (built in 1907), which provided a "moving picture and illustrated song performance" seven nights a week. For the less culturally inclined, Fremont Street hosted a motley array of drinking establishments, ranging from the cheaper bars in the red light district of Block 16 to the area's pretentious Arizona Club.[15]

While some townsmen were content to spend their free time reveling in the bawdy atmosphere of Block 16, other residents longed for more fulfilling activities. To accommodate this need, Las Vegans wasted little time establishing a vigorous social life to ease the loneliness of desert living. Among the first groups to organize were the Eagles, who met on August 21, 1905 and formally created a fraternal lodge on September 15. Within months they raised enough money to purchase a lot on Fremont near First Street (today part of the Golden Nugget) and erect a building. The organization promoted a variety of community events, including an annual Thanksgiving celebration, occasional sports contests for children, civic fund-raising campaigns for polio victims, and other worthy causes. Similarly, the Las Vegas Elks owed their existence to Elk settlers and members from nearby towns who helped organize the local chapter. In April 1906, a group of Elks met at the Hotel Nevada and formed a lodge. While a formal Elks charter was not obtained until June 1923, the "Stray Elks" nonetheless sponsored dozens of parties and entertained numerous gatherings of regional Elks in Las Vegas's hotels and clubs. Moreover, they marked each Independence Day with a gala and fireworks show at the Old Stewart Ranch.

Many of these same men also founded the town's Masonic Lodge in 1907. Led by banker John S. Park, the club would eventually count most of the town's major business and professional men as members. Within two years of their founding, the Masons had purchased a lot on South Third Street and erected a lodge upon it. The structure formally opened in September 1909 with the help of a visiting delegation of Tonopah Masons who came to Las Vegas for the occasion. While the Masons and Elks were the major social clubs in early Las Vegas, there were a number of smaller organizations, including a chapter of the Odd Fellows—a club which had seen its Nevada debut during the early Comstock boom.[16]

Of course, Las Vegas women were also active in the community-building process. As early as May 1906, local women formed the "Help One Another Club" to ease the transition of living in a new town. Local Christmas tree festivals and parties for the children began in 1906. Although many women and children left

Las Vegas in the summer months, women's groups were active during the rest of the year. In 1911, women from the town's most prominent families formed the Mesquite Club, which held frequent meetings devoted to civic causes and educational programs. The group, for instance, sponsored lectures in Nevada history, Indian basketry, and other cultural topics. The club was also committed to improving the town's appearance and quality of life. On Arbor Day 1912, women organized a "plant a tree and bless the earth" campaign, which provided Las Vegas with two thousand desperately needed shade trees. Then in June 1915, Mesquite Club members lobbied county and school board authorities for creation of a kindergarten in town. A year later, members held a benefit to raise money for a Las Vegas library, which opened in April 1917, stocked with five hundred books donated by the club. Supplementing this organization was a local Women's Club, which quickly allied with regional affiliates. By 1912, thanks to railroad and later auto stage lines, Las Vegas women joined with their counterparts across Nevada in attending annual conventions and participating in programs of statewide interest.[17]

In addition to various club activities, the community's women played an active role in aiding American troops during World War I. In May 1917, Frances McNamee, wife of prominent attorney Leo McNamee, joined with a group of other women to form the Clark County chapter of the American Red Cross. Headquartered in the county courthouse, this organization collected hundreds of sweaters, shirts, and coats (either donated or made by local women) for Allied troops and war refugees. In many ways the war united the city and region as never before. One manifestation of this community spirit was southern Nevada's response to the national war bond drive. By June 1917, "patriotic Clark County residents," led by Las Vegas, had purchased over $87,000 worth of bonds, with railroad employees in the repair shops alone contributing $2,500 in just one week! A year later, county residents triumphed again, easily meeting their quota for the third Liberty Loan drive. Locally, there were other sacrifices. During America's year-and-a-half participation in the war, patriotic Las Vegans observed meatless days once and sometimes twice a week to conserve food for the military. Moreover, residents freely cooperated with the Clark County

Defense Council (formed in March 1918), even supporting the council's request to close down gambling operations (beginning in August 1918) until war's end. Following the armistice, Las Vegas welcomed home its returning veterans. Like their compatriots across the country, local servicemen wasted no time organizing; by September 1919, they had formed a local post of the American Legion. Three years later in 1922, twenty-eight female residents, including an army nurse, established the women's auxiliary to the American Legion.[18]

In addition to public festivals, fraternal organizations, civic clubs, and veterans' groups, local churches were also important. As it had been elsewhere in Nevada and the West, religion was an integrating force which glued the young community together. On a desert frontier beset by violence, hard drinking, and prostitution, religion provided a measure of social control. Services began in the town's first year of existence. The Methodists held their first service in June 1905 in a tent near refreshing Las Vegas Creek. While the initial Presbyterian service antedated the May 1905 auction, the first pastor did not arrive until 1910—a delay which led some of the more restless communicants to Methodism. Although Las Vegas hosted a substantial number of Catholics, no church was built immediately. Instead, priests from the Diocese of Salt Lake City (Nevada did not become a diocese until 1931) came to Las Vegas every few weeks to say mass in a tent or donated room. Finally in 1908, the Catholics erected a small chapel on South Second Street which evolved into their first parish, St. Joan of Arc.

Similarly, the Episcopalians began modestly with occasional services held by visiting priests and even bishops from Utah. Then in 1908, the Las Vegas Land and Water Company donated land for an Episcopal church, which opened for services in 1909. Close on the heels of these denominations were the Baptists, who formally organized their worship services in 1910, although a church structure itself was not erected on Fremont and Seventh Streets until 1924. Oddly enough, the Mormons, who had originally pioneered the area in 1855, were among the last groups to establish an official presence. Bishop Ira Earl was the driving force behind the Mormon's Carson Street chapel and the city's first stake and ward church in 1923.[19]

Las Vegans also struggled to guarantee the town's survival

and growth by diversifying its economy. Veterans of earlier town-building efforts, both native Americans and immigrants, recognized that every successful town must engage in what might be called future making—the process by which a young community, through its own initiative, tries to shape and ensure a prosperous future for itself. Imbued with the independent spirit and restless opportunism so characteristic of frontier people, Las Vegans like Jake Beckley, Ed Von Tobel, and other members of the business fraternity sought to multiply their town's advantages beyond railroading by securing other industries. Of course, the railroad was the lifeblood of early Las Vegas, especially in 1905, after construction began on Senator Clark's Las Vegas and Tonopah Railroad. Thanks to this project, carloads of rails, ties, and other supplies arrived almost daily from San Pedro for transshipment to the grading and track-laying crews headed northwest toward Rhyolite and Goldfield. It was this junction of Clark's Salt Lake and Tonopah lines at Las Vegas which brought the locomotive repair shops in 1909. The expanded payroll (175 new jobs immediately) sparked a real estate boom in 1911 which saw Peter Buol, James Ladd, and other developers open new housing additions north, east, and south of the existing town. Yet, as other Nevada towns could testify, reliance upon the railroad was a two-edged sword. Disastrous floods in 1907 and again in 1910 cut service between Las Vegas and Salt Lake for months at a time, short-circuiting local prosperity.

Even more disturbing were high railroad rates, which stifled local promotion. Anxious to secure the lion's share of regional transportation, Charles Squires and other Las Vegas businessmen maintained constant pressure upon the railroad to reduce high passenger and freight rates. As early as 1905, local editors demanded price cuts to help fulfill "the mission that has designated Las Vegas as the greatest commercial city of all the southwest." The plea for lower fares continued into the 1920s, when auto highways finally eased the town's dependency. In addition to prices, service was also an issue. Clearly, the railroads hampered Nevada's efforts to build a thriving intrastate economy. In June 1917, Squires argued for better railroad service to northern Nevada. Observing that it was cheaper and easier to travel to Reno by either the Barstow-Sacramento or Salt Lake routes, Squires requested direct service and lower fares through Tono-

pah. Such an improvement, he argued, would encourage ship-
ment of northern Nevada flour, sugar, lumber, and livestock to
Las Vegas, which, in turn, could trade southern Nevada products north. The commerce would benefit all. As Squires reasoned, "The promotion of intra-state business would increase
our wealth by keeping our money within the state." But the railroads were not impressed, and Squires's dream had to await the
truck era.[20]

While floods, poor service, and high rates were always both-
ersome, the permanent shutdown of service posed an even
greater danger to the young town's economy. Las Vegas slowly
lost its once booming trade with the Bullfrog Mining District in
the years after 1912. As World War I drew to a close and the demand for high-grade ore began to slow in the Goldfield area, the
Las Vegas and Tonopah Railroad cut its service in 1917 to a tri-
weekly schedule. A year later, on October 31, 1918, railroad
vice-president J. Ross Clark announced the termination of all
service on the line.

Three years later, Las Vegas absorbed another blow when
Senator Clark revealed his plans to sell the San Pedro, Los Angeles and Salt Lake Railroad to the Union Pacific. The change of
masters marked the end of an era. Everyone knew that the paternalistic treatment which Clark had reserved for his Las Vegas
progeny would cease once executive decisions began emanating
from the Union Pacific's boardrooms in Omaha and New York.
Subsequent events only confirmed this fear. In October 1921, a
brief wildcat strike in the Las Vegas yards followed the discharge
of sixty local shopmen. Then, during the national railroad strike
of 1922, Governor Emmet Boyle dispatched the state police to
Las Vegas after violence flared between scabs and striking workmen. With so much of the town's business community dependent upon the patronage of railroad employees, support for the
picketers was strong. So, in apparent response to the city's pro-
union sentiments, Union Pacific officials decided to punish the
community later that year by moving the repair shops to Caliente.
Coming on the heels of the postwar recession and devastating
strike, this was a major blow for Las Vegas.[21]

Yet, as had been the case in other Nevada towns, economic
adversity only toughened the resolve of business leaders to cast
off the yoke of railroad control by diversifying the city's port-

folio. Charles Corkhill spoke for many when he noted that for seventeen years Las Vegas had been little more than a "parasite" living off the railroad. For too long, dependency upon the shop payroll had been the "curse of the city," because the community "lacked the incentive to go ahead and accomplish what it can accomplish." To buttress his view, Corkhill emphasized the recent arrival in Las Vegas of developer W. F. Holt, the man who "gave Imperial Valley to the world." Holt's earlier success in southern California and his expressed desire to purchase the Winterwood Ranch near town raised hopes that he would build railroads, irrigation systems, banks, and "cities and empires" in the Las Vegas Valley. Complaining that Las Vegas was "sick and tired of being treated like a child," Corkhill confidently announced that if Holt decided to invest, he would "replace the Union Pacific shops in twenty-four hours." Such a move would liberate citizens and businessmen alike from the town's stifling dependency upon the railroad. In Corkhill's mind, the era of diversification was fast approaching. Not only would commercial agriculture catalyze the process, but so would the construction of Boulder Dam (the Colorado River Compact would be signed in November), which would encourage the arrival of the Atchison, Topeka and Santa Fe Railroad and, with it, lower passenger and freight rates. Ultimately, with new industry and competitive railroad rates, Las Vegas would assure its destiny as "one of the greatest cities in the great southwest." [22]

Of course, the diversification effort did not begin in 1922. The farsighted and independent people who built the frontier community recognized the value of developing an agricultural hinterland. Both the Las Vegas Board of Trade (founded in August 1905) and the later chamber of commerce (established in 1911) pushed various crop experiments. As early as 1905, the successful drilling of artesian wells demonstrated that underground water supplies were more than sufficient to irrigate the valley. Indeed, many contemporaries shared the optimistic view of one Salt Lake reporter, who in 1905 predicted that Las Vegas would "one day be the center of an agricultural region of wondrous wealth." Local investors struggled to fulfill the prophecy. The opening of Clark's townsite encouraged the planting of more farms in the valley and experiments to develop a cash crop economy. In 1912, forwarding merchants Ed Clark and C. C. Ronnow planted thirty-five acres of alfalfa, which eventually sold for $4,000. In that same year, local lands yielded forty bushels an acre of wheat and forty-five of corn.

Two years later, determined to expand the area's list of crops and duplicate the success of Churchill County, Moapa Valley's Isaiah Cox and former Las Vegas mayor Peter Buol (now president of the Southern Nevada Land and Development Company) planted forty acres of cantaloupes on land leased by Buol. Local newspapers praised the effort to initiate commercial-scale production of the crop and hoped the move would "induce the ranch owners of the valley to plant at least a portion of their acreage to cantaloupes" so that shipments this season can be made "in carload lots." For its part, Senator Clark's railroad did its utmost to promote local farming. In 1911, for instance, the company leased one thousand square feet of space at the Land and Products Exposition at the Los Angeles Exhibit Building. Clark then encouraged the Las Vegas Chamber of Commerce to provide as many exhibits as possible (to be transported at railroad expense) to impress the forty thousand expected investors "seeking new investments or locations brought into southern California by the railroad." Unfortunately, the alkali content of the Las Vegas valley's soil ultimately doomed efforts to duplicate the success of the Imperial and San Joaquin valleys.[23]

On another front, Las Vegans struggled to profit more from their rich mining hinterland. Hopes were fueled by the building of Senator Clark's railroad, which connected Las Vegas with the Pioche-Delamar districts to the northeast and the Bullfrog-Tonopah districts to the northwest and projected roads linking the city with Searchlight and El Dorado in the south. The signing of the Colorado River Compact in 1922 boosted expectations even further that low-cost dam power would team with convenient transportation to make Las Vegas a smelting hub. In headlines which screamed "Steel Mills for Las Vegas," Charles Corkhill boldly predicted that within a few years Las Vegas would become the greatest milling and smelting center in the Southwest. Subsequent events seemed to justify this optimism. After all, World War I had inspired development of large-scale manganese operations only fifteen miles southeast of Las Vegas, while just southwest of town, Blue Diamond's gypsum quarries and plasterboard factory promised significant shipping if not milling profits. But, once again, nature denied Las Vegas its triumph, as southern Nevada's mineral boom died almost as quickly as it had begun.[24]

Fortunately, the town's efforts to diversify its economy extended beyond agriculture, mining, and even the dam. From its earliest days, Las Vegas was a fun spot. In 1905, when the railroad advertised lots for sale in the new Las Vegas Townsite, it carefully reserved Blocks 16 and 17 (bordered by Fremont, Second, Third, and Stewart) for the sale of intoxicating liquors. Almost immediately, a jungle of tent bars sprang up in the zone. The Star, Gem, Red Onion, Arcade, and a host of other dives thrived twenty-four hours a day, catering to travelers and locals anxious to quench their thirst, gamble, and carouse with the legion of "ill-famed women" who plied their trade in the infamous cribs outside. Most popular of all was the Arizona Club, built in 1905 by the flamboyant Scotsman James O. McIntosh. Thanks to the booming trade that first year, McIntosh opened a pretentious new building in 1907 featuring solid oak doors, beveled glass windows, and fine imported whiskey. For the next twenty years Las Vegas maintained its reputation as an entertaining refuge for weary travelers and regional businessmen.

The city's potential as a resort city stemmed from its mild winter climate as well as its recreational attributes. In July 1905, Las Vegas Land and Water Company president C. O. Whittemore advised townsmen that in all of its advertising in the eastern states the railroad was marketing Las Vegas "as a sanitarium—a haven for the winter tourist and a blessing to [those] subject to pulmonary complaints." Then, in an effort to reassure local businessmen who were suffering through a mild recession and their first scorching summer in Las Vegas, Whittemore predicted that by December the town would have "an activity and liveliness to compare with beach resorts for its salutary winter climate."[25]

Schemes for resorts were both plentiful and ephemeral. In December 1918, for instance, prominent New York investor Charles Hubbell came to Las Vegas with plans to build a one-hundred-room tourist hotel somewhere in Nevada and perhaps even in Las Vegas. Hubbell reasoned that projected highways opening access to the Grand Canyon and Utah's Zion Canyon would ultimately spark a substantial tourist trade. Local booster

"Pop" Squires greeted the statement with unrestrained glee, predicting that the effect of such a resort "on every class of business would be marked." Moreover, he predicted that the town's smaller lodging houses would also benefit from the many people "attracted by the big hotel, who after a short stay there would seek more modest quarters for a longer period." As early as 1918, Squires glimpsed the value of using a famous hotel as a magnet for luring tourists to Las Vegas—a marketing ploy which future Las Vegans would raise to the level of an art.[26]

Though Hubbell never built his hotel, he nonetheless encouraged the chamber of commerce (which already had appointed a Hotels Committee) to look beyond mining and agriculture. While no major resorts graced Las Vegas before the dam era, there was a steady stream of smaller enterprises catering mostly to locals. Typical was the effort of developer David Lorenzi, who, after arriving in 1911, acquired eighty acres of land west of town for the sumptuous resort he planned to build. Construction began shortly after World War I, with workmen struggling to dig two lakes fed by artesian wells. When it opened in 1921, Lorenzi's Resort (today Lorenzi Park) featured dancing, boating, sailing, and the largest swimming pool in Nevada. Future plans included a casino and tavern (once Prohibition had ended) as well as a ranch house for guests. As the 1920s wore on and more highways were opened linking the West and East, the notion of building a ranch-style hotel became more plausible. Convinced of Las Vegas's potential as a winter tourist center, Edward Taylor, an eastern investor, purchased the old Kiel Ranch in 1924 from banker John S. Park and announced plans to convert the property into a dude ranch for eastern tourists. Later in the 1920s, speculator Leigh Hunt bought much of the land south of town for resort development. However, little came of these and other schemes. For the most part, Reno's dude ranches, located on the main New York–Chicago–San Francisco auto and rail routes, snared most of the divorcees and tourists bound for dude ranches, while Palm Springs, Scottsdale, and even New Mexico spas largely monopolized the winter vacation business.[27]

But these setbacks were only temporary; later decades would vindicate the faith of Squires and the other pioneers. To be sure, the roots of Las Vegas's modern-day success lie deep in the city's past. The native and immigrant people who built the town were an ambitious and determined group. In just ten years they established a city, invented a county, and organized a community. Moreover, they developed a vision of what Las Vegas could become. Convinced that their city was destined for greater things than whistlestop status, they dreamed of steel mills, chemical plants, rolling farmlands, and winter resorts. Their hopes were misplaced, but their optimism fueled a momentum which carried them through the lean years. Led by a booster press, they were not content to remain a railroad town, and, even after Hoover Dam's completion in 1936, they were not satisfied with being a mere "gateway town" for tourists. The winning formula eluded townsmen until 1940, when Thomas Hull finally demonstrated the feasibility of combining casinos with year-round resorts.

In the end, Charles Corkhill and the others were correct: the key to Las Vegas's success was not the railroad. Nor was it gambling. The real key lay in the spirited town-making effort of the first twenty years and, more precisely, in the stubborn independence, restless opportunism, and sense of destiny exhibited by the city's pioneers—an infectious spirit transmitted to succeeding generations of Las Vegans.

NOTES

1. Wilbur Shepperson, *Restless Strangers: Nevada's Immigrants and Their Interpreters* (Reno: University of Nevada Press, 1970). Several works provide helpful introductions to the subject of town making on the western frontier. See, for instance, Rodman Paul, *Mining Frontiers of the Far West, 1848–1880* (New York: Holt, Rinehart and Winston, 1963); Thomas Noel, *The City and the Saloon: Denver, 1858–1916* (Lincoln: University of Nebraska Press, 1982); Duane Smith, *Rocky Mountain Mining Camps: The Urban Frontier* (Bloomington: Indiana University Press, 1967).

2. U.S. Department of Commerce, Bureau of the Census, *Nevada, 1910*, 53–62.

3. Stanley Paher, *Las Vegas, As It Began—As It Grew* (Las Vegas: Nevada Publications, 1971), 104–5. For more on early Las Vegas, see Patricia Holland, "Las Vegas Business District, 1905–1930," unpublished paper; Ralph Roske, *Las Vegas: A Desert Paradise* (Tulsa: Continental Heritage Press, 1986), 51–70; Perry B. Kaufman, "The Best City of Them All: A History of Las Vegas, 1930–1960," Ph.D. dissertation, University of California, Santa Barbara, 1974, 15–20; and Michael S. Green, "Boosting Beginnings: *The Las Vegas Times*, 1905–1906," unpub-

lished paper, passim. For creation of the county division club, see *Las Vegas Age*, August 1, 8, 1908, 1. For more on the north-south split, see James Hulse, *Lincoln County, Nevada: 1864–1909, History of a Mining Region* (Reno: University of Nevada Press, 1971), 77–79, and Charles Squires's "Clark County" chapter in Samuel P. Davis, ed., *The History of Nevada*, 2 vols. (Reno: Elms Publishing Co., 1913), vol. 2, 795–805.

4. For the city's incorporation, see *Statutes of Nevada*, chap. 132, March 6, 1911, 145–83. For the actual organization of the city government, official salaries, and business license fees, see Board of City Commissioners, *Minutes*, vol. 1, June 22, 1911, A–B; July 5, 1911, C–H.

5. Green, "Boosting Beginnings," 1–2.

6. *Las Vegas Review-Journal*, June 10, 1979, 3J–5J. Gay was briefly deposed in 1918; see *Las Vegas Age*, October 26, 1918, 1.

7. *Las Vegas Times*, June 10, 1905, 1. The city established two hose companies in 1911 and provided three dollars to the chief and two dollars to each member for each fire they fought. City Commission, *Minutes*, vol. 1, July 5, 1911, 1.

8. *Las Vegas Age*, May 27, 1911, 1.

9. Florence Lee Jones, "Las Vegas, Golden Anniversary Edition," special ed. of the *Las Vegas Review-Journal*, February 28, 1955, "Las Vegas First Edition," 4; *Clark County Review*, September 18, 1909, 1; *Las Vegas Review-Journal*, November 12, 1978, 3J–5J.

10. Florence Lee Jones and John Cahlan, *Water: A History of Las Vegas*, 2 vols. (Las Vegas: Las Vegas Valley Water District, 1975), vol. 1, 37; *Clark County Review*, October 23, 1909, 1; May 15, 1915, 1; Jones and Cahlan, *Water*, vol. 1, 33–34.

11. *Las Vegas Review-Journal*, November 14, 1982, 6L–7L; Jones, "Las Vegas," 13.

12. *Clark County Review*, October 9, 1909, 3; City Commission, *Minutes*, vol. 1, August 2, 1911; September 9, 1911, 1–3. The sewer bond issue passed by 183 to 11. See ibid., October 10, 1911, 20; *Clark County Review*, November 6, 1909, 1.

13. *Las Vegas Times*, June 17, 1905, 2; September 2, 1905, 1; *Clark County Review*, January 10, 1914, 1; March 28, 1914, 1; May 15, 1915, 1; May 22, 1915, 1.

14. *Clark County Review*, March 14, 1914, 1; Jones, "General Section," 9; *Las Vegas Age*, February 8, 1919, 1; *Las Vegas Review* (formerly *Clark County Review*), March 24, 1922, 1; May 4, 1923, 1; Jones, "Construction Section," 11.

15. *Las Vegas Times*, July 22, 1905, 2; *Clark County Review*, September 18, 1909, 1; September 4, 1915, 1; July 20, 1912, 3; September 18, 1909, 3.

16. Jones, "Las Vegas Second Edition," 10; idem, "Construction Edition," 8; idem, "Las Vegas Second Edition," 10.

17. Jones, "General Section," 9; *Clark County Review*, November 6, 1915, 1.

18. Jones, "Las Vegas Second Edition," 12; *Las Vegas Age*, June 16, 1917, 1; Jones, "Construction Edition," 2. For the wartime ban on gam-

bling, see City Commission, *Minutes,* August 12, 1918, 247–48; Jones, "Construction Section," 3.

19. Jones, "Las Vegas First Edition," 12.

20. Paher, *Las Vegas,* 97–99, 113–19; Roske, *Las Vegas,* 58–60; *Las Vegas Times,* July 8, 1905, 2; *Las Vegas Age,* June 30, 1917, 1.

21. Jones and Cahlan, *Water,* vol. 1, 53; *Las Vegas Age,* September 28, 1918, 1, 4.

22. *Las Vegas Review,* July 14, 1922, 1.

23. *Clark County Review,* February 21, 1914, 1; January 31, 1914, 1; *Las Vegas Age,* February 25, 1911, 1.

24. *Las Vegas Review,* June 9, 1922, 1; Jones, "Construction Section," 11.

25. *Las Vegas Review-Journal,* June 10, 1979, 3J–5J; *Las Vegas Times,* July 22, 1905, 1.

26. *Las Vegas Age,* March 8, 1919, 1.

27. Jones, "Construction Section," 8.

MIDDLE GROUND AND MARGINAL SPACE: SENSE OF PLACE IN THE MIDDLE WEST AND THE GREAT BASIN

ELIZABETH RAYMOND

In a nation of identical fast food franchises and television newscasts, regionalism seems strangely irrelevant. The hegemony of a national culture fabricated in New York and Los Angeles easily overpowers any subtle local variations among America's geographic sections. Nonetheless, regional identities stubbornly persist, and students of American culture continue to explore richly variant patterns of regional literature, art, ethnicity, economy, or religion.

The obvious key to this persistence of American regions is geography. Regional differences are grounded both literally and figuratively in the environment, which provides the crucial physical context in which any distinctive local culture develops. Consideration of two particular American regions will reveal the extent to which geographic factors are implicated in the perpetuation of American regionalism by focusing on the development of a characteristic regional sense of place in each.

Of course, the American landscape is not merely a regional phenomenon. It plays an important symbolic role in the shared national culture as well. Indeed, Americans have traditionally taken particular pride in the physical extensiveness of their country. In the United States, nationalism is defined not only by loyalty to republican political institutions but also by esteem for a bountiful land, "beautiful for spacious skies and amber waves of grain." The North American continent is at once the setting for and the proof of American achievement. Americans see themselves as a great nation in part because they inhabit such spectacularly productive space. Thus, figuratively, American nature and culture are inextricably intertwined.

Students of American society have long observed and discussed this interrelationship. The symbolic role of nature in American culture has been fruitfully explored by many scholars.[1] They have pointed out that the fertility and productivity of the eastern two-thirds of the United States helped shape optimistic national expectations of plenty for all. New England colonists, for example, asserted their status as God's chosen people in part by pointing out the divine favor that led them to stumble into such a productive wilderness.[2] Later, in his famous 1893 frontier thesis, historian Frederick Jackson Turner greatly enhanced the valuation of the American landscape when he argued that the exigencies of the American wilderness actually combined to *produce* its vaunted republican form of government. According to Turner, it was the prolonged frontier experience that accounted for the emergence and preservation of American democracy.[3]

Other scholars of American nature have examined the physical evolution of the American landscape as successive generations have altered the environment in order to make it conform more closely to their expectations of it.[4] These studies have suggested that the nature which Americans value so highly is in reality anything but natural, that the landscape has been and continues to be profoundly altered by human occupation, even when it appears to be empty. Early English settlers introduced bluegrass and honeybees, drained swamps, and filled bays to create new land. Americans have changed the direction of rivers, imposed the rectangular survey on the surface of the land, and introduced life-giving water to arid environments. In attempting to remedy environmental problems they have imported kudzu and starlings and inadvertently poisoned their wildlife refuges. By dividing and conquering the continent, they have established not only a new civilization but an altered geography as well.

This new geography—the landscape that Americans have created by their changes—is the setting for regionalism, which can be defined, after historian Donald Worster, as that which "emerges as people try to make a living from a particular part of the earth, as they adapt themselves to its limits and possibilities."[5] Regional consciousness, or sense of place, is thus a blend of both symbolic and physical aspects of nature. It grows out of the particular and distinctive patterns of interaction between people and place as inhabitants both change the land and are in turn changed by it. Sense of place is the means by which people give meaning to their specific experience of nature, and it varies, as nature itself varies, between the hills of West Virginia, for instance, and the plains of west Texas. Perception of place can be more clearly traced by considering two specific American regions, the agricultural heartland of the Middle West and the ranching and mining territory of the Great Basin.

The Middle West, America's breadbasket, is the epitome of environmental triumph. According to the regional myth, it is formerly empty and trackless prairie that has been tamed by the superhuman efforts of generations of settlers into extraordinarily fertile farmland. The measure of their achievement is the contemporary regional landscape, replete with overflowing corn cribs, section-line roads that meet at neat right angles, and rich black dirt fields. The Great Basin, on the other hand, defies the national mythology of abundance. An arid region that stubbornly resists agricultural productivity, it remains largely a sinister and disturbing desert. It is celebrated for the degree to which it remains unchanged by human occupation. Despite the manifest differences between them, however, both regions have developed a distinctive regional sensibility that is based on longstanding patterns of interaction between human residents and local environment. In both places, people have attributed specific meaning to the landscape, but the content and development of that meaning vary considerably between the two regions.

Both regions are nominally western, but similarities between them are few. For the sake of geographic precision, the extensive Middle West is subdivided into an area including all or portions of the present states of Iowa, Nebraska, Minnesota, and North and South Dakota. It is distinguished from the more western plains states west of the 100th meridian on the basis of Walter Prescott Webb's three criteria of topography, vegetation, and rainfall.[6] Like Webb's more western plains states, this Prairie Midwest is an immense area of level, treeless, relatively featureless land. However, unlike Webb's plains, the prairie was originally covered by tall native grass plants, reaching as high as six to eight feet. Moreover, in most years it receives sufficient rainfall for traditional methods of humid agriculture.

The Prairie Midwest is further distinguished, on the basis of social and cultural factors, from the prairie states of the Old Northwest, east of the Mississippi River, and from the border states of Kansas and Missouri. These regions, although they share abundant rainfall and areas of indigenous tallgrass prairie, developed in a distinctive fashion due, in the former case, to the economic influence of industry centered around the Great Lakes and, in the latter case, to the political divisions of the battle over slavery.

In the Prairie Midwest, even today, agriculture is paramount. The landscape is open and exposed, except for groves of trees surrounding numerous evenly spaced farmhouses which command the adjacent fields. Urban areas are few, and most are based on the processing and transportation of raw agricultural products from the farms. In this place steeped in agricultural productivity, the major subject of writers is the many nuances and variations of human relationships to the land. Writers from the Prairie Midwest dwell on the process of making and keeping this land productive. They take pride in what has collectively been achieved in transforming the prairie from barren openness to America's breadbasket. The theme of Prairie Midwestern writing is the creation and perfection of farmland, of making the inert dirt into significant space.

The Great Basin, on the other hand, is characterized by sterility rather than fertility. Its most distinctive feature, the fact that all of its rivers are inward flowing and never reach any ocean, was identified by John Charles Frémont in 1843–44. Bounded on the east by the Wasatch Mountains of Utah and on the west by California's Sierra Nevada, the Great Basin is a unique geographic province containing most of the state of Nevada and portions of California, Oregon, Idaho, and Utah. Extremely arid, with average rainfall of fewer than ten inches annually, it is a region of high altitude and great topographical variation. Narrow desert valleys are bounded by north-south-tending mountain ranges at intervals of twenty to eighty miles. If the Prairie Midwest is predominantly horizontal and extensive, the Great Basin is a preeminently vertical land where weather varies with altitude.

Native vegetation in the valleys is limited to desert shrubs such as sagebrush, while the mountains support the scrubby piñon pine and mountain juniper. Formerly covered by giant pre-historic lakes, much of the soil is alkali. Agriculture is therefore of minimal importance, since it is limited to valley areas of good soil that can be irrigated. Given the character of the soil and the paucity of water, such areas are necessarily few. Historically, the economy of the region has been based on the exploitation of lim-ited natural resources in the form of ranching and mining and, in Nevada, on the tourism attracted in the twentieth century by the legalization of behavior prohibited elsewhere, such as gam-bling, divorce, and prostitution.

Because of these limitations, regional population in the Great Basin remained low and is sparse even today. Mining boom-towns came and went with depressing regularity, despite the discovery and exploitation of major deposits like Nevada's Com-stock Lode and Ely Copper Belt. Instead of being spread evenly across the landscape, the population of the Great Basin is clus-tered into only a few major cities, including most prominently Las Vegas, Reno, and Salt Lake City. The rest of the region re-mains today as it has seemed throughout much of its history, an eerily empty barrier to be crossed hurriedly on the way to some-where more convincingly attractive or prosperous.

The Great Basin, too, has a tradition of regional writing, but in contrast to the Prairie Midwest it is neither unified nor op-timistic. Instead of portraying a satisfying historical progression in which the landscape first overwhelms but then is slowly bent to human purposes, Great Basin observers remark on the funda-mentally unchanging nature of their regional environment. This desert place stubbornly resists conformity to national norms of abundance and productivity and becomes instead an implicit challenge.

Great Basin writers, whether they despise the desert as a foreboding wilderness or cherish it as a landscape of ineffable beauty and mystery, agree on its fundamental intractability: "As they [pioneers] saw it, so can we see it today; so little has man disturbed the landscape. Nature's visible processes are slow, and few people find their way here, for mankind to make 'improve-ments.' The broad, far-reaching picture remains, as the still years slip by, mostly unchanged."[7] People do not modify the desert environment of the Great Basin; either they leave it hurriedly and in relief, or they remain and learn through a painful process of trial and error to adapt themselves to it. With the sole exception of the Mormons, to be discussed below, there is no environmental triumph evinced in this regional literature.

Geographical differences between the two regions thus differentiate them not only physically but also psychologically, in terms of prevailing attitudes toward the natural environment. The Prairie Midwestern sense of place as significant and important contrasts with images of the Great Basin as merely empty or marginal space. Systematic comparison will further illuminate the central importance of landscape in regional perception.

The earliest accounts of both regions come from explorers and travelers who were not favorably impressed with the land they encountered in either place. Due to the absence of trees that were traditionally used as indications of soil fertility, the Prairie Midwest was contemptuously dismissed as "wholly unfit for cultivation" and "nearly as bad as the Lybian Desart [sic]."[8] The Great Basin was characterized by Frémont as sterile, and one 1849 traveler described the Humboldt River Route in decidedly uncomplimentary terms: "It is a *dirty, muddy, sluggish, indolent stream,* with but little grass at the best of times. . . . A friend of mine remarked, it was fit for nothing else but to sink to the 'Lower Regions,' and the quicker it done it the better. He much preferred calling it the Hellboldt River."[9]

Yet differences in the two began to appear with the arrival of longer-term residents. In the Prairie Midwest, pioneer settlers began to make changes almost immediately. They built houses and fenced the land, and, most significantly, they broke the native prairie sod to plant crops. Initially, their accounts of this process emphasize obstacles and restrictions rather than accomplishments. Diaries, county histories, and autobiographies all stress the heroic achievements of the pioneer generation against considerable natural odds in the form of blizzards, lack of fuel, tornadoes, hailstorms, and grasshopper plagues. They recount the hardships of the struggle to impose order and civilization on an open, featureless, and initially forbidding land. Farmers' journals joyfully catalogue not acreage planted but the hallmarks of social life: the arrival of the railroad, construction of the first post office or church, organization of a school district. A

North Dakota lawyer's wife in the 1880s emphasized the tremendous importance of people: "The Northern Pacific [is] the greatest asset this country ever had. Hundreds of thousands of intelligent and cultivated people flocked to the north, who would never have considered it had not a railroad paved the way."[10] As depicted by writers at the time, the Prairie Midwest appears as an alien and austere environment, which they set about to improve by swiftly reproducing familiar institutions in order to render it more congenial. As Willa Cather in O Pioneers! described the initial stages of the process, "There was nothing but land: not a country at all, but the material of which countries are made."[11]

Once the settlement process was completed, however, Prairie Midwesterners celebrated their accomplishment not only in establishing social institutions but also in effecting significant environmental changes. When Hamlin Garland describes such changes in his Son of the Middle Border, his sense of satisfaction in the cumulative environmental transformation is evident: "Day by day the settlement thickened. Section by section the prairie was blackened by the plow. . . . Lanes of barbed wire replaced the winding wagon trails, our saddles gathered dust in the grain sheds, and groves of Lombardy poplar and European larch replaced the towheads of aspen and hazel through which we had pursued the wolf and the fox."[12] Garland's contentment is typical of many later fictional accounts of the Prairie Midwest which celebrate the efforts of the first generation and the humanized agricultural landscape which they constructed out of raw prairie: "There was nothing secret in that land. Beyond the long pitch and roll of the Iowa Prairie there was no mountain dominating the low country, nor ocean where the remote horizon was always water and sky. In every grove of trees a house. In every house a family. The crops held the under shape of the earth."[13] Here, clearly, is the tantalizing potential of American nature made manifest in Iowa's fertile farms. The ostensibly barren earth has been brought to bear wonderful fruit against numerous obstacles.

In the Great Basin, by contrast, chronology is not so orderly and the fruits of human labor are of many different sorts. The process of settlement in the Great Basin began scarcely twenty years later than in the Prairie Midwest, but for two reasons accounts of the former region circulated much more widely in the rest of the United States. One was the anomaly of the Mormon state of Deseret, established on the eastern edge of the Great Basin in 1847 and laying claim to most of the region. The Mormon outpost at Salt Lake City attracted attention because of the open practice of polygyny (the practice of having plural wives) and the general notoriety of its founders. A variety of visitors passed through it on their way elsewhere, and consequently there were many accounts that described the settlements and the character of the land on the eastern edge of the Great Basin. The discovery of gold in California in 1848 was the other factor in the growing reputation of the Great Basin. Because the most practicable wagon trail to the gold fields followed the Humboldt River through Nevada (although it involved negotiating a two-day stretch without grass or palatable water for the animals at the end), another large group of travelers was attracted to the Great Basin without any intention of settling there. Both these migrant streams left copious records of their experiences, with the result that, unlike the Prairie Midwest, the Great Basin was already known by reputation to many who later ventured into it.

What they had learned of it no doubt left them with a certain amount of trepidation. One 49er summarized his trip in a typical letter published in the hometown newspaper:

> We traversed a desert 300 miles long, and for sixty miles we saw not a blade of grass, nor drop of water, and all that cheered our imaginations was a boiling spring, which gave some variety to the monotonous uniformity of the scenery. It was necessary to travel day and night, so as to pass this cheerless solitude as fast as possible, lest our animals and ourselves should be prostrated by pitiless thirst.[14]

Newcomers to the Great Basin almost universally assess their surroundings in terms of these previous accounts. Either they are grateful because the desert is not quite so forbidding as they expected, or they are disillusioned after having trusted in positive reports. The latter is the sorry case of one overland traveler who relied on popular guidebooks and came to question his faith:

> I would ask the learned and descriptive Mr. Frémont and the elegant and imaginative Mr. Bryant, where was the beautiful valley, the surpassingly lovely valley of Humbolt [sic]? Where

was the country presenting the most splendid "agricultural features"? Where the splendid grazing, the cottonwood lining the banks of their *beautiful and meandering stream*, and everything presenting the most interesting and picturesque appearance of any place they every saw?[15]

Knowledge about the Great Basin thus preceded and shaped actual contact with it. The predicament of Mrs. Orsemus B. Boyd in 1867 graphically illustrates the influence of expectation on environmental perception. Having been forewarned of the grandiose scale of western scenery, her disappointment in Nevada is apparent in her reminiscences: "As the very tiniest streams in the West are designated rivers, we were always expecting, only to be disappointed, great things in that line. At last, when we reached Austin, and saw that the Reese River could be stepped across, all expectations of future greatness in the way of rivers were relinquished."[16] Her disillusionment is complete after endless days of seeing nothing but sagebrush, and she finally resolves to relieve the monotony by visualizing the individual sagebrush as sheep, which are, to her, both more familiar and more tolerable than the disappointing western reality.

Many who came to the Great Basin, like Mrs. Boyd, were temporary sojourners rather than residents. They came along the major transportation routes west, or to seek riches in mining booms, or, like Mrs. Boyd, to follow a husband in the military. In any event, the pattern of settlement in much of the Great Basin was spotty and temporary. Towns founded on the vaguest hints of gold or silver dry up and blow away when the promise proves illusory. Men and women come to live for a while and then, like Samuel Clemens in Virginia City, move on to seek a broader scope for their ambitions elsewhere. They observe the Great Basin in passing but do not invest their labor in settling it. It remains a desert after they move on, just as it was before they arrived. Unlike their counterparts in the Prairie Midwest, settlers in the Great Basin exploit rather than nurture.

The only exception to this pattern is the area of Mormon settlement in the eastern half of the region. There an agricultural ethic imported directly from the midwestern states by the itinerant Mormons prevailed even in the face of adverse environmental circumstances. Irrigation projects were established in Utah through church initiative and communal labor. Since then, the contrast between areas of Mormon settlement and the rest of the desert has been noted by most observers. Even an 1858 traveler remarked with surprise that the Mormons were practicing field agriculture:

> Utah is their promised land and the city they have built in this district is their Zion.
> The land irrigated by this new Jordan and by other rivers produces excellent pastures. In the spring, grass grows there in abundance very quickly. The same valley also produces vegetables and cereals of every kind. Apple trees and peach trees thrive there well; the vine has been introduced recently and they are starting to build sugar and beet refineries.[17]

The same man also recorded in passing the risks of agriculture in the high desert when he added that "certain years despite the most intensive precautions everything withers and dies."

These risks, in addition to the tremendous costs of building irrigation works in a day and age before government subsidy, were sufficient to discourage agriculture in most of the Great Basin. Although Mormons continued to prosper in their settlements, they were sustained by a communal ethic peculiar to them and a firm religious belief in the value of an agricultural economy. For those lacking such an ethic and the spiritual and economic support that the church provided, agriculture was a more formidable and less successful undertaking. Indeed, in Great Basin mining communities such as Virginia City, cherishing the earth was regarded as misguided. Flannery Lewis recalls an uncle as "a very difficult man for Virginia City to understand. He had a garden, for one thing, and a garden in Virginia City, in such a dry and sullen land, was preposterous."[18]

Residents of the Great Basin more commonly regarded it as a resource to be exploited for their private enhancement. They mined or logged or built ranches. The miners lived in constant expectation of some future wealth that never materialized, and even the ranchers experienced environmental catastrophe before they recognized the necessity of grazing responsible numbers on the public land and making some provision to sustain their herds through the winter.[19] The Gentile society that developed in the Great Basin took pride in what it extracted rather than what it nurtured. Even today observers of Nevada's gambling industry suggest that the extractive mentality persists, as residents jeopardize the splendors of nature in favor of increased income from imported tourists:

> There is not much difference between the proud new Sunbelt cities and the old mining camps. They are both temporary Woodstocks of wanderers hell-bent on plundering. They will exhaust the place and then move on. . . . All over the region I see my handiwork: the ghost towns, the mine scars, the butchered grazing tracts, the dull cities, the highways full of traffic racing to get nowhere, the crap tables, the damned and maimed rivers. We have taken our main chance and the results only look good on the Dow Jones.[20]

Even those who fully appreciate the wild beauty of the desert colors and who celebrate the majesty of its scale never entirely come to terms with the insignificance of human presence there:

> It seemed to me the oldest country I had ever seen, the real antique land, first cousin to the moon. Brown, bony, sapless, like an old man's hand. We called it new because it was not thick with history, not a museum and guidebook place. Man had been here such a little time that his arrival had not yet been acknowledged. He was still some season's trifling accident.[21]

For Great Basin writers, there is something disconcerting about a landscape where human beings are an intrusion, where people and nature are in perpetually unresolved conflict. The high desert country is equally as compelling as the open prairie, but the environmental tale here is of compromise with rather than conquest of the land. People in the Great Basin remain there only on the sufferance of an extremely exacting nature. Even the green Mormon fields are overshadowed by gray-brown hills that symbolize the precariousness of their hold in the arid environment. The seductive glitter of Las Vegas is reinforced by the threatening drabness of the desert around it.

Each of these geographical regions has thus developed a distinctive sense of place, a regional consciousness grounded in some characteristic relationship to the land. In the Prairie Midwest, the productivity of the land is central to self-definition. When an Iowa banker in Ruth Suckow's novel *The Folks* tours California, he is contemptuous of the pettiness of western agriculture: "But when he thought of . . . putting all this care into keeping a lawn green and queer plants flourishing, it seemed to him a puttering sort of life. Nature here didn't do anything; it was like hothouse gardening: Annie might enjoy the great roses and geraniums, but he couldn't interest himself in things that seemed to be mostly for show." [22] In the Prairie Midwest, nature is definitely not for show. It is fundamentally important, a genuine force in people's lives, not only regionally but in the rest of the world as well. The prairie produces basic foodstuffs in almost unimaginable quantity, sufficient to support the world. California's superficial landscape, by contrast, produces hothouse roses. In the regional perception, there is no question as to which is the more significant.

The power of the prairie landscape is central to regional identity even in an era of agricultural depression and overproduction. The modern protagonist of Douglas Unger's *Leaving the Land* is ambivalent about inheriting the family farm in Dakota. He returns only reluctantly to the moribund small town where he was raised and has no desire to operate the farm, where he has never lived:

> The point was food, quantities of food. It all looked so easy, that tractor driver in his air-conditioned cab, that wonderful machine crawling across the face of the same earth it would have taken my ancestors forty years to plow. What matter if a whole style of life was gone? What matter if the earth no longer served a single family, a small parcel of immortality for the common man? . . . All that mattered was food, the wheat on the hill, the hay in the meadow, the mutton under my boot. Whatever method could raise them best and most efficiently would win the prizes of the earth. There was little beauty to it, in my mind. [23]

Yet when the moment of decision arrives and his mother offers him the deed to the family farm, he cannot refuse it. This land that has been in his family for generations is not simply a means to make money, it is a responsibility. Its proper use will define his life as it has defined the lives of the rest of his family since they came to it. Perhaps there is some previously unsuspected beauty remaining after all.

In the Prairie Midwest, the environment has been profoundly and enduringly altered by human presence. The modern agricultural landscape is a created space, a cultural artifact of which residents are proud. Through their collective efforts, over time, they have produced a cultivated middle ground located comfortingly between the excesses at either side—empty, untamed prairie on the one hand and modern urban congestion on the other. They find pleasure in its richness and its regularity and take pride in their role in bringing it to fruition. They sing the native beauties of this agricultural landscape, knowing full well that it is a human construction. In the words of one contemporary celebrant of the prairie: "The eye for beauty is the eye for love. We find our beauties in the things that alter nature according to our own visions: in immaculate lawns, in polished pillars of marble, in cornfields, straight as an arrow and clean as a company dinner plate."[24]

Great Basin nature, by contrast, is remote and intractable. Human impact here is negligible, and the scale of the landscape dwarfs its human residents. Far from celebrating their ability to challenge and change the land, desert dwellers denounce its power to minimize their efforts:

> "It's the place!" he thought. "People came, and passed by, and even lived here, and they left mementos of themselves—chips of obsidian, or tin cans, or an ancient wagon, or even a whole house with most of what it had ever contained. And yet they passed on. And the place, that is, the spring and the meadow and the hummocks and the black rock that looms above—the place remained. They could not change it. It was too strong for them."[25]

Even those who are not sojourners in the Great Basin feel their hold on the place is tenuous. They learn, sometimes painfully, that water is limited and resources few, that the richest of mines are eventually exhausted, and even, perhaps, that the gambling industry is not invulnerable to economic recessions. In this delicate environment of natural limits and little change, human tenure is precarious. Only the dry and distant mountains are triumphant.

In order to endure here, people must make their peace with an elemental and unchanging land. They cannot expect to alter it greatly or for very long. Even the green oases of irrigated cities are merely cosmetic. They conceal but do not eliminate the desert: "the leaves and branches are so thick in places that one may cheat himself into a pleasant fantasy of green and wooded slopes and grassy vales beyond. We have managed to hide here and there, the bleak hills and sere brown mountains of the distant horizon and the middle ground. . . . the illusion, as of a country of gentle slopes and wide-stretching woodland is very welcome and *almost deceptive*." [26] The illusions of the desert are many and beautiful. Its fascinating colors at sunrise and sunset are widely remarked. The lure of riches just waiting to be uncovered in some yet unexplored hill or casino is perpetual. Yet these attractions do not suffice to make the desert lovely. For all its charms, the Great Basin is not a humanized landscape. Instead it remains formidable and alien, a region that is at best tangential—if not openly hostile—to the American environmental dream of abundance and productivity. Admirers of the desert extol it not because it gives scope and shape to human ambition but because it so totally resists them. Despite the efforts of many who have come to it, the Great Basin remains for the most part a marginal space.

Sense of place in the complacent and self-congratulatory Prairie Midwest is thus far different from sense of place in the obdurate and forbidding Great Basin. But the writing of each place is characterized by a strong regional identity that is based on the historical experience of its peoples as shaped by a particular local geography. Their regional identities are determined by the interaction of a specific nature and culture. Similar forces and nuances continue to sustain and nourish American regionalism even in the face of all the considerable pressures for a single, pervasive American nationalism.

NOTES

1. E.g., Henry Nash Smith, *Virgin Land* (Cambridge: Harvard University Press, 1950); Leo Marx, *The Machine in the Garden* (New York: Oxford, 1964); Roderick Nash, *Wilderness and the American Mind* (New Haven: Yale University Press, 1982, 3d ed.).

2. Edward Johnson, *The Wonder Working Providence of Sion's Saviour,*

ed. F. Jameson (New York: Scribners, 1910); William Cronon, *Changes in the Land: Indians, Colonists, and the Ecology of New England* (New York: Hill and Wang, 1983).

3. Frederick Jackson Turner, "The Significance of the Frontier in American History," in Ray A. Billington, ed., *Frontier and Section: Selected Essays of Frederick Jackson Turner* (Englewood Cliffs, N.J.: Prentice-Hall, 1961).

4. E.g., John B. Jackson, *American Space* (New York: W. W. Norton, 1972); John R. Stilgoe, *The Common Landscape of America, 1580 to 1845* (New Haven: Yale University Press, 1982); Donald Worster, *Rivers of Empire* (New York: Pantheon Books, 1985).

5. Donald Worster, "New West, True West: Interpreting the Region's History," *Western Historical Quarterly* 18 (April 1987): 149.

6. Walter Prescott Webb, *The Great Plains* (New York: Macmillan, 1931).

7. Ida Meacham Strobridge, *In Miner's Mirage Land* (Los Angeles: Baugarat Publishing Co., 1904), 15.

8. Report of the 1821 Stephen H. Long Expedition, quoted in Harlin M. Fuller and LeRoy R. Hafen, eds., *The Journal of Captain John R. Bell* (Glendale, Calif.: Arthur H. Clark, 1957), 282; Thomas Woodward, "Diary of Thomas Woodward while Crossing the Plains of California in 1850," *Wisconsin Magazine of History* 17 (March, June 1934): 350.

9. David M. Potter, ed., *Trail to California: The Overland Journey of Vincent Geiger and Wakeman Bryarly* (New Haven: Yale University Press, 1945), 191.

10. Kate Eldridge Glaspell, *Incidents in the Life of a Pioneer* (Davenport, Iowa: Sawden Brothers, n.d.), 33.

11. Willa Cather, *O Pioneers!* (Boston: Houghton-Mifflin, 1913), 8.

12. Hamlin Garland, *A Son of the Middle Border* (New York: Grosset and Dunlap, 1917), 144.

13. Paul Engle, *Always the Land* (New York: Random House, 1941), 174.

14. S. Knudson, quoted in Walker D. Wyman, ed., *California Emigrant Letters* (New York: Bookman Association, 1952), 68.

15. Potter, *Trail to California*, 190.

16. Mrs. Orsemus B. Boyd, *Calvary Life in Tent and Field* (New York: J. Selwin Tait, 1894), 67.

17. Auguste Nicaise, *A Year in the Desert*, ed. and trans. Edward J. Kowrach (Fairfield, Wash.: Ye Galleon Press, 1980), 57.

18. Flannery Lewis, *Suns Go Down* (New York: Macmillan, 1937), 171.

19. See James A. Young and B. Abbot Sparks, *Cattle in the Cold Desert* (Logan: Utah State University Press, 1985), for an environmental history of the cattle industry in the Great Basin.

20. Charles Bowden, *Blue Desert* (Tucson: University of Arizona Press, 1986), 36.

21. J. B. Priestly, *Midnight on the Desert* (New York: Harper and Bros., 1937), 2-3.

22. Ruth Suckow, *The Folks* (New York: Literary Guild, 1934), 672.

23. Douglas Unger, *Leaving the Land* (New York: Ballantine Books, 1984), 282.

24. Paul Gruchow, *Journal of a Prairie Year* (Minneapolis: University of Minnesota Press, 1985), 125.

25. George R. Stewart, *Sheep Rock* (New York: Random House, 1951), 11.

26. Henry R. Mighels, *Sagebrush Leaves* (San Francisco: Edward Bosqui and Co., 1879), 148, my italics.

CULTURAL FALLOUT IN THE ATOMIC AGE

A. COSTANDINA TITUS

Most things which fundamentally alter the entire basis of existence occur gradually, being more discernible to historians in later years than to the individuals who experience them. This was not the case, however, with the dawning of the Atomic Age.[1] It came from nowhere, literally bursting upon the scene in August 1945 with the destruction of Hiroshima and Nagasaki, and its impact was immediate, instantly and irrevocably changing the human landscape.

Since that time, the ever-present reality of the atomic bomb has had a pervasive influence on American culture. Not only are we constantly reminded by the news media of the potential dangers of nuclear war, but "objets d'atom" have also invaded our physical space. Daily excursions bring us in frequent contact with nuclear power plants, military restricted zones, weapons testing centers, research laboratories, and civil defense facilities. And everyone has special "nuclear memories." As *Scientific Monthly* stated in September 1945, "Just as people recall the circumstances under which they first heard the news of the attack on Pearl Harbor, so they will remember how the atomic bomb first burst upon their consciousness."[2] Who does not recall watching the mushroom cloud rise above the Nevada desert; finding an atomic viewer ring in the bottom of a cereal box; getting an x-ray; hearing the clock tick as it climbed toward 11 A.M. on October 25, 1962; going with a special date to see *Dr. Strangelove*; explaining to a child what "nuclear winter" means? So fully does nuclear reality pervade our consciousness that one might argue that the bomb has become a category of being, much like space and time, which, according to Kant, are built into the very structure of our minds, giving shape and meaning to all our perceptions.[3]

Following initial shock over the atomic bomb's destructive power, Americans quickly rallied and took the awesome new weapon in stride. It became an extremely popular subject for entertainers of all sorts. Comedians joked about Japan's "atomic ache," and one newscaster commented that Hiroshima looked like "Ebbetts Field after a game between the Giants and the Dodgers." Bob Hope read the following valentine on his radio show, February 14, 1946: "Will you be my little geranium, until we are both blown up by uranium?" Hollywood jumped on the bandwagon and quickly revised a nearly completed spy thriller, *The House on 42nd Street*, to make the object of an enemy agent's quest be "Process 97, the secret ingredient of the atomic bomb." This was soon followed by *The Beginning or the End?*, an MGM movie billed as the true story of the building of the bomb. In the music industry, the Slim Gaillard Quartet recorded "Atomic Cocktail" in December 1945; the Golden Gate Quartet followed with "Atom and Evil"; a California company marketed a line of jazz recordings under the "Atomic" label, complete with mushroom cloud; and "When the Atomic Bomb Fell" quickly became a country music favorite.

Businesses also capitalized on the atomic theme. Department stores ran "atomic sales" and advertisers offered "atomic results." A New York jewelry store advertised atomic jewelry, "as daring to wear as it was to drop the first atom bomb." General Mills offered an atom bomb ring for fifteen cents and a cereal box top; and in 1947 the Manhattan phone book listed forty-five businesses with the word "Atom" in the title, including the Atomic Undergarment Company.[4]

Along with this public acceptance of the bomb came a flurry of imagined potential uses for atomic power which, as the *St. Louis Post-Dispatch* declared on August 7, 1945, could be "a blessing that will make it possible for the human race to create a close approach to an earthly paradise." These wonderful new inventions included atomic-powered rockets, airplanes, ships, and automobiles. Other suggested uses focused on environmental improvement themes: melting the polar ice cap and controlling the weather through the use of artificial suns mounted on tall steel towers, digging canals, breaking open mountain chains, and generally tidying up the awkward parts of the world. Still others emphasized possible medical advantages and economic benefits. In short, many felt that the introduction of atomic energy as a destructive force was an unfortunate twist of history which distorted the true significance of the atom. As Gerald Johnson wrote in the *American Scholar* in early 1946: "Atomic fission seems to open the way to such improvements in the condition of life as the race has never known. It also opens the way to sudden, violent death, but what of that? So did steam; so did electricity. Yet we have made use of them, in spite of their dangers."[5]

In the midst of these technological prophecies, American philosophers, scholars, and social critics were attempting to grapple with the moral and political implications of the bomb. Atomic themes dominated their writing and discourse throughout the years immediately following the war as they looked at the effect of the bomb on the consciousness and character of the American people. Some were hopeful; some pessimistic. Chancellor Robert Hutchins at the University of Chicago organized the Office of Inquiry into the Social Aspects of Atomic Energy, which brought together economists, sociologists, political scientists, and religious leaders to discuss the matter, and hundreds of conferences were held around the country where such people gathered to share their insights on the new world. A survey of thirteen American educational journals of the period shows that teachers were likewise deeply engaged in the effort "to define their unique professional responsibility" in the Atomic Age. American sociologist Talcott Parsons pleaded the case for more funding for social science research because the bomb had dramatically underscored "the potentialities of modern scientific technology for destruction and disruption of social life" and a social science response was imperative. Finally, a 1949 U.S. Office of Education study concluded that the "Atomic Age" phrase had been widely adopted by authors and editors as "a good interest-catcher . . . which proves their book is 'up-to-date.'"[6]

The religious community also focused on the morality of the bomb. The Atomic Age had begun with a prayer when a chaplain on Tenian Island blessed the crew of the *Enola Gay* as it left for Hiroshima. From that point on, the American clergy were very involved in the public's development of attitudes toward the bomb, particularly from the standpoint of its use in Japan. Americans generally took the position that God had given us the secret and we had used it to end the war and save lives. As Arthur Compton, a leading Protestant layman, told a 1946 symposium on "The Moral Meaning of the Atomic Bomb" organized by the Episcopal church, "Atomic power is ours and who can deny that it was God's will that we should have it?" By 1947 both the Protestant and Catholic churches in the United States had formally addressed the issue and both had condemned the concept of total war, the deliberate terror bombing of civilians, and the destruction of Hiroshima and Nagasaki. They stopped short, however, of condemning the atomic bomb as an instrument of war and even granted moral legitimacy to the retaliatory use of such a weapon under certain circumstances. Likewise, the Jewish community was generally supportive; while some hailed the bomb as having ended the war and others took pride in the significant role played by Jewish scientists in the bomb's development, the overriding ethical issue for Jews was not the bomb but the Nazi holocaust.[7]

The bomb's influence was also felt in the pages of the literary world. At first, some of the well-established writers of the time, including William Faulkner, Archibald MacLeish, Lionel Trilling, Saul Bellow, Norman Mailer, and Wallace Stevens, seem to have made deliberate efforts to omit any mention of the bomb from their works. Scholars today suggest that their writings, however, were profoundly shaped by the threat of atomic annihilation, reflecting a "counter apocalyptic sensibility which begins to see the world as saved." Despite this initial resistance, as the years passed the atomic theme began to play a larger role in literature. Numerous hortatory poems appeared by such writers as Edgar Guest, Hermann Hagedorn, Aaron Kramer, William Rose Benét, and Karl Shapiro. John Hersey wrote *Hiroshima;* and Carson McCullers used a newspaper account of the bombing to introduce the principal characters in *Member of the Wedding.* Poet Irene Orgel wrote of a woman physicist's role in building the bomb in "Sonnet to Lise Meitner"; Randall Jarrell referred to the bomb as "the first human sun" in "The Death of the Gods"; and Milton Kaplan explored the "bomb's effects on the stratagems by which we inure ourselves to inexorable death" in "Atomic Bomb."[8]

While the general literary response to the bomb was somewhat tentative, the science fiction writers of the day took up the theme with vigor. Hundreds of short stories appeared in popular magazines, including "Thunder and Roses" and "Memorial" by Theodore Sturgeon, "Nightmare" and "To Still the Drums" by Chandler Davis, "The Answer" by George O. Smith, and "The Highway" by Ray Bradbury, who also wrote a collection of stories compiled as *The Martian Chronicles*. Three novels appeared: Pat Frank's *Mr. Adam,* Ward Moore's *Greener Than You Think,* and George Stewart's *Earth Abides.* In these works, the outlook is persistently bleak, nuclear holocaust an ever-present reality—sometimes as a looming or barely averted cataclysm, sometimes as an event that has already occurred.[9]

One would expect the public's interest in the bomb to wane as time passed and the novelty wore off. This, however, was not to be the case; rather than diminishing with time, attention to the bomb actually increased during the fifties. This can be attributed to several factors: (1) the Soviets' acquisition of an atomic bomb in September 1949 and the end of the United States' monopoly; (2) the beginning of atmospheric testing in the Nevada desert near Las Vegas in January 1951, which firmly implanted the mushroom cloud on the horizon; (3) the extensive public relations campaign mounted by Lewis Strauss, powerful chairman of the Atomic Energy Commission (AEC) in the mid-fifties; and (4) the self-protection drills and activities carried out by the Federal Civil Defense Administration, an agency created by Congress in December 1950 to prepare the country for nuclear attack.

In addition to these political reasons for escalated interest in the bomb, three psychological factors also account for the continued fascination with the mushroom cloud throughout the fifties. First, atomic power was mysterious, new, and unknown; as such it sparked tremendous imagination and provided great potential for creativity. Second, atomic power was so awesome, so scary, so threatening and overwhelming that making it familiar was the only way people could deal with it, a principle similar to whistling in the dark. Finally, it was so American that the bomb became a political symbol of freedom almost equal to the eagle or the flag. It was a patriotic reminder throughout the Cold War of our efforts to protect the democratic way of life from evil Communist aggression.[10]

Governmental activities greatly shaped the atomic culture of the fifties. Not only were AEC press releases front-page news on an almost daily basis, but regularly scheduled air raid drills were frequently held. People soon came to recognize the universal radiation logo which marked the location of bomb shelters; school children met Bert the Turtle and learned to "duck and cover" if attacked; and Civil Defense films, such as *Atomic Survival, Survival City,* and *Survival under Atomic Attack,* were commonly shown for entertainment as well as educational purposes at social club and church meetings. The U.S. Post Office issued an "Atoms for Peace" stamp in 1953, and the Joint Committee on Atomic Energy in Congress provided a special atomic film to all congressmen to show in their home district or state. Perhaps most impressive of all the public relations efforts were the AEC's publication and dissemination of a little green booklet entitled *Atomic Tests in Nevada.* Distributed throughout southern Nevada and neighboring Utah, the book was designed to assure those residents living near the test site that they would not be in any danger if they followed a few simple precautions.[11]

These efforts by the government to sell the American people on the bomb were successful, as evidenced by the public acceptance of the program expressed throughout the fifties and early sixties. Gallup polls of the day show high levels of support for continued testing and development of the H-bomb; pro-testing politicians were reelected to Congress and the presidency; and the mushroom cloud became a benign symbol of the era. Signs for Atomic Cafe and Atomic Motel were fairly common along major cross-country highways. A small town in southern Idaho near an AEC facility became known as Atomic City. Even Walt Disney got into the act, publishing a book for children entitled *Our Friend the Atom.* The Boy Scouts created an atomic energy merit badge, and two atomic energy museums were opened, one at Oak Ridge, Tennessee, and the other at Los Alamos, New Mexico.

Again the entertainment industry was heavily involved in perpetuating the atomic culture of the times. Lowell Blanchard and the Valley Trio equated the second coming of Christ with a nuclear detonation in the popular song "Jesus Hits Like an Atom Bomb," while Little Caesar compared his love to an atomic blast:

> Boom! Something exploded down inside
> And rushed teardrops to my eyes,
> Oh yes,
> I have that funny feeling,
> I guess it's my atomic love, for you (oooh).[12]

Tom Lehrer's satirical song about a nuclear age cowboy roaming the test sites of the Southwest in lead underwear was a favorite on college campuses, and *Mad Magazine* published a nuclear war "Hit Parade" featuring postholocaust parodies of current popular songs.[13]

Novels like Nevil Shute's *On the Beach*, Helen Clarkson's *The Last Day*, Walter Miller's *A Canticle for Leibowitz*, Eugene Burdeck and Harvey Wheeler's *Fail-Safe*, and Kurt Vonnegut's *Cat's Cradle* also explored scenarios of nuclear war and human extinction. Science fiction writers followed suit, as illustrated by Isaac Asimov's story "The Gentle Vultures" and Mordecai Roshwald's *Level 7*. Poets Thomas Merton in "Original Child Bomb" and Robert Lowell in "Fall 1961" offer additional observations on life in the Nuclear Age.[14]

At the movies, in addition to typical Cold War films about subversion and battlefield confrontations with Communists, Hollywood produced two kinds of films that dealt specifically with atomic warfare. They either delivered a pro-testing message in a straightforward, quasi-documentary fashion not unlike official government films or they employed a more subtle approach using fantasy and science fiction to create doomsday situations. Among the realistic dramas were *The Atomic City*, released in 1952 by Paramount, and *Hell and High Water*, a 1954 film so realistic it has been compared to Orson Welles's radio version of "The War of the Worlds." Far more popular at the box office were the sci-fi movies, a genre which some scholars feel rose to prominence during this period by capitalizing on the paranoia, loss of identity, and fear of the unknown which were the prevalent attitudes of the time. Some of the more popular of these films include *Invasion, USA, The Atomic Kid, The Amazing Colossal*

Man, The Day the Earth Caught Fire, Panic in the Year Zero, The H-Man, The Blob, It, Attack of the Crab Monsters, The Incredible Shrinking Man, and *Them!* [15]

Likewise, television during the fifties featured several popular series, especially "The Outer Limits" and Rod Serling's "Twilight Zone," which frequently dealt with topics related to nuclear war and the effects of radioactivity.[16] The first documentary series to consider the impact of nuclear war was "Air Power," filmed in 1956. The various programs chronicled the defense action that might be taken in the event of an air attack. It was not until the sixties, however, that a television documentary examined the moral implications of atomic weapons.[17]

Journalists, invited by the AEC to witness and report on detonations, were also fascinated by atomic phenomena and the mysterious "goings on" in the Nevada desert. Dozens of well-known reporters, including Walter Cronkite, Dave Galloway, John Cameron Swayze, and Bob Considine, frequently perched on bleachers atop News Nob, a small hill some ten miles from ground zero; from here they witnessed the blasts and covered the awesome story for the American public.

Several major nationally distributed publications also ran stories on Las Vegas and its reaction to the testing program. In 1952 Daniel Lang wrote a piece entitled "Blackjack and Flashes" for the *New Yorker.* A similar story by Samuel Matthews, "Nevada Learns to Live with the Atom," appeared in a 1953 edition of *National Geographic.* Gladwin Hill wrote "Desert Capital of the A-Bomb" for a 1955 *New York Times* Sunday travel section; and the famous shot of the mushroom cloud rising over "Glitter Gulch" became *Life Magazine's* "Picture of the Week" in 1951.[18]

Throughout this period, language, perhaps the most important aspect of culture, was also profoundly affected by the bomb. From the beginning, the government promoted euphoric visions of nuclear development. The discovery of x-rays promised a technological "Garden of Eden"; the "philosophers' stone" and the "elixir of life" had been found at last. During the days of the Manhattan Project, Los Alamos was picturesquely referred to as "the Hill"; the bomb was called a device, a gadget; and the first test was somewhat heretically named "Trinity" from the John Donne poem in which the poet asks a "three-personed God" to use his power to "break, blow, burn, and make one new." A detonation is an "event," and the target is referred to as "ground zero." Peaceful uses of atomic power were promoted by referring to "waving the radioactive wand," "the sunny side of the atom," or "the atomic genie in the bottle." There were also the "super bomb" and the "clean bomb," "Atoms for Peace," and "Plowshare." This reliance on euphemisms was really brought home in 1965 when Hal Stroube of Pacific Gas and Electric, speaking at an American Nuclear Society meeting, stressed the need to eliminate "objectionable words from the atomic lexicon," suggesting instead that the AEC come up with some "palatable synonyms" for "scare words."[19]

The impact of the bomb on American culture was even more apparent in those areas immediately connected to its production and testing. This is certainly true at both Hanford, Washington, where during the early days of the Manhattan Project the first plant was constructed to produce plutonium, and in Las Vegas, Nevada, the city closest to the Nevada Test Site. The people in both locales remain tied strongly to the atomic operations there, in terms of economics and political loyalty, and have developed local cultures which go beyond the national trends in their levels of acceptance and support.

Begun in 1944, the Hanford Nuclear Reservation in southeast Washington is the largest nuclear facility in the world, covering 570 square miles and employing a total work force of some fourteen thousand people. The complex includes the world's first full-scale reactors and largest known radioactive waste site, a billion-dollar test facility for breeder technologies, and three commercial nuclear power plants. Furthermore, it has produced the plutonium for over half the atomic weapons in the American arsenal.[20]

Most of the workers at the reservation live in the Tri-Cities (Richland, Pasco, and Kennewick), where the local culture is characterized by "atomic banality."[21] Richland High School boasts a mushroom cloud as its emblem and has athletic teams called the Bombers. There are also streets in town bearing names which reflect the reservation's influence: Proton, Argon, and Nuclear Lanes. Businesses include Atomic Body Shop, Atomic Foods, Atomic Bowling Lanes, and Atomic TV Service. At a recent office Christmas party, two reservation workers who had been contaminated received T-shirts that read, "I'm Hot Stuff."

Other commonly given gag gifts included "a pair of safety glasses to John, who never wears his"; "a glove for Rick, who burned his hands"; and "suntan lotion for Roy, who always stands right next to the radiation source."

Since 1948, the city of Richland has held an annual western-style celebration known as Atomic Frontier Days which features a parade, a beauty contest (won one year by future Hollywood actress/tragic figure Sharon Tate), and a barbecue to which the whole town turns out. The Central United Protestant Church has as its motto, "Where the atom is split, the churches unite." At one time a giant sign stood along the trans-Hanford highway that winds around the reservation perimeter; it announced that red lights would flash when radiation danger was present. Many people felt, however, that the sign was too menacing and so it was taken down in the seventies. Also in the seventies, when President Nixon proposed closing down N reactor due to the surplus of plutonium, the Tri-Cities rallied behind the cause; the communities called in all their clout with Washington senators Warren Magnuson and "Scoop" Jackson and the schoolchildren wrote letters to Nixon explaining why such an act would cause a great hardship on their families.[22]

This attitude may soon be gone, however, as more and more of the "old hands" who came to Hanford in the early days, a proud group of dedicated and skilled craftsmen, are replaced by the new "boomtown cowboys" who are more transient and interested primarily in the high salaries they can earn. The older generation believed unquestioningly in the product; they came to Hanford to do a special job for the government and keep quiet about it. They deny any adverse implications of their work and refuse "to talk about the bad things"; they have faith in both the government and scientific technology. The young employees, however, are very cynical, trusting neither experts nor truths; they "deny the possibility of worthwhile human action and denigrate even attempts to link moral vision to day-to-day choices." They scoff at safety precautions and feel no ideological commitment to what they are doing at the reservation. These two groups currently coexist at Hanford, but the underlying culture is bound to change as one gradually replaces the other with the passage of time.[23]

This invasion of the A-bomb into the culture of an area has

been even more evident in southern Nevada. It is not surprising that the actual neighbors of the test site would be more attuned to atomic phenomena than either the nation at large or Hanover, where operations are less "glamorous." Following the first atmospheric test in Nevada in January 1951, it was not long before the mushroom cloud was vying with the showgirl for top billing along the Las Vegas strip. The "atomic hairdo," originally designed by GeeGee, hairstylist at the Flamingo Hotel, was a popular request for special occasions. The hair was pulled over a wire form shaped like a mushroom cloud and then sprinkled with silver glitter at a cost of only seventy-five dollars. The "atomic cocktail" was also a big seller in bars along the Strip. Made from equal parts of vodka, brandy, and champagne, with a dash of sherry, the potent drink was served at breakfast parties following the predawn shots. In the Desert Inn Sky Room, Pianist Ted Mossman first played his boogie-woogie tune, "Atomic Bomb Bounce," which soon had people swinging all over town. Another local entertainer, Jackson Kay, billed himself as the "Original Atomic Comic." And a musical group known as the Atom Bombers boasted that they were the "Detonators of Devastating Rhythm." The Sands Hotel sponsored a Miss Atomic Bomb Contest which featured beautiful young contestants wearing puffy white mushroom clouds pinned to their bathing suits. One of the stage props was a small replica of a detonation tower labeled "Yuk Yuk Flats."

Local merchants also capitalized on the atomic theme: car salesman "Boob" Jones proudly advertised "Atom Drops on High Prices." Allen and Hanson, Las Vegas haberdashers, placed a barrel full of broken plate-glass window fragments in front of their downtown store with a sign, "Atomic Bomb Souvenirs—Free." Within an hour the barrel was empty. On March 13, 1953, Sheppard's Furniture Store advertised a "Great Atomic Bomb Sale" which "starts the minute the 'St. Pat' atomic bomb is exploded." The ad went on to say, "We've blown our top too." Free five-dollar gift certificates were promised to "the first ten customers to enter our store after the explosion."

The gambling industry attempted to use the testing program as an additional draw for boosting the tourist trade in Las Vegas. The Chamber of Commerce provided tourists with up-to-date shot calendars so they could schedule their visits and with road maps pointing out several vantage points around the test site. Many of the hotels packed box lunches for bomb watchers to carry to picnics at Angel's Peak, a mountain in the Charleston Range forty-five miles away, from which tourists could experience the blast and watch the rising mushroom cloud. One establishment even called itself the "Atomic View Motel," claiming that guests could witness the flash without ever leaving their poolside lounge chairs. Although they promoted the tests as an additional attraction to Las Vegas, gambling establishments also devised certain precautions against the effects of the shots. Several casinos posted signs warning that if a tremor from a bomb blast caused dice to turn or roulette balls to jump from one slot on the wheel to another, the house ruling was final.

The mushroom cloud was further institutionalized as a fixture on the Nevada cultural scene when it made its way into printed material. In the fifties the official Clark County seal, which today bears the picture of a Joshua tree, was designed around a large mushroom cloud. The cover of the 1953 Las Vegas High School yearbook, the *Wildcat Echo*, also featured such a scene. Likewise, the telephone directory for Clark County depicted a map of Nevada on its cover with a mushroom cloud emerging from the southern part of the state. One of the best-selling postcards of the era was a color shot of "Glitter Gulch" with Vegas Vic waving in the foreground and a mushroom cloud rising over the Union Pacific Railroad station in the background.[24] And the feature story for the June–December 1955 issue of *Nevada Highways and Parks* was about the Nevada Test Site with a "typical mushrooming cloud of fire, smoke, sand, and radioactive particles" pictured on the cover.[25]

Not everyone enthusiastically embraced the new AEC operations. A few local critics emerged from time to time, including Howard Hughes (who ironically was the government's largest defense contractor at the time of his protest); but, in the main, most southern Nevadans have consistently supported the test site since its opening. Test site contractors EG & G described this cooperative attitude of the local community to prospective clients and personnel in a 1961 report: "There have been so many detonations of nuclear devices at the test site in the past ten years that the community [of Las Vegas] is completely accustomed to, and unconcerned about, radiation hazards from such operations."[26]

When the Limited Test Ban Treaty went into effect in 1963, public interest in the bomb subsided. Ironically, over the next ten years, while the government steadily increased its weapons stockpile, the bomb gradually disappeared from the American cultural scene. The aphorism "out of sight, out of mind" seemed to describe the country's reaction to the conversion in 1963 to exclusively underground testing. Gone was the mushroom cloud on the horizon that previously had served as an ominous reminder of the testing program. Furthermore, many people felt that conducting the tests in underground tunnels eliminated the danger of radiation exposure, which had been a primary objection of most of the program's earlier critics. On the international scene, the Cold War of the 1950s was being replaced by a policy of détente between the two superpowers despite the ongoing conflict in Southeast Asia. And at home, the media turned their attention away from the seemingly mundane activities of the AEC to focus instead on civil rights, antiwar protests, and the antics of the flower generation. Love beads and gimme caps superseded the mushroom cloud as significant manifestations of the contemporary culture.[27]

Responding to the low interest rate, Hollywood produced few atomic films after the test ban went into effect. Those which did appear, while not overtly antibomb, were less supportive than their predecessors. They focused primarily on technology, presenting it as basically evil and potentially even more dangerous if not controlled. Inherent in such films was the warning that man should not rely on technology at the expense of humanity and civilization. Films which exemplify this theme include *Five, The World, the Flesh, and the Blood, On the Beach, Dr. Strangelove, Hiroshima, Mon Amour, Ladybug, Ladybug, Fail Safe,* and *The Bedford Incident.*[28]

Television, the medium of the era, followed suit and also paid little attention to atomic themes, with the exception of a few documentaries. Fred Freed's "The Decision to Drop the Bomb" attempted to advance the public's awareness of the nuclear problem by focusing on historical, social, and scientific perceptions. He followed this in 1966 with another NBC documentary entitled "Countdown to Zero," which was concerned with the proliferation of nuclear weapons. From 1969 to 1973 three additional network documentaries studied the problem in depth: "Footnote on the Atomic Age," "Arms and Security: How Much

Is Enough?," and "And When the War Is Over—The American Military in the 70's." Each program subtly urged a restructuring of nuclear power and suggested that the longer the arms race continues the less security we have. In addition, the British Broadcasting Corporation produced a forty-seven-minute documentary, "The War Game," which won the 1966 Oscar for the Best Feature Documentary.[29]

By the seventies, the American people had become accustomed to living with the bomb. Faced with a kaleidoscopic combination of nuclear images since 1945, they had developed attitudes toward nuclear weapons which were at once accepting and avoidance seeking. These mixed signals about atomic power had come from various sources over the years. The image of the bomb promoted by the political elite was that atomic weapons were useful tools to be brandished for diplomatic gain. On the other hand, the image of the bomb projected in the science fiction literature of the age reflected severe pessimism, even fatalism; the bomb was not presented as a winning weapon but as a genocidal geode. The image projected by Hollywood was more like that of literature than of the elites, but it was much less stark and direct, less monolithic and more "sugarcoated." While Hollywood presented monsters created by radiation, in the end such mutants always lost out to science and/or the military. Additional conflicting images of the bomb had been fostered by the atomic scientists who first were overcome by technological infatuation, later suffered from ethical misgivings about their role in the bomb's creation, and finally out of patriotism resigned themselves to the course of events. As a result of these contradictory messages, the American public, left with no coherent image of the bomb, simply chose to pretend it was not there.[30]

Such acquiescence is currently being challenged, however, as the bomb returns, after a twenty-year hiatus, to the center stage of the American cultural scene. The antitesting movement has gained momentum, being joined by numerous Hollywood celebrities and international political figures. Meanwhile the Strategic Defense Initiative, or "Starwars," is being hailed by the president as a critical addition to our own arsenal. Nuclear waste has become a major issue on the agenda, and court cases involving "downwind victims" are making front-page news. The TMI and Chernobyl accidents have alerted the public to the dangers of radiation, and the United States and the Soviet Union are exchanging surveillance teams to observe weapons-testing procedures.

Within such a climate of extreme turbulence and intensified concern, American culture has already begun to reflect the re-emergence of the mushroom cloud. New atomic movies and television specials are being produced; nuclear songs are once again hitting the charts; and the familiar cloud is reappearing on bubble gum cards, tee shirts, and record albums. Scholars and politicians alike speak in nuclear jargon about "credible super-criticality events," "major airborne releases," "collateral damage," and "surgical strikes." It is yet to be seen, however, which direction this cultural development will take. As the twenty-first century dawns, will the cloud come to represent a benign umbrella protecting those who gather in its shadow? Or will it be portrayed as an ominous specter, looming over our lives and threatening those who fall within its reach?

NOTES

1. Paul Boyer, *By the Bomb's Early Light: American Thought and Culture at the Dawn of the Atomic Age* (New York: Pantheon Books, 1985).

2. *Scientific Monthly* (September 1945), cited in Boyer, *Bomb's Early Light*, 3.

3. T. V. Smith and Marjorie Grene, eds., *Philosophers Speak for Themselves* (Chicago: University of Chicago Press, 1957), 253–62.

4. Boyer, *Bomb's Early Light*, 10–26.

5. Ibid., 109–30; Gerald W. Johnson, "The Liberal of 1946," *American Scholar* 15 (Spring 1946): 156.

6. Boyer, *Bomb's Early Light*, 133–77; Dorothy McClure, "Social-Studies Textbooks and Atomic Energy," *School Review* 57 (December 1949): 542.

7. Boyer, *Bomb's Early Light*, 211–29; Arthur H. Compton, "The Moral Meaning of the Atomic Bomb," in William Scarlett, ed., *Christianity Takes a Stand* (New York, 1946), 57–71.

8. Boyer, *Bomb's Early Light*, 243–56.

9. Ibid., 257–65; Albert Berger, "The Triumph of Prophecy: Science Fiction and Nuclear Power in the Post-Hiroshima Period," *Science-Fiction Studies* 3 (July 1976): 144–56; Ray Bradbury, *The Martian Chronicles* (Garden City, N.Y., 1950); Ward Moore, *Greener Than You Think* (New York, 1947).

10. A. Costandina Titus, *Bombs in the Backyard: Atomic Testing and American Politics* (Reno: University of Nevada Press, 1986).

11. Ibid., 70–85.

12. Ibid., 86–93.

13. Ibid., and Boyer, *Bomb's Early Light*, 353.

14. Boyer, *Bomb's Early Light*, 353–54.

15. A. Costandina Titus, "Selling the Bomb: Hollywood and the Government Join Forces at Ground Zero," *Halcyon* (1985): 17–30; idem, "Back to Ground Zero: Old Footage through New Lenses," *Journal of Popular Film and Television* (1983): 2–11.

16. J. Fred MacDonald, "The Cold War as Entertainment in Fifties Television," *Journal of Popular Film and Television* (1978): 3–31; Boyer, *Bomb's Early Light*, 354.

17. Jack G. Shaheen, ed., *Nuclear War Films* (Carbondale: Southern Illinois University Press, 1978), 83–174.

18. Titus, *Bombs in the Backyard*, 94–95.

19. Stephen Hilgartner, Richard C. Bell, and Rory O'Connor, *Nukespeak: The Selling of Nuclear Technology in America* (New York: Penguin Books, 1983), 2–79.

20. Lynn Simross, "Chernobyl and Hanford: Nuclear Author Draws Parallels," *Los Angeles Times*, May 7, 1986.

21. Paul Loeb, *Nuclear Culture: Living and Working in the World's Largest Atomic Complex* (Philadelphia: New Society Publishers, 1986).

22. Ibid., 21–184.

23. Ibid., 185–257.

24. Titus, *Bombs in the Backyard*, 86–100; Georgia Lewis, "'Atomized' Las Vegas Danced 'Atomic Boogie,'" *Las Vegas Review Journal*, January 23, 1983; A. Costandina Titus, "A-Bombs in the Backyard: Southern Nevada Adapts to the Nuclear Age, 1951–1963," *Nevada Historical Society Quarterly* (Winter 1983): 235–54.

25. Titus, *Bombs*, 93–94.

26. Ibid., 98–100.

27. Ibid., 101.

28. Shaheen, *Nuclear War Films*, 3–82.

29. Ibid., 83–174.

30. Michael J. Strada, "Kaleidoscopic Nuclear Images of the Fifties," *Journal of Popular Culture* (1986): 179–98.

GAMBLING LANGUAGE AND NEVADA LAW

THOMAS L. CLARK

Vocabulary words in a language find various degrees of acceptability among the populace. Along the spectrum of vocabulary used by members of a society are many levels of usage: slang, colloquialisms, informal conversation, standard language, formalisms, and a variety of special language uses such as argot and jargon. The language used in the gaming industry in Nevada and, consequently, the language that gets into statutes exhibits features of all these language styles, with the exception of vulgarisms. And some people argue that even the use of vulgarisms is common enough in Nevada gaming and enforcement of the Nevada Gaming Control Act to warrant its inclusion in a list of vocabulary types found in the gaming industry.

Three aspects of language are dealt with in this article. First, we will see how standard English has been modified by both legal and illegal gambling activities. Part of this modification has involved moving some of the vocabulary that might be considered slang into standard English by utilizing it in the formal setting of state statutes. The second aspect here deals with the inadequacies of the gambling-related definitions in the Nevada statutes. The mere fact of including certain language in official documents has the effect of raising the level of some slang to the status of acceptability as standard English. Finally, we deal with one aspect of the vocabulary of gambling, the names of games in state statutes. The extension of the list of games and the particular games named illustrate some of the lively political wrangling that takes place anytime legislators involve themselves in morality and the law.

Nevada was not the first state in which legalized gaming flourished. Betting on horse races was a public activity in many states long before Nevada became a territory, much less a state. But the enactment of the Nevada gaming statute in 1931 marked the beginning of a legitimate enterprise that would outshine all previous legalized betting in any part of the globe. The history of gambling activity in Nevada, as traced in Nevada statutes, illustrates changes in the language, reinforcing certain words as standard English, marking the shift in words from slang to standard or even formal English, and demonstrating syntactic style of the most convoluted and interesting sort.

Daniel J. Boorstin wrote, "Nevada gambling flourished as a border industry—just over the border from illegality and other states."[1] Las Vegas borders on California, Arizona, and Utah. Reno is a dozen miles from the California border and a direct drive from San Francisco. Lake Tahoe, with its active gaming centers, is literally on the border of California and Nevada. On the opposite side of the state, Wendover sits on the border of Nevada and Utah. The Utah end of town looks like many other western desert waystations on the highway, while the Nevada end of town is tricked out in neon and the bright lights that beckon gamblers. Even more recently, gambling centers are built close to the border, never in the middle of the state. The town of Jackpot has been a thriving gambler's haven on the Idaho border since the mid 1970s, and in the mid 1980s Laughlin is booming at the southernmost tip of Nevada where Arizona and California meet.

But Boorstin also notes metaphorically that gambling in Nevada has flourished just over the border from illegality. And this flourishing has brought to Nevada many gamblers who find themselves legitimate very soon after leaving states where they were illegitimate. They bring with them their language, particularly the language of what in their old states had been considered illegal: gaming and gambling, betting and wagering, punting and booking.

Language historians are fond of pointing out that territorial language helped in a major way to preserve and perpetuate the freshness and exuberance of American English, especially vocabulary, nouns, and naming. The explanations for this exuberance in language vary.

One of the most frequently offered [explanations] has been the freedom of the frontier, and the escape from conventional restraints in other matters, including morals, which encouraged an analogous liberty in language. It is true that the frontier has been an extremely important element in our national life. Many historians have followed the lead of Frederick Jackson Turner in finding that the "really American part of our history" must be traced to the men who grew up under frontier conditions. The belief—myth, if it is that—has been so strong that John Kennedy, one of the most popular presidents of the twentieth century, made his national appeal in terms of developing a "New Frontier."[2]

The notion that loose morals in the American West are reflected in a looseness of language does not necessarily hold true when one looks at the language used in historical documents and, moreover, the intentions of those people using the language. Nevada's lawmakers wanted their new state to reflect high moral character right from the beginning. On page after page of the statutes, beginning in 1864, morality is being legislated at every turn. Gamblers, thieves, and riffraff are generally abused, yet abused in a language that is exuberant, lively, sometimes exhilarating and exulting.

From the earliest days of the western states, gambling has occupied the minds and lawbooks (and language) of the people. For example, in 1864, the same year that Nevada achieved statehood, the Montana legislature outlawed "three-card monte, strap games, thimble-rig, black and red, the ten dice game, faro, and any other game where fraud and cheating was easy, practiced, or rampant."[3] Ties between Montana and Nevada, especially those ties reinforced by the regular interchange of people in the ranching industry and the mining industry, had an effect on Nevada. And both states had to deal with the itinerant professional gamblers as well as the miners and ranch hands. Nevada legislators looked to their Montana brethren for inspiration in dealing with gamblers, especially the itinerant professionals.

Cheating and cheating games were common all over the West. The same games banned in Montana and even other games were condemned in Nevada. In 1875 an "act to prohibit cheating" became part of Nevada law.[4] In addition to the games mentioned above, it also specifically outlawed the "California dice" game, also known as "twenty-one" (not the card game) and the "top and bottom" game. Also condemned were "hogging games."

Nevada's legislators voted on-again, off-again periods of legalized gambling. While Nevada was still a territory, gambling was illegal but tolerated in the area. In 1864, Nevada became the "Battle Born" state, though, as Daniel J. Boorstin has pointed out, Nevada actually had been "the creature not of freedom's battle, nor of tradition, nor of nature, but of politics and silver."[5] The wealth of the Comstock Lode and Lincoln's need for votes made Nevada. On February 23, 1865, representatives at the first session of the legislature of the new state approved a bill titled "An Act to Prevent Gaming."[6] In fact, gambling was so much a part of the life of Nevadans that participation in gambling was regarded as a misdemeanor. A few years would pass before participation would come to be considered a felony.

That first bill in the first legislative session of 1865 contained four short sections and essentially replaced the 1861 territorial prohibition of gambling. Fewer than 350 words were required to declare gaming illegal in the state. By contrast, Assembly Bill 144 in the forty-ninth legislative session, approved March 30, 1959, ran to thirty-one closely packed pages.[7] More than 15,000 words were required to revise the statute and create the Nevada Gaming Commission. At present, the *Nevada Revised Statutes* treat gaming and gambling in six chapters of the law, running to 211 pages.[8]

The games named in the 1865 act were not so numerous as those listed by the Montanans the year before. But the list was to grow over the years. Table 1 shows some key dates in the history of Nevada gambling statutes and the names of the games listed at the time. The lists here are alphabetical, though they were not listed so in the statutes. In every case, however, the first three games listed in the statutes were faro, monte, and roulette, in that order. Whether this speaks to the popularity or frequency of the three games we can only guess. The order of the rest varied.

The language used in the statutes is often so convoluted and obtuse that no one, not educated citizen, gambler, lawyer, law-enforcement officer, gamester, or mobster, can get through certain passages without becoming frustrated. After tortuous meanderings through often lengthy passages, the reader comes up against one dead end after another. Let

TABLE 1.

GAMES NAMED IN NEVADA STATUTES IN VARIOUS KEY YEARS

	1865 (Act to Prevent Gambling)	1869 (Act to Legalize Some Gambling)	1879 (Refining Legal Games)	1909 (Act to Prevent Gambling)	1931 (Act to Legalize Gambling)	1959 (Create Nevada Gaming Commission)
1.	faro	faro	fantan	bridge whist	big injun	big injun
2.	lansquenette	lansquenette	faro	craps	blackjack	bingo
3.	monte	monte	juargusnette	fan-tan	craps	blackjack
4.	rouge et noir	rondo	keno	faro	draw poker	craps
5.	roulette	*rouge et noir*	monte	five hundred	fan-tan	draw poker
6.		roulette	red and black, or diana	frog	faro	fan-tan
7.			red, white, and blue	hokey-pokey	keno	faro
8.			rondo	klondyke	klondyke	keno
9.			rouge-et-noir	lansquenette	monte	klondyke
10.			roulette	monte	roulette	monte
11.			twenty-one	poker	seven-and-a-half	roulette
12.				rondo	stud poker	seven-and-a-half
13.				rouge et noir	twenty-one	slot machine
14.				roulette		stud poker
15.				seven-and-a-half		twenty-one
16.				solo		
17.				stud-horse poker		
18.				tan		
19.				twenty-one		
20.				whist		

us trace what looks like a straightforward example. At the
beginning of the 1959 bill that created the Nevada Gaming
Commission, various words and terms used in the bill are defined. One simple paragraph reads, "'Operation' means the
conduct of gaming" (428). This type of definition is called a
definition by stipulation. That is, the second part of the phrase
specifies the sense of the first part of the phrase by using a
longer set of words to transmit a synonymous sense of the
shorter initial term. This is one of several types of *informal*
definitions. Other informal definitions use antonyms, examples, analogies, illustrations, or various other expanded
paragraphs involving longer explanations, history of a term,
etymology, and such.

In formal documents, and statutes are certainly formal
documents, nearly any language scholar would prefer to see
a *formal definition* used in place of an informal definition. Let
us look at another definition. From the same 1959 Assembly
Bill 144: "'Gaming device' means any mechanical contrivance
or machine used in connection with gaming or any game"
(428). Again, note that this is an informal definition. The
fulcrum word is *means*. It serves as an equal sign, equating
the term on the left with the phrase on the right. And the
phrase on the right *stipulates* the sense of the term in the form
"*x* means *y*." A drawback to the informal definition is that
the equivalent or synonymous phrasing on the right-hand
side may not be any clearer to the reader than the term on the
left. This particular definition for "gaming device," however,
reflects a more serious problem with informal definitions.
The word *gaming* occurs in both the left-hand term and the
right-hand term. Any lexicographer will point out that a
word or phrase cannot effectively be defined in terms of itself. An additional complication is that the left-hand term is
made up of an adjective (gaming) derived from a participle
by way of a gerund, followed by a noun (device). In the right-
hand term, "gaming" could be either a participle or a gerund,
given the context of the phrase, but it functions syntactically
as a noun. The compound function connects the term to the
noun in the following phrase "or any game."

Notice how the phrasing above differs from a *formal* definition. The format of a formal definition is "*B* is a *specie* of *genus*

FIGURE 1.

PARTS OF A FORMAL DEFINITION

B	=	subset of A	with C
gaming device	is	mechanical contrivance or machine	used in wagers for money or its representative

labeled *A* with specific *differentiae* labeled *C*." Figure 1 illustrates this more graphically. The content of *B* is *gaming device*, the term to be defined. The equal sign (=) is the equivalent of the verb "to be" and indicates that the term to the left of *is* is equal to the sum of terms on the right. The term *A*, "mechanical contrivance or machine," is the general category of which *B* is only one of several members. Finally, *C* lists the characteristics that distinguish *B* from all the other items in the general category of *A*. Thus, there are many "mechanical contrivances or machines," but only "gaming device" as one of those machines will allow wagers for money or its representative. Note also that the differentiae under *C* have been modified to avoid defining a word in terms of itself.

But the definition for "gaming device" in the 1959 bill did use the word "gaming" as part of the definition. And a nearby paragraph in the bill defines that word in turn: "'Gaming' or 'gambling' means to deal, operate, carry on, conduct, maintain or expose for play any game as herein defined" (428). The distinction between *gaming* and *gambling* in Nevada statutes I have dealt with extensively elsewhere.[9] And we have just seen the drawbacks to the structure of the informal definition. All that is left is to see the reference to "any game as herein defined." We look for a nearby paragraph that will define *game* and find it quite close indeed:

> "Game" or "gambling game" means any banking or percentage game played with cards, dice, or any mechanical device or machine for money, property, checks, credit or any representative of value, including, without limiting the generality of the foregoing, faro, monte, roulette, keno, bingo, fan-tan, twenty-one, blackjack, seven-and-a-half, big injun, klondyke, craps, stud poker, draw poker or slot machine, but shall not include social games played solely for drinks or cigars or ciga-

rettes served individually, games played in private homes or residences for prizes or coin machines operated solely for cigars, cigarettes, drinks or golf balls. (428)

This definition looks exhaustive on the surface but finally leads us to the dead end predicted so many paragraphs ago. The very details listed in this definition are finally its downfall. The reader might expect as much simply by noting the reference to "coin machines operated solely for cigars, cigarettes, drinks or *golf balls*" (emphasis mine). On the one hand, few citizens still smoke cigars. On the other hand, coin machines dispensing golf balls were a short-lived novelty.

The passage quoted demonstrates the pitfall found in many statutes. By trying to include every possibility and contingency, the lawmakers wind up with long and convoluted sentences in which the meaning is lost in a maze of syntax. Further, the games named are not defined and the social conditions described in the statute are mutable. The overall result is a dated statute that has little relevance to any time after the immediate session in which it was enacted.

Similar problems of dated information and lack of definitions carry over to the specific games named.

The games listed here are found among all those listed in Table 1. Various games such as big injun, klondyke, or seven-and-a-half may not be generally known and therefore require defining. On the one hand, a legal argument might be made that the general vocabulary in a statute requires no definition but rather carries common dictionary meaning or the meaning understood by a member of the general public, the average educated citizen. Depending on the context of the games, the average citizen may be familiar with the games. Now it happens that bingo, keno, roulette, twenty-one, craps, and slot machines are found in every sizable casino in the state. There are few visitors to casinos who have not seen those games operating and have some idea about what they might be. Stud poker and draw poker may not be so common to casinos as the preceding games but are widely known even in areas of the country where keno might be considered exotic or rare. Although fan-tan was still being played in some casinos in 1959 when this bill was composed, it is no longer common. Fan-tan serves as a demonstration of what happens to many vocabulary words. As the referent falls into disuse, so does the term. Few of the people who frequent Nevada casinos today even know whether fan-tan is a card game or a dice game (it's a card game).

Even further along the road to oblivion is monte. The term itself has referred to several types of card games over the years. An old dishonorable scam was played by moving three cards around face down on a table and challenging a bettor to pick a specific card, usually the queen of spades, from among the three. The game was originally called three-card monte. But terms used with a high degree of frequency are often shortened, and the game was often called monte. In the latter part of the nineteenth century, the distinction between monte and three-card monte appears to have been preserved. The Act to Prohibit Cheating, passed in the Seventh Session (1875), lists three-card monte among other notoriously crooked games that are being especially targeted for eradication (50). Four years later, the Act to Restrict Gaming, passed in the Ninth Session (1879), lists monte among other such "respectable" games as faro, roulette, fantan (*sic*), and twenty-one (115).

So we see that common understanding of certain forms of vocabulary requires familiarity, frequency of use, and adequate dictionary definition. Failing any or all of these criteria would seem to require that a word or term be defined within the statute. We have seen the function of familiarity and frequency of use in the 1959 bill. But what of dictionary definition?

The games listed in Table 1 were important enough at the time to be listed without definition. But just a few years can create problems with a vocabulary. In the various statutes referred to, thirty-nine different names are used to refer to games. Some of the names refer to the same game, some names are no longer used, and a few of the games are unknown today. Let us look more closely at categories of these games and see how words change over the years, along with the meanings signified.

The first group of games are those well known to residents of Nevada, since they are found in any casino that currently offers both table and machine gambling. Such games include slot machines, bingo, keno, roulette, craps, and card games such as poker and blackjack.

The card game known as twenty-one has been played for

years in this country and before that in England, where it was usually called by its name as imported from France, *vingt-et-un* (literally translated as "twenty and one"). The language process demonstrated by this is called *loan translation*, or *calque*. Only more recently has it been called blackjack in this country. In fact, in the 1931 act that legalized Nevada gambling, blackjack is listed right after twenty-one, as though the framers of the bill knew the game equally by both names and therefore included both names to prevent confusion. Interestingly, in the Nevada statutes, the name in 1875 referred to a cheating game played with dice but in 1879 was listed with legitimate games, and the term apparently referred to the card game.

The game of seven-and-a-half, referred to in every act from 1909 forward, was played the same way as blackjack or twenty-one, except that the Spanish forty-card deck (minus tens, nines, and eights) was used. Aces counted as one point, face cards for one-half point. The aim was to get seven and one-half points without going over.

In the game referred to in the 1879 act as red and black, or diana, the banker dealt five cards on the table. The players could bet whether three or more would be of the same color. A variety of other wagers could be made also.

Webster's Ninth New Collegiate Dictionary (hereafter cited as W9), a desk dictionary published in 1985 and found on the shelf above most students' desks (as opposed to the unabridged *Webster's*, found on a separate platform in the reference room of the library), carries the earliest citation date for many of the games listed in Table 1.[10] The dice game of craps, listed in Nevada acts of 1909, 1931, and 1959, is listed in W9 as dating from 1843 in this country. Keno, listed in the 1879 Nevada act, dates from 1814 in W9, where the etymology lists the word as stemming from French *quine*, referring to "five" (winning numbers), from the original rule requiring that five numbers selected by the player must be called in order to win anything at the game. Roulette, one of only three games listed in every act in Nevada from 1865 onward, has always been a popular gambling game and is listed in W9 as being common to English since 1745. Bingo, listed in the Nevada act of 1959, has been extant, according to W9, since 1936.

The slot machine as we know it has been referred to in Nevada statutes since 1909. But from the previous century, law-makers seemed to make a distinction between slot machines that yielded money or tokens of worth and devices called "nickel-in-the-slot machines" that yielded premiums like cigars, cigarettes, sticks of gum, or pieces of candy. The hyphenated first part, "nickel-in-the-," seems to have been dropped when two things became obvious: first, the machines could be rigged to take any coin from a penny to a silver dollar or token; second, the machines were used regularly for gambling for money, mostly illegally, no matter what ruse was used as a cover (such as golf balls, as recorded in the 1959 act).

Quite often people think only in terms of cards or dice when they think of gambling. But notice that of the games so far listed in the first group, one is played with cards, one with dice, one with a wheel and a ball, one with coin slots, and two with drawn balls. But finally, card games outnumber all others in our list.

Poker was a relative latecomer to the gambling scene of the American West. In spite of the impression that most people have from watching cowboy movies, the earliest reference to poker in this country dates from 1834. W9 lists draw poker from 1849 and stud poker as late as 1864. In fact, there was no reference to poker in Nevada statutes until 1909, and that act referred to poker and stud-horse poker. Draw poker and the more recent version of stud poker would have to wait for recognition by Nevada lawmakers until 1931.

The second group of games listed in Table 1 have an earlier history and are now either dead or nearly so.

The favorite game in the early years of western settlement was faro. It is referred to in every Nevada act, from the beginning to the present, even though it is rarely played anymore. A few old-timers among retired dealers still recall the final days of the game being played in casinos. W9 reminds us that the first reference to the game in print dates from 1735. It moved west with the first settlers and prospectors. But other games caught the attention of gamblers and replaced this, the most popular game of the frontier towns.

Monte was a popular game among cowboys, who brought the game northward from Texas and Mexican cowboys. This Spanish card game dates from 1824 in W9 and was mentioned in every Nevada act from 1865 onward. There is occasional confusion between this game, usually played with a forty-card deck, with cards dealt out to several players, and the hustler's cheating game more commonly referred to as "three-card monte," in which the hustler puts three cards face down on a table and asks onlookers to pick a particular card after making a wager.

The Chinese in the early American West played fan-tan, as attested from 1878 in the *Oxford English Dictionary*. The game was played by betting whether, after a handful of beans or coins was divided into groups of four, the remainder would be zero, one, two, or three. Nevada statutes legalized a game of the same name in 1879. But in Nevada, the game was played with a deck of cards. It was sometimes spelled fantan, more often hyphenated as fan-tan. The 1879 reference in the Nevada statutes may mark the earliest citation to the card game of fan-tan. The first reference to any word or term is notable and this is a rarity indeed. No reference to the game is to be found in the *Dictionary of Americanisms* or the *Dictionary of American English*, the two major sources for vocabulary peculiar to American English.[11]

We will see below that little is known about some games, partly because there are often variant terms for referents. The way this operates in American English (in any language, for that matter) is hinted at by what we *do* know of fan-tan. The game was once tremendously popular, so more has been written about it than about some of the other games that achieved popularity only briefly or only in a restricted locale. An encyclopedia of games tells us about the class of games which includes fan-tan: "This game belongs to a family of games called *stops*. The generic *stops* games feature: the play stops or is interrupted temporarily or finally, when a card specified to be played next is not available."[12] The description goes on to list variant names for fan-tan: sevens, Parliament, card dominoes, play or pay, five or nine, Swedish rummy, eights. It is also sometimes called crazy eights, crazy jacks, etc., depending on the rank chosen as wild. If the person drafting the act in 1879 had known the game by one of the variants, that variant might have been used in addition to, or even instead of, fan-tan. My contention is that such a process took place with some of the other games whose names we will examine.

Although the game of rondo is named in statutes in 1869, 1879, and 1909, thereby indicating that it enjoyed popularity, little is known about the game as it was played in Nevada. The *Dictionary of American English* attests a game played with balls on a large table, rather like billiards or pool, as early as 1797. But it is not until 1849 that the *Dictionary of Americanisms* lists rondo as a gambling game. *W9* does not even carry the term. If the gambling game was played on a table, then it would be similar to betting on bar pool today. But we also must remember that listing the game in successive statutes may have been the result of a bill drafter who simply used the language and vocabulary from the previous statute without knowing anything about the games listed, or perhaps without caring which names were being listed, since any game can be used for wagering.

The French game rouge et noir has long been popular in this country as well as abroad. Unlike roulette, another game of French origin, this one caused problems for the statute writers, not the players. First referred to in Nevada in the 1869 act, the game was italicized in the 1869 act, then hyphenated in the 1879 act. By 1909 the old spelling was back, without the italics. The name of the game translates to "red and black" in English, but this English name may refer to a different game. Both rouge et noir and red and black are listed in the 1879 act. But the double listing may have been an accident, since the 1879 act has several other problems, not the greatest of which was hyphenating the name of the game for the only time in the statutes we are examining. *Webster's Second International Dictionary*, the unabridged version of 1934, listed the game as the same as "trente et quarante" but called "rouge et noir" because of the colors bet on.[13] The multivolume *Century Dictionary* says the same but adds that the game is also called red and black.[14] But in Nevada law, as mentioned, and as we shall see in detail, red and black is something different.

Difficulty with the 1879 Nevada act is hinted at in the preceding paragraph. Another problem in that act was with announcing a legal game called juargusnette. This is the only reference ever found to such a game and leads me to believe that it is a misspelling for lansquenette, which was listed in the acts of 1865, 1869, and 1909, but *not* in 1879. Lansquenette has also been spelled "landsquenet" and called "the precursor of faro." It might be noted that, precursor or not, the game was listed along with faro in all acts up to 1931. The name of the game is

French, but it was borrowed from German, and named for the *landsknecht* (*land,* "country" + *knecht,* "boy"), a foot soldier. Specifically, the foot soldier was a mercenary and the game was introduced by these foot soldiers into a number of countries, one of which was France. The game was a banking game that did resemble faro.

The last game in this group is klondyke. In all the references to be found in Nevada statutes, the spelling is with a *y.* All other references to a card game of this name are spelled klondike and refer to either a gambling solitaire game also called canfield or a banking game similar to six-card stud. There is a poker dice game used for betting in bars that has the same name, but this latter version appears to be of a later date. The name of the gambling solitaire game dates from 1902 in the *Dictionary of Americanisms.* As will be seen in the discussion of the next group of game names, the problem of determining whether the reference is to the banking game or the solitaire game is made difficult because, while the game was listed in the 1959 and the 1931 acts, it was first listed in the act of 1909. The name may have been carried over to the later acts by a drafter of bills who did not know anything about the game. We have every indication that phrasing, including names of games, was copied from one act to the next modification.

The third group of games are to be found only in the 1909 act. In that year, the antigambling contingent fought to make all gambling illegal in the state. Since some forms of gambling had been legal for forty years, the attempts to make all gambling illegal caused a good deal of hard feeling in the state. The progambling coalition managed to force certain concessions, such as delaying the date for enforcement by more than a year. In addition, several games played more for social activity than for gambling purposes were included in the bill in order to make the act as obnoxious as possible to the antigambling forces in the state.[15]

The problem of distinguishing a social game from a gambling game has plagued lawmakers for years. After all, wagering at bridge is common, and more than one college student has used the game for supplementing income. In the various attempts to make the distinction, certain characteristics seem to suggest themselves. First, a gambling game is generally public. It is played in a place where persons who are strangers to one another can congregate and participate, such as a casino, bar, or saloon. Second, a social game is generally more private; the participants often know one another and socialize in other ways also; the activity often takes place in a home, club, or church. Third, the primary purpose of the gambling game is to win or lose money; there may be secondary reasons listed by the player, such as enjoyment, excitement, or socialization. Finally, the primary purpose of the social game is for entertainment and diversion, generally with friends and acquaintances; any winning or losing of money is secondary. A number of games named in the 1909 Act to Prevent Gambling would, under consideration of the preceding, be classified as social games rather than gambling games.

Bridge whist was more commonly called bridge. Says Morehead, "The game of Bridge-Whist superseded Whist as the favorite club game in about 1896, but was itself superseded by Auction Bridge and is now obsolete" (176). That bridge whist was still relatively new to Nevadans is evident from the fact that whist, played around the world since 1663, is named separately in the act as being prohibited.

Several of the games mentioned in this act may have been placed there for the same reason. In 1904, five years before the Nevada act, the rules for five hundred were copyrighted. Five hundred is a card game based on euchre and was designed to be a social game intermediate in difficulty between euchre and whist. Says Morehead, "Five Hundred was an instant success, and it *remained the foremost social game for a decade,* until supplanted by Auction and Contract Bridge" (210; emphasis mine).

Two of the games mentioned in the 1909 act were frog and solo. They may have been different names for the same or a very similar game. Although there is a solitaire card game named frog, the chances are that the act referred to a three-handed card game that enjoyed international popularity. Says Morehead, "In German this game is Tapp or wuerttembergischer Tarok; in French, Solo or *Sans Pendre;* in English, Solo, Heart Solo, Slough, Sluff, or Frog. It has even been called Rana, after the frog genus. But the name Frog is derived (by ear) from the German *frage* (I ask), the lowest game that can be bid in Skat and similar games" (327).

The other game mentioned both in the act and in Morehead's description is solo. There were a number of popular card games in which one person played against others: in Spanish, *el solo*, in England, solo whist. It has been described as a simplification of ombre (or *hombre* or *l'hombre*), with the forty-card Spanish deck being used. It shared similarities with other games whose names seemed to be used almost interchangeably: quadrille, skat, frog, tarok, and whist (or "whisk"). Like frog, it was a three-handed card game. But more importantly to our purposes, it was popular at the time the 1909 act was composed. Says Morehead, "Players in the western United States developed this game *early in the present century* by elaboration of Heart Solo or Frog" (330; emphasis mine).

There can be little doubt that certain lawmakers did add the names of social games to the list of gambling games to be prohibited in 1909, and perhaps some of the names were thrown in whimsically. Hokey pokey is fairly well known as a children's singing game ("You put your left foot in, you put your left foot out, you put your left foot in, and you shake it all about. Do the hokey pokey and you turn yourself around, that's what it's all about"), but it is not known as a gambling game or a card or dice game. The *Dictionary of Slang and Unconventional English* lists a cheating scam by the name of hokey pokey, but use of the phrase in this way may derive from "hocus pocus," meaning prestidigitation or close card or coin manipulation as performed by closeup magicians.[16] No reference can be found to the game of tan as listed in the 1909 act. One might suppose the name to be a clipped form of fan-tan but that game is already listed in the act. In other Nevada acts there are similar games listed close together, so *tan* may or may not be related to fan-tan.

A fourth group of games are primarily cheating scams or bunko frauds. The 1875 act to specifically prohibit cheating mentions the California dice game, also called twenty-one and top and bottom. No dictionary lists a cheating scheme known by these names. However, in a book published in 1891, there is a description of a duping scheme called top and bottom.[17] The scheme is based on the little-known fact that the pips on opposing faces of a die add up to seven. On three dice, the total of the tops and bottoms would be twenty-one. And in fact three dice were used in the scam described. Once the dupe was pulled into an elaborate scheme to cheat another (who turned out to be an accomplice of the game rigger), the dupe was victimized with a fake dice switch. This seems to indicate that the California dice game in our act was the same scam and known also as twenty-one and top and bottom.

A counter dice game that used ten dice and was sometimes called twenty-six may have been the game referred to in the Montana statute quoted earlier. The game was notorious among saloonkeepers because they knew the odds in the game were greatly in their favor and the payoff negligible, while any customer willing to play the game was ignorant of the odds. Games like twenty-six are known as hogging games because, while not truly fixed or crooked, the odds are so high against the player as to make the person running the game look like a person who is hogging all the money on the table or counter. The first reference to a hogging game in the *Dictionary of Americanisms* is not until 1880, which makes the citation of the term in the 1875 Nevada statute the earliest citation known. Not often do we find a citation earlier than that discovered by the lexicographers in their historical dictionaries.

One of the cheating games mentioned in the 1864 Montana act, black and red, is mentioned nowhere else, not in Nevada or any other gambling source. Other games, however, are mentioned in both the 1864 Montana source and the 1875 Nevada act, including thimble-rig, three-card monte, and the strap game. The shell game, using three walnut shells with a pea hidden under one, was the basis of thimble-rig, and three-card was the same type of rigged game, using three cards face downward. Despite the fact that strap games were notorious enough to be listed in the statutes of both Montana and Nevada, not much is certain about how the scam was perpetrated. In the middle of the 1890s, Quinn describes one type of strap or belt game that may have been similar to the ones referred to in the statutes. Called also the O'Leary Belt, the contraption was a sort of wheel of fortune affair that was taken around to fairgrounds and carnivals by hustlers looking for easy prey.

Of all the games mentioned, with all their variants, only two have eluded description. The game called red, white, and blue and listed only in the 1879 act seems to have eluded all game books, descriptions, and aliases. This is not unusual for a game that might have been of limited appeal or rarely found. But the other game, big injun, was listed in both 1931 and 1959, indicating that the game was well known for some thirty years. I have been unable to find anything written about the game. I have listed the name in a set of standard questions I ask old-time dealers and players when I am conducting oral histories, so something may turn up in the oral tradition.

In the foregoing paragraphs, we have accounted for several lexical items peculiar to Nevada statutes, and we have been observers at what lexicographers call a parade of language. Along the way, we have seen several language processes at work. Language is constantly changing, constantly being renewed with fresh vocabulary while older vocabulary terms slip into obsolescence from lack of use. As time has passed, the statutes connected with gambling and gaming have become somewhat less lively and exuberant, more turgid and staid. In the effort to cover all contingencies, lawmakers have sometimes sacrificed clarity and precision. In attempting to define everything, many terms, especially names for games, are left undefined, and it is not difficult to find imprecision in Nevada statutes generally. The significance of imprecision in language hardly needs belaboring. The lesson for us here is to attend to vagaries in language where we find them, and when we find them in formal English, we have a duty to expose them.

But the syntax of language is only part of the study. For a lexicographer, watching new words come into the vocabulary, march past with vigor, then pass slowly out of sight as time goes on gives a sense of historicity comparable only to living to a venerable age, as Wilbur Shepperson has done. May we all enjoy life in similar fashion.

NOTES

1. Daniel J. Boorstin, *The Americans: The Democratic Experience* (New York: Random House, 1973), 75.

2. Albert H. Marckwardt and J. L. Dillard, *American English* (New York: Oxford University Press, 1980), 91, 92. It should be pointed out, in fairness to the memory of Albert Marckwardt, that Dillard, the reviser of his book, twisted the thrust of the message from Marckwardt's original version of *American English*, published in 1958. Marckwardt quoted Turner and went on to state that understanding language inno-

vations took place over the three-hundred-year history of American English and *that* time period should be used as the basis for Turner's "frontier." He made no mention of myth—that was an addition by Dillard who, through misguidance or treachery, misunderstood or violated Marckwardt's original intent.

3. U.S. Department of Justice, Law Enforcement Assistance Administration, National Institute of Law Enforcement and Criminal Justice, *The Development of the Law of Gambling: 1776–1976* (Washington, D.C., 1977), 388.

4. Nevada State Legislature, *Laws of Nevada*, Seventh Session (1875), 50–53.

5. Boorstin, *The Americans*, 65.

6. Nevada State Legislature, *Laws of Nevada*, First Session (1865), 169.

7. Nevada State Legislature, *Laws of Nevada*, Forty-Ninth Session (1959), 427–57. In the rest of this article, where the statute and session referred to are clear in the context, I place the page number in parentheses within the text.

8. State of Nevada, *Nevada Revised Statutes*, Title 41, "Gaming, Horse Racing, Sporting Events" (1985), vol. 13.

9. Thomas L. Clark, "Gaming and/or Gambling: You Pays Your Money . . . ," *Verbatim* 10, no. 4 (Spring 1984): 20–21. In that article I noted that the indexing system for the *Laws of Nevada* volumes was mixed, sometimes using "gaming," sometimes "gambling," to refer to items by page. Out of the sixty-three sessions (through 1985), the index in the volumes carries no reference to gaming or gambling in twenty-one of those sessions—mainly, the sessions during the years before gaming became big business around 1939. In twelve of the sessions before 1909, the term "gaming" was used in the index. "Cheating" and "gambling" were used as finder words only once each during those years. The 1909 session, during which wagering was again made illegal, the reference is to "gambling." And so were the references in 1915 and 1931 sessions. But from 1939 to 1985, "gambling" is used in every index. Beginning in 1959, both terms are found in the index. It is notable that corporate thinking had entered the Nevada gaming scene from about 1957 onward, and apparently the word "gaming" sounds better, cleaner, and more businesslike than "gambling." But gambling is apparently more acceptable to Nevadans. Already by the Fiftieth Session (1960), the term "gaming" in the index carries the legend "See Gambling." And so it has pretty much remained, in spite of the fact that most amendments to the *Nevada Revised Statutes* now deal with the operations of the Nevada *Gaming* Commission and the State *Gaming* Control Board (emphasis mine).

10. Frederick C. Mish, ed., *Webster's Ninth New Collegiate Dictionary* (Springfield, Mass.: Merriam-Webster, 1985).

11. These two works are the standard references to all words thought to be of American origin or used primarily in America: William A. Craigie and J. R. Hulbert, *Dictionary of American English* (Chicago: Uni-

versity of Chicago Press, 1938); Mitford M. Matthews, *Dictionary of Americanisms* (Chicago: University of Chicago Press, 1951).

12. Albert H. Morehead and Geoffrey Mott-Smith, *Culbertson's Hoyle: The New Encyclopedia of Games with Official Rules* (New York: Greystone Press, 1950), 217. Further references to Morehead in the text will include only the page numbers from this book.

13. William Allan Neilson, ed., *Webster's New International Dictionary of the English Language*, 2d ed., unabridged (Springfield, Mass.: G. and C. Merriam Co., 1934/1940).

14. William Dwight Whitney, ed., *Century Dictionary* (New York: Century Co., 1889/1914).

15. Ralph Roske, "Nevada Gambling, First Phase, 1861–1931," unpublished manuscript, Special Collections, University of Nevada, Las Vegas (paper read at the Western Historical Association meeting, 1977), 10.

16. Eric Partridge, *Dictionary of Slang and Unconventional English*, 8th ed. (New York: Macmillan Publishing Co., 1984).

17. John Philip Quinn, *Fools of Fortune* (Chicago: The Antigambling Association, 1891), 281.

EUROPE

BRITAIN, RACE, AND AFRICA: RACIAL IMAGERY AND THE MOTIVES FOR BRITISH IMPERIALISM

MICHAEL S. CORAY

Between 1870 and 1914 Britain acquired vast territorial holdings in tropical Africa. The particular motives behind this expansion of empire have been identified by Richard Faber, who found them to be common threads in the fabric of imperial development from ancient times: (1) the colonizing motive; (2) the economic motive; (3) the aggressive motive; (4) the strategic motive; (5) the missionary motive; and (6) the leadership motive.[1]

Faber's description of the content of these six primary motives underscores that they may occur in any possible combination despite often inherent contradictions in content. He viewed the colonizing motive as a form of imperialism which might "more correctly be called 'colonization,'" for it is primarily an attempt to acquire new territories expressly for the purpose of eliminating the pressures of surplus population at home. The economic motive is primarily a "lust for loot and tribute" but may also take the more sophisticated form of a desire to secure both "markets and materials" for continued economic development. Such security also implied, according to Faber, that development would be to the mutual benefit of both the metropolitan and acquired territories. The aggressive motive could be as simple as the "desire for revenge, excitement, power or prestige, whether for the fun of it or to impress others." Yet this motive also springs from "the simple urge to trample on weak but refractory peoples, or to advertise power and strength." Its most recent expressions have taken two characteristic forms: "empire-building to keep up with the Joneses" and the social Darwinian fight for survival, where "the race will be to the fleet and the fight to the strong, . . . [where] nature is fierce and bloody and . . . people must either come out on top or go under." The strategic motive is based on simple self-preservation, whether it is in the need to protect existing dependencies or in the extension of lines of communication from the metropolitan area to those dependencies. The missionary motive centers on "the ambition to proselytize; to convert other peoples to a religion, a culture or a way of life." The leadership motive is based on the clearly ethnocentric "conviction of superior ability to provide orderly government, whether as a permanent proprietor or as a temporary trustee."[2]

Faber also cautioned that "the original cause of imperial advance may not, of course, be the same as the reasons given later to justify it—either because it does not look good enough, or because another object has in fact intervened." Yet, of all the motives, "the last two, when sincere, may be thought altruistic. The others make no pretence to be so." Moreover, "because of their apparently altruistic character the 'Missionary' and 'Leadership' motives are most likely to be invoked by civilized peoples who feel the need to justify their expansion."[3] The intent of this essay is to investigate one of the sources of these last two motives by surveying British images of Africans from their formation in the mid-sixteenth century to the onset of widespread British territorial acquisitions in Africa during the late Victorian period.

Before undertaking this task, a brief overview of the larger historiographical problem surrounding the question of motives will prove helpful, for the simple identification of commonly acknowledged motives does not begin to suggest the depths of the scholarly debate on the causes of Britain's expansion into the wet tropics generally and into tropical Africa in particular.

For the past thirty years the debate on motives has centered on the relative primacy of the economic, aggressive, or strategic motive as well as upon their interaction between the 1870s and World War I. Substantial has been the disagreement regarding the primacy of any one of the specific motives, even with modification, as an explanation of Britain's imperial thrust into Africa.

The oldest argument, and perhaps the progenitor of all others, is the economic motive. As early as 1902, John A. Hobson developed a hypothesis that came to be regarded as the most influential non-Marxist economic interpretation of imperialism.[4] Hobson's original theory, published in *Imperialism: A Study* (1902) and later refined and modified by others, most notably by V. I. Lenin's *Imperialism: The Highest Stage of Capitalism* (1917), proposed that the inevitable decline of the profitable investment in industrialized economies during the last three decades of the nineteenth century forced potential investors to undertake the relatively more risky venture of investing in the undeveloped regions of the world. Since these captains of capital were able to manipulate their national governments, such investment brought additional pressures upon those governments to provide the kind of protection for investment which only outright annexation could secure.[5] Hobson's theory viewed imperialism as the inevitable handmaiden of an expanding finance capitalism. Its purpose was clearly to exploit known and unknown resources, and its occurrence was triggered in Africa by economic crises in industrial Europe following 1870.[6]

This interpretation of the primacy of the economic motive dominated the historiography of British imperial expansion into Africa until the end of World War II. Since then it has been attacked on several fronts, most notably in the work of Ronald Robinson and John Gallagher. In three deeply influential collaborative efforts these authors stood orthodox historiography on its head.[7] Not only did they challenge the primacy of economic motives as an adequate explanation of Britain's African imperialism by suggesting the primacy of strategic motives, but they also challenged the notion of periodization, which had formed the bedrock of the economic interpretation. According to Robinson and Gallagher, Britain's expansion into Africa during the last decades of the nineteenth century was not a marked departure from practices which began during the second decade of that century. Rather than a discontinuity born of European economic crises, imperial expansion represented a basic continuity of thought and action.

Nor was imperialism the product of the machinations of the capitalist class. Instead, it was the product of the "official mind" of policymakers and bureaucrats who, in the words of Wm. R. Louis, a principal interpreter of the Robinson and Gallagher thesis, "acted on strategic calculations in a way quite differently from what they would have done had they based their decisions on economic advantages as such. Economic interests were involved but were not determinative. 'The official mind' translated economic calculations into strategic concepts drawn from long-rooted experience of the worldwide empire."[8]

Robinson and Gallagher also attacked the essentially Eurocentric bias of the old economic interpretation. British imperialism in Africa was, they maintained, a response by the "official mind" to crises on the periphery rather than in Europe. To defend this hypothesis, the authors argued that African subimperialism (the sociopolitical crisis of African origin which took place on the local or regional level) often prompted the larger imperialism of European nation-states. Because this subimperialism stood beyond the direct control of metropolitan policymakers, it often required actions by Europeans which may not have otherwise taken place. British responses to such crises were characteristically reluctant but occasionally precipitous. British imperialism was the product of the collision between the expansive forces of Europe and unmanageable forces of indigenous African politics. It was born of Anglo-African collaboration and the need to meet local crises, such as the Egyptian rebellion of 1882 or the Boer War. Such events simply precipitated the expansion of British control, be it formal or informal. But such expansion, when and where it occurred, was predicated on strategic rather than economic grounds.

The Robinson and Gallagher thesis, then, challenged the utility of economic motives as an explanation for Britain's expansion into nineteenth-century Africa. Since the publication of "The Imperialism of Free Trade" in 1953, a lively and continuing debate has occurred among economic historians in the pages of the *Economic History Review* and among both Africanists and historians of British imperialism in the pages of the *Journal of African History*. Additional comment, support, criticism, and exploration have taken book form as other scholars join the fray. The debate on the causes of British imperialism has itself become a thriving historiographical field.[9]

It will not be necessary to accept or reject the validity of the emergence of a "new imperialism" between 1870 and 1914 to pursue the objectives of the current essay. Faber's missionary and leadership motives, it shall be argued, sprang from a set of British images of Africa and its peoples and from the shifting courses of action implied by that imagery in the face of changing ideas about Britain's role in world affairs. It will be argued that the content of these images was established in the mid-sixteenth century and that this content persisted in relatively static form through the late nineteenth century. What changed was not so much the content of the images but the significance attached to it.

The remainder of this essay will attempt to demonstrate this relationship by exploring the changing significance of some of the most prevalent British images of Africans from the period of initial contact to the 1870s. Although they were not the only sources of such change, particular emphasis will be given to the racialist science and moral philosophy of the nineteenth century.[10]

It must be stressed from the onset that European contact with tropical Africa began in the fifteenth-century maritime revolution which enabled the Portuguese, as well as their later Dutch, Danish, British, and French competitors, to gain first access and finally control of the world's major sea lanes. It was not until the end of the eighteenth century, however, that Europeans began to have a quantifiable impact on the continent or its peoples, largely as a result of their increasing involvement in the slave trade. This involvement provided wider exposure to Africans in their native habitat and in the Americas.[11]

Winthrop D. Jordan, in his monumental study of Anglo-American attitudes toward blacks from the sixteenth to the early nineteenth centuries, established several clusters of perception which would continue to prevail in the English mind. They emerged during the mid-sixteenth century, when English traders and travelers established contact with sub-Saharan Africans for the first time. They predate the advent of extensive British participation in the slave trade during the next century and were largely the product of an emotional, yet comprehensible, xenophobic reaction that may be typical of any initial contact between alien peoples and cultures.[12]

According to Jordan, "Englishmen found the natives of Africa very different from themselves. Negroes looked different; their religion was un-Christian; their manner of living was anything but English; they seemed to be a particularly libidinous sort of people."[13] More specifically, Jordan's clusters include seven related perceptions, each of which gave rise to separate though interlocking questions regarding African character, achievement, and potential. He has labeled them (1) the blackness without; (2) the causes of complexion; (3) defective religion; (4) savage behavior; (5) the apes of Africa; (6) libidinous men; (7) the blackness within.[14]

In his analysis of these clusters, Jordan emphasized several key points. Early English travelers were consistent in their mention of African skin color, which was routinely described as "black." This depiction, according to Jordan, is evidence of the powerful reaction of Englishmen to peoples whose outward appearance was so startlingly different from their own. The classification of themselves as "white" simultaneously placed the two color groups in instant opposition to one another. Each came to be viewed as the negation of the other.

Physical distinctions based on skin color triggered ethnocentric tendencies which depicted other physical features (such as hair texture, the thickness and shape of the nose and lips) as repulsive. Questions regarding the causes of skin color brought forth a wide range of explanations, the two most popular of which centered on the operation of climatic forces and on a biblical interpretation commonly referred to as the "Curse of Ham."[15] The first explanation introduced environmental determination as a cause of human variation, while the second associated variation with divine intention and the infallibility of the Bible. The importance of this latter association cannot be overstated, for the Curse of Ham became one of the primary defenses for the enslavement of Africans. It also established a hierarchical relationship in which the paternity of Europeans, Asians, and Africans was traced to three of Noah's sons. That the black sons of Ham stood on the bottom rung of this hierarchy and were consigned to serve their cousins as slaves left a lasting imprint on European thought regarding the status of the Negro.[16] But as explanations for African skin color, neither proved satisfactory. The cause of the Negro's complexion would remain a matter of speculation. Still, the fact of such an obvious physical difference, with or without causal explanation, did much to shape the other clusters of perception. It intensified the negative connotations that would be assigned to them in the English mind.

The perception that Africans suffered "defective religion" depicted them as heathens. Although that condition could be remedied by conversion to Christianity, its existence, as a distinct African attribute, became deeply intertwined with other ascriptive traits. The combination of black skin color and heathenism often produced an image of Africans as the living incarnation of the devil.[17] Heathenism also suggested the content of the next cluster, which portrayed Africans as savage men who exhibited savage behavior.

Jordan's description of this cluster emphasizes that the condition of savagery, construed in the broadest sense, was simply "the failure to be civilized." Civilization, as the English of the period understood it, was something of a catchall category which included such aspects of culture as language and government; moral standards or their absence; economic practices; and even clothing styles and table manners. It included the ways by which people lived, particularly with respect to their mastery over the natural world as evident by their ability to exploit it. When the English compared the standards of their life-styles with those of Africans they found much to applaud but more to condemn. African social systems and forms of government were favorably compared to the English system when they included the familiar sociopolitical hierarchy of kings, counselors, and commoners, of gentlemen and lesser classes. Far more common was the observation "that Negroes would behave better under improved circumstances." Others believed "the Africans naturally wicked, but even these observers often used 'natural' only to mean 'ingrained.'" None would ask, until well into the eighteenth century, "whether the Negro's non-physical characteristics were inborn and unalterable." Still, the deep fascination with African savagery gave rise to speculation that Africans were, by their behavior, closer to brutes than to civilized men.[18]

This speculation served as the essential link to the notion that a primordial but continuing relationship existed between the African and the great apes of the continent. Most prominent within such speculation was the chimpanzee, which contemporaries called the "orang-outang." British contacts with the peoples of tropical Africa and with anthropoid apes occurred "at the same time and in the same place. The startlingly human appearance and movements of the 'ape' . . . aroused some curious speculations" which influenced the English perception of Africans.[19] The English were quick to affirm a "similarity between the man-like beasts and the beast-like men of Africa. A few . . . went so far as to suggest that Negroes had sprung from the generation of ape-kind or that apes were themselves the offspring of Negroes and some unknown African beast." This sexual association with bestiality underscored the English perception of the Africans' defective religion and savagery. It also contained "an inner logic which kept it alive without much or even any factual sustenance."[20]

The English used such practices as polygyny to construct a broader sexual mythology for Africans. Males were commonly considered to have been endowed with exceptionally large genitalia, and African females were portrayed as characteristically wanton in their behavior. Africans of both genders were said to be aggressively hypersexual and driven to rampant promiscuity.[21] What, after all, could constitute clearer evidence of their savagery? Lasciviousness coupled with nakedness became the mark of the beast. That such wanton displays of sexuality could be so pervasive and so apparently free of guilt may have added to the belief that Africans were a personification of the demonic being.[22] As Philip Mason has suggested, "For lack of a Devil, we had to seek some other image upon which to focus that mixture of dislike and yet repressed desire that we feel for sexual licence, cruelty and malignity."[23]

The content of the first six clusters combined to form the content of the "blackness within." Jordan writes that the Elizabethan period and the Protestant Reformation which spawned it were characterized by "the twin spirits of adventure and control, and while 'adventurous Elizabethans' embarked upon voyages of discovery overseas, many others embarked upon inward voyages of discovery. Some men . . . were to do both." In the process, English perceptions integrated "sexuality with blackness, the devil, and the judgment of a God who had originally created man not only 'Angellike' but 'white.' These running equations lay embedded at a deep and almost inaccessible level of Elizabethan culture." Such was the result of an age which emphasized obedience to both heavenly and temporal authority; an age which equated vagabondage with social disruption and a lack of inward control; an age which decried its own growing avariciousness.[24]

Africans became a negative counterpoint to the positive images which Englishmen held of themselves. The content of Jordan's "blackness within" gave meaning and value to the other clusters of perception. It provided the context within which "a society in a state of rapid flux, undergoing important changes in religious values, and comprised of men who were energetically on the make and acutely and often uncomfortably self-conscious of being so, came upon a people less technologically advanced, markedly different in appearance and culture."[25] The notion of inward blackness transformed the African into the personification of all that the English had sought to reject and repress in themselves. From the initial period of contact to the late Victorian era, this and the other clusters were constant features of Anglo-African interaction.

British contact with Africa increased in the seventeenth and eighteenth centuries, largely as a result of involvement in the transatlantic slave trade. But it was only during the Enlightenment that a serious reevaluation of British images of Africa began. The emergence of rationalism as the basis for understanding the universe produced the empiricism which generated new theories and philosophies regarding the nature of God, man, and the universe. Fed by a skepticism of religion and the classical traditions of the past, Enlightenment thinkers in Britain and continental Europe sought to use the power of reason to discern the eternal truths expressed by natural law. Old judgments, and the assumptions upon which they were based, were challenged, rejected, and reinterpreted. So too was the significance ascribed to the content of many of Jordan's clusters.

A beginning was made in Britain with the development of new ideas regarding the significance and cause of variation in skin color. John Ray, considered by many to be the founder of modern botany and zoology, began this reevaluation by suggesting that differences in the skin color of men were no more significant than color variation in plants and animals. Color did not indicate fundamental distinction in kind. That some men were black and others white did not indicate that they were fundamentally different beings. This suggestion was amplified by Edward Tyson, Ray's collaborator and rival and the acknowledged founder of comparative anatomy, who suggested that skin color was conditioned by climate and its effects on glands located beneath the surface of the skin. But it was Tyson's comparison of the structure of the chimpanzee and man that would suggest two theories that would become important in British thought.

The first of these theories was based on the idea that the ape was the "brother to man." It suggested, in the words of Leon Poliakov, that the European was "a monkey or a Negro who had been able to better himself." So close a relationship between ape and man was unacceptable to many thinkers, but the allusion to blacks as primitive Europeans who continued to live in a state of natural savagery gained wide currency among intellectuals. The second and more widely supported theory held that apes and Africans were "hopelessly retarded men." In this view, Europeans were considered the most intelligent and beautiful members of the human family because they were the farthest removed from "brute creation." The measure of distance was physical and cultural and was no less subjective than the measurements established during the Elizabethan Age.[26]

The intelligentsia was not the only group which reevaluated the meaning of the imagery surrounding the African during the eighteenth century. Another more popularly based reassessment began in the earliest decades of the eighteenth century and followed two largely xenophobic trends. Among those who had continuing contact with Africans, either as traders or planters, a distinction existed between the individual and the generic Negro or African. African customs could be condemned as repugnant, but it was not axiomatic that individual Africans were bereft of ability, virtue, or intelligence. African slaves could be described as "obstinate, rebellious, thievish, and lazy," but so too were the servile classes of Europe. Among those who viewed Africans from a distance, however, such distinctions were often lost. The tendency to generalize the attributes of specific and sometimes idealized individuals into characteristics of an entire group was much more pronounced here.[27]

It was within this context that the eighteenth-century image of Africans retained a certain continuity with images of the past. Much of the popular commentary during the early decades of the century centered on the African physical environment and reveals that the continent had acquired a dual image. On the one side stood the fantasy of a luxuriant continent which contained vast exploitable wealth. Fed by Spain's success in exploiting its territories in the New World, this image suggested a natural paradise where nature, in a grand display of beneficence, endowed the African with a world of plenty in which labor was unnecessary for subsistence. Lush tropical vegetation also suggested that African soils, under enlightened management, could supply the agricultural needs of Europe as well as of Africa.

On the other side stood an image which focused on the reality of an oppressive climate, dangerous plants and animals, and the near certainty of death to Europeans from pestilential disease. For the African, moreover, the tropical environment had a debasing effect. It lay at the root of his savagery and his stagnation; it obviated the necessity of hard labor upon which all civilization and progress were based. Without the need to labor and the requisite discipline which labor required, African development had been arrested, frozen in time.[28]

This dualism played an indirect role in the speculation of moral philosophers on the substance, cause, and meaning of cultural diversity and was prominent in shaping British thought on life in the tropics. This was particularly the case among Scottish philosophers, who proposed that human development, progress, and history could be defined and measured in economic terms. This rather circular and value-laden hypothesis was based on the untested assumption that human societies progressed through various stages, beginning with the most primitive and ending with the most refined. Each stage was characterized by a specific type of economic endeavor, and the value assigned to the relative sophistication and efficacy of each type established its place along a progressive scale. The most usual configuration placed hunting (and presumably gathering) economies at the base and moved upward to pastoralism, agriculture, and finally to commerce. This simple schema also provided for the classification of cultures as savage, barbarous, or civilized.[29] The stage was now set for a wider debate on the reasons for different levels of advancement.

It was within this context that the dual image of Africa assumed new importance. The prevalence of noncommercial economies on the continent suggested that the physical environment of the tropics was responsible for the failure of Africans to progress beyond the stage of barbarism. Despite the general tone of Enlightenment philosophy and its stress on the equal potential of all men to progress through the agency of education and improved environment, economic theory was blended with environmental determinism where Africa was concerned. Environmentalists maintained that the tropics produced character traits which were antithetical to those required for civilization.[30] The tropics affected mental ability by draining the intellect.[31] They produced timidity instead of courage, laziness rather than industry, and aggressive sexuality in the place of restraint.[32] The development of civilization, in such physical circumstances, was impossible.

These arguments were rejected by two of the more outspoken groups in the eighteenth-century debate on the character of Africans. One group included individuals who had begun to question the unity of mankind. Spurred perhaps by the religious skepticism and anticlericalism of the Enlightenment and the pre-Adamite theory of the seventeenth century, the theory of polygenesis again reared its head.[33] Polygenesists, as well as whites in the West Indies, were particularly opposed to environmental determinism because of its implications regarding the ability of whites to bring civilization to the tropics. They agreed with the environmentalists on the quality of African backwardness but proposed an alternative cause. The characteristics which prevented the African from rising above barbarism were an inherited racial legacy.[34]

The other opponents of the environmentalism of the eighteenth century were the evangelicals and abolitionists who viewed the defects in African character as institutional and therefore amenable to change. Instruction in civilized behavior and proper sociopolitical organization, they argued, would lead to African progress. The major cause and primary expression of African barbarism was the continued operation of the slave trade. Defective character and the expression of barbarism could be curbed by the simple expedient of abolishing the slave trade and replacing it with a more "legitimate" system of commerce. Africa would thus be pushed and pulled toward civilization.[35]

By mid-century, these conflicting views were on a collision course in the growing discourse on the slave trade. Both polygenesists and humanitarians agreed that African progress might be accelerated by wider contact with a superior culture and civilization. The major disagreement concerned the conditions under which such contact should take place. Polygenesists, and the supporters of slavery generally, argued that the traits of barbarism could be controlled, if not eliminated, by the coercive labor and forced acculturation of civilized behavior required by slavery. The humanitarians saw slavery as the key to barbarism and its elimination as the key to progress. Borrowing from the moral philosophers, they trusted the power of "legitimate" trade to nourish the development of the mental and moral traits necessary for civilization.

By the late eighteenth century the British were also in nearly unanimous agreement on another key point. The Africans' physical characteristics were linked to their life-styles as freemen in Africa or slaves in the Americas. "Once this association was made," according to Philip Curtin, physical characteristics "became unconsciously linked with social views, and with the common assessment of African culture." Perceptions of physical difference, and the value associated with such difference, allowed "cultural prejudice" to merge with "color prejudice." [36] This confluence would shape and direct the scientific investigation of race from its beginning in the late eighteenth century until it coalesced in the late nineteenth.

Britain's contact with Africa simultaneously acquired a new dimension and urgency. Continuing involvement in the slave trade had produced strong and vocal opposition at home. The demand of the humanitarians for the substitution of a "legitimate" trade acquired a new political importance. [37] Direct physical involvement by British nationals, meanwhile, moved beyond the west coast and into South, Central, and East Africa by the 1870s. Each of these developments would sharply alter Britain's relationship with the African continent and its people.

From 1790 to 1875 British commercial activities expanded beyond the tiny coastal trading enclaves and into ever-widening stretches of the African interior. At the crest of this expansion was the technological and industrial revolution of the mid-nineteenth century. According to Daniel R. Headrick, this revolution brought an equally revolutionary change in the relationship between Asia, Africa, and Europe:

> In the year 1800 Europeans occupied or controlled thirty-five percent of the land surface of the world; by 1878 this figure had risen to sixty-seven percent, and by 1914 over eighty-four percent of the world's land area was European-dominated. The British Empire alone, already formidable in 1800 with a land area of 1.5 million square miles and a population of twenty million, increased its land area sevenfold and its population twentyfold in the following hundred years.[38]

The development of steamboats allowed the British to penetrate the navigable reaches of the Niger as early as 1832.[39] The widespread adoption of quinine as a prophylactic against the ravages of *Plasmodium falciparum* malaria, the most common form of the disease in West Africa that was nearly always fatal to those who contracted it as adults, sharply reduced the mortality rates of Europeans in the region by the mid-1860s.[40] This ended the image of Africa as "the white man's grave" and led to a dramatic increase in the number of European explorers who ventured into the deep interior after mid-century. Such exploration, and the conflicting claims to African territory which it produced, played a major role in the process of formal partition which began during the 1880s.[41]

Equally important advances occurred in firearms technology, as the smoothbore muzzle-loading flintlock muskets of the early decades of the century gave way to rifled breechloaders and percussion cap technology in the 1860s. These in turn were replaced by repeating rifles during the 1880s. Even these gave way to the greater firepower of the Maxim and other machine guns beginning in 1884.[42] The disparity in firepower between Europeans and non-Europeans between the 1880s and 1920 was as broad as it would ever be.[43] Despite the certainty that contemporary Europeans could not have realized the temporary nature of this disparity, they focused upon its existence as a benchmark against which differences in raw power, both real and potential, might be measured. It was only a small step to adopt technological development as a basic measurement of more subjective distinctions. The British, from their position in the forefront of the industrial, technological, medical, and military innovations of the period, would lead this broader reassessment. In the process, Europe's technological advance and Africa's apparent stagnation were consciously and unconsciously linked to differences in the character of the peoples of these continents.[44]

Expanding British contact with Africa, meanwhile, provided a second basis for the reassessment. Old images were recast with subtle but often important changes. Then began a period during which the image of Africans became more harsh and less flexible. But always, like some vestigial remnant sealed within the inner recesses of a collective memory, lay those initial impressions of Africans.[45]

A third basis for reassessment rose from the changing circumstances of British imperial control during the late eighteenth century. The new examination of Africa and its potential role within British imperial policy began with the loss of the American war and the growing recognition that reforms would be required in the West Indies.[46]

By the late eighteenth century, the British had access to much more information regarding the diversity of African peoples than had been the case for those travelers and traders whose accounts contributed much of the substance for Jordan's clusters of perception. The growth of geographical and ethnographical studies, together with information recovered from medieval Arabic texts, provided new materials for the interested. Most interest centered, however, on aspects of African life which bore directly or indirectly on British trading opportunities. Some attention was given to indigenous systems of slavery, but the often subtle differences between these systems and those prevalent in the West remained unrecognized. An emerging romanticism, and the convention of the "noble savage" which it spawned, required that the more titillating aspects of African social behavior and ritual be reported in great frequency and detail, even though Africans were not included in the "noble" category of savagery.[47]

At the heart of this new discussion was the theme of "the Negro's place in nature."[48] It built upon the speculations of the earlier decades and was joined, again, by publicists, travel writers, antislavery advocates, humanitarians, and missionaries. It also became a basis for scholarly debate in fields as diverse as natural history and moral philosophy. The most important new development was that this discussion made use of the newly popular language of "race."[49]

As the transition in terminology occurred in the mid-eighteenth century the dualism of the earlier period underwent a subtle change. The earlier gap in the depiction of Africans between travelers and traders, as opposed to armchair speculators, began to close. Descriptions of individual Africans in the travel literature of the later decades continued to leave room for the range of virtues and abilities which the British admired in themselves. But when travel writers discussed Africans in the aggregate as "Negroes" or "Africans" depictions became increasingly demeaning. Individuals might be described as trustworthy or cultured, but "Africans" in the abstract were seen as inhuman savages.[50] The previous distinctions between the individual and the group were beginning to blur among those Britons who had the closest contact with Africans. The practice of linking group characteristics and culture to individual personality was increasing.

This tendency was even more extreme among biologists and other naturalists. The attempts to bring intellectual order to chaos led to the systematic classification of nature according to rational patterns of relationships.[51] The ancient idea of the "Great Chain of Being" influenced an acceptance of the existence of a divinely imposed hierarchy of relationships within the whole of animate nature. The systems of racial classification that were developed in the late eighteenth and early nineteenth centuries continued this emphasis on hierarchy by first defining races according to physiognomic traits and then ranking each race according to subjective criteria.[52] This process both allowed and promoted the qualification of racial traits without requiring that the qualitative criteria be determined scientifically.

Adherence to the uniform hierarchy implied by the "Great Chain of Being" was by no means universal. The broad range of variation among individuals who were classified within the same racial category forced William Lawrence and James Cowles Prichard, two of the most important figures in British physical anthropology during the first half of the nineteenth century, to discard the logic of that ancient idea. Lawrence, for his part, accepted the prevailing categories of racial classification as a convenient but arbitrary construction. The darker races were, to his mind, but "degenerate" by-products of superior Europeans. Whites were superior "not as the highest term in a series but as the single superior race standing above all of the 'dark races' grouped together at a lower level." The basis of white superiority, for Lawrence, lay in the aesthetics of color and in the superior mental and moral traits required for civilized behavior and worldly achievement. Lawrence's conception of racial traits as "a kind of average for the whole group," meanwhile, led him to concede that individual Africans might rise above the average of their group and achieve "the usual standard of the white race." [53]

Prichard, who like Lawrence was an opponent of slavery and the slave trade, was the more earnest humanitarian of the two. He was also a staunch monogenesist who would not allow his disdain for the barbarism of African life to overshadow his belief that there was "no physical limitation to the *potential* achievement of any people, no matter what their race." Prichard also dismissed racial classification by physical characteristics alone and replaced it with a system which combined physical and linguistic distinctions. His concern here was that classifications of race based entirely on physical characteristics served to obscure significant similarities which transcended racial categories. Physical traits, moreover, might be ephemeral. His emphasis on language reflected a belief that it was "the only valid criteria for classifying the peoples of the world" because linguistic differences were "perhaps much more ancient distinctions than the varieties of form and colour." This physical-linguistic system of classification, in Prichard's view, would tidy up many of the confusing loose ends caused by transcendent physical characteristics. But this use of language as a characteristic of race also demonstrates the consistency with which even the defenders of African equality accepted xenophobic judgments of the meaning of cultural variation. It also demonstrates the depths of the continuing confusion of race with culture. [54]

The fact that Europeans assigned themselves the highest rank on every racial scale is important but not surprising. Doing so established divergence from European norms as the basis for the measurement of qualitative differences. This, in turn, led to the equation of physical traits with cultural attainment, both demonstrated and potential. [55] But because Europeans and Africans were perceived as the ultimate extremes in the range of physiognomic diversity, the placement of Europeans within the highest rank made the consignment of the generic "African" to the lowest nearly axiomatic. This equation of physical appearance with character and mental ability maintained a continuity with much of the content of Jordan's clusters of perception.

Late eighteenth-century attempts to explain the origins of human variation also renewed the polygenesist challenge to the orthodox Christian belief in monogenesis and the unity of mankind which it implied. This assault was launched on the Continent, where religious orthodoxy was more transient than in Britain, and would not become a prominent feature of British racial science until the 1840s.[56] By that time, the intellectual community on the Continent had partially succeeded in cloaking the philosophical speculation of the polygenesists with the status of science.

The new polygenesis was firmly grounded in two widely popular but easily refutable beliefs. One asserted that differences in anatomical structure proved Europeans and Africans were the products of separate creations. The African nervous system, for instance, was said to be more acute in sight than that of Europeans but less sensitive to pain and taste. The African brain and internal body fluids were described as darker and African genitalia as larger than those of other races. Polygenesists also insisted that African women experienced less painful childbirth and menstruation than did European women. The second basic argument was more simple. Africans were said to be closer to animals than Europeans because of their early sexual maturity and shorter life expectancy. Both of these arguments were corrected by Thomas Winterbottom's observations of numerous Africans in Sierra Leone during the 1790s, but his work received attention only from those who defended the idea of African equality.[57]

The work of the quantifiers of racial differences continued to emphasize the depths of the physiognomic distinctions between the races. It was used as evidence by polygenesists to support their contention that each race was the product of a separate, independent creation event. Races were not, as a result, simply quantifiable units within the human family; they were biologically determined branches of creation.[58] Racial characteristics, as expressions of behavior and culture, were immutable. They

could not be improved through the adoption of more enlightened economic systems or by interaction and borrowing from
higher civilizations. Most polygenesists agreed that the African
was, at best, an intermediate creature who fell somewhere on
the scale of animate nature between the manlike apes and the
true human being. The quantifiers of racial characteristics placed
the African at the bottom of the human family; the science of
polygenesis denied him membership in that family.[59]

The 1840s also brought racial interpretations of history into
vogue in Britain. These interpretations were influenced by the
observation that the aboriginal peoples of the Americas tended
to "die out' with the onset of white settlement. This phenomenon
had been seen as evidence of providential beneficence toward the
English in the eighteenth century. But during the nineteenth-
century expansion into Canada and Australia it took a new tone.
It was now seen as "divine intervention in the cause of civilization" and became a confirmation of "the law of human progress."
The racial histories of the mid-century attempted to link the extinction of nonwhites to "some natural law of race relations."[60]

Africa became part of this new literature because the differences in mortality there, as demonstrated above, contradicted
the basic model of the rest of the world and challenged its
standing as natural law. It was within this context that moral
philosophers used the findings of science to develop racial interpretations of history. The most prominent feature of these interpretations was their effort to assess the relative superiority of
the various "tribes" or groups which composed the Caucasian
race. Thomas Arnold, former headmaster at Rugby and Regis
Professor of History at Oxford in 1841, was among the first to
use this theme to revive Berkeley's idea that "the torch of civilization passed successively from one race [nationality] to another, each of them, as soon as it had accomplished its task, dis-
appearing from the scene of history." The Teutonic race, and
especially its Anglo-Saxon relative, was assigned the special
mission of passing Christianity and Western culture to the other
races. As the last great race, the Anglo-Saxons expanded their
control over the world as an expression of divine providence.[61]

Thomas Carlyle, the first major British writer to take up this
theme, also lauded the superiority of the Teutonic race as evident by its ability to subjugate the world. Anglo-Saxons, in par-

ticular, had been given two special tasks: "the industrial task of conquering 'half or more' of the planet, 'for the use of man,' and the constitutional task of sharing the fruits of conquest, and showing other peoples how this might be done." For Carlyle, "Africans were not inferior merely by chance or for the time being. They had been created inferior *in order* to serve their European masters." [62]

The young Disraeli took up the same theme but replaced the Germans with Jews as the vanguard of the Caucasian race because of their secret spiritual powers. [63] In what proved to be a prophetic harbinger of the anti-Semitic arguments of the 1930s, Disraeli revealed his understanding of contemporary racial thought: "The fact is, you cannot destroy a pure race of the Caucasian organization. It is a physiological fact . . . And at this moment, in spite of centuries, of tens of centuries, of degradation, the Jewish mind exercises a vast influence on the affairs of Europe." Such influence was not a product merely of the laws and literature which had been borrowed from Judaic tradition, "but of the living Hebrew intellect." "You never observe a great intellectual movement in Europe," he continued, "in which the Jews do not greatly participate. The first Jesuits were Jews; that mysterious Russian Diplomacy which so alarms Western Europe is organized and principally carried on by Jews; that mighty revolution which is at this moment preparing in Germany, and which will be . . . a second and greater Reformation . . . is entirely developing under the auspices of Jews, who almost monopolise the professorial chairs of Germany." [64] Disraeli's hierarchy of human achievement placed Jews at the top and reserved the second rung of the ladder for the Anglo-Saxons because they were best suited "to receive the 'light of Jewish spirituality.'" [65]

Robert Knox, the British surgeon who has been described as "the real founder of British racism and one of the key figures in the general Western movement towards a dogmatic pseudo-scientific racism," challenged Disraeli's hierarchy but not his assertion of the importance of race in history. [66] On this point, Knox offered the central dictum of mid-century British science: "that the race in human affairs is everything, is simply a fact, the most remarkable, the most comprehensive, which philosophy has ever announced. Race is everything: literature, science, art—in a word, civilization depends on it." [67] For Knox, the Saxons

and Celts had been given the task of dominating the world because it was they who manifested the racial traits required to do
so. Knox shared the belief of other British scientists that races
were distinct entities endowed with specific traits that could not
be changed by the external environment nor by interbreeding
with other races. The course of history, for Robert Knox, was
determined by biology. It was played out in an evolutionary
struggle between the races. The darker races had developed earliest. Their period of achievement had run its course. They were
now locked into a long period of stagnation, and the future promised only their extinction at the hands of their pale superiors.[68]

Knox's system of "transcendental anatomy' proposed that the
history of animate nature was the product of an unfolding struc-
tural plan. Racial variation arose from arrested development at
the embryonic stage of human growth. The superiority of the
Saxon race, then, was a product of its uninterrupted development and its ability to adhere to a unified organic plan. Knox
also argued that the same racial traits which insured Saxon supremacy in western Europe denied Saxon hegemony in Africa.
The biological traits which allowed Saxon civilization to flower
in the temperate regions precluded survival in tropical Africa.
This idea prompted two important corollaries. First, the African,
by reason of his ability to survive in the tropics, became the
"natural enemy" of the European. Second, the combination of
African military prowess with the inability to be civilized suggested that Africans might withstand a European attack indefi-
nitely. The logic of these arguments was straightforward. Despite their "natural physiological and psychological inferiority,"
Africa was best left to Africans. British colonies could only be
sustained by "the labour of the races indigenous to the region
and by steady migration from the Saxon homeland." History
had become "a matter of each race attempting to dominate its
own homeland and construct its own government, laws and civilization according to its distinct, inner nature."[69]

The pre-Darwinian decades of the nineteenth century also
witnessed the end of the relatively primitive morphological and
biblical systems of British racial analysis. These gave way to increasingly sophisticated new techniques derived from such new
areas of formal study as biology, paleontology, and histology.
The investigation of human variation, even among monogene-

sists, became more "scientific" and more explicitly racist.[70] In this context racism is best described as a "system of thought in which group characteristics of human beings, of a non-somatic nature, are considered to be fixed by principles of descent and in which, in general, physical attributes (other than those of sex) are the main sign by which characteristics are attributed."[71]

The abstract quality of the "Negro" continued to be central to these new studies, and race continued to be viewed as a measurable typological construct. "To the typologist," as Nancy Stephan explains, "every individual human being belonged in some way or another to an undying essence or type. However disguised or hidden the individual's membership in the type might be, the scientists expected to be able to see behind the individual to the type to which he belonged. The result was to give a 'mental abstraction an independent reality,' to make real or 'reify' the idea of racial type when in fact the type was a social construct which scientists then treated as though it were in fact 'in nature.'"[72] Racial classification thus became openly quantitative as well as qualitative.

The British scientific community continued its earlier emphasis on comparative anatomy but shifted the direction of such studies toward measurements of the skull and other indexes of "nigrescence." The conflict between mono- and polygenesists over the degree and significance of racial differences continued, even though the theorists of both schools accepted the notion that culture was the product of physical type. Both of these developments changed the nature of the debate on race by introducing biological determinism as the explanation for both behavior and its social expression as culture. The early eighteenth-century emphasis on the essential similarity of humankind was replaced by an emphasis on human differences. Races, even for many monogenesists, were no longer seen as the mutable products of specific physical and cultural environments; they had become fixed, unchanging types.[73]

The growing influence of the science of phrenology was as culpable as any other field of inquiry in bringing about this hardening of attitudes. Initially a reformist science which attempted to refute biological determinism, phrenology became essentially "innatist and typological" and influenced both scientist and nonscientist alike. Basing their studies on the notion "that the brain was the organ of the mind," such internationally renowned researchers as Johann Frantz Gall, J. G. Spurzheim, George Combe, and Samuel Morton succeeded in convincing many that "biology, not philosophy or metaphysics, was . . . the key to animal and human action." By establishing the importance of the physical structure and function of the brain to all human activity, the phrenologists helped to popularize biological determinism as an explanation for all racial (and national) characteristics. That such characteristics were the product of an unchanging biological inheritance was the given in this equation. All that remained was to extrapolate generalizations from the findings on individuals to the racial types which they supposedly represented. Much of this task would fall to post-Darwinian anthropology. Despite the eclipse of phrenology as a science in Britain by the 1840s, many of its principles influenced a new generation of physical and social scientists.[74]

By the time of the publication of Darwin's theory of evolution by natural selection in 1859, British racial scientists were agreed, according to Stephan, on three propositions. First, "intrinsic animality and intelligence" were determined by physical structure and could be measured along a graduated scale. Second, the differing structures of the brains of each race were inherent and could be measured by "the appearance of the head." Third, racial characteristics were not determined by the environment, nor were the traits acquired by individuals through adaptation to the circumstances of their lives inheritable. "Races were now seen," Stephan continues, "as forming a natural but static chain of excellence, whether on the basis of nervous organisation, skull shape or brain size. The hierarchy of races was believed to correspond to, and indeed to be the cause of, what most people took to be the natural scale of human achievement in the world, with the European on top and the African or aboriginal Australian invariably at the bottom." These ideas won public favor because they were backed by a rigorous new scientific method, and because the conclusions reached by that science catered to "the Europeans' sense of themselves in the world."[75]

Darwin's theory brought no immediate change to the function of race as a social construct. It did challenge, however, one of the basic premises of earlier studies of natural science—the idea that species were fixed or static entities. In addition to asserting that species experienced continuous change "by a natural process of variation, struggle and the selection of traits favourable for survival," Darwin also proposed that adaptation was the essential mechanism by which new species emerged from the old. This construction linked species through "time and space by descent." By implication, it linked man and animal more firmly than had been the case in earlier scientific theory.[76]

Among British racial theorists, Darwin's beliefs that man emerged from "some unknown animal ancestor, and that the distinction between species and varieties was continually being broken down by evolutionary change," caused but brief concern.[77] Such minor inconveniences had been smoothed over before.[78] Within a decade of the publication of Darwin's theories, evolutionism had been incorporated into existing racial ideas. Rather than weakening them, evolution provided racialist physical and social scientists with the "scientific" vocabulary of "survival of the fittest."[79] Racialist arguments, as a result, acquired greater appeal, prestige, and persuasion than they had enjoyed in the pre-Darwinian nineteenth century.

Darwin's theories also begot social Darwinism. In its most crude form, social Darwinism involved the application of evolutionary theory to human societies.[80] Its importance to the image of Africans lay in the stress within evolutionary theory on the idea of progress. Darwin's vision of "individual and racial struggle" as the cause for the "moral, intellectual and social progress of mankind" undermined the fixity implied by earlier social and racial theories.[81] The character and abilities of individuals were still linked firmly to race, but individual and collective advancement up the scale of civilization became a clearer possibility. Christian reformers and humanitarians could again argue that the acceptance of Christianity would lead not only to individual salvation but to "progress" as well.[82]

The continued acceptance of a social, cultural, and historical hierarchy was implicit in the social Darwinian notion of progress. It "served most effectively to bolster up the complacency and self-satisfaction of those who felt justified in claiming that their society had 'advanced furthest,'" but it also intensified their contempt "for those who could now be described as 'lower' or 'inferior' races. 'Savages' could be regarded as the 'contemporary ancestors' of Europeans, occupying a stage which 'civilized' people had left behind many centuries ago." The older ranking of human societies from savage to civilized was maintained, but savages were now described as "children" rather than beasts.[83]

The increasingly common use of a familial term such as *children* to describe members of an "inferior" racial group demonstrates the connection between domestic social concerns and the continuing debate on wider racial questions. For the Darwinist, the same features which delineated racial typologies also delineated British class structure. It became convenient, therefore, to apply the language used in discussions of the lower classes to discussions of inferior races. Both groups shared a common subordination. It became common for social Darwinists to speak "in terms of dependence, of development, of benevolent and paternal supervision and of the 'child' or the childlike qualities of the 'primitive' people. This allowed a theory of the inherent dependence and inferiority of certain groups to be combined with the assumption that an underlying identity of common interest existed in spite of it." This idea of common interest reinforced earlier notions of a British racial destiny and assigned the task of fulfilling it to the upper and middle classes.[84]

The convergence of the idea of a British racial destiny and the possibility for African progress was an important source of the missionary and leadership motives for British imperialism in Africa. These motives reflected, in their most benign form, the moral obligation and Christian duty of a master to a ward. Superior peoples were charged to use their unique talents to lift the burden of savagery from the shoulders of a backward race. A long period of tutelage would allow an inferior people to assimilate as much of the moral and cultural basis for civilization as their racial capabilities might permit. In their most malevolent form, these motives reflected a racial determination to become, in the words of V. G. Kiernan, "the lords of human kind." The inherent imitative abilities of the inferior race would allow it to simulate the outward trappings of civilized behavior, but limited intellectual capacity would prevent any understanding or appreciation of the virtues of such behavior. The "natives" would remain on the razor-edged margin between barbarism and civilization. Keeping them in their place would require a firm hand.

These two forms of the missionary and leadership motives

represent opposite extremes. The middle ground was vast. Innumerable variants occurred. But each displayed a distinctive pedigree that can be traced to the sixteenth century. The content of British images of Africa and Africans in the late nineteenth century was little different from that of the sixteenth. What had changed was the British interpretation of the significance of that content.

The key to these new interpretations in the late nineteenth century was the transformation of race from a scientific concept into a "social construct." This change created its own reality. Race, despite the fact that it was "a value-judgement bailed out by science," supplied both question and answer, cause and effect.[85] It gave meaning to the diversity of human physical traits by linking them inextricably to personal and group behavior, character, and mental endowment—the acknowledged foundations of civilization and cultural achievement. The perceived grandeur of British civilization and culture was attributed to superior racial traits.[86] The perceived depravity of African civilization and culture, whether in the African homeland or abroad, was viewed as the natural outcome of inferior racial traits. The collision of these key ideas, and their linkage to the social construct of race, invoked the missionary and leadership motives for British imperialism in Africa.

NOTES

1. Richard Faber, *The Vision and the Need: Late Victorian Imperialist Aims* (London: Faber and Faber, 1966), 15–16.

2. Ibid.

3. Ibid., 16–17.

4. Winfried Baumgart, *Imperialism: The Idea and Reality of British and French Colonial Expansion, 1880–1914* (1975; reprint, Oxford: Oxford University Press, 1982), 92; William G. Hynes, *The Economics of Empire: Britain, Africa and the New Imperialism 1870–95* (Bristol: Longman, 1979), 4–5.

5. Hynes, *Economics of Empire*, 4–5; L. H. Gann and Peter Duignan, "Reflections on Imperialism and the Scramble for Africa," in Peter Duignan, ed., *Colonialism in Africa: 1870–1960*, vol. 1, *The History and Politics of Colonialism 1870–1914*, ed. L. H. Gann and Peter Duignan (Cambridge: Cambridge University Press, 1969), 104–8; Paul Kennedy, "Continuity and Discontinuity," in C. C. Eldridge, ed., *British Imperialism in the Nineteenth Century* (New York: St. Martin's Press, 1984), 22–23; James Sturgis, "Britain and the New Imperialism," in Eldridge,

British Imperialism, 85–86; A. P. Thornton, *The Imperial Idea and Its Enemies: A Study in British Power* (1959; reprint, New York: St. Martin's, 1985), 73. Baumgart reminds us that Hobson's notions were anticipated by Adam Smith, Karl Marx, John Stuart Mill, Karl Kautsky, and Alexander Helphand and that his expression of those ideas in 1902 was an attempt "to join the political debate of the day [regarding the Boer War], especially to address himself to the causes and consequences of the war . . . Hobson tried to expose the causes of the war and at the same time to show an alternative for their elimination. He shared the view of many of his contemporaries that the capital interests behind the South African mining industry were responsible for the outbreak of the conflict, and he used the deep public interest in the war to popularize the social-reform proposals he developed . . . He was not really concerned about imperialism, but about the social question in England" (Baumgart, *Imperialism*, 91–94).

6. Baumgart, *Imperialism*, 96.

7. The arguments included here are based on Wm. Roger Louis, ed., *Imperialism: The Robinson and Gallagher Controversy* (New York: New Viewpoints, 1976), 2–38. The works alluded to include John Gallagher and Ronald Robinson, "The Imperialism of Free Trade," *Economic History Review*, 2d ser. 6, no. 1 (1953): 1–15; Ronald Robinson and John Gallagher with Alice Denny, *Africa and the Victorians: The Official Mind of Imperialism* (London: Macmillan, 1961); Ronald Robinson and John Gallagher, "The Partition of Africa," in F. H. Hinsley, ed., *The Cambridge Modern History*, vol. 11, *Material Progress and Worldwide Problems, 1870–1898* (Cambridge: Cambridge University Press, 1962), 593–640; Ronald Robinson, "Non-European Foundations of European Imperialism: Sketch for a Theory of Collaboration," in E. J. R. Owen and B. Sutcliffe, eds., *Studies in the Theory of Imperialism* (London: Longman, 1972), 117–42.

8. Louis, *Imperialism*, 8.

9. For examples of the diversity of the elements in this debate, see ibid. and Eldridge, *British Imperialism*. The former volume includes critical responses from such notable historians as D. C. M. Platt, George Shepperson, and Eric Stokes. It also includes commentary from A. J. P. Taylor, W. W. Rostow, Henri Brunschwig, Hans-Ulrich Wehler, Roger Owen, Richard Graham, Akira Iriye, Ernest R. May, and Sydney Kanya-Forstner. Eldridge's more recent study includes, in addition to those cited earlier, contributions from Peter Burroughs on "Colonial Self-Government," R. J. Moore on "India and the British Empire," A. E. Atmore on "The Extra-European Foundations of British Imperialism: Towards a Reassessment," Christine Bolt on "Race and the Victorians," M. E. Chamberlain on "Imperialism and Social Reform," and Eldridge on "Sinews of Empire: Changing Perspectives."

10. Contributing factors which cannot be treated here in any detail include the role of domestic politics, the treatment of blacks in Britain, and the wider dimensions of British social history. See Geoffrey Alder-

man, *Modern Britain 1700–1983: A Domestic History* (London: Croom Helm, 1986); François Bedarida, *A Social History of England 1851–1975*, trans. A. S. Forster (London: Methuen, 1979); Roger Cooter, *The Cultural Meaning of Popular Science: Phrenology and the Organization of Consent in Nineteenth-Century Britain* (Cambridge: Cambridge University Press, 1984); L. P. Curtis, Jr., *Anglo-Saxons and Celts: A Study of Anti-Irish Prejudice in Victorian England* (Bridgeport, Conn.: Conference on British Studies, 1968); Peter Fryer, *Staying Power: Black People in Britain since 1505* (Atlantic Highlands, N.J.: Humanities Press, 1984); Douglas A. Lorimer, *Colour, Class and the Victorians: English Attitudes to the Negro in the Mid-Nineteenth Century* (New York: Holmes and Meier Publishers, 1978); Eric Hobsbawn and Terence Ranger, eds., *The Invention of Tradition* (Cambridge: Cambridge University Press, 1983); J. A. Mangan, *Athleticism in the Victorian and Edwardian Public School: The Emergence and Consolidation of an Educational Ideology* (Cambridge: Cambridge University Press, 1981); Paul B. Rich, *Race and Empire in British Politics* (Cambridge: Cambridge University Press, 1986); Edward Scobie, *Black Britannia: A History of Blacks in Britain* (Chicago: Johnson Publishing Co., 1972); James Walvin, *Black and White: The Negro and English Society 1555–1945* (London: Allen Lane, Penguin Press, 1973).

11. Robin Hallett, "Changing European Attitudes to Africa," in John E. Flint, ed., *The Cambridge History of Africa*, vol. 5, *From c. 1790 to c. 1870* (Cambridge: Cambridge University Press, 1976), 458–60.

12. Philip Curtin, *The Image of Africa: British Ideas and Actions, 1780–1850* (Madison: University of Wisconsin Press, 1964), 28–30.

13. Winthrop D. Jordan, *White over Black: American Attitudes toward the Negro, 1550–1812* (Baltimore: Penguin Books, 1968), 3.

14. Ibid., 4–43; Charles H. Lyons, *To Wash an Aethiop White: British Ideas about African Educability, 1530–1960* (New York: Teacher's College Press, 1975), 6–9, 16.

15. Jordan, *White over Black*, 4–20; Nancy Stephan, *The Idea of Race in Science: Great Britain 1800–1960* (Hamden, Conn.: Archon Books, 1982), 8.

16. Leon Poliakov, *The Aryan Myth: A History of Racist and Nationalist Ideas in Europe*, trans. Edmund Howard (New York: Basic Books, 1974), 7–8.

17. Jordan, *White over Black*, 26.

18. Ibid.

19. Ibid., 28–29.

20. Ibid., 31–32.

21. Ibid., 158–60; Poliakov, *Aryan Myth*, 136.

22. Jordan, *White over Black*, 32–40.

23. Quoted in Michael Banton and Jonathan Harwood, *The Race Concept* (New York: Praeger, 1975), 15.

24. Jordan, *White over Black*, 41–42.

25. Ibid., 43.

26. Poliakov, *Aryan Myth*, 155–59. The physical contrasts between

Europeans, Africans, and apes presented eighteenth-century scientists, particularly those on the Continent, with a continuing problem of where to place the Negro in the great scheme of humankind. Poliakov's treatment of mono- and polygenesism in anthropology during the Enlightenment asserts that "it looks as if European narcissism needed a clear dividing line between 'them' and 'us.' Psychologically a demarcation was required but it could be drawn in different ways . . . A relationship can be detected between Christian orthodoxy and the choice of dividing lines." This relationship was forcefully illustrated in a controversy involving Pieter Camper, the Dutch monogenesist anatomist who would later develop the measurement of "facial angle" as a gauge of intellectual ability, and Johann Meckel, an atheist German surgeon. Meckel's dissections of the bodies of several Negroes in 1757 led him to argue that "their brains were of a darker colour than those of Europeans, and that their blood was black." He concluded that such differences in internal structure made Negroes "almost another species of man." Camper castigated Meckel's obvious aversion to the Negro's skin color and used his own belief in the monogenesist model of creation, as well as his anatomical expertise, to argue that "Negroes were genuine human beings" who lacked the "upper intermaxillary bone" that was essential for classification within the "simian species" (ibid., 161–62). But arguments over the proper placement of the Negro did not end here. For a full exploration of the currents of anthropology in continental Europe, see ibid., chap. 8.

27. Curtin, *Image of Africa*, 34–35.

28. Ibid., 58–63; Keith Thomas, *Man and the Natural World: A History of Modern Sensibility* (New York: Pantheon Books, 1983), 25. Thomas also suggests that "contemporary theology . . . provided the moral underpinnings for that ascendancy of man over nature which had by the early modern period [1500–1800] become the accepted goal of human endeavour" (Thomas, *Man and the Natural World*, 22). Curtin amplifies this judgment by asserting that this emphasis on the value of labor sprang from the Protestant ethic and Calvinism. By the late eighteenth century, labor was viewed as inherently good in itself. It was also basic for civilization as the British defined it (Curtin, *Image of Africa*, 62).

29. Curtin, *Image of Africa*, 63–65.

30. Ibid., 63–67.

31. Lyons, *To Wash an Aethiop White*, 20.

32. Curtin, *Image of Africa*, 65–67.

33. Lyons, *To Wash an Aethiop White*, 38–40; Poliakov, *Aryan Myth*, 132–33.

34. Curtin, *Image of Africa*, 66.

35. Ibid., 67–69.

36. Ibid., 30.

37. The British movement to abolish the slave trade picked up momentum from the 1760s to the final achievement of abolition in 1807. The 1760s and 1770s saw increasing agitation for the abolition of the

slave trade emerge from such organizations as the English Evangelical movement and the Methodist and Quaker churches. Some of the most important figures in the abolition movement included John Newton, founder of the Evangelical movement; John Wesley, founder of Methodism; Grenville Sharp, who argued that existing English law could be used to protect the rights of blacks; Thomas Clarkson, who challenged the profitability of the triangular trading system and proposed the efficacy of free trade; and William Wilberforce, who was the main spokesman for abolition in Parliament. By the 1790s and the French and Haitian revolutions, the popularity of abolition had moved beyond the humanitarian and religious community to include Britain's radical correspondence societies as well. Yet strong resistance from proslavery lobbies, principally the West India Committee, succeeded in delaying abolition of the slave trade until 1807. Michael Craton, James Walvin, and David Wright, *Slavery, Abolition and Emancipation: Black Slaves and the British Empire* (New York: Longmans, 1976), 231–35. For a brief but useful summary of the abolition movement, see ibid., 231–82.

38. Daniel R. Headrick, *The Tools of Empire: Technology and European Imperialism in the Nineteenth Century* (New York: Oxford University Press, 1981), 3.

39. Ibid., 27–28, 60–62.

40. Ibid., 58–70; Philip Curtin et al., *African History* (Boston: Little, Brown and Co., 1978), 446.

41. Robin Hallett, *Africa since 1875: A Modern History* (Ann Arbor: University of Michigan Press, 1974), 44. Also see Robert I. Rotberg, ed., *Africa and Its Explorers: Motives, Methods, and Impact* (Cambridge, Mass.: Harvard University Press, 1970).

42. Headrick, *Tools of Empire*, 83–100; Hallett, *Africa since 1875*, 45; Curtin, *African History*, 447.

43. Curtin, *African History*, 448.

44. Hallett, "Changing European Attitudes," 472.

45. Curtin, *Image of Africa*, v–vi.

46. Ibid., 33–34.

47. Ibid., 22–24, 34; Hallett, "Changing European Attitudes," 473–74; Poliakov, *Aryan Myth*, 136. Poliakov makes the further point that while the indigenous peoples of the New World were portrayed in such a way as to become "a positive pattern of the enigmatic 'natural man,' of that non-European who was to serve henceforth as a mirror to Europe," the convention of the noble savage used the "Black Man" to mirror the "hidden and negative side" of European character (Poliakov, *Aryan Myth*, 136).

48. Curtin, *Image of Africa*, 34; Hallett, "Changing European Attitudes," 472.

49. The first use of the term *race* as a classification of human groups according to such phenotypical traits as skin color, hair texture, etc., was undertaken by François Bernier in 1684. The eighteenth century

witnessed a lively debate in Europe and the United States among scientists, theologians, scholars, philosophers, and laymen regarding the status of Negroes more generally. It was within this context that the first systematic classification of human races, Johan Friedrich Blumenbach's *On the Natural Variety of Mankind*, was published in 1775. By the early nineteenth century the English used the term *race* to designate divisions within mankind which were also recognizable as social and biological units. In this respect, "race" could also be a synonym for "nationality" or even for peoples who spoke the same languages. Banton and Harwood, *The Race Concept*, 13, 24–25; Poliakov, *Aryan Myth*, 135; Curtin, *Image of Africa*, 36; Stephan, *Race in Science*, 9.

50. Curtin, *Image of Africa*, 36.

51. Ibid. Thomas's study of man and nature in early modern Britain argues that man's dominance of other species became the central theme of the "conjectural history" of the eighteenth-century European Enlightenment. The study of natural history, formalized during this period, was initiated by "practical and utilitarian" motives. "Botany began as an attempt to identify the 'uses and virtues' of plants, primarily for medicine, but also for cooking and manufacture. . . . Zoology was equally practical in its intentions. The Royal Society encouraged the study of animals with a view to determining 'whether they may be of any advantage to mankind, as food or physic; and whether those or any other uses of them can be further improved'" (Thomas, *Man and the Natural World*, 27–28).

52. Curtin, *Image of Africa*, 38–40. The idea that physical appearance indicated such traits as mental capacity is at least as old as classical Greek philosophy. Lyon, *To Wash an Aethiop White*, 21–22.

53. Curtin, *Image of Africa*, 231–32.

54. Ibid., 232–33, 365 (emphasis in original). The compatibility between separate creation and the classification of race by language was quickly seized by polygenesists. Differences in language became evidence of polygenesis.

55. This was particularly the case with mental capacity. The racial classifications of Linnaeus and Buffon's theory of racial degeneracy were combined with the anatomical investigations of the late eighteenth century to establish a scientific measure of mental capacity. The work of Blumenbach, Samuel Thomas Sommering, Peter Camper, John Hunter, Charles White, and others was important to the classification of the Negro race as mentally inferior to all others. This widely trumpeted conclusion was amplified and challenged in the nineteenth-century speculations of the Comte de Gobineau and Francis Galton on the one side and James Cowles Prichard and William Lawrence on the other. The debate also included scientific polygenesists such as Georges Pouchet and Carl Vogt and spokesmen for Aryan supremacy such as G. Vacher de Lapouge and Houston Chamberlain. John R. Barker, *Race* (New York: Oxford University Press, 1974), 24–30, 32–50; Lyon, *To*

Wash an Aethiop White, 34–35; Poliakov, *Aryan Myth*, 161–63, 165–69, 173; Jordan, *Black over White*, 497–506; Curtin, *Image of Africa*, 37–38; Stephan, *Race in Science*, chap. 1.

56. Stephan, *Race in Science*, 3. Curtin argues that the polygenesism of the earlier eighteenth century declined in British anthropology at the turn of the century because of theological opposition to rationalism and the general evangelical and revivalist tenor of the time. It reemerged, however, in the 1850s. Curtin, *Image of Africa*, 229, 368.

57. Curtin, *Image of Africa*, 229.

58. Stephan, *Race in Science*, 2–4.

59. Ibid., 2–4, 14–19, 29; Banton and Harwood, *Race Concept*, 26–30; Jordan, *White over Black*, 216–65; Ashley Montagu, *Man's Most Dangerous Myth: The Fallacy of Race*, 5th rev. ed. (New York: Oxford University Press, 1974), 3–38; Hallett, "Changing European Attitudes," 475–77.

60. Curtin, *Image of Africa*, 372–74.

61. Ibid., 375–76; Poliakov, *Aryan Myth*, 231.

62. Reginald Horsman, "Origins of Racial Anglo-Saxonism in Great Britain before 1850," *Journal of the History of Ideas* 37 (1976): 399–401; Curtin, *Image of Africa*, 380 (emphasis in original).

63. Poliakov, *Aryan Myth*, 231–32.

64. Quoted in ibid., 232.

65. Ibid.; Horsman, "Origins of Racial Anglo-Saxonism," 403–4.

66. Curtin, *Image of Africa*, 377.

67. Quoted in Poliakov, *Aryan Race*, 232; Curtin, *Image of Africa*, 378.

68. Curtin, *Image of Africa*, 379; Poliakov, *Aryan Myth*, 232–33; Stephan, *Race in Science*, 41–43. Knox was, obviously, a pre-Darwinian evolutionist. His theory proposed that evolution followed a single creation in which "all existing species were implicit, but not present. They later evolved according to a great original plan." Once they had been created, however, the slow pace of evolutionary change made human races more or less permanent. Curtin, *Image of Africa*, 369.

69. Curtin, *Image of Africa*, 379–80; Stephan, *Race in Science*, 42–43; Poliakov, *Aryan Myth*, 233. While Knox also argued that Anglo-Saxons were a "vigorous, acquisitive, aggressive race, natural democrats," he also pointed to their deficiencies. They did not produce "men of artistic genius or abstract thought. They were a race 'of all others the most outrageously boasting, arrogant, self-sufficient beyond endurance, holding in utter contempt all other races and all other men.' What is more, although no race perhaps exceeded them in a sense of justice and fair play, this was '*only to Saxons.*' They did not extend their love of justice to other races" (Knox's emphasis; Horsman, "Origins of Racial Anglo-Saxonism," 406).

70. Stephan, *Race in Science*, xiv, 5; Curtin, *Image of Africa*, 39, 42, 228.

71. Robert Ross, ed., *Racism and Colonialism: Essays in Ideology and Social Structure* (The Hague: Martinus Nijhoff Publishers, 1982), 1.

72. Stephan, *Race in Science*, xviii.

73. Ibid., xviii, 4–41; Hallett, "Changing European Attitudes," 477.

74. Stephan, *Race in Science*, 20–28, 44–46. Although phrenology was abandoned by serious scientists it continued to influence British popular thought. The emphasis within phrenology on the superiority of the Caucasian race was especially strong among the American contributors to the discipline. Morton's investigation of cranial capacity was inspired by the Swiss, Anders Retzius, whose craniometry had developed the cephalic index. Morton's measurement of cranial capacity in cubic inches inspired Josiah C. Nott and G. R. Gliddon to use the findings of phrenology and craniometry as the basis for their defense of the inherent inferiority of nonwhites. Innate inferiority justified the enslavement of blacks and the extermination of Indians. Such measures were deemed necessary because the structure of the brains of the non-Caucasian races limited their ability to improve by exposure to higher cultures. In Britain, meanwhile, phrenology became the basis of Anglo-Saxon ascendancy within the Caucasian race. Curtin, *Image of Africa*, 367–68, 372; Horsman, "Origins of Racial Anglo-Saxonism," 397–99.

75. Stephan, *Race in Science*, 45–47.

76. Ibid., 47.

77. Ibid., 48–49.

78. As early as 1810, Prichard had proposed a rudimentary evolutionary theory to explain color variation within mankind. Adam and Eve, he argued, were black. Their progeny became white as they became civilized. This equation of whiteness with civilization confirms the continuing importance of the content of Jordan's cluster by reiterating the use of skin color as an indication of worldly achievement. The significance of Prichard's notion of evolutionary change, however, fell largely upon deaf ears. Poliakov, *Aryan Myth*, 211.

79. The terminology of "survival of the fittest" was created by Darwin's contemporary, Alfred Russel Wallace, who suggested it as an alternative to Darwin's "natural selection." Greta Jones, *Social Darwinism and English Thought: The Interaction between Biological and Social Theory* (Atlantic Heights, N.J.: Humanities Press, 1980), 143. Two aspects of Darwin's evolutionary system are especially important here. Darwin viewed human races as "discrete mental and moral units based on biological differences." His argument that an "anatomical, mental and moral continuity" existed between man and animals gave greater weight to the use of physical and cultural differences as measures of the distance between the two. Existing racial gradations took on new importance as the races which were lowest on the scale of human achievement were regarded as closest to the animal antecedents of man. Savagery became a synonym for beastliness and, like mental and moral ability, had a hereditary biological cause. The so-called lower races formed the base of the evolutionary scale of mankind. Darwin's idea of progress was equally important, for his emphasis on competitive struggle for survival made adaptation the engine of progress and the key to the continuation of all organic life. Living creatures which failed

to develop the traits necessary for survival faced the inevitability of extinction. Those which adapted insured their own survival. And because such traits were hereditary, successful adaptation also insured progress. For Darwin, "racial extinction and progression" walked hand in hand. "Natural selection worked on individual and racial variations to select, during racial struggle, the most fit races and to raise them up in the scale of civilization." This process had brought the European to the pinnacle of civilization. It also assured the march of the higher races to ever-greater achievements. Stephan, *Race in Science*, 48–49, 53–59.

80. The difficulty in developing a precise definition for this multi-dimensional term is addressed in R. J. Halliday, "Social Darwinism: A Definition," *Victorian Studies* 14 (1971): 389–405.

81. Stephan, *Race in Science*, 80.

82. Hallett, "Changing European Attitudes," 479. The role of both groups is discussed in Curtin, *Image of Africa;* and Christine Bolt, *Victorian Attitudes to Race* (London: Routledge and Kegan Paul, 1971).

83. Hallett, "Changing European Attitudes," 479–80.

84. Jones, *Social Darwinism and English Thought*, 144–45. A somewhat different perspective on the relationship between the issues of race and class is provided in Lorimer, *Colour, Class and the Victorian*.

85. Leon Poliakov, "Racism from the Enlightenment to the Age of Imperialism," in Ross, *Racism and Colonialism*, 55.

86. Stephan, *Race in Science*, 45–47.

NOSTALGIA FOR THE GOOD OLD DAYS: IMAGES OF MEDICINE'S PAST AMONG FRENCH PHYSICIANS OF THE FIN DE SIÈCLE

MARTHA L. HILDRETH

In 1901 Dr. Aymard of Seine-et-Oise, France, stated, "It is a banal observation that in our modern society the medical profession has lost the influence, respect, and sympathy with which it was surrounded in the old days."[1] In 1897, Dr. Justin Bach of Toulouse bemoaned the passing of "the good old days when the doctor carried out his double mission of curing and calming suffering by creating a climate of trust and confidence, and a retiring doctor could proudly pass on a loyal clientele to his worthy son."[2] In 1907, Dr. Lucien Dore of Cadours, Haute-Garonne, observed, "The doctor in the old days [was] semidivine . . . how far we are from enjoying the respect our fathers had."[3]

In the late nineteenth and early twentieth centuries observations of this kind were commonplace among French private practitioners. These were the doctors who called themselves *petit practicien, médecin du village, médecin du quartier.*[4] They constituted the mass of general practitioners in France as distinguished from an elite within the profession holding posts in hospitals, medical faculties, and the bureaucracy.[5] In France, medical prestige accrued from such educational, governmental, and hospital positions. Ordinary private practitioners claimed that doctors attached to these institutions also attracted the most lucrative practices and dominated the upper-class clienteles while they struggled to make what they could call a decent living from small-town and urban neighborhood practices.[6]

Tensions between the medical elites and private practitioners involved ideological issues as well as jealousies over clienteles and prestige. By the 1880s and 1890s, few practitioners were unaware that they lived in an era in which the new science of bacteriology was beginning to transform medicine's understanding of disease. While many basic questions about the nature of specific microscopic pathogens and the phenomenon of contagion remained yet to be resolved, it was clear that bacteriology would have far-reaching consequences for the practice of medicine. For private practitioners of the era, the most critical question was not the matter of whether or not one believed in the existence of germs, but rather how bacteriology would affect the day-to-day practice of medicine and the relationship between physician and client. As Russell Maulitz has explained, the major source of tension within the profession was between the alternative visions of medical practice in the laboratory or at the bedside.[7] Physicians of the fin de siècle wondered if in the future their entire contact with patients would consist of only a brief contact to obtain samples of microorganisms and their main medical role would be to examine germs under a microscope. Maulitz points out that physicians did not divide neatly into two camps, one rushing into the laboratory and the other stubbornly guarding the cherished terrain of the bedside and examining room. Rather, these alternative images of bedside and laboratory provide a way of understanding the tensions created within medical practice with the beginning of the era of laboratory medicine.[8] Private practitioners worried about their social role and the nature of their profession in a future in which the scene of diagnosis and of medical action would so radically alter.

In France, these tensions were exacerbated by the long-standing divisions between the institutional and bureaucratic medical elites and the private practitioners. Laboratories were yet another institution connected with the medical faculties and the hospitals, territory normally off limits to French private practitioners. Thus, while members of the elite welcomed a new era in medicine at the fin de siècle, ordinary practitioners overwhelmingly expressed concern that they were in the process of losing their traditional role and status in society, that clienteles were becoming unreliable, and that relations with patients were becoming increasingly difficult. While deploring the unwelcome changes of the present, private practitioners looked with nostalgia back toward a past when the practice of medicine seemed to have been more stable and relations with clients more harmonious.

Idealizing the past and lamenting its loss is a general phenomenon. It is a way in which a culture expresses its present concerns and intentions. For example, historians often contrast the Enlightenment's worship of classical images with the Romantics' fascination with the gothic. With the Reagan presidency America has also witnessed a certain nostalgia for the 1950s which seems to reflect an unease with the social changes of the 1960s and 1970s. Historical nostalgia occurs also at other levels and centers often around specific concerns. Family historians have been continually frustrated in their efforts to destroy the deeply cherished myth that the family is currently in crisis because of certain historically determined changes in its structure. A growing body of research indicates that the large, extended, two-parent family has probably never been typical of any culture or time. Yet popular culture clings to this image, clearly as a way of expressing current concerns. One can make the same observation about the working woman. As much as historians, again, have shown that women have always worked, the popular culture insists that this is a new phenomenon.

In these last two examples, the views of present-day historians stand in conflict with the popular myths of their own societies. In addition to being at odds with the popular views of their own era, historians can also sometimes be contradicted by the very historical subjects they study. Generally, medical historians regard the 1880s and 1890s as the beginning of medicine's rise to the status of a modern science, with the development of a theory of disease which could be scientifically validated and which resulted in some new and notably effective treatments. Likewise, historians view the medical professions of the 1880s and 1890s as on the threshold of a golden era in social prestige and status. According to this view, the period before the late nineteenth century, while seeing some periodic progress, was generally a dark age. The picture that French physicians of the fin de siècle expressed about their own present and about the immediate past of their profession was quite different. For them, the golden era was in the past, and the present was one of crisis.

From the standpoint of the present day it seems ridiculous

that physicians of the fin de siècle would confidently state their opinion that the profession was in peril and that private practice was about to disappear. Historians tend to ignore such obstinate contradictions to what the historical record, compiled in retrospect, reveals. However, when such disaffirming opinions were so widely believed, as indeed they were among the practitioners of the era, it seems they merit some serious attention. An examination of these views reveals that developments in the medical profession, in how medical practice is carried out and in how disease and patients are viewed, involve much more than what historians usually concentrate on; that is, on the history of medical science. There is no direct relationship between science and practice, between scientific insight and changes in medical treatments and methods. Rather, this relationship is mediated by many other considerations which occupy the minds of the practitioners who must, after all, choose to reject or accept innovation. The images which physicians hold of their profession, of its past history and its current place in society, reveal these mediating concerns. The images that physicians of the fin de siècle held about themselves and their past reveal the considerations that would affect how the insights of bacteriology would be incorporated into medical practice. Further, in the process of building and discussing these images of the profession, physicians constructed a kind of discourse through which they created a consensus among themselves and within their society about the role of the physician in the future.

According to contemporary private practitioners, around 1900 the profession faced a severe crisis: a general decline of status and income which had begun in the 1870s.[9] Doctors spoke openly of the "impoverishment" of the profession.[10] They widely complained that they were faced with a smaller and smaller number of clients who, unlike their fathers' patients, quarreled over fees and hopped from one practitioner to another. The public, doctors felt, was becoming disrespectful and often preferred non-licensed practitioners to the physician. Dr. Auguste Cézilly of Paris observed that "the peasant does not call a doctor until after exhausting the arsenal of charlatanism.—He calls the doctor to find out what he is going to die of. He takes care to stipulate that the doctor should not return unless he is called for, and that call never comes, unless it is to attest to the cause of death."[11]

Doctors blamed overcrowding in the profession as the major cause of their loss of status. Overcrowding, they reasoned, led to intense competition. This in turn led to unethical practices such as overprescribing and conspiring with pharmacists to receive kickbacks. Doctors also complained that they could no longer assure a place in the profession for their sons, a time-honored practice. In the words of one doctor, "The son of the concièrge of the Faculty of Medicine is becoming a doctor, while the son of the doctor is reduced to role of concièrge at the Faculty because the medical profession will become overcrowded with the sons of concièrges." [12] Doctors blamed overcrowding on several factors. They argued that more medical students were attracted to the profession because of the positive publicity generated by public awareness of the new discoveries in bacteriology. In addition, thanks to educational reforms, more young Frenchmen were receiving the requisite secondary education. Finally, there was more space available for them in medical schools because after 1885 medical students were allowed to complete the first two years of their training at the departmental medical colleges. [13]

Low status was also blamed on increased stratification in the profession. Private practitioners pointed out, usually in scornful tones, that the elites of the profession were ones who of late had been receiving all the prestige from the positive publicity given to Pasteur's discoveries. Established practitioners complained that patients were flocking to the clinics at the great hospitals, faculties, and Pasteur Institutes but not to the private practitioners. Patients in the countryside deserted their old practitioners as soon as a young doctor appeared in town, assuming that the recent graduate had access to important new knowledge. [14] Physicians further maintained that the press, while it lauded Pasteur and his disciples, continued, in the tradition of Molière, to be highly critical of everyday medical practice. [15] Thus, private practitioners argued simultaneously that while new scientific discoveries had brought prestige to some in medicine they had brought woe to the private practitioner. Dr. Bach argued also that the elites of the profession, or the "Princes of Science," as he called them, helped to generate public hostility by their enormous fees. [16] Private practitioners also complained that they were scorned and ridiculed by medical students who

were encouraged by these same "Princes of Science" to denigrate traditional practitioners.[17] The result of all this, in the eyes
of general practitioners, was a public that was disrespectful, dis-
loyal, and increasingly penurious toward their doctors. In a dramatic essay, one doctor described the typical practitioner as
"ruined, his own deep aspirations, affections and honor attacked by an imbecilic public and blind justice, reduced to transforming himself into a salesman to survive."[18]

Against this gloomy picture of the present, doctors envisioned a more noble past when families gave faithful patronage
to one doctor whom they paid regularly and gladly. In these
good old days the rich always added a little to their bills to make
up for the free care the doctor gave to the poor; the bourgeoisie
paid quickly and fully and considered their doctor a member of
the family; workers and peasants paid what they could in goods
and services and with their recognition and veneration.

A variety of evidence suggests that the good old days were
not at all as doctors of the fin de siècle perceived them. Jacques
Léonard has meticulously studied the lives of three thousand
French doctors from 1805 to 1892, focusing particularly on social
and economic status. He reports generally that throughout much
of the century their professional lives were difficult. Few physicians made a living simply by practicing medicine. Competition
was intense; illegal healers were popular and seldom seriously
bothered by legal authorities. Although a small, mostly urban
elite enjoyed high status, most physicians did not. If they had
no property, they struggled to survive.[19] Léonard argues that
this began to change with the advent of the Third Republic
(1870). He points out that with the fame of the discoveries of
Pasteur and Koch growing in the 1880s and 1890s, physicians
became heros, Paris streets were named for them, and monu-
ments were erected to them.[20] The doctors' perception of overcrowding in the profession in the 1880s and 1890s is also not
borne out by available statistics. The ratio of licensed practitioners to population, counting both *docteurs* and *officiers de
santé*, reached its low point in 1847: 1 practitioner for every 1,959
as a national average.[21] After that time, the number of practitioners began to decline drastically and the population grew
slightly, so that in 1886 there was 1 practitioner for every 2,585.
Between 1886 and 1896, the ratio stayed relatively constant. By
1901 it had fallen slightly to 1 practitioner per 2,278.[22]

The statistical evidence for increased clienteles and Léonard's picture of social and economic improvement after 1870 are vividly contradicted by the opinions of physicians of the era. Physicians maintained that their status had been declining since 1870 and that a sort of golden age had existed before that time. Also, physicians did not perceive that the profession was statistically less crowded in the 1880s and 1890s than in the preceding four decades. On the contrary, the so-called crisis of overcrowding is a constant theme: no less a concern in the relatively uncrowded 1880s than in the slightly more crowded 1890s. But perhaps their alarms were not groundless. Enrollments at the faculties were increasing dramatically: 590 diplomas were issued in 1889, and 1,152 in 1901.[23] More importantly, national statistics do not provide a complete picture of the potential clientele available to an individual practitioner. Physicians were quite unevenly distributed in France. For example, in 1896, the Department of the Seine (Paris and surrounding suburbs) had a ratio of 1 practitioner per 1,035 population, while the Department of Haute-Loire had a much lower concentration of practitioners, 1 per 6,738.[24] Generally, physicians were concentrated in established urban areas, especially in the cities which had faculties or schools of medicine. They were also more heavily concentrated in the prosperous farming areas, where villages had relatively high populations. They were most absent in poor, sparsely populated rural areas and also in the new, rapidly growing industrial areas. To sum up, physicians concentrated among the bourgeoisie and among more prosperous peasants, and it may have been that various factors were causing this clientele to decline.

Social change and the rebellion of patients against certain therapies may have adversely affected clienteles. France faced several agricultural crises in the 1880s and 1890s which may have affected the ability of farmers to pay physicians. There was a general transfer of population to urban areas, and doctors were generally very reluctant to follow rural clients to working-class neighborhoods. In addition, city doctors were increasingly able to extend their practices into the countryside thanks to improved transportation. This created more competition for rural practitioners. Other factors may also have adversely affected available clienteles. Several authors have argued that potential clients of the physicians were frightened away by the techniques associated with the era of heroic medicine.[25] Even in the 1890s doctors still used techniques and medicines which were very unpleasant and quite harmful. Purging and bleeding continued to be widely utilized. Although bleeding was recognized increasingly as dangerous, it was recommended for a variety of conditions from digestive complaints to cerebral hemorrhage and intestinal lesions, and it was included on fee schedules as late as 1892.[26]

New technical developments and scientific discoveries did not necessarily result in reasonable or helpful treatments. Electricity was a popular all-purpose remedy, utilized for conditions including paralysis, anemia, pale skin, and chorea. Electric shock was used for gynecological and obstetrical problems, including direct application of electric current to the uterus in case of hemorrhage, hysteria, melancholy, fibroid tumors, lesions, and abdominal swelling.[27] Bacteriological theory initially produced some drastic and dangerous treatments. It became popular to "disinfect" internal organs, with the stomach and, again, the female reproduction organs as the main targets. Strong antiseptic solutions were employed, necessitating the conjunctive use of cocaine.[28] Clients seemed to have rebelled against such treatments. Sarah Stage has suggested that the great patent medicine boom of the late nineteenth century was due to a desire to self-medicate and avoid the harsh treatments prescribed by physicians.[29] French physicians observed a drastic increase in malpractice suits around 1900. It is not clear, however, what caused them.[30] They may have had their source in a rebellion against heroic medicine, or they may have been an expression of rising expectations on the part of the public at a time when medicine could not deliver commensurate therapy. Whatever the motivation, this evidence suggests that physicians were accurate in their observations that more clients were rebelling against their practitioners and seeking out nonlicensed healers.

It is difficult to know what to make of all this conflicting information about the rising or falling status of the profession. Jacques Léonard suggests that a better era for medical practice arrived after 1870, while physicians of the early Third Republic were equally convinced that the "good old days" existed before 1870 and that their own age was one of crisis characterized by malpractice litigation and public disrespect. Certainly it is true that society was at one and the same time issuing testimonials to physicians and suing them in court. Léonard's picture of a rising status for physicians with the advent of the Third Republic may be too optimistic or too generalized. It is based largely upon analysis of physicians' income and property. It is perhaps dangerous to equate too closely income and status. More seriously, Léonard's assessment of medicine's status after 1870 tends to ignore the deep divisions in the profession. It may have been true, as the private practitioners noted, that the fame of the bacteriological revolution only rubbed off on the elites of the profession.

On the other hand, some evidence suggests that the status of the ordinary private practitioners was not quite as bad as they often portrayed. After 1870, when France became a republic, physicians began to enjoy tremendous political influence. It is a commonplace notion among French historians that the village doctor replaced the village priest as community adviser and arbitrator of village affairs. These political doctors included not only the elites but many of the so-called average private practitioners as well. There were 108 physicians in the National Assembly (Chamber of Deputies and Senate) in 1896, and hundreds of village mayors were drawn from local private practitioners. Physicians often bragged about their political influence. It would seem, therefore, that far from suffering a decline in status, physicians were enjoying unprecedented social deference and political power in the Third Republic.[31]

This ambiguity in both the physicians' understanding of their position in society and in society's attitude toward practitioners reflects a time in which a complex of changes within society and within medical ideology was affecting the practice of medicine. What truly distinguished the period before 1870 from the period after was simply the stability of medical practice in the good old days. While demographic and economic factors were changing their clienteles, the development of bacteriological theory seemed about to overturn the whole nature of medical practice, creating a sense of crisis in the profession. As for the public, medical science was receiving a great deal of attention, and it was, at one and the same time, lauded for its advances and punished for its inability to produce any tangible therapeutic results based upon those advances. Private practitioners, then, were in a certain sense correct in their appraisal that the famous scientists had benefited while the many ordinary practitioners had suffered in the area of prestige. While, generally speaking, most private practitioners may have been better off after 1879, no doubt many individual physicians were driven from practice by changes in their clienteles and by increased competition. Others were discouraged and disheartened by the increased tendency of their clients to sue for malpractice.

In this era of tension and change, private practitioners were well disposed to believe in the existence of a golden era of medical practice. Martin Pernick has noted that American physicians in the mid-nineteenth century also believed in a golden era of medical practice existing sometime in the indeterminate past. He argues that no such golden age ever really existed.[32] He maintains that this American medical mythology developed during the Jacksonian era, when physicians were feeling the effects of rapid social change and a general attack on the idea of social deference.[33] French doctors of the late nineteenth century were also facing a challenge to their traditional concept of their profession, for the age of the bacteriological sciences brought with it much discussion of new roles for physicians. Public health reformers of the 1880s and 1890s advocated an image of the physician as public hygienist. Dr. F. Ranse, editor of the *Gazette Médical de Paris*, observed in 1889:

> Formerly the doctor's terrain did not go beyond the limits of the family. Today the role of the doctor has been extended considerably. The revolution in medicine from microbial doctrines has caused public health to take wings . . . The result is that for the first time the physician has a true social role to fill . . . The old "family doctor" has become the guardian of the public health, the "public doctor."[34]

Dr. Paul Brouardel, in many ways the leader of the public health movement and a pioneer in many medical areas, wrote several books addressing what he called the transformation of the medical profession at the end of the nineteenth century. Brouardel's essential message was that the physician was about to become the "hygienist" of society where his role would be one of prevention and surveillance.[35] A. J. Martin, secretary of the *Société de médecine publique*, envisioned a bureaucratic order of physicians under the National Public Health Committee (*Comité consultatif d'hygiène publique*, chaired by Brouardel), whose purpose would be to carry out the directives of a centralized antibacterial authority.[36] These issues were much discussed in medical, governmental, and public circles in the 1880s and 1890s.[37] The hygienists assumed that private physicians would be only too happy to comply with the program, becoming the advance troops of the new hygienic order. Private practitioners, however, rebelled against this image. They insisted that they would not become functionaries directed by a hygienic hierarchy of great scientists. To resist this hygienic vision, they organized a national professional movement to promote a contrary idea of medical practice.

Private practitioners organized the Union of Medical Syndicates in 1881. The union was the French medical profession's first association dedicated to the aggressive promotion of professional interests. It united a growing number of local physicians' organizations, called syndicates, into a national movement. By 1892, there were about two hundred syndicates in France, covering the entire nation; roughly half of these were affiliated with the national union. (Nonaffiliated syndicates were usually organized in regional federations and they generally followed the policies and programs of the Union of Medical Syndicates.)[38] The Union of Medical Syndicates was founded by a group of doctors who were private practitioners in the departments around Paris; they were led by Dr. Auguste Cézilly. Cézilly was inspired by the British Medical Association to form the first French organization which would address "the much neglected role of the doctor outside of medicine, narrowly defined."[39]

A number of newsletters and journals dealing with professional issues were published under the auspices of the Union of Medical Syndicates, local syndicates, and another organization, Le Concours médical, which operated in affiliation with the Union of Medical Syndicates. This professional medical press provided a forum for the expression of anxieties about the present, the nostalgic vision of the past, and ideas for the future. In their press, private practitioners openly opposed the vision of a comprehensive public health bureaucracy promoted by the National Public Health Committee. Union writers claimed that the prestigious National Public Health Committee, made up of some of Pasteur's most important disciples, was "incompetent" when it came to the actual practice of medicine.[40] The union movement frankly stated that its goal was to preserve private practice against this bureaucratic onslaught and the hygienist vision of the future of medical practice.

To counter the image of the physician-hygienist, the union engaged in an extensive program of image creation. Members carefully described their notion of the traditional practitioner of the good old days, focusing on his relationship with his clientele. They used a variety of means to promote the image. These means included a legislative lobbying program, articles in the union press to publicize the image among doctors, and the creation of codes of professional conduct.[41] The union's campaign of image building provides a clear picture of its goals. This campaign promoted certain notions implicit in the ideology of the good old days: a close confidential relationship between family and physician and reciprocal loyalty and respect. A basic part of all these ideals was the perception that certain aspects of professional relationships had to be shielded from the public. Competition, arrangements to share patients, buying and selling of clienteles, overlapping territories of practice, problems over the collections of fees—all needed to be managed by physician organizations but in such a way that the public was unaware of these activities. These efforts would control and manage the effects of the perceived overcrowding in the profession. They would make the profession respectable. They would also convince both the profession and the public of the importance of preserving the "traditional" model of practitioner.

Dr. Grellety of Vichy wrote the most thoroughgoing description of the union notion of the "good practitioner." In the eighties and nineties, his articles on this subject appeared regularly in Le Concours Médical, one of two union journals. Grellety characterized the private rural practitioners as

> isolated in the uttermost ends of the most obscure departments. . . . Let us follow them in their long peregrinations of night and day, along narrow tracks, in winter's wind and snow and summer's broiling sun. With a tender respect we must speak of their mission so often little appreciated and inadequately remunerated . . . Their life is certainly not made of the cloth of silk and gold . . . The world expects that doctors are men of mercy and charity, never allowed repose, never allowed fatigue; the hour of their repast is exactly when

one comes to fetch them or when the patient arrives to consult. The doctor can never be irritated at these interruptions,
often made for the most frivolous reasons . . . His zeal, love of
his patients must be constant, otherwise one says he is not
worthy of his mission which imposes upon him the most ar-
duous lowly tasks without hope of recognition.[42]

The popular literature of the late nineteenth and early twentieth centuries is full of the picture of the devoted village doctor.
But what is interesting here is that Grellety's audience was made
up of physicians. As he explained it, the union press was aimed
at the physicians of the villages and urban neighborhoods, exactly the groups he was describing with such idealism. The
union presented articles which articulated the fears of the private practitioners about issues such as overcrowding, lack of
opportunities in medicine for their sons, and the detrimental
effects of the bureaucratic medicine of the bacteriological revolution. But it also presented articles like Grellety's which sought to
create a sense of unity and professionalism around an image of
self-sacrifice and service to the family. These sorts of articles
were the cornerstone of a movement which sought to achieve
public recognition for the services of private practitioners as well
as to build a consensus among physicians about their social role.
Grellety's themes were echoed in the writings of other ideologues
of the union movement.

The role of the family doctor and the notion of "self-sacrifice"
were the major foci of the union's image. They were central to
the concept of the "good old days" when the "good practitioner" was primarily the family friend, adviser, and confidant.
As Brouardel described it, the family doctor's medical decisions
were intertwined with his duty to promote the family interests
and protect family sensibilities.[43] Union writers told their colleagues that they should create illusions to spare the patient and
family a dismal prognosis and to make themselves more welcome in the household. One writer advised:

never let yourself be carried away with the skepticism so
justly rejected by Pasteur. You can have a much happier influence on your patients. You can relieve even if you cannot
cure. You can give hope of inestimable importance which
gives the desperately ill [the] illusion of a future even if it will

not happen. You spare them the cruelty of seeing that the
road of life is blocked. Your visit will thus be heartily welcomed and salutary.[44]

Pasteur's name is invoked here in a revealing way. Before
Pasteur, the greatest breakthrough in medical thought was the
development of the clinical approach to medicine among Paris
hospital physicians of the early nineteenth century. The clinical
school focused on empiricism, pathology, and disease specificity.
Its approach to therapy was one of extreme skepticism. This
skepticism was widely rejected by physicians all over the Western world who continued with what they believed to be their
tried and true medications and treatments, including the heroic
medicine described above. Bacteriology marked the next great
breakthrough, but like the clinical insights it resulted immediately in few useful medical therapies.[45] Yet it promised much,
and physicians did not hesitate to invoke Pasteur as their cham-
pion against the skepticism in medical therapy expressed by the
medical elites while admitting in the next breath that they still,
perhaps, could not cure. Clearly what was most important was
the positive image of Pasteur for medicine's prestige. The most
obvious application of bacteriological theory was in public health
activity to assure clean water, food safety, and sanitation. It was
precisely such bureaucratic and state activity that struck fear in
the hearts of private practitioners and caused them to promote
alternative images of medicine to which they then, ironically, associated Pasteur's name.

Private practitioners used the idea of the family doctor as a
bulwark against the onslaught of public health programs. The
public health establishment planned to create a system of reporting and tabulating cause of death and cases of contagious disease throughout the nation. These statistics would be the basis
of the public health authority and action. The program was
modeled on the *Bureau de statistique de la ville de Paris,* founded in
the 1860s by Jacques Bertillon, and upon the model of public
health organizations in Britain and New York City. The idea of
systematic statistic gathering was supported by the *Société de
médecine publique et d'hygiène professionnelle,* the *Association gé-
nérale des médecins de France,* the National Public Health Committee, the Academy of Medicine, and all of France's leading
hygienists.[46] Private practitioners in the union, however, were

adamantly opposed to these plans. This program, they argued, was a direct challenge to their vision of their relationships with the family. It was a violation of the code of professional secrecy.[47] As Dr. G. Drouineau wrote in Le Concours, "the Doctor possesses the confidences of all the family, the [knowledge of] the most appalling moral miseries, the most shocking facts." These would be thrown to the wind, Drouineau argued, if the doctor had to reveal his professional secrets.[48] One union doctor wrote, "We are repelled by the idea of becoming the family's informer."[49]

Public authorities insisted in vain to private practitioners that cases of contagious disease must be gathered as a basis of effective epidemic control. Union writers maintained that there were no contagious diseases that families would willingly disclose publicly. They cited examples such as the following. A mother would not want it known that her daughter had had typhoid, for it was widely believed that this disease, if suffered in youth, brought about loss of hair and teeth in middle age. Thus, the daughter's marriage chances would suffer.[50] The union writers advocated putting the responsibility for declaration on the head of the household. In this way the doctor's privileged relationship with the family would not be tarnished.

The declaration of cases of tuberculosis was a major concern to private practitioners. In 1899, hygienist Dr. Jacques Joseph Grancher launched a campaign against this all too common scourge with the founding of the Commission permanent contre la tuberculose. The union opposed the plans of the antituberculosis commission to identify cases of the disease geographically in order to establish what sort of housing conditions fostered it. The union complained that if faced with the impending publicity, patients would not visit their physician. They would go instead to a pharmacist to receive medication, as the latter was not obliged legally to declare their case.[51] Dr. Lemaire of the Lille physicians' syndicate argued against informing the tuberculosis patient himself if that patient was a child or youth; "after all why spoil the ten to fifteen good years left to the patient." Lemaire also claimed that public knowledge of tuberculosis could make a family pariahs in the community.[52]

Union leaders argued that the obligation of declaration presented a moral and economic dilemma for doctors. Doctors feared losing clients who were anxious to guard family skeletons.

Small businessmen feared that public knowledge of disease in the shop would keep customers away. Union critics argued that scrupulous proprietors and scrupulous doctors would be discriminated against; the public would patronize shopkeepers who hid their contagion and shopkeepers would patronize doctors who misdiagnosed and otherwise covered up dangerous diseases.[53] In Cézilly's words, a physician would be caught between "his personal interest and his duty."[54] In spite of the opposition of private practitioners, two laws, the 1892 Law on the Practice of Medicine (*Loi Chevandier*) and the 1902 Public Health Law, required the declaration of cause of death and cases of contagious disease by physicians. Doctors were subject to a fine if they did not comply. However, this provision was rarely enforced and physicians regularly violated the law.[55] Union writers advised their colleagues to circumvent the regulations by using vague terms such as "intestinal troubles" when reporting cause of death to cover up disease which might embarrass the family.[56]

A special campaign to promote the model of the family doctor was organized for the industrial working class. The image of family doctor was based on the relationship of the physician to his patients among the bourgeoisie and petite bourgeoisie. Much of the lower classes, urban and rural, did not utilize private practitioners.[57] Urban lower classes were cared for in city hospitals and clinics, *bureaux de bienfaisance*, or increasingly by physicians employed by mutual aid (insurance) societies.[58] In the 1890s, two laws, the 1893 Medical Assistance Law and the 1898 Work Accident Law, helped to underwrite medical care for some members of the lower classes. In response, the union undertook several measures to ensure that the monies allocated under these programs would be spent for private care rather than hospital care or care under mutual aid societies. Part of these efforts involved the spreading of the image of the family doctor among the working classes. In the words of Dr. Chevandier, the union's spokesperson in the Chamber of Deputies, it was a point of "democracy" that all people in France should have the same sort of medical care.[59] The union emphasized to workers that they now had the ability to demand the same medical care enjoyed by the bourgeoisie.

The union's campaign to convince workers to use private practitioners was run by Dr. Diverneresse. Diverneresse organized a program of lectures and pamphleteering to advise workers of their "rights" under the new legislation. Many of these lectures were given at the *universités populaires*, night schools sponsored by the *bourse de travail*, working-class associations. The Work Accident Law required employers to pay the medical bills of workers injured on the job. Employers generally sought to fulfill this obligation by organizing mutual aid societies which in turn employed physicians. Some employers were also in the habit of sending injured workers to hospitals for treatment that was often free, or at least low cost. Diverneresse told workers that under the law they had the right to be cared for by the doctor of their choice. He warned the workers that their employers would try and force them to go to a "company doctor." He told them not to let the company physicians so much as fill out the paperwork pertaining to their accident but to have this done by their private physician. He argued that most injuries could be taken care of at home, admitting, however, that patients suffering from compound fractures and injuries to the spine probably should be hospitalized.[60]

Diverneresse painted a grim picture of the hospitals in contrast to his glowing portrait of the private practitioner. He warned that workers would be treated "like an indigent" at the hospital and advised that "medium range" injuries such as simple fractures, burns, and cuts requiring sutures were "exactly the sort of injuries that the hospitals like to have their interns practice on."[61] In contrast, Diverneresse described the kindly *médecin du quartier*, who, he said, "would treat the workers as a friend." It was always better for the patient, he said, to be cared for at home, surrounded by family, friends, and the neighborhood doctor, who would have his best health and "moral" interests at heart, rather than by the "mercenary nursing" staffs of hospitals. If surgery was necessary, Diverneresse told the workers, they were probably better off having it done at their homes. He assured them that antiseptic conditions could be created there and a special surgical room was not necessary. Furthermore, they were better off trusting the surgical skills of their neighborhood doctor or one of his colleagues rather than the "great scientists" and interns of the hospital, who, he implied, were more interested in experimentation than in care.[62]

In promoting the image of the family doctor, physicians reflected a sensibility of the family's need to be protected from the state. Family historians have commented upon the separation of the private and public in the course of the nineteenth century and upon the family's withdrawal from the public, or, in Christopher Lasch's words, its becoming a "haven in a heartless world." [63] This analysis focuses upon the bourgeois family. In their emphasis on protecting family secrets, upon resisting the intrusive public health bureaucracy, and upon illusion and delusion in reporting illnesses and cause of death, private practitioners clearly supported this notion of the family as a haven from a world which was becoming at least overly snoopy if not altogether heartless. What is notable about the program run by Diverneresse and other similar activities on the part of the union is that private practitioners made a concerted effort to promote this image of the family as private among the lower classes. Thus they told the working-class and peasant families what secrets they should hide, and in fact in the process defined for those families what constituted "unmentionable" information. The working class was told that they, like the bourgeoisie, should protect their secrets and their bodies from the public institutions of the hospital, clinic, mutual aid societies, and public health establishment. Based upon the nostalgic, idealized picture of medicine's past, the private practitioners reconstituted themselves as coconspirators in the family's resistance to the intrusive state.

The nostalgic image of medical practice also became, for the profession itself, a source of unity and resistance. It is not at all clear that the role whose loss physicians lamented had ever been a reality for more than a few practitioners before 1870. The image of respected and even venerated family confidant and adviser with high status and stable clientele must have been a highly idealized vision of the past. But whatever its reality, this image was important for its power as a cultural myth. The "family doctor" of the past did not become the "public doctor" of the future. The leading voices among the private practitioners were able to utilize the powerful and persuasive image of the family doctor to promote an alternative to the hygienic, public model of the physician-bureaucrat or physician-functionary. The image of the family doctor not only unified the profession but ultimately persuaded the culture at large to accept this idea of medical practice in the name of preserving the physician's historical role. This image of the past helped to shore up and expand private practice as the basis for medical care when other models, derived from the implications of new scientific concepts, threatened to destroy it.

NOTES

1. Dr. Aymard, "Les Premiers Effets de l'encombrement," *Bulletin des Syndicates Médicaux de France* (May 1901): 1038 (hereafter cited as *Bul. des Syn. Méd. de Fr.*).
2. Dr. Justin Bach, "Clients réfractoires," *La Fédération Médicale* (February 1897): 5.
3. Dr. Lucien Dore (founder of the physician's syndicate of Haute-Garonne), "Le Role social du médecin dans l'état," *La Fédération Médicale* (June 1907): 7–10.
4. Dr. J. Noir, "Auguste Cézilly," *Bulletin Officiel des Syndicates Médicaux de France*, November 5, 1902, 446; Auguste Cézilly, "A nos adherents," *Le Concours Médical*, July 5, 1879; idem, "Aux members du concours," *Le Concours Médical*, January 7, 1888, 1; Dr. Gassot, "Historique de la Société du concours médical," *Bul. des Syn. Méd. de Fr.* 37 (1889): 322–23.
5. For a more detailed discussion of the differences between the medical elites and the private practitioners of the union movement, see Martha L. Hildreth, "Medical Rivalries and Medical Politics in France: The Physicians' Union Movement and the Medical Assistance Law of 1893," *Journal of the History of Medicine and Allied Sciences* 42 (January 1987): 5–29.
6. I use the terms *clientele* and *clients* to refer to those individuals and families who were regularly seen by a particular physician. The term *patient* implies one who is sick; physicians frequently interacted with and influenced clients who were not necessarily ill.
7. Russell C. Maulitz, "Physician versus Bacteriologist, the Ideology of Science in Clinical Medicine," in Morris J. Vogel and Charles E. Rosenberg, eds., *The Therapeutic Revolution, Essays in the Social History of American Medicine* (Philadelphia: University of Pennsylvania Press, 1979), 91–107.
8. Ibid.
9. Bach, "Clients réfractoires."
10. Gassot, "Historique."
11. Dr. Auguste Cézilly, "Un médecin par commune!," *Le Concours Médical*, June 18, 1887, 292–94.
12. Dr. "X," "L'Encombrement médical," *Bul, des. Syn. Méd. de Fr.* (February 1900): 887–88.
13. Aymard, "Les Premiers Effets."

14. Dr. A. Coriveau, "Probité professionnelle," *Le Concours Médical,* January 25, 1902, 49.

15. "H.J.," "La Paille et la poutre entre la presse et les médecins," *Le Concours Médical,* March 15, 1902, 161.

16. Bach, "Clients réfractoires."

17. Dr. Grasset, *Bulletin des Sociétés Médicaux d'Arrondissement,* September 20, 1900, 547–48.

18. Dr. P. Vigne, "Lettre au corps médical français," *La Fédération Médicale* (March 1906): 15.

19. Jacques Léonard, "Les Médecins de l'ouest au XIXème siècle," dissertation for the *doctorat d'État,* University of Paris, 1975 (Paris: Lille-Champion, 1978).

20. Jacques Léonard, "Le Corps médical au début de la IIIème République, ou l'heureux dénouement d'un malaise professionnel," in *Médecine et philosophie à la fin du XIX siècle,* under the direction of J. and J. L. Poirier, l'Institut de recherche universitaire d'histoire de la connaissance des idées et des mentalités (n.p., 1983?); idem, "La Médicalisation de l'état, l'exemple des premières décennies de la IIIème république," *Annales de Bretagne* 86 (1979): 313–20.

21. The *officiers de santé* were a kind of second-class doctor. They were created in 1805 to replace the surgeons, whose profession was officially abolished. The *officiers* were educated for two years at departmental medical schools and then served a two-year apprenticeship with a *docteur en médecine* and were examined by departmental medical juries. Their practice was slightly restricted in that they were forbidden to perform some major operations. In reality, the public recognized little difference between *officiers* and *docteurs;* both were called *médecin* and both carried on the same sort of medical practice. For a discussion of the roles of the *officiers de santé,* see George Sussman, "The Glut of Doctors in Mid-Nineteenth-Century France," *Comparative Studies in Society and History* 19 (July 1977): 287–303.

22. *Annuaire statistique de la France* (1930): 11–12; *Recueil des travaux du Comité consultatif d'hygiène publique de la France* 16 (1886): 124–25 (hereafter cited as *RTCCHP*).

23. Paul Brouardel, *La Profession médicale au commencement du XXème siècle* (Paris: J. B. Baillière, 1893), 39.

24. Dr. Maurice Lesieur, *Répértoire officiel de la médecine et de la pharmacie française* (1896).

25. Léonard, "Les Médecins de l'ouest"; Sara Stage, *Female Complaints: Lydia Pinkham and the Business of Women's Medicine* (New York: W. W. Norton, 1979), chap. 1; Eliot Freidson, *Professional Dominance: The Social Structure of Medical Care* (New York: Atherton Press, 1970), 20–21.

26. "Traitement de l'hemmoragie cérébrale," *Le Concours Médical,* August 9, 1879, 71; the recommended treatment was bleeding from a vein in the arm 180 to 200 grams of blood; *Le Concours Médical,* February 27, 1892, 105; *Le Courrier Médical,* December 2, 1892, 419.

27. *Gazette Hebd. des Sciences Médicales de Bordeaux,* May 31, 1891, 353;

Gazette Médical de Liège, August 17, 1893, 547; *Le Concours Médical,* November 5, 1892, 536.

28. "Les Laveurs vagino-uterins, dit Vide-Bouteilles," *Gazette Hebd. des Sciences Médicales de Boreaux,* March 6, 1892; *Le Courrier Médical,* January 24, 1891, 40.

29. Stage, *Female Complaints.*

30. H. J., "Constatations encourageantes," *Le Concours Médical,* March 19, 1902, 193–94.

31. Jacques, Léonard, *Médecine entre les savoirs et les pouvoirs* (Paris: Aubire Montaigne, 1981), 281–82.

32. Martin Pernick, "Medical Professionalism," in *Encyclopedia of Bioethics* (New York: Macmillan, 1978), 1030.

33. Ibid.

34. Dr. F. Ranse, "Le Médecin et la médecine de nos jours," *Gazette Médical de Paris,* ser. 7, April 6, 1889, 165.

35. Brouardel, *La Profession médicale,* 226.

36. A. J. Martin, *Essai d'organisation de la médecine publique en France* (Paris: Masson, 1880).

37. Martha L. Hildreth, *Doctors, Bureaucrats and Public Health in France, 1888–1902* (New York: Garland Press, 1987), 108–63.

38. "Les Syndicates médicaux," *Gazette Médicale de Liège,* October 27, 1892; Gassot, "Historique," 322–32; see also Hildreth, *Physicians, Bureaucrats and Public Health,* 36–107.

39. Aymard, "Les Premiers effets," 1039; Cézilly, "A nos adherents," 2.

40. *Le Concours Médical,* July 30, 1892), 369.

41. Hildreth, *Doctors, Bureaucrats and Public Health,* 67–71.

42. Dr. Grellety, "Apologie du médecin de campagne," *Le Concours Médical,* June 6, 1891, 266–68.

43. Brouardel, *La Profession médicale.*

44. Louis Renon, "Les Rapports professionnels du médecin avec ses malades et avec ses confrères," *La Fédération Médicale* (September 1905): 9–16.

45. Thomas McKeown, "Food, Infection, and History," in Robert I. Rotberg and Theodore K. Rabb, eds., *Hunger and History* (Cambridge: Cambridge University Press, 1983), 29–50.

46. *RTCCHP* 18 (1888): 410–26; 20 (1890): 51; *Lyon Médical,* August 2, 1891, 479.

47. The law on professional secrecy was part of the civil code.

48. Dr. G. Drouineau, *Le Concours Médical,* August 23, 1879, 280.

49. Anonymous, *Le Concours Médical,* February 19, 1901, 57–58.

50. Dr. Alphonse Jaumes, *La Déclaration des causes de décès et des maladies épidémiques* (Montpellier: Boohm, 1889), 14–15.

51. Grancher was one of France's most important hygienists. He was a member of the National Public Health Committee, the Academy of Medicine, the Faculty of Medicine of Paris, and the Pasteur Institute of Paris. Other important hygienists on the antituberculosis committee

were A. J. Martin and Paul Brouardel. See Yvonne Knibiehler, "La Lutte antituberculeuse," *Annales de Bretagne* 86, no. 2:321–22; *Recueil des travaux du Comité permanent contre la tuberculeuse* 1 (1903–5); Dr. G. Lemaire, "La Loi sur la protection de la santé publique," *Bulletin des Syndicates Médicaux du Nord et du Pas-de-Calais* 17 (May 1902): 258–65.

52. Dr. G. Lemaire, "Rapport sur la déclaration et la désinfection obligatoire," *Bulletin des Syndicates Médicaux du Nord et du Pas-de-Calais* 4 (February 1902): 213–22.

53. Ibid.

54. Cézilly, *Le Concours Médical,* July 20, 1892), 369.

55. Fernand Widal, "Rapport général à M. le Président du Conseil Ministre de l'Intérieur, sur les épidémies en 1906," *Bulletin de l'Academie de Médecine,* June 16, 1908; *La France Médical,* March 25, 1893; *Gazette Médical de Paris,* June 20, 1893, 293.

56. Dr. Mauvais-Chadigne (of Flèche, Sarthe), "Le Secret médical et les administrations," *Le Concours Médical,* June 13, 1887, 283.

57. Jacques Léonard, "Les Guérisseurs en France au XIXème siècle," *Revue d'Histoire Moderne et Contemporaine* 27 (July–September 1980): 501–16.

58. Martha L. Hildreth, "Les Syndicates médicaux et la mutualité: Le Début du conflit au commencement du vingtième siècle et l'exemple du syndicat Toulousain," trans. Guy Wagener and Miriella Mellara, *La Revue de L'Economie Sociale* 10 (January 1987): 7–21.

59. Hildreth, "Medical Rivalries and Medical Politics," 27–29.

60. Dr. Diverneresse, "Addresse à l'Université populaire Voltaire, à l'Université populaire la fraternelle, et à l'Université populaire de Montreuil: Les Droits des blesses du travaille depuis la loi de 1898," *Bulletin Officiel de l'Union des Syndicates Médicaux de France,* June 20, 1902, 231–40; July 5, 1902, 241–49; July 20, 1902, 269–74; October 19, 1902, 366–67.

61. Ibid.

62. Dr. Diverneresse, "Pour les médecins des campagnes," *Bulletin Officiel de l'Union des Syndicates Médicaux de France,* October 5, 1902, 361.

63. Christopher Lasch, *Haven in a Heartless World: The Family Besieged* (New York: Basic Books, 1977).

ALCHEMY, THE TECHNICAL OPTION, AND THE NUCLEAR AGE

BRUCE T. MORAN

When alchemists in the sixteenth and seventeenth centuries sought to justify their projects of transmuting base metals into gold and silver, they often turned to Scripture. The Old Testament was a fruitful source for passages that could be given alchemical meaning. Solomon's wisdom, many thought, included alchemical understanding, by reason of which he had attained his fabulous wealth and maintained his political predominance. In the book of Exodus, Moses' response upon finding his followers worshiping a golden calf assumed the status of a *locus classicus* among biblical references legitimating alchemical procedures:

> As he approached the camp and saw the calf and the groups dancing, Moses' anger blazed. He threw down the tablets he was holding and broke them at the foot of the mountain. He seized the calf they had made and burned it, grinding it into powder which he scattered on the water; and he made the sons of Israel drink it. (Exodus 32: 19–21)

From the alchemical perspective, Moses had prepared an *aurum potabile*, a drinkable gold, which he used to promote the health and well-being of his people and to bring them back to the proper worship of Yahweh. In both instances, Moses and Solomon could be shown to have employed their alchemical knowledge as a means of sustaining religious and political authority. Thus, not only alchemy itself but its use as a political-religious tool received scriptural legitimation. To ruling princes in Europe who patronized alchemy for their own political purposes this latter justification was especially appealing. And it is this view of al-chemy as a political expedient, considered in both its traditional and its more modern, scientific forms, that defines the general parameters of the study that follows.

Even a brief survey of alchemical patronage reveals the close connection between alchemical interest and political ambition. By relying, at least in part, upon alchemical intervention, many princes and kings in the later Middle Ages and Renaissance chose to depend upon a new sort of technical option in con-fronting threats to their political power. The consequences of that commitment were often tragic. Despite the claims of al-chemical enthusiasts, the discovery of a philosophers' stone that would turn base metals into gold remained an illusion. But what if it had been real? The question may be ahistorical, but it is not absurd. Indeed, owing to discoveries in nuclear physics at the beginning of the twentieth century, the type of power sought for in vain by alchemical patrons has become, in our own world, a scientific reality. Ernest Rutherford, one of the founders of nu-clear physics, described it in 1937 as the "newer alchemy." I want to suggest that such power is no less a narcotic and its uses sustained by similar kinds of illusions as were present in tradi-tional forms of alchemical patronage. We might, in fact, refer to the type of elemental transmutation made possible by radio-active decay and particle bombardments as a modern equivalent of the alchemist's philosophers' stone.

It is important not to be misunderstood at this point. By link-ing the uses and illusions of nuclear power to alchemy, I am not attempting, in any literal way, to tie modern science and tech-nology to the world of medieval and Renaissance alchemists. Nor am I arguing that the same political and social ambitions have been necessarily supported by appeal to alchemical and nuclear power, respectively. Nevertheless, like the earlier sort, the "newer alchemy" has been invoked frequently as a technical option in safeguarding the authority of the state, as a way of keeping social and political chaos at bay, and as a means of pro-tecting the security of both individual and popular interests. The question is, however, whether modern alchemy of the nu-clear sort is any more useful as a political expedient than its chimerical predecessor. Viewed solely in terms of a technical option in solving political problems, there is a sense in which commitment to the modern alchemy of nuclear deterrence may amount to worshiping a false idol, another golden calf. To find the illusion in the technical option of both older and "newer" alchemies, we must begin with an examination of the political purposes served by alchemical patronage at times quite remote from our own. Once reconstructed, that distant vision of alchemical illusion can help us cut through to the realities of our own nuclear predicament.

During the course of the thirteenth and fourteenth centuries, alchemists acquired a social identity apart from other professions and artisan activities.[1] What most prompted the recognition of alchemy as an independent occupation was the legitimacy that alchemists obtained by being increasingly called upon to serve at princely and royal courts. What first accounted for the need of alchemical skills at court was a crisis of political economy.

In the period around 1300 a general lack of precious metals in Europe obstructed the expansionist plans of many territorial rulers and made their own claims to regional authority more vulnerable. To stretch their resources, some courts turned to the practical skills of assayers and alchemists, who, by alloying gold and silver with other metals, provided the court with a means of producing more coins from the usually modest amount of gold and silver at its disposal. The budgetary advantages of such processes were obvious. In England, Edward III (1312–1377) ordered that two alchemists, John le Rous and William of Dalby, be brought to him with or without their consent. The king valued their technical skills as politically significant since, he reasoned, "per artem illam nobis et regno nostro per factionem huiusmodi metelli multum prodesse poterunt" (by that [alchemical] art, and through the making of metals of this sort, they will be able to do much good for us and for our kingdom).[2]

While the growth of secular monarchies was, at least in some cases, facilitated by the debasement and counterfeiting of coins, the Church, which struggled against the rising tide of secular strength, found it necessary to condemn alchemy outright and labeled alchemists as nothing more than simple forgers. Two views of alchemical activity tied to political ambitions had, by the early fourteenth century, quite clearly emerged. To territorial rulers, whose revenues from personal demesne lands were generally unequal to their political ambitions, alchemy offered a technical solution to generating wealth and extending political power. For this group alchemy was wreathed with abundant virtue. From the point of view of the Church, however, whose much larger landed holdings provided extensive wealth already and at whose expense territorial rulers sought to increase their own authority, alchemy and alchemists were bad. Thus, in the *Romance of the Rose*, Jean de Meun, who supported the secular rights of princes, valued alchemy as a true science.[3] Shortly thereafter, however, a papal bull, *Spondent quas non exhibent* (They promise that which they do not produce), which was proclaimed by Pope John XXII in 1317, condemned alchemists for practicing deceit and for counterfeiting coins.[4] From the pope's viewpoint, alchemists were to be dealt with as criminals and their property confiscated. Where clerics were involved in alchemy they were to be stripped of their benefices and removed from whatever offices they held. Regardless of which perception was preferred, alchemy was treated as "state of the art" technology. In most cases, where it benefited the ambitions of state, it gained respect and was encouraged. Where it threatened the authority and stability of the existing political and social order, it was condemned.

As a technical option, alchemy attained its most vigorous patronage at times of intense competition between rival political factions. In the fourteenth and fifteenth centuries, the Hundred Years War provided just such an environment. To help him in his campaigns against the French, the English king Henry VI (1421–1471) sought alchemical assistance from the English clergy. Since he believed that priests transubstantiated bread and wine into the body and blood of Christ as part of the daily Mass, Henry considered that they, above all others, could offer the technical assistance he required in transmuting base metals into gold. The clergy, however, were outraged by the comparison and refused to cooperate.[5] Henry had better luck attracting lay alchemists and provided a large number of them with royal privileges. At the same time, however, he made alchemical activity outside the aegis of the state illegal and appointed a three-man commission to prosecute anyone found practicing alchemy without a royal charter.[6]

Although Henry never discounted the possibility of transmuting metals, he was most interested in the more immediate rewards that alchemists could supply by means of counterfeiting royal coins. To meet political challenges from the French and to deal with similar challenges arising within England as a result of the rivalry between the houses of York and Lancaster, royal decrees emphasized the need to increase the number of gold and silver coins in the king's treasury so as to satisfy the creditors of the crown.[7] Alchemy became economic policy for Henry, who appointed royal commissions, made up of high-ranking ecclesiastical figures, royal officials, and "men learned in natural philosophy," who were to report to him concerning whatever they learned about the alchemical art.

Both Henry and his successor, Henry VII (1457–1509), who employed at one time an entire company of soldiers to assist in alchemical projects, made use of alchemy as a technical option in solving economic woes. The results of their patronage were twofold. On the one hand, the debasing of coins led to a rapid deterioration in the worth of English currency. The problem became so severe that, later in the century, the Scottish Parliament had to forbid all commerce with England. On the other, the respect given to alchemists at the English court occasioned a sudden increase in popular attention to alchemy and alchemical practitioners.[8] The first alchemical works written in English verse appeared in the second half of the fifteenth century. Ripley's *Book of the Twelve Gates* and Thomas Norton's *Ordinall* were both composed at this time. Their works were not aimed at the court but at a much wider audience. Having gained legitimacy through the court, however, alchemy could be offered as something akin to household science. Thus the works of both authors appeared with the expressed purpose of instructing the multitude, and even the unlearned, in the alchemical art.

While alchemy was being treated as a technical solution to improving the state budget in England, its symbolic value was not lost in the support of political ambitions in northern Europe. One of the most interesting German alchemical treatises from the early fifteenth century is a work known as *Das Buch der heiligen Dreifaltigkeit* (The book of the sacred trinity), whose author is thought to have been a Franciscan monk named Ulmannus. To historians of alchemy *Das Buch der heiligen Dreifaltigkeit* has always been intriguing for the parallel it constructs between the

suffering, death, and resurrection of Christ and the process of
creating the philosophers' stone (the *lapis philosophorum*).[9] What
has come to be called the *Lapis*-Christ parallel emphasized a
strong spiritual dimension in the work of the alchemist.[10] Yet it is
also clear that Ulmannus intended his treatise to serve a political
purpose, singling out, in his dedication, the Elector Friedrich I
of Brandenburg (r. 1415–1440) as the one whom God had chosen
to understand and make use of all the wondrous alchemical
medicines which had been created through Christ's holy suffering. The recipes in the book were, then, part of a divine revelation by means of which, it was hoped, Friedrich would become
emperor and through which he would be able to reestablish a
pure Christian religion.[11]

The significance of this dedication can only be understood as
it fits into the confused social and political climate within the
Holy Roman Empire near the end of the medieval period. There,
the violence and insecurity that had affected the whole of western Europe throughout the fourteenth century had become especially severe. The German states lacked a really effective central government that could be called upon to curb the constant
bickering among German princes and to settle economic and social disputes. The turmoil inspired thoughts of political and economic reform, with many seeking a revival of imperial power as
a way to check social, economic, and political disintegration.
Some reflected nostalgically on the *gute alte Zeiten*, the "good old
days," when imperial authority had been able to resolve conflicts between princes and their estates and to protect weaker
states from the aggression of neighboring princes. The theme of
the revival of imperial power became especially strong at the
Council of Constance (1414–1418), which elected a new emperor, Sigismund (r. 1410–1437). Later, in the 1430s, there appeared the *Reformation of the Emperor Sigismund*, a pamphlet
which emphasized imperial rights as a means of easing social
discontent. At the same time, the German cardinal Nicholas of
Cusa painted a grim future for northern Europe if a way was not
found to augment imperial authority. In his *Concordia Catholica*
(1433) Cusa wrote that "a mortal disease has befallen the German *Reich*, if it is not speedily treated, death will inexorably
ensue. Men will seek for the realm of Germany and will not find
it; and in time strangers will seize our habitations and divide
them among themselves."[12]

Although much hope for political reform fell to the Emperor Sigismund, there arose also a popular myth that the older power of the empire, which had seen its most glorious days during the reigns of Friedrich Barbarossa (1123?–1190) and Friedrich II (the *Stupor Mundi*; 1194–1250), would be regained with the return of the "just Emperor Friedrich." At least for some, Friedrich of Brandenburg, who traced descent through his mother to the house of Hohenstaufen (the imperial family of the earlier Friedrichs), was the "just emperor" who, according to prophecy, would construct an empire of justice and secure peace once again throughout the various German states.[13] This is the role that was allotted to Friedrich in the dedication of Ulmannus's alchemical treatise. Coming as a gift from God, the philosophers' stone was made part of a spiritual revelation empowering Friedrich, by divine right, to restore the ancient imperial dignity and represent divine justice within a reconstituted Holy Roman Empire.

However great the symbolic content of the text, Friedrich also sought in it practical advice, becoming himself an active alchemical patron as a way of protecting his authority in Brandenburg, especially during the violent years of the Hussite Wars (1419–1436). Alchemy even entered into the prince's treaty agreements. In 1437, for instance, Friedrich concluded a treaty with Duke John of Sagan in which the duke promised to teach Friedrich's son the art of alchemy within three years. Friedrich's youngest son, the margrave Albrecht Achilles, also looked upon alchemy as a political tool and, in 1477, obliged the knight Henry of Freyberg to pledge himself to the practice of alchemy in his behalf as part of the knight's swearing of a peace oath, or *Urfehde*.[14]

Although considerable attention had already been given to alchemy by kings and princes in the later Middle Ages, the heyday of alchemical patronage did not occur until much later, the opening years of the seventeenth century and just prior to the outset of an unprecedented northern European catastrophe known as the Thirty Years War (1618–1648). Alchemical patronage was never more intense than in these years, a time which coincided with the outset of the so-called Age of Reason. The same generation that saw some of the most important thinking of the Scientific Revolution, that witnessed the work of Galileo,

Kepler, Bacon, Descartes, Grotius, and others, also believed in
magic and persecuted witches more energetically than any other
period before it. The claims of alchemists had by then become
frenzied, their collections of recipes voluminous. And yet it
would be wrong to characterize this time in terms of a struggle
between science and superstition, or between reason and irra-
tionality. After all, there was nothing new about the use of reason in the Age of Reason. Appeals to reason had been a steady
feature in medieval scholastic argument. Of course, within the
framework of scholastic debate, the authority of the Church determined the limits and inner contours of rationality. In other
words, what appeared rational depended upon which authorities one trusted in interpreting the world. In this way, too, alchemy itself could be made to rest upon a consistent set of religious, philosophical, and empirical premises which functioned
to provide logical coherence to its arguments and to promote its
practical-technical worth among European rulers. As threats to
the political and social security of princes in northern Europe
grew increasingly acute, the logic of alchemy, offering the possibility of a technical fix to political and economic problems,
became increasingly attractive. Although the patronage of alchemy within such a context may have been a patronage of de-
spair, we must not lose sight of the fact that it was, nevertheless,
viewed as a reasoned approach to stemming the tide of political
disintegration and to curbing the erosion of personal political
power.

When German historians reflect on their own history, they
find two moments when organized society disappeared from
their world entirely. The example nearest at hand stems from the
devastation of the Second World War. The other relates to the destruction of the Thirty Years War. No one could have missed the
indications leading to rebellion and to the outbreak of bitter
fighting in 1618. No one, however, was able to avert the disaster.[15] Most German princes sought to protect their religious-
political interests by organizing themselves into protective
leagues and by relying upon their collective power as a means of
intimidating opposition. On the one side stood the Catholic
Holy Roman Empire, which was bent upon protecting its traditional rights and privileges against advancing Protestantism.
Particularly dangerous, from the imperial perspective, were

those Protestant princes who used the new religious ideology to pursue separatist politics within the empire. Yet viewing the Thirty Years War as a war of religion (i.e., Catholics versus Protestants) would be a ridiculously simplistic appraisal. Politics and religion were cut from the same cloth, a relationship that helps explain the many divisions within the Protestant camp and the fact that, at one time or another during the course of the war, Protestants could be found fighting on the Catholic side, Catholics on the Protestant. Neither should one overlook the basic dynastic and territorial ambitions of the major powers involved in the war: the Austrian Hapsburgs (reigning family of the Holy Roman Empire), their cousins the Spanish Hapsburgs, the Danish and Swedish states, and last but not least the French. However complex the reasons for division on the eve of the war, there is, nevertheless, a germ of truth in describing northern Europe as split into two rival camps, two empires, in 1618—the one imperial, Catholic, based still upon a mainly agrarian economy and represented still by a feudal social structure, the other princely, Protestant, urban, and characterized by new entrepreneurial interests.[16] No one considered reconciliation between the two ways of life possible. Thus, in the several decades before the outbreak of war, both the emperor and many German princes turned to the alchemical arts in order to find a technical advantage in dealing with the opposing world view.[17]

Since princes sought to advance private ambitions through alchemical patronage, cases of alchemical deceit, or instances where alchemists became suspected of withholding secrets, were often dealt with as forms of personal betrayal and civil apostasy. At such times alchemists might be dealt with in ways geared to emphasize the authority of the prince. At Dresden, the elector August of Saxony established, in the last quarter of the sixteenth century, a court laboratory known as the *Goldhaus*. Several alchemists were employed in the laboratory, as a result of whose work the elector could confide in 1578 that he was already so far advanced in the alchemical art that out of eight ounces of silver he could, in six days, produce three ounces of purest gold.[18]

The best-known member of the Dresden alchemical community was David Beuther, who resided at August's court from 1575 to 1582. His preferred position, however, did not protect him from incurring the prince's displeasure when August began to suspect him of hiding alchemical secrets. Beuther was consequently arrested and thrown into prison, where, after being threatened with execution if he would not reveal his secrets entirely, the alchemist took his own life.[19]

At Stuttgart, Friedrich of Württemberg supported a succession of alchemists near the end of the sixteenth century, some of whom he maintained in a sort of alchemical commune at Gross-Sachsenheim. Friedrich was no less tolerant of secrecy and deceit than the elector August. One court alchemist found guilty of misdealings at the Stuttgart court was ordered executed by the prince on a gallows made from the iron that he had promised to turn into gold. To add to the humiliation, Friedrich ordered that the gallows be covered with a gold-colored metal and that the alchemist be hanged wearing a gown decorated with gold tinsel.[20] Rather than dismantling the gallows following the execution, Friedrich maintained it and brought it back into use later in dealing with the suspected deceit of other alchemists. Not all alchemists at the Stuttgart court received such harsh treatment. Some who were unable to deliver earlier promises escaped the court just in the nick of time. The well-known Scottish alchemist Alexander Seton (d. 1604) was one of these. After refusing to provide Friedrich with one of his tinctures, Seton fled the court, finding safe harbor finally at the imperial court of Rudolph II in Prague, where the emperor maintained his own court circle of alchemists, astrologers, and magicians.[21]

One of the most interesting examples of how commitment to alchemical patronage led ultimately to political disaster during this time is the case of the German landgrave Moritz of Hessen-Kassel (1572–1632). In Moritz's view alchemical wisdom was reserved for a privileged few in society. It was, after all, privileged learning, and he based his claim to possess it on the same divine foundations that supported his noble rights. Aristocratic privilege would, he assumed, bring him alchemical insight, and alchemy itself would protect, thereafter, his elite social and political position. To bring alchemical wisdom to his court, Moritz created a circle of alchemical adepts and mystical physicians, maintaining an intense correspondence with its members and orchestrating numerous alchemical projects from his position at the circle's privileged center.[22]

How alchemical patronage served Moritz's self-perceived role among Protestant German princes can best be understood from the rhetoric of petitions sent to him by those wishing to bring their alchemical secrets and skills to the Kassel court. Most share the same general tone of discourse. However, one letter, a document of over two hundred folio pages, stands out from the rest.[23] In this petition, Moritz is represented as a chosen philosopher-prince who would use the alchemical gift for the benefit of all Christians. If successful in his long search for alchemical wisdom, the petitioner writes, Moritz would employ his knowledge to help overcome the two greatest enemies of the Christian world—the papacy and the Turkish empire. One need not look far to find an implicit message. By means of alchemical secrets, Moritz would rise to a place of political prominence among European kings and princes. Overcoming the papacy meant displacing the Catholic Hapsburgs. By also subduing the infidel Turks, Moritz would be left the Protestant ruler of a new, and vastly extended, Christian empire. The language turns on a division of good and evil and makes the possession of the philosophers' stone a political as well as a moral right. By means of alchemy, Moritz is told, he can best guard against, and ultimately overcome, "den teufflichen bösen Reich" (the devilish evil empire), in this case certainly an allusion to the Catholic Hapsburgs.

In pursuit of the political ideal outlined in this and many other petitions received at court, Moritz nurtured numerous alchemical adepts representing a wide range of theoretical and procedural opinions. The extent of that patronage diminished only slightly with the compounding of political problems brought about by the participation of Hessen-Kassel in the early years of the Thirty Years War. Finally, with imperial armies bombarding Mortiz's towns, with the loss of support of his own estates and *Ritterschaft*, and with no other options remaining to him except the failed alchemical one, Moritz had no choice left but to abdicate in 1627.[24] Yet, even now, exiled from Kassel and with imperial troops in possession of much that had once been his, Mortiz refused to give up hope of alchemical salvation. He built a new laboratory and sought to recover his lost authority through the patronage of further alchemical schemes and by his own participation in alchemical projects.

And why not? There were, after all, numerous accounts of alchemical successes and of the rich rewards that had been be-
stowed upon those who had participated in them. In particular,
stories relating to the activities and discoveries of the alchemist
Alexander Seton fascinated the Kassel court. Through his own
emissaries, Moritz learned of Seton's flight from the court of
Friedrich of Württemberg and learned from another correspondent of a peculiar incident at Strassburg occurring in the wake of
Seton's brief residence there, one that involved both the king of
France and the Holy Roman emperor.

According to the report,[25] a goldsmith in Strassburg named
Philip Jacob Gustenhover had in some way obtained from Seton
a tincture for transmuting metals. Gustenhover's claims for transmuting metals became generally known and brought him to the
attention of both the king of France and the emperor, each of
whom demanded that he be delivered to his respective court.
Faced with royal and imperial injunctions, the goldsmith sought
the protection of his city. However, the Strassburg city council
remained unconvinced of the truth of Gustenhover's claims and
ordered his imprisonment until it could establish whether he
was actually able to make gold. A date was thereafter set for the
goldsmith to demonstrate his alchemical skills. Yet, as the time
approached, Gustenhover announced that he was not able to
proceed with the proof of his alchemical talents since he had en-
trusted his transmuting tincture to his wife for safekeeping and
could not tinge gold without it. Rumors about the secret location
of the tincture ran throughout the city, and Moritz's informant
commented that "she says that she has sent it overland so as to
preserve it in a trusted site, several here, however, say that it has
been sent to a monk, others say no, that she has it with her in a
secret place, *in monte Veneris.*

Without the tincture Gustenhover languished in the Strassburg city prison. Yet not everyone was convinced that the prepared tincture was crucial to his alchemical successes, and
Moritz's correspondent saw in the gradual declining health of
the incarcerated goldsmith the circumstances of French intrigue.
A prostitute, he reported, known to be in the service of the
French, had become one of Gustenhover's regular visitors. On
one occasion she had been found carrying *Mercurius sublimatus,*
which she explained was necessary to kill rats in her house.

Moritz's contact, however, guessed that the poison was actually being administered in some way to Gustenhover, making him progressively weak and affecting him to the point of taking leave of his senses, in which state he would be enticed to divulge his secrets to the woman and through her to the deputies of the French king.

Gustenhover's problems were not only with the French. Without the protection of the Strassburg city council, the emperor Rudolf II could demand that he be sent to him at Prague. As he had done before, Gustenhover protested that he could no longer produce gold since his original supply of the tincture received from Seton was now exhausted. Rudolf considered the excuse a ruse. The remainder of the story survives only in the lines of the court poet, de Delle.

> Er ist in weissen Thurn gebracht,
> Kam aber weg in einer Nacht.
> Ward zu Strassburg wider gefangen.
> Der Keyser trug gross Verlangen,
> Bis er wieder nach Prage kam.
> Muss im weissen Thurme sitzen
> Und vor grosser Angst schwitzen.
> Was das End wird weisen aus,
> Erfahren wir aus Keysers Haus.[26]
> (He was brought to the White Tower
> But got away one evening.
> He was caught again at Strassburg.
> The Emperor made great demands
> Until he came again to Prague.
> Now he must sit in the White Tower
> And sweat with fear.
> What will come of it in the end
> We will learn from the emperor himself.)

Alchemical commitment of the type represented at the Kassel court and by the treatment of alchemists who failed to make good on their claims were really motivated by the same assumptions. The ability to transmute metals was possible, was based upon the authority of ancient philosophical opinion, could be justified on religious grounds, and had attained, at least on the basis of some reports, empirical verification. It made good sense to expect that the alchemical option would produce results, and princes, therefore, willingly allocated great resources to alchemical pursuits. If individual processes failed, it was not a problem of alchemy but a matter of ill-advised procedure or personal dishonesty. Yet even when not accompanied by instances of legerdemain, attempts to obtain a philosophers' stone capable of transmuting metals always failed. Nothing in the theory or practice of alchemy in the medieval or early modern period could have produced it. Nevertheless, faith in those pursuits as constituting technical solutions to complex sociopolitical problems hardly diminished. Although alchemical failures were always disappointing and led to the political destruction of not just a few reigning monarchs and princes, such rulers were, in a way, lucky. Part of the predicament of the present age, in fact, stems in large part from a modern alchemy which is all too successful.

The alchemists were not entirely wrong. It is possible to change one element into another, albeit for very brief moments. Viewed today from the atomic level, the difference between lead and gold is, in fact, by no means great. As almost everyone knows from even a casual acquaintance with modern physics, each of the elements utilizes the same basic building blocks in its construction. The smallest bit of gold, its elemental atom, possesses a nucleus made up of 118 neutrons and 79 protons. Around the nucleus itself orbit 79 electrons. By contrast, an atom of lead contains a nucleus consisting of 126 neutrons and 82 protons, around which circle 82 electrons. The difference, then, between lead and gold turns out to be nothing more than 8 neutrons, 3 protons, and the same number of electrons. Find a way to rearrange these, and at least part of the alchemist's dream becomes plausible.

It is, however, not easy to dislodge discrete protons and neutrons from an atomic nucleus. To do so one would have to have enough energy to move a particle of matter so fast that it could break through the barrier created by the orbiting electrons. A power of that magnitude could hardly have been conceived of by early alchemists, even in their wildest imaginings. Nevertheless, it is precisely such a power that twentieth-century science has been able to recreate, and by so doing has manufactured the true philosophers' stone.

In 1902, physicist Ernest Rutherford (1871–1937) and chemist Frederick Soddy (1877–1956) witnessed an event that had the effect of overturning the contemporary conception of the nature of matter. They observed that the atoms of two well-known elements, uranium and thorium, were spontaneously transforming themselves by a process of radioactive decay.[27] According to Soddy's later recollections, the mood of the two scientists at the time of the observation was one of alchemical dismay. Soddy turned to Rutherford, declaring that "this is transmutation: the thorium is disintegrating and transforming itself into an argon gas." Rutherford, who recognized the complications in such a description of nature, responded: "For Mike's sake, Soddy, don't call it transmutation. They'll have our heads off as alchemists."[28] The two carefully chose to use the term *transformation* in their published accounts, but no one was fooled. William Crookes, the editor and publisher of one of the most widely consulted chemical journals, the *Chemical News*, pronounced that the discovery "undermined the atomic theory of chemistry, revolutionized the foundations of physics, revived the ideas of the alchemists."[29] Later, in the year of his death, Rutherford himself wrote a popular account of his work, giving it the title *The Newer Alchemy*.[30]

Spontaneous radioactive decay was, however, only one sort of transmutation. In 1919, Rutherford bombarded nitrogen atoms with helium nuclei that were emitted from radium and found that the rapidly moving particles from the helium nucleus occasionally broke through the atom's enclosing seven electrons, colliding thereafter with the nitrogen nucleus itself. In the encounter he determined that the two neutrons and two protons belonging to the helium nucleus had stuck to the nitrogen's seven neutrons and seven protons. The impact, however, was so violent that one proton was dislodged, leaving an atom whose nucleus possessed eight neutrons and eight protons which surrounded itself with eight electrons; that is, an atom of oxygen.[31] Not exactly changing lead into gold, but it was elemental transmutation nevertheless.

In one sense such changes have gone on since the origins of the universe, consequences of the thermonuclear reactions taking place at the core of every star, including our own sun. Yet what is produced naturally in the storehouse of the universe we are able to duplicate, to a modest extent, with the nuclear knowledge at our disposal. Heavy hydrogen, for example, briefly transmutes into helium and heavier elements in the explosion of the hydrogen bomb. Our philosophers' stone is the result of the rigorous use of mathematical reasoning and experiment. It is expressed in terms of hard science and sophisticated technology. Our information is analytical and precise. If, as was necessary in the early 1970s, we wanted to know about the effectiveness of Soviet ICBMs against the stationary U.S. Minuteman force, we could compute the destruction with the following equation: $P_K = 1 - e - cy2/3 / H2/3 (CEP)^2$. P_K equals the "single shot probability" (the probability that a target will be destroyed by a single warhead); y equals the yield or energy of the attacking warhead; H equals the hardness of the target (in this case the Minuteman silo); CEP equals the circular error probability (the area around the target within which the warhead has a 0.5 probability of landing); finally, c is a constant dependent upon the units of measurement. The results are expressed in terms of "kill probability."[32] There is certainly little room for illusion here. And yet, what we may expect of our nuclear option and our analytical wisdom in political, cultural, and social spheres could be just as chimerical as the expectations of the original alchemists themselves.

Like the earlier attempts to find a philosophers' stone as a way of dealing with a political adversary or of securing social privilege, commitment to finding a nuclear-technical solution to political problems is dangerous—dangerous because it also is based, to a large extent, upon illusion. In this case the illusion is not with the thing itself but in what reliance upon it leads people to believe about their world. In reflecting upon Rutherford's experiments involving transmutation, J. Robert Oppenheimer observed that some of Rutherford's most noteworthy work was undertaken during the time of the First World War and that such experiments had "led, among [other] things, to man's release of atomic energy, [and] to what may someday be judged the most compelling argument of all for putting an end to war itself."[33] Oppenheimer, as scientific director of the Manhattan Project, was himself instrumental in creating the first nuclear weapons. Yet the development of nuclear arsenals has by no means compelled men to put an end to war, nor has the logic of mutually assured destruction prevented the threat of using nuclear arms. In fact, the assumption that the horror of nuclear destruction obstructs its possible occurrence is one of the most common of nuclear illusions.

On more than twenty occasions U.S. presidents have threatened to resort to nuclear war during crises. Perhaps the best-known example of "nuclear blackmail" is Dwight Eisenhower's threat of nuclear attack unless China agreed to a settlement of the Korean conflict along lines proposed by the United States. In 1954, Eisenhower sent Strategic Air Command bombers to Nicaragua to support U.S. interests in Guatemala. Later, in 1958, he told the Joint Chiefs of Staff to resort to the use of nuclear weapons, if necessary, to limit the spread of revolution in Iraq. John F. Kennedy's aides reckoned the odds at between one-third and one-half that the United States would launch a nuclear attack during the Cuban Missile Crisis. Presidents Nixon and Carter have also resorted to nuclear threats or have themselves been threatened by the use of nuclear arms, especially in regard to confrontations in the Middle East.[34] Threats are, of course, not actions, but they are generally of no effect unless there is also a commitment to make good on them. Moreover, no one can deny that with nuclear arsenals in place the world has not suffered a major conflagration for over forty years. Yet, the world is not at peace. Hostilities between world views continue to be intense, although ideological struggles are now fought out over the corpses of bystanders in the Third World. If there has been a time of happy quiescence, at least for the populations of the world's superpowers and their allies, it is necessary to remind ourselves that such apparent equilibrium has been, and is being, bought by robbing many of those living in the world's poorer nations of their lives and happiness and by constantly placing at risk all of mankind and the entire future of the world community.

The first deception leads to another—that reliance upon a nuclear arsenal makes us safer. Perhaps there was a time when it could be argued that having more guns than the opposition might have made sense as a deterrent to foreign aggression, although competition for armaments has seldom made the world at large a safer place in which to live. Yet the logic that argues more is better simply no longer applies. In relation to nuclear

arsenals, and the potential for destruction which even one nuclear mishap promises, "more" definitely does not mean "safer."

There are other illusions too: that the actual use of nuclear
weapons could be of limited scope and result in winners and
losers as in a "conventional" confrontation (a distinction that itself is becoming more and more obsolete),[35] or that the pre-
sumed safety of a nuclear defence makes it unnecessary to try to
bridge political, social, and ideological divisions as a way of
securing peace. This last deception is particularly distressing
since, like those princes who sought political salvation through
their total commitment to alchemy, the exclusive reliance upon
the nuclear option today has turned our focus away from whatever possibilities might exist that could promote a climate of accommodation and reconciliation between political and ideological systems. Like Europe poised on the brink of the Thirty Years
War, we too think in terms of absolutely good and absolutely
bad, of the morally right and the "evil empire." At just the point
when an ecological consciousness has, more than ever, emphasized the interrelatedness of all things, when communication
and commerce can operate instantly on a worldwide basis, and
when we are finally able to identify the image of earth as seen
from the remote perspective of space, insistence upon the nuclear option frustrates the exploration of what some authors
have regarded as the necessity of a "holistic world picture."[36]

Alchemical knowledge has always been upheld as privileged
knowledge. In fact, most alchemical treatises explained their use
of a highly symbolic and allegorical language as a means of
obscuring an alchemical message so that only the truly deserving and enlightened would comprehend their secrets. If those
secrets were to become common knowledge, these same texts
insist, great chaos and harm would be brought into the world.
The fifteenth-century *Ordinall* of Thomas Norton warns:

> If one evill man had hereof all his will
> All Christian Pease he might hostilie spill
> And with his Pride he might pull downe
> Rightfull Kings and Princes of renowne
>
> . . . .
>
> If Vicious men mought lerne this Science
> They would therewith doe wondrous violence
> And with Ambitiousnesse grow evermore
> Worse of Conditions then they were before.[37]

Fortunately, the secrets of medieval and early modern alchemy remained obscure and ineffective, even to those who claimed an understanding of them. The knowledge of twentieth-century alchemy, on the other hand, has enormous consequences not only for our own lives but for that "common world," that historical world of collectivities that we are born into and which we now have the power to destroy.[38] Few need to be convinced that nuclear war is undesirable, but many are content to maintain illusions about the nuclear peace. Freeing ourselves of the illusions surrounding our own philosophers' stone will be the crucial step in taking control of our future and in securing the futures of the many generations to follow. We need to begin depending less upon the politics of modern alchemy and instead look for ways to achieve the type of real security that comes as a result of mutual respect among peoples even where ideologies and systems of government differ. By seeing through the illusion of the technical fix, we may, unlike those unfortunate alchemists at the Stuttgart court, still escape the gilded, cast-iron scaffold on which we stand.

NOTES

Note: I wish to thank James Hulse and David Harvey for their valuable comments and suggestions. Any errors, inaccuracies, or misperceptions are, of course, entirely my own.

1. For the social origins of alchemists and alchemy, see Barbara Obrist, "Die Alchemie in der mittelalterlichen Gesellschaft," in Christoph Meinel, ed., *Die Alchemie in der europäischen Kultur-und Wissenschaftsgeschichte* (Wolfenbütteler Forschungen 32) (Wiesbaden: Otto Harrassowitz, 1986), 33–59.

2. Ibid., 51. Cf. Dorothea Waley Singer, *Catalogue of Latin and Vernacular Alchemical Manuscripts in Great Britain and Ireland Dating from before the 16th Century,* 3 vols. (Brussels, 1928–1931), vol. 3, 777–78.

3. "It is a notable thing that alchemy is a true art. Whoever worked wisely in it would find great miracles . . . For those who are masters of alchemy cause pure gold to be born from pure silver. They add weight and color to it with things that cost scarcely anything. They also make precious stones, shining and desirable, from pure gold; and they deprive other metals of their forms, to change them into pure silver, by means of white liquids, penetrating and pure" (Jean de Meun, *The Romance of the Rose,* trans. Charles Dahlberg [Princeton: Princeton University Press, 1971], 272–73).

4. John XXII's bull, listed also by the title *De crimine falsi,* is quoted by Robert Halleux, *Les Textes alchimiques* (Typologie des sources du Moyen Age occidental 32) (Turnhout, 1978), 124–25.

5. See H. L. Ogrinc, "Western Society and Alchemy from 1200 to 1500," *Journal of Medieval History* 6 (1980): 119.

6. Ibid., 119–20.

7. On Henry's financial woes, see Ralph Griffiths, *The Reign of King Henry VI: The Exercise of Royal Authority 1422–1461* (Berkeley: University of California Press, 1981), chap. 15, "In Search of Money."

8. Wilhelm Ganzenmüller, *Die Alchemie im Mittelalter* (1938; reprint, Hildesheim: Georg Olms, 1967), 108–10.

9. Wilhelm Ganzenmüller, "Das Buch der heiligen Dreifaltigkeit," *Archiv für Kulturgeschichte* 29 (1939): 93–146; Herwig Buntz, "Das 'Buch der heiligen Dreifaltigkeit.' Sein Autor und seine Überlieferung," *Zeitschrift für Altertumskunde und Literatur* (1971): 150–60; Marielene Putscher, "Das *Buch der heiligen Dreifaltigkeit* und seine Bilder in Handschriften des 15. Jahrhunderts," in Meinel, *Die Alchemie*, 151–78.

10. An extensive treatment of the Lapis-Christ parallel is included by C. G. Jung in his *Psychology and Alchemy* (Bollingen Series 20), trans. R. F. C. Hull (Princeton: Princeton University Press, 1968). On the spiritual content of alchemy, see Wilhelm Ganzenmüller, "Alchemie und Religion im Mittelalter," *Archiv für die Geschichte des Mittelalters* 5 (1942): 329–46; H. J. Sheppard, "Gnosticism and Alchemy," *Ambix* 6 (1957): 86–101; idem, "The Redemption Theme and Hellenistic Alchemy," *Ambix* 7 (1959): 42–46. Most recently spiritual alchemy has been made the focus of the work of Karl Hoheisel, "Christus und der philosophische Stein. Alchemie als über- und nichtchristlicher Heilsweg," in Meinel, *Die Alchemie*, 61–84.

11. Ganzenmüller, *Die Alchemie im Mittelalter*, 110–12; idem, "Alchemie und Religion," 329–46.

12. Geoffrey Barraclough, *The Origins of Modern Germany* (New York: Capricorn Books, 1963; first published 1946), 340, n2.

13. Ganzenmüller, *Die Alchemie im Mittelalter*, 110–12.

14. Karl Christoph Schmieder, *Geschichte der Alchemie* (Halle, 1832), 226; Emil Ernst Ploss et al., *Alchemia: Ideologie und Technologie* (Munich: Heinz Moos, 1970), 165.

15. Still a basic guide to the Thirty Years War, emphasizing its futility and political meaninglessness, is C. V. Wedgwood, *The Thirty Years War* (London: Jonathan Cape Ltd., 1938). Another important study is Georges Pagès, *The Thirty Years War*, trans. David Maland and John Hooper (New York: Harper and Row, 1970; first published 1939).

16. This view has been suggested by Josef V. Polišenský, "The Thirty Years War," *Past and Present* 6 (1954): 31–42; idem, *The Thirty Years War*, trans. Robert Evans (Berkeley: University of California Press, 1971); idem, *War and Society in Europe, 1618–1648* (Cambridge: Cambridge University Press, 1978).

17. Hermann Kopp, *Die Alchemie in älterer und neuerer Zeit*, 2 vols. (1886; reprint Hildesheim: Georg Olms, 1971), vol. 1, 125–29, 187–99; R. J. W. Evans, *Rudolf II and His World: A Study in Intellectual History 1576–1612* (Oxford: Clarendon Press, 1973).

18. Karl von Weber, *Anna Churfürstin zu Sachsen . . . Ein Lebens-und Sittenbild* (Leipzig, 1865), 273; Kopp, *Die Alchemie*, vol. 1, 127.

19. Kopp, *Die Alchemie*, 127.

20. Ibid., 181–84.

21. On the circle of the Emperor Rudolf II, see Evans, *Rudolf II and His World*.

22. I have described the design of Moritz's circle in "Privilege, Communication, and Chemiatry: The Hermetic-Alchemical Circle of Moritz of Hessen-Kassel," *Ambix* 32 (1985):110–26.

23. Murhardsche Bibliothek der Stadt Kassel und Landesbibliothek, 2° MS Chem 17, 1–202.

24. A thorough discussion of the events leading up to Moritz's abdication is provided by Christoph von Rommel, *Geschichte von Hessen* (Kassel, 1835–37), vol. 7, 528–681.

25. Murhardsche Bibliothek der Stadt Kassel und Landesbibliothek, 2° MS Chem 19, vol. 2, 170r–85r.

26. Schmieder, *Geschichte der Alchemie*, 332–33.

27. E. Rutherford, *Radioactive Transformations* (New Haven: Yale University Press, 1906). Rutherford's early papers pertaining to elemental transmutations have been collected by Alfred Romer, ed., *The Discovery of Radioactivity and Transmutation* (New York: Dover, 1964).

28. Lawrence Badash, "How the 'Newer Alchemy' Was Received," *Scientific American* 215 (1966):91.

29. Ibid.

30. Ernest Rutherford, *The Newer Alchemy* (Cambridge: Cambridge University Press, 1937).

31. E. N. da C. Andrade, *Rutherford and the Nature of the Atom* (New York: Doubleday, 1964), 164ff.

32. Michael Nacht, *The Age of Vulnerability: Threats to the Nuclear Stalemate* (Washington, D.C.: Brookings Institute, 1985), 68–69.

33. J. Robert Oppenheimer, *Science and the Common Understanding* (New York: Simon and Schuster, 1953), 31.

34. Joseph Gerson, "What Is the Deadly Connection?" in Joseph Gerson, ed., *The Deadly Connection: Nuclear War and U.S. Intervention* (Philadelphia: New Society Publishers, 1986), 10–13.

35. Cf. Robert Jervis, *The Illogic of American Nuclear Strategy* (Ithaca and London: Cornell University Press, 1984), 109ff.

36. Robert Jay Lifton and Richard Falk, *Indefensible Weapons: The Political and Psychological Case against Nuclearism* (New York: Basic Books, 1982), 241–43. Cf. Richard Falk, *A Study of Future Worlds* (New York: Free Press, 1975); also Richard Falk, Samuel S. Kim, and Saul H. Mendlovitz, eds., *Toward a Just World Order* (Boulder, Colo.: Westview Press, 1982).

37. Thomas Norton, *The Ordinal of Alchimy*, in Elias Ashmole, *Theatrum Chemicum Britannicum* (1652; reprint, New York and London: Johnson Reprint, 1967), 14, 38.

38. The distinction between the world of the individual, the "private

world," and the "common world" which "transcends our life-span into
past and future alike" and which nuclear generations, for the first time
in the history of civilization, have the power to destroy was first described by Hanna Arendt in *The Human Condition* (Chicago: University of Chicago Press: 1958). Most recently the distinction has been
employed by Jonathan Schell, who refers to the death of history and
all other parts of the "common world" as "the second death" in his
important study of the nuclear threat, *The Fate of the Earth* (New York:
Alfred A. Knopf, 1982).

HUMANITIES

HUMANISM AND LANGUAGE IN CHAUCER'S DREAM VISIONS

PHILLIP C. BOARDMAN

It is a pleasure to contribute to a volume in honor of Wilbur Shepperson, and it may be particularly appropriate to offer here a study of Chaucer, for this greatest of medieval English poets displays qualities that have been central to Shep's interests during a distinguished career of teaching, research, and public service. Chaucer, after casting a skeptical eye upon the tumultuous political scene of the late fourteenth century, chose then to engage it with humor, creativity, and continued personal involvement. An accomplished satirist, Chaucer nevertheless maintained a deep respect for English culture and institutions. And Chaucer was a humanist, in broad and narrow senses, devoting an important part of his career to revitalizing traditions and texts and planting seeds in generations of poetic followers.

Linked to all these qualities was an extraordinary public dimension, underlying both the life and poetry of this man who, in his poetic self-portraits, shows himself as superficially private and confidential. That Chaucer appeared at public occasions is not to be doubted. His works continually refer to an audience of listeners as well as readers, and, as a frontispiece to one of the manuscripts of his *Troilus and Criseyde*, we have a marvelous illustration showing him reciting at a podium for an audience of courtiers in a garden outside a castle.[1] One member of the audience may even be King Richard II. Chaucer was a public presence, and he attained some public prominence from a lifetime in civil posts, including membership in Parliament, embassies to France and Italy, and offices in Works and in Customs.[2] He is a

presence in his works as well, most often as the speaking character we have come to call the narrator. When, as in *Troilus and
Criseyde*, he is absent as a character in the poem, his striking
voice still creates the illusory presence of an independent narrator.[3] In a superficial way, of course, part of Chaucer's "humanism" attaches to this voice, in our hearing (reading) an extraordinary humanness in his approaches to character and story. But
Chaucer's humanism lies much deeper than that, and, in this essay, I will trace its roots through a general characterization of
Chaucer's three early dream visions, the *Book of the Duchess*
(ca. 1369), the *House of Fame* (ca. 1379), and the *Parliament of
Fowls* (ca. 1381). These three poems, all experiments in one of
the most popular genres of the Middle Ages, established the
concerns of the poet in the period before his masterpiece, *Troilus
and Criseyde* (ca. 1385). After *Troilus*, Chaucer returned to the
dream vision form with the *Legend of Good Women*, the Prologue
to which is an epitome of the three early poems. The Prologue
introduces a collection of tales about good (and therefore unhappy) women, and thus the poem serves as a rehearsal for the
much more successful framed collection, the *Canterbury Tales*,
left incomplete at Chaucer's death.

The early dream visions trace a continuing conflict between
authority and experience, between belief and knowledge. The
narrator proves especially adept at raising these issues, for he
always relies on books as the authoritative sources of truth.[4] His
belief in books is general, extending to all old stories, and, because he is afraid to face experience himself, he is not able to
resolve conflicts within the literary tradition by turning to personal experience. He has no effective way to measure or evalu-
ate what he reads. Furthermore, books provide the narrator-
poet with his only inspiration; he has only one way of writing:

> I hope, ywis, to rede so som day
> That I shal mete som thyng for to fare   [*dream*
> The bet, and thus to rede I nyl nat spare.
>   (*PF*, 697–99)[5]

As a matter of course, he must read a book so that he can dream
some material for a poem.[6] The poem, which is simply a retelling
of both the book and the dream, amounts to a self-conscious
description of the process of composition. This concern with

composition, with sources and with rhetorical *inventio*, has particular significance in relation to the Christian tradition within which Chaucer is writing, as I will show.

By raising the composition of each poem constantly into the consciousness of the reader as a subject of the poem, Chaucer exploits a range of effects which occur as the traditional strategies of language start to break down. Not only does his use of these traditions raise moral questions, but it also draws to an extraordinary degree upon the reader's awareness of language itself. He conveys both the pressing need to communicate and the recalcitrance of the medium through which he must speak. R. P. Blackmur has brilliantly characterized a similar poetic moment:

> It is arguable that Greek tragedy came at the analogous moment in Athenian history, when the gods were seen as imaginative instead of magical myths. The advantage for the poet is in both instances double and pays in poetry for the burden. There is the advantage of the existing machinery of meaning in the specific culture, which is still able to carry any weight and which is universally understood; and there is the advantage of a new and personal plasticity in the meanings themselves. Faith, in the agonized hands of the individual, becomes an imaginative experiment of which all the elements are open to new and even blasphemous combinations, and which is subject to the addition of new insights.[7]

The dream visions comprise just such an imaginative experiment. Indeed, Chaucer manipulates the important elements of his dream visions—waking experience, the authoritative tradition of books, the imaginative dream experience—so that they are "open to new and even blasphemous combinations."

The dream visions are examinations of the traditional strategies of poetry. In each of the poems, the dream drops the narrator-poet into a poetic "situation," one already served by established poetic tradition; in fact, Christianity offers a ready solution to the problems the poet confronts in each dream. The affirmation of eternal life in the face of death is one of the great themes of Christian literature and would provide the narrator of the *Book of the Duchess* a clear strategy of consolation. Christianity, in addition, offers a host of material on the right and wrong uses of fame and of love, potential solutions for the poetic problems in the *House of Fame* and the *Parliament of Fowls*. Throughout the dream visions, however, Chaucer pushes his narrators into the dreams with a seeming commitment not to turn to Christianity as a solution within his art. Through his narrators, who represent comic models of humanist stances, he chooses to work outside of explicit Christian responses to the problems of a poet, holding a range of secular artistic solutions up alongside the *a priori* Christian answers. But it must also be remembered that Chaucer can move away from developed Christian responses not in spite of, but because of, the strength of the Christian tradition.

The dream vision, of all common literary forms, was perhaps most capable of calling up both Christian and secular associations. There were numerous examples of good and bad dreams, true and false dreams, beautiful and ugly dreams in both the classical and Christian traditions. Because of the Christian ability to subsume classical works through allegorical reading, all dreams, especially those of Cicero and Boethius, reverberated with Christian moral significance. The usual Christian use of the dream vision, nevertheless, involved rather specific Christian revelation, from the *Dream of the Rood* and the *Divine Comedy* to *Pearl* and *Piers Plowman*. Chaucer, however, avoids revelation. The confused exposition of dream theory at the beginning of the *House of Fame*, like the comic argument between Chanticleer and Pertelote over dreams in the Nun's Priest's Tale, does much to blunt the possibility of a bright Christian revelation during the sleep which follows. Even in the *Book of the Duchess*, where Christian revelation could offer both profound consolation and spiritual hope, Chaucer nowhere invokes Christianity; Christian consolation is merely suggested, and then only in the inadequate language of courtly love.[8] Chaucer omits from his account of the book he reads, Ovid's "Ceyx and Alcyone," the part which could symbolically figure forth the consolatory hope of heaven, when the lovers are changed into immortal birds.

We can understand Chaucer's refusal to commit himself to any of these traditions by looking more closely at the consolation in the *Book of the Duchess*. The *consolatio* typically involves a confrontation between head and heart, between detached wisdom and the overwhelmed ego. The natural outlet for sorrow is lament. Boethius's Lady Philosophy responds with educational instruction rather than human sympathy. Consolation comes when reason, quickened by the clear statements of truth, overtakes grief. In this structure, sustained emotion can only be registered through the weakness of the sufferer, for the teacher is always more stern than sympathetic. The Christian *consolatio*, based on Christian interpretations of Boethius, substitutes Christian doctrine for the teachings of Lady Philosophy, as in *Pearl*. It can be seen how clearly the *Book of the Duchess* departs from this structure. We find, for example, two grieving humans who seek consolation, one an unrequited lover, the other a bereaved and mourning lover. There is no Lady Philosophy in the poem: each man represents a different sort of authority, neither of which is Christian. The dreamer is a lover-by-the-book; he lacks the experience which would give his love depth and fulfillment. The knight has the experience of fulfilled love; he lacks the consolatory assurances which old authoritative stories like "Ceyx and Alcyone" could give him. By bringing these two humans and their respective authorities together, Chaucer attempts a different strategy for offering consolation, one based on developing a poetic language which can express human understanding and human love while accommodating an otherworldly realization of the transience of beautiful human things: "To lytel while oure blysse lasteth!" (*BD*, 211).

If the emphasis on language seems unusual, we must remember that, as a poet, Chaucer was writing at a time when the understanding of language was shifting in a way similar to that described by R. P. Blackmur above. In the traditional view, the poet was not concerned to create value and meaning in the world. The materials for poetry came from the books of the past and from the great Book of Nature. All things existed in a hierarchy to which objective values were attached. The fact that the medieval writer did not subjectively determine these values freed him to treat subjects as "matter" to be taken up and shaped, as described here by the medieval rhetorician Geoffrey of Vinsauf: "follow, as it were, the technique of the metalworker. Transfer the iron of the material, refined in the fire of the understanding, to the anvil of the study. Let the hammer of the intellect make it pliable; let repeated blows of that hammer fashion from the unformed mass the most suitable words."[9] Because truth lay outside him in patterns which were familiar and ever-present, the medieval poet was called upon to be not an original creator but rather the commentator on existing material, as described here by Horace: "It is hard to be original in treating well-worn subjects, and it is better for you to be putting a Trojan tale into dramatic form than that you should be first in the field with a theme hitherto unknown and unsung. A theme that is familiar can be made your own property as long as you do not waste your time on a hackneyed treatment." [10] In the Middle Ages, artists were concerned to capture and imitate essences in their art; in Dante's words, "Your art, as far as it can, follows nature as the pupil the master, so that your art is to God, as it were, a grandchild." [11]

The kind of imitation described here must be distinguished from the high-order mimesis of the Renaissance. The high-mimetic poet, according to Northrop Frye, was "pre-eminently a courtier, a counsellor, a preacher, a public orator or a master of decorum." [12] The Renaissance poet pronounced with great authority on moral affairs, and did so by virtue of his calling as a poet. He spoke, in Sidney's view, with the "force of a divine breath," so that he became a better "maker" than Nature: "he bringeth things forth far surpassing her dooings. . . . Her world is brasen, the Poets only deliver a golden." [13]

The late medieval poet like Chaucer, not so exalted as Sidney's Renaissance creator, was also not so confident as the early medieval theoreticians about the easy correspondence of language and reality. [14] The sense of a fully external and apprehensible reality had fallen prey to what C. S. Lewis has called "that great movement of internalisation, and that consequent aggrandisement of man and desiccation of the outer universe, in which the psychological history of the West has so largely consisted." [15] Chaucer's statements about language mostly recognize the likelihood of failure. Chaucer was consistently aware of the ability of language only partially to comprehend reality, even to "falsen som of my mateere" (CT, I, 3175).

Alongside imitation—a respect for the integrity of the material—lay another function of poetic language, this based in the integrity of the audience. Chaucer, schooled in the Horatian dicta of profit and delight, speaks often of sentence and solace, game and ernest, corn and chaff. The necessity to offer the audience moral instruction and worthy ensaumples, all couched in language which was fit and pleasing, placed the artist in the long rhetorical tradition running from classical times through the eighteenth century.[16] The rhetorical handbooks, like that of Geoffrey of Vinsauf cited above, provided proven techniques for fitting language to the necessities of the audience. The medieval poet, a student of rhetoric accustomed to the transmission of poetry through public recitation, was necessarily awake to the strengths and weaknesses of poetic language as a way to teach and delight his audience.

Attempting to be true to both material and audience, the medieval poet was, then, caught in the middle. His object was the communication of truths from both past traditions and external reality, in as pleasing and entertaining a way as possible. He was a "mediator," a "critical commentator," or what Maurice Evans calls simply "the purveyor of honest recreation."[17] Chaucer's narrators in the dream visions are, in effect, the dramatization of this role. Their materials—books and dreams—are made objects within the poems so that we can watch the narrator-poets attempt to explain to us what they can barely comprehend themselves. Their comic naiveté, their oft-stated professions of insufficient wit, and their lack of experience all contribute to their confusions, of course, but the real source of their difficulties lies in sorting through the confusing and contradictory materials which go into the poetry and somehow making the value of those materials available to people in the fourteenth century.

If the theoretical role of the poet just described—that of the imitative and rhetorical artist—completely accounted for the medieval poet's position, so that, as D. W. Robertson argues, he had merely "to reflect a reality outside of himself,"[18] a Christian poet like Chaucer should encounter few real difficulties. As if to show how such theories are always exploded in practice, however, Chaucer makes the narrators in all his poetry slavish adherents of Robertson's view. Each professes a doctrine of imitation; each is removed as far as possible from responsibility for the content of his poem (and his "little wit" is sufficient apology for the form). In the dream visions, the narrator cannot be held accountable for book or dream, for they come from higher authorities. The dream form itself frees the narrator from having to resolve his themes, for it always provides an easy mechanical ending and a safe return to his books. In *Troilus and Criseyde*, the narrator begs the excuse of imitative translation: his old source is responsible for the bad turn his love story takes. In the *Canterbury Tales*, the narrator is a simple reporter, not to be blamed if the vulgar stories offend his audience: he must be true to his subjects and tell what he saw and heard.

The poetic language which Chaucer works toward in his poetic experiments—the language which he feels can capture the essences of reality for his audience in an entertaining way—grows directly from his narrators' slavish imitation. It is a language of irony and double vision, a language which suggests that any close look at poetic tradition, at external reality, and at human nature will reveal not singular truth and unity but contradiction and manifest confusion. It is a language which looks at what the world offers without committing itself to any point of view about that world: it admits all possibilities without rejecting any of them out of hand. This open-minded acceptance of all things in effect attaches its own more human set of values over against the divinely given hierarchy of values we noted earlier. We can take the *Parliament of Fowls* as an example.

Most critics argue that the *Parliament* sets up a clear opposition between a rather shady Venus and a more attractive Nature.[19] But Nature is not able, actually, to supplant Venus in the poem. Venus, after all, represents as important a force in human love as Nature does, and a *more* important force in love poetry. Thus, while the poem *defines* Nature as ruler (after Alanus de Insulis), it *shows* her as sergeant-at-arms, one whose advice on the selection of a mate is not even accepted by the formel. Venus, who occupies only a side-chapel in Priapus's temple, has a similarly mixed portrait. Significantly, her effect in the poem is extended, but made diffuse, when she is addressed at different places in the poem by three different names, Cytherea, Venus, and Cypride. She is, nevertheless, the goddess to whom our narrator prays for inspiration as he sets out to tell his story at the beginning of the poem, *after* he has seen her true nature revealed in his dream.

Chaucer's poetry, because of the myopia of the ever-present narrator, operates as if the clear hierarchy of Christian values did not exist, as if everything had to be looked at and sorted out from the beginning. And thus when D. W. Robertson says that medieval art has no tension in it, he is looking only at the grand hierarchical constructions of the mythographers and not at Chaucer's poetry.[20] Chaucer is full of tension. Although the hierarchical world view maps a clear way upward for people to choose what is good and valuable, they as often as not choose the lower course, the path of least resistance and greatest apparent beauty; they make this choice as if kept from seeing beyond externals to what the attractive appearances actually represent. It is this very fact which informs the humanist moral tension in Chaucer's poetry. Chaucer's Parson says, "Manye been the weyes espirituels that leden folk to oure Lord Jhesu Crist and to the regne of glorie. / Of whiche weyes ther is a ful noble wey and a ful covenable, which may nat fayle to man ne to womman that thurgh synne hath mysgoon fro the righte wey of Jerusalem celestial; / and this wey is cleped Penitence" (CT, X, 79–81). While the Parson's sermon is an exposition of the "ful noble wey," Chaucer's major poems, from the dream visions onward, are explorations of the "many weyes espirituels."[21] Chaucer's irony holds out the possibility that moral truth can be found in the persistent short-sightedness of people, in their "slydynge of corage" (wavering of heart) (TC, V, 825). The poet knows that *game*, as well as *ernest*, can lead to truth.

If game can lead to truth, however, only earnest can finally be counted on to bring salvation, and the recognition of this informs Chaucer's Retraction, his final statement about his art. But it is important to recognize that the Retraction makes full use of the poetic language which Chaucer developed and has itself a double vision. It starts:

Now preye I to hem alle that herkne this litel tretys or rede, that if ther be any thyng in it that liketh hem, that therof they thanken oure Lord Jhesu Crist, of whom procedeth al wit and al goodnesse. / And if ther be any thyng that displese hem, I preye hem also that they arrette [attribute] it to the defaute of myn unkonnynge [lack of skill] and nat to my wyl, that wolde ful fayn have seyd bettre if I hadde had konnynge. / For oure book seith, "Al that is writen is writen for oure doctrine," and that is myn entente. (CT, X, 1081–83)

This *apologia* invokes the same vision of art found in Chaucer's dream visions. The incomplete *House of Fame*, in the absence of closing words from the man of great authority, rests on the twice-stated doctrine that the good effects of dreams must finally come from God: "God turne us every drem to goode!" (*HF*, 1, 58). The Pauline statement, "Al that is writen is writen for oure doctrine," takes us right into the center of the discussion in the Prologue to the *Legend of Good Women*, where the narrator spells out Chaucer's intention:

> it was myn entente
> To forthere trouthe in love and it cheryce,   [*cherish*
> And to be war fro falsenesse and fro vice
> By swich ensaumple; this was my menynge.   [*such*
>   (*LGW*, G, 461–64)

Chaucer's purpose throughout his poetry was moral, and his intentions were of the highest kind. But wishes and accomplishments are two different things, a recognition we noted earlier. Just as the statement of intentions in the Prologue backhandedly suggests the possibility that art may succeed in ways the poet could not have anticipated, even while his moral purpose is thwarted, so the Retraction goes on to admit Chaucer's apprehension that some of his poems, in spite of his intentions, might not work in favor of his personal salvation: "Wherfore I biseke yow mekely, for the mercy of God, that ye preye for me that Crist have mercy on me and foryeve me my giltes; / and namely of my translacions and enditynges [writings] of worldly vanitees, the whiche I revoke in my retracciouns" (*CT*, X, 1084–85). Chaucer is finally unwilling to let the question of his personal salvation rest on the moral success of his artistic explorations of the "manye weyes." In the end he disavows all those works for which he has just claimed a moral purpose, for the authoritative doctrine of the Church says he must.

If there is a tension in the two parts of the Retraction (the statement of intentions in which he apologizes only for his lack of skill and the general confession in which he retracts his most "skillful" works), it is like the tension which Chaucer developed in the dream visions, where he evolved a language capable of serving both tradition and experience while reserving a critical, even skeptical, attitude toward them. Because of this tension the critic groping for a phrase which characterizes Chaucer's art must finally take refuge in pairs of nearly opposed tendencies: Chaucer is "involved yet objective, detached yet sympathetically moved"; his art strikes an "ironic balance between realism and idealism," characterized by comic seriousness, mirth and morality, skeptical fideism and moral realism.[22] All these phrases recognize a humanist stance which was neither easy nor inevitable; it emerged from years of experimenting, compromising, and even failing. A comparison of the early F version and the later G revision of the Prologue to the *Legend of Good Women* betrays Chaucer as a conscious artist and a court poet, shaping his poetry to very practical exigencies. He was no mystic; his poems do not burn with the *incendium amoris* of the lyrics of Richard Rolle or of *Piers Plowman*. He had to work his way through the traditions, through the rhetorical techniques and poetic tactics, in order to do the job of every poet—finding the language which will yield a whole vision of his fellow humans and, more important, the language which will capture the essence of his relationship with God. This language, largely the result of his continuing experiments in his dream visions, helped Chaucer realize his main achievement, which Sidney recognized, "that he in that mistie time, could see so clearly."[23]

NOTES

1. The best study of this illumination is Elizabeth Salter, "The Troilus Frontispiece," in *Troilus and Criseyde: A Facsimile of Corpus Christi College, Cambridge MS 61* (Cambridge: D. S. Brewer, 1978), 15–23. Most recently, see Laura Kendrick, "The Troilus Frontispiece and the Dramatization of Chaucer's *Troilus*," *Chaucer Review* 22 (1987):81–93. Some of the research for this essay was undertaken with the support of a sabbatical leave, and for that I am grateful to the president and the board of regents of the University of Nevada, Reno.

2. Donald Howard's recent biography, *Chaucer: His Life, His Works, His World* (New York: Dutton, 1987), provides the best account of his many documented activities and their relationship to his works and cultural traditions.

3. See, for a summary of arguments about the narrator, Alice R. Kaminsky, *Chaucer's Troilus and Criseyde and the Critics* (Athens: Ohio University Press, 1980), 83–93.

4. In this essay I will speak of Chaucer's narrator as a single continuing presence in the works. Although each poem has a narrator who is, potentially at least, a figure of that work alone, nevertheless the narrative voice throughout his works is consistent enough that we can hear it as a set of variations on the comic public persona of the poet himself.

5. All quotations from Chaucer are taken from *The Riverside Chaucer*,

3d ed., ed. Larry D. Benson (Boston: Houghton Mifflin, 1987) and are cited parenthetically by work and line number.

6. Charles A. Owen, "The Role of the Narrator in the *Parliament of Fowls*," *College English* 14 (1953):266–67.

7. R. P. Blackmur, *Language as Gesture: Essays in Poetry* (New York: Harcourt Brace, 1935), 32–33.

8. See Phillip C. Boardman, "Courtly Language and the Strategy of Consolation in the *Book of the Duchess*," *English Literary History* 44 (1977):567–79.

9. Geoffrey of Vinsauf, *Poetria Nova of Geoffrey of Vinsauf*, trans. Margaret Nims (Toronto: Pontifical Institute of Mediaeval Studies, 1967), 41–42.

10. Horace, "On the Art of Poetry," in *Classical Literary Criticism*, trans. T. S. Dorsch (Baltimore: Penguin, 1965), 83.

11. Dante, *Inferno*, trans. John D. Sinclair (New York: Oxford University Press, 1939; reprint 1970), XI 103–5 (149).

12. Northrop Frye, *Anatomy of Criticism: Four Essays* (1957; reprint, New York: Atheneum, 1965), 58.

13. Sir Philip Sidney, "An Apologie for Poetrie," in James Harry Smith and Edd Winfield Parks, eds., *The Great Critics* (New York: Norton, 1932; 3d ed., 1951), 196, 195.

14. Examining references to the nature of language in late medieval writings, Marianne Novrup Børch concludes: "What is obvious from this is that the meaning of words is not stable, that words can therefore give no unambiguous account of the truth, and that Reason cannot be held responsible for every verbal utterance" (*The Failure of Reason: Experience and Language in Chaucer*, Mindre skrifter udgivet af Laboratorium for folkesproglig Middelalderlitteratur ved Odense Universitet 6 [Odense, Denmark: Odense Universitets Trykker, 1982], 5).

15. C. S. Lewis, *The Discarded Image* (Cambridge: Cambridge University Press, 1964; reprint 1967), 42. It is this "psychological history of the West" that Raymond Tripp has identified with humanistic tradition and, like Lewis, in largely a negative way (Raymond P. Tripp, Jr., *Beyond Canterbury: Chaucer, Humanism, and Literature* [n.p.: Onny Press Ltd., 1977], esp. 2).

16. See particularly Payne's *Key of Remembrance: A Study of Chaucer's Poetics* (New Haven: Yale University Press, 1963); Ernst Robert Curtius, *European Literature and the Latin Middle Ages*, trans. Willard Trask (New York: Harper and Row, 1963); Rosemond Tuve, *Elizabethan and Metaphysical Imagery: Renaissance Poetic and Twentieth-Century Criticism* (Chicago: University of Chicago Press, 1947); and Paul Fussell, *The Rhetorical World of Augustan Humanism: Ethics and Imagery from Swift to Burke* (New York: Oxford University Press, 1965; reprint 1969).

17. Maurice Evans, *English Poetry in the Sixteenth Century*, 2d ed. (New York: Norton, 1967), 22; "mediator" and "critical commentator" are from A. C. Spearing, *Criticism and Medieval Poetry* (1964; 2d ed.,

London: Edward Arnold, 1972), 77–78. The theoretical and, indeed, medical grounds for the notion of literature as recreation has been studied by Glending Olson, in *Literature as Recreation in the Later Middle Ages* (Ithaca: Cornell University Press, 1982).

18. D. W. Robertson, *A Preface to Chaucer: Studies in Medieval Perspectives* (Princeton: Princeton University Press, 1962), 15.

19. See, for instance, Charles O. McDonald, "An Interpretation of Chaucer's *Parlement of Foules*," *Speculum* 30 (1955):444–57. More recently, Bruce Kent Cowgill, "The *Parlement of Foules* and the Body Politic," *Journal of English and Germanic Philology* 74 (1975):315–35, has registered this opposition between Venus and Nature in mythographical terms.

20. Robertson, *Preface to Chaucer*, 10–12, 17.

21. Trevor Whittock, *A Reading of the Canterbury Tales* (Cambridge: Cambridge University Press, 1968), 296.

22. The two direct quotations are from Charles Muscatine, *Poetry and Crisis in the Age of Chaucer* (Notre Dame: University of Notre Dame Press, 1972), 145, 114; "comic seriousness" is from Ian Robinson, *Chaucer and the English Tradition* (London: Cambridge University Press, 1972), 8–9, 69; "mirth and morality" is the phrase of Helen Storm Corsa, *Chaucer: Poet of Mirth and Morality* (Notre Dame: University of Notre Dame Press, 1964), 38–39; "skeptical fideism" is from Sheila Delany, *Chaucer's House of Fame: The Poetics of Skeptical Fideism* (Chicago: University of Chicago Press, 1972), 34–35; "moral realism" is used both by Alain Renoir, "Tradition and Moral Realism: Chaucer's Conception of the Poet," *Studia Neophilologica* 35 (1963):199–210, and by E. Talbot Donaldson, *Speaking of Chaucer* (New York: Norton, 1970), 9–10. More generally, see Peter Elbow, *Oppositions in Chaucer* (Middletown, Conn.: Wesleyan University Press, 1975).

23. Sidney, in Smith and Parks, *Great Critics*, 224.

NEWMAN ON "TOLERATION"

JAMES F. HAZEN

N ewman professed liberalism," said an angry Lord Acton of his former friend and mentor, "when in fact he was in favour of the Inquisition."[1] The remark is literally mistaken on both counts, but like many angry and wrongheaded outbursts it grasps in a crude way something of the many-sidedness of a great and complex man. In his own time, especially during the period of the Oxford tracts (1833–1841), John Henry Newman (1801–1890) seemed to many Englishmen to embody the very soul of an antique, perhaps Inquisitorial, dogmatic austerity in religious matters, a spirit of extreme intolerance—and there is truth in such a view of him. In our time, the name of Newman is, on the other hand, linked with the Second Vatican Council and with the spirit of reform and "updating" which has rocked the Roman church for the past twenty years. In particular, Newman's ideas about the "development" of Christian doctrine, about collegial and diffused rather than centralized authority in the church, and about the important role of laymen in the church's affairs have made Newman seem the apostle of modernization, change, and toleration of diverse views rather than a stern inquisitor—and there is much truth in this view too. Thus, a brief consideration of Newman's career in the light of the ancient and honored concept of "toleration" will, I hope, shed some light on the man, his time, and our own.

The idea of religious toleration has a long pedigree in the history of Western thought and is usually said to have had a benign influence upon our civilization. Toleration is generally counted a virtue in individuals, in governments, and in peoples or nations,

while its opposite is generally counted a vice. Even those who
consider themselves decidedly "in the right" on any given issue
would not like for that reason to be called "intolerant." On the
other hand, insofar as "toleration" implies, or can be seen to im-
ply, a laxity, a merely half-hearted commitment to what one
thinks or believes, then it can be, and sometimes is, regarded as
a weakness if not a vice. The career and writing of John Henry
Newman—in his youth a fervent Evangelical Christian, at Oxford a High Church critic of Anglicanism and leader of the Oxford Movement for its reform, in middle age a Catholic convert
and an ally of liberal rather than conservative elements in his
new church, and finally, in old age, a revered cardinal of the Roman church—exposed him to nearly every problem and dilemma, personal and political, connected with the principle of
toleration in the religious sphere.

At least three distinct meanings of the concept of toleration
may be discerned in its evolving history: (1) political toleration, the official commitment by states or governments to allow,
through legislation or decree, religious liberty in their domains;
(2) social or civil toleration, the unofficial disposition or unwritten law developed in the people of a nation to allow the same in
everyday life; (3) dogmatic toleration, the practice within corporate religious bodies themselves, such as the Anglican or Roman
Catholic churches, of allowing some diversity of belief, shade of
opinion, or variety of interpretation regarding their own specific
creeds. It can be said in general that the first of these, political
toleration, was simply an established fact (or at least a fact rapidly becoming established) in Newman's time and especially in
the political world of England. The second, civil toleration, was
on the other hand not an established fact at all, and Newman felt
its absence keenly and personally in the years following his conversion to Rome in 1845. With regard to the third, which concerned Newman most in his thought and writing and which
is also the most complex of the three, we can say (somewhat
baldly, perhaps) that Newman found the Anglican church of his
time too tolerant, the Roman church of his time not tolerant
enough.[2]

Before turning to Newman's involvement with the first of
these issues, political toleration, it may be useful to consider
briefly something of its history. The Roman Empire at the time

of Constantine is generally credited with originating, in the
Edict of Milan (A.D. 313), the first explicit program of religious
toleration in the Western world. After nearly three hundred
years of a persecution alternately mild and severe (depending
wholly on the taste and energy of a variety of Roman emperors),
Christianity at last received an official charter acknowledging
and allowing its existence. It was the great founding moment in
the history of religious toleration, but only a moment, for in
short order, with the conversion of Constantine, came a very
different dispensation, as the newly converted Constantine himself became the chief persecutor of dissent within the Christian
church and of paganism without. In the words of Gibbon, "the
edict of Milan, the great charter of toleration, had confirmed to
each individual of the Roman world the privilege of choosing
and professing his own religion. But this inestimable privilege
was soon violated: with the knowledge of truth the emperor im-
bibed the maxims of persecution; and the sects which dissented
from the catholic church were afflicted and oppressed by the triumph of Christianity."[3]

Gibbon's sarcastic phrase "with the knowledge of truth" highlights the fundamental problem inherent in the ideal of religious
toleration in all times and places—it is very difficult for those
who think themselves in possession of truth to tolerate the existence of error. And when the truth in question is a religious
truth affecting all of life in the most profound and diverse ways,
the temptation toward persecution of "error" is nearly irresist-
ible. So long as Constantine himself vacillated between the ancient religion of his own people and that of the Christians (until
about his fortieth year), he espoused toleration; when he embraced Christianity with the zeal of the convert, toleration was
forgotten.

As the empire of Constantine and his successors "declined
and fell" in succeeding centuries, Christianity flourished and
rose, secure and confident in its own "knowledge of the truth."
That truth, and the church built around it, dominated the nations of the Western world until the time of the Renaissance,
when the new and rival truths of humanism, natural science,
and Protestantism began to challenge the medieval hegemony.
In Newman's own nation of England, Protestantism created a
small hegemony of its own in the form of the established Angli-

can church, a church which included much diversity yet was a powerful and coherent hegemony for all that. Newman himself characterized the diversity of Anglicanism in these strong and witty words: "as the English language is partly Saxon, partly Latin, with some German, some French, some Dutch, and some Italian, so this religious creed is made up of the fragments of religion which the course of events has brought together and has imbedded in it, something of Lutheranism, and something of Calvinism, something of Erastianism, and something of Zuinglianism, a little Judaism, and a little dogmatism, and not a little secularity, as if by hazard." [4] A national church so diverse in itself was scarcely in a position to oppose strenuously the toleration of other Protestant creeds, and, in fact, English history from the seventeenth century on has been marked by the steady growth of official religious toleration.

In Newman's time, however, the issue of political toleration came to a sharp focus in the agitation for Catholic Emancipation during the 1820s. The energies behind this cause came chiefly from Ireland, whose five or six million citizens had been electing their own members to the Parliament in London since the abolition of the Irish Parliament in 1800. The penal laws in force required those elected members to disavow any actual or potential political allegiance to the Church of Rome before taking their seats. But in the summer of 1828 the flamboyant Irish political leader Daniel O'Connell forced the issue. Running for the seat in County Clare, O'Connell announced that "as a Catholic I cannot and of course never will take the oaths at present prescribed to members of Parliament; but the authority which created these oaths—the Parliament—can abrogate them." [5] O'Connell was elected, and the Parliament did abolish the penal laws in the Catholic Emancipation Act of 1829.

Newman was at that time a young Fellow of Oriel and a recently ordained priest of the Anglican church; he was mainly intent upon fulfilling his pastoral duties and making the beginnings of his personal career as a scholar and writer. A Tory by inclination, he was not then or ever a political activist, but the issue of Catholic Emancipation did draw him out. In letters to his mother and sisters he expressed several reactions: "You know I have no opinon about the Catholic Question, and now it is settled I shall perhaps never have one; but still, its passing is

one of the signs of the times, of the encroachment of Philo-
sophism and Indifferentism in the Church" (to Jemima, February 8, 1829).[6] A few weeks later he writes to another sister: "I am
clearly in *principle* an anti-Catholic; and, if I do not oppose the
Emancipation, it is only because I do not think it expedient, perhaps possible, so to do. I do not look for the settlement of difficulties by the measure; they are rather begun by it, and will be
settled with the downfall of the Established Church. If, then, I
am for Emancipation, it is only that I may take my stand against
the foes of the Church on better ground, instead of fighting at a
disadvantage" (to Harriet, March 16, 1829).[7] He is for emancipation only in the sense that he is not against it; he sees the whole
issue mainly as a "sign of the times," and his deeper worries
center on the future of the Anglican church in an age of increasing, and even already ascendant, indifferentism on matters of
religion.

In this same letter, he comments mainly on what he sees as
the duplicity of Sir Robert Peel, Tory leader in the Commons and
M.P. for the University of Oxford. "That the anti-Catholic party,
who have by far the majority of number, should have been be-
trayed by its friends suddenly, craftily, and that the government
should have been bullied by Mr. O'Connell into concessions, is
most deplorable." Peel had made, on his election some years before, a clear commitment before his Oxford constituents to oppose Catholic Emancipation. With O'Connell's election in 1828,
he had changed his view and presided over the passage of the
Emancipation Act. Thus Newman and many at Oxford felt be-
trayed, victims of political "craft." When Peel stood for relection
in the spring of 1829, the Oxford parsons, including Newman,
took their revenge and defeated him. Newman wrote to his
mother: "We have achieved a glorious victory. It is the first public event I have been concerned in, and I thank God from my
heart both for my cause and its success. We have proved the independence of the Church and of Oxford" (March 1, 1829).[8]

The last sentence strikes the keynote so far as Newman and
"political toleration" are concerned. The politicians of the day
were quite simply committed to the principle of religious liberty,
and so were the people who elected them; there was no stop-
ping the drift toward complete toleration, no matter what that
might mean for the established church. Newman finds himself

here torn between loyalty to a beloved church and loyalty to the principles of democratic rule. He was always a man who believed strongly, on traditional Christian grounds, in the sovereignty of existing civil authority. As he wrote in his essay on the "Fall of de la Mennais," commenting on the abbé's involvement in the July Days of 1830, "He does not seem to recognize, nay, to contemplate the idea, that rebellion is a sin."[9]

In general, Newman had a horror of political revolutions, and of the French Revolutions of 1789 and 1830 in particular, an aversion expressed repeatedly in his writings and illustrated graphically in a well-known passage of the *Apologia Pro Vita Sua* (1864). Writing of his Mediterranean journey of the spring of 1833, Newman recalls (without any hint of a subsequent change of mind) his abhorrence of the revolutionary flag of France and all things associated with it: "A French vessel was at Algiers; I would not even look at the tricolour. On my return, though forced to stop twenty-four hours at Paris, I kept indoors the whole time, and all that I saw of that beautiful city was what I saw from the Diligence."[10] He averted his eyes from the tricolor, he was "forced" to stop in Paris, he "kept indoors"—these are vivid but not exaggerated expressions of his principle that "rebellion is a sin."

In England there was no rebellion in Newman's time, but the evolution of English political life during the entire history of the Anglican church amounted to a quiet but fundamental revolution in the political and social atmosphere, and such a "rebellion" had been fostered by the governmental authority itself, the English Parliament. That Parliament had passed, as early as 1689, the Act of Toleration and, in Newman's early youth, the Trinity Act in 1813, abolishing all penalties in law connected with nonbelief in the Trinity. It had, in 1828, repealed the Test Act and thus opened all public offices in England to people who were not necessarily members of the Anglican church, and in 1829, with the Catholic Emancipation Act, it granted Roman Catholics specifically the right to sit in Parliament (providing that they took an oath barring the pope from interfering in English political affairs). Since these and other pieces of legislation were the laws of the land, expressions of the sovereign will of the English people, Newman was bound to support them as expressions of that sovereignty. Thus, "political toleration" of religious liberty, being the established principle of the age, was not for Newman any longer a debatable issue. Hence the kind of reluctant acceptance seen in the letters above.

In addition to this respect for established and legitimate political authority, there was also, growing in Newman at this stage of his life but not as yet fully formed, a conviction about the need for a total separation of church and state. This principle, so familiar to Americans, did not wear the same colors for an Anglican clergyman of Newman's time as it wears for us. Newman tells us in the *Apologia* of his exposure to it during his early years at Oxford (about 1822) under the tutelage of Richard Whateley, Fellow of Oriel and a man who, in Newman's words, "emphatically, opened my mind, and taught me to think." [11] Whateley, a staunch anti-Erastian, was an early and controversial advocate of the disestablishment of the Anglican church. Of the wisdom of this course neither Whateley nor anyone else could ever convince Newman, but Newman *was* persuaded that the church was itself "a substantive body or corporation" independent of the state, and that, in Whateley's words, it was a "profanation of Christ's kingdom" for either the state to interfere with spiritual affairs or the church with temporal. [12] This general principle was the immediate cause of the Oxford Movement which Newman led in the 1830s, and, as the letters cited above suggest, it was also very much at the heart of Newman's thinking during the Catholic Emancipation crisis. It was simply not the business of the state to look after the spiritual welfare of its people—that was the business of the church, and even in a state having a national church, that church must assert its own powers, independently of the politicians.

Such a principle is easy to enunciate and even to implement in a country having no established national church. But in England, with its Anglican church supported by taxation, its Parliament holding the purse strings for both state and church, and its king as nominal head of the church and defender of the faith, what can "separation of church and state" possibly mean?

Newman's hope was that the Oxford Movement of 1833 to 1841 would bring about a fundamental revitalization of the Anglican church, enabling it to survive and flourish no matter how many other religious bodies were "tolerated" by the English Parliament. A clear formulation of what the Anglican church stood for and believed, Newman hoped, would rally the energies and commitments of English believers in such a way as to restore Anglicanism to what it once believed itself to be, the one true church, distinct from the corruptions of Rome on the one hand and from the ever-multiplying sects of Protestant dissent on the other. But the Oxford Movement failed, the famous tracts were discontinued on orders from the bishop of Oxford, and Newman's own belief in the Anglican church collapsed in the period 1843 to 1845. Anglicanism was not the one true church Newman had in the past hoped and believed it was; on the contrary, it was simply a small, almost irrelevant sect, hopelessly dependent upon the civil power of the land and in a state of schism from the larger and older church out of which it had grown.[13] Newman's personal solution was simply to leave it and to announce his conversion to the Church of Rome. In doing that, he opened up his life to a new range of tolerationist issues, which I have called "social" or "civil."

In theory, social toleration should be the practical and immediate consequence of political toleration. Once the people's elected representatives enact laws ensuring the toleration of religions, that toleration should be at once the ruling spirit of the land. But in practice, of course, it is not so. No doubt political toleration, expressed in the form of legislative acts or royal decrees, signals and expresses an important change in the social and moral atmosphere of a country, but once the laws are made, old antagonisms, hostilities, and prejudices do not immediately die, they merely sleep. Thus, in England, despite the Toleration Act of 1689, the Trinity Bill of 1813, and Catholic Emancipation in 1829, prejudice and bigotry were still abroad in the land, waiting only an appropriate provocation to awaken them. Such a provocation was Newman's own conversion to Rome in 1845, given the notoriety his name had achieved through the Oxford Movement, and great was the public outcry over that single conversion. But a weightier occasion came a few years later.

On September 29, 1850, Pope Pius IX formally restored the Roman Catholic hierarchy in England (a country which had since the later seventeenth century been considered a missionary field by Rome and where Catholic affairs had been supervised by the College of Propaganda), a move which was little more than a logical consequence of Catholic Emancipation but which was greeted by the English public, press, and even the prime minister as an act of "Papal aggression."[14] Two weeks after the restoration, the *Times* launched a ferocious attack, and it is no exaggeration to say that the whole nation was soon up in arms. The prime minister, Lord John Russell, referred to Roman Catholicism as a religion of superstition and mummery in a public "Letter to the Bishop of Durham" (November 4, 1850).[15] Riots broke out in London and other large cities; the pope was burned in effigy; priests and even Catholic laymen were attacked in the streets. While Newman and his fellow English Catholics greeted the formal restoration of the Roman church in England as "Christ upon the Waters" (the title of Newman's sermon on the installation of William Ullathorne as the first bishop of Birmingham, October 27, 1850), it was clear that most of their countrymen did not.

Throughout the last months of 1850, protest and outcries about the "papal aggression" continued, often coming to Newman's very doorstep at the Birmingham Oratory. One of the Oratorians, Father John Cooke, had died on November 12; at his funeral service the following evening, a large and tumultuous mob assembled in the street outside the Oratory and attempted to force an entry. Newman had to call the police, and the service was continued behind closed doors. "We had a great row last night," Newman wrote to Richard Stanton, "and had to send for the police—and tonight also. The people are making a great row under my window now, while F. Joseph is preaching."[16] In early December, Newman wrote that "some furious Protestants here threatened to tear our gowns off us in the street."[17] There was constant talk and press notices of possible legal action against the Roman church, of enforcing the laws against wearing certain kinds of ecclesiastical garb, of "kicking out" the Catholics from England, and of the government "laying its paws on our property" (as Newman expressed it to Faber).[18] The pope himself was amazed, and so was Newman, but something needed to be said or done to restore the spirit of toleration which had seemed to be prevalent before the new "aggression."

In the summer of 1851 Newman delivered his *Lectures on the Present Position of Catholics in England* and published them as a book that same year. These lectures are among the most eloquent pleas for religious toleration produced in the nineteenth century and constitute one of Newman's liveliest, wittiest, and most immediately engaging controversial works. His method is to engender and encourage toleration through a slashing attack upon intolerance. From the opening sentence his style is high spirited and anecdotal. As a former Protestant himself, and as a lifelong Englishman, he knew full well the extent and depth of his fellow citizens' prejudice. His target is, and the first lecture is called, "The Protestant View of the Catholic Church." That view, he says in subsequent lectures, is based upon fable, indifferent to true testimony, logically inconsistent, rooted in prejudice and ignorance, and maintained solely by tradition. "By tradition is meant," he says wittily, "what has ever been held, as far as we know, though we do not know how it came to be held, and for that very reason think it true, because else it would not be held." [19]

The Protestant view of the Catholic church is analogous to the view a mob of Russians might take to the English nation were its knowledge of England based solely on selected passages of Blackstone's *Commentaries on the Laws of England*. Newman imagines at length and with hilarious vigor a scene in Moscow, a demagogic, anti-British orator, an angry mob, and the orator reading out certain statements from Blackstone. "I open the book, gentlemen, and what are the first words which meet my eyes? *'The King can do no wrong'* . . . this British Bible, as I may call it, distinctly ascribes an absolute sinlessness to the King of Great Britain and Ireland. Observe, I am using no words of my own, I am still but quoting what meets my eyes in this remarkable document." [20] Newman continues painting this dramatic and parodic scene; the orator cites other passages from Blackstone which refer to "the legal UBIQUITY of the King," his omnipresence in his courts of law, his customs offices, his postal service, everywhere the power of Britain extends. Climactically, the demagogic orator finds in Blackstone a further amazing statement: " 'In the law,' says Blackstone, 'the Sovereign is said *never to die.'* " [21] At this point the Russian mob imagined by Newman breaks out in clamorous protests against the arrogant English who ascribe such powers to their monarch and to themselves.

The point and the parallel are clear. The Protestant view of the Catholic church is based upon such partial and ignorant views of realities as the Russian demagogue presents to his angry listeners. At the close of the first lecture, Newman sums up: "I say deliberately, and have means of knowing what I say, having once been a Protestant, and being now a Catholic— knowing what is said and thought of Catholics, on the one hand, and, on the other, knowing what they really *are*—I deliberately assert that no absurdities contained in the above sketch can equal—nay, that no conceivable absurdities can surpass— the absurdities which are firmly believed of Catholics by sensible, kind-hearted, well-intentioned Protestants. Such is the consequence of having looked at things all on one side, and shutting the eyes to the other." [22] In subsequent lectures, Newman refers to and disposes of, with wit and relish, such typical Protestant ideas as that the pope is Antichrist, the late medieval church was corrupt throughout, the Jesuits are crafty and duplicitous, the nunneries are havens of depravity, and the like. Never did Newman appear to enjoy himself more before a public audience and to give such free rein to his biting wit, power of epigram, and dramatic sense as he did in these lectures. His immediate audience was Catholic, but the meaning of his words was felt throughout the land; the book sold widely, and it may well be, as Chesterton implies, that by itself, and certainly in connection with the *Apologia* of 1864, *Lectures on the Present Position of Catholics in England* was a palpable influence in dispelling the intolerant way of thought it exposed. [23]

The third kind of toleration with which Newman was concerned is usually called "dogmatic toleration," the internal toleration on the part of religious bodies or institutions themselves of dissent, disagreement, or divergence of opinion within the fold. Throughout his long career, from his youthful days as Fellow of Oriel and Anglican priest to his last years as a cardinal of the Church of Rome, Newman was most interested in this aspect of toleration, and it is also this aspect of the issue which most concerns the Roman church today. [24] As suggested above, the Anglican church into which Newman was born included a good deal of diversity and variety; it was in many ways Catholic and Protestant at once. It incorporated High Church and Low Church parties; it had room for Evangelicals (Newman himself had been one, until he got to Oxford), for Calvinists, for Anglo-Catholics, for Puritans and for nonjurors, and for hosts of laymen and even priests who held widely varying beliefs on many points of doctrine. In short, the Anglican church was very diverse, tolerant, and "English," and as Newman's use of the word "indifferentism" above suggests, this degree of internal tolerance within Anglicanism disturbed the young Newman a great deal.

One of his best-known early sermons bears the title "Tolerance of Religious Error" (in *Parochial and Plain Sermons*, volume 2) and is a forthright statement of an antitolerationist position. Preaching on St. Barnabas's Day, Newman uses the saint himself as an example of how, even in one of the worthiest of the Apostles, an excess or misdirection of Christian love may lead to toleration of what should not be tolerated—Barnabas was too friendly to certain Jews of his acquaintance and adopted some of their ways and habits, earning the clear censure of Paul in Galatians 2 and Acts 15. Although Charity is certainly the "first and greatest" of the Christian commandments, Newman argues, it is by no means the only one, as the story of Barnabas should remind us. There is also the commandment of keeping the faith and loving our fellowmen "in the Truth." It is possible, and necessary, for Christians to be "at once kind as Barnabas, yet zealous as Paul."[25]

It was the error of Barnabas to live by Charity alone, and that same error is, Newman argues, the characteristic error of the present day. "Liberality is always popular," and it is always pleasant to get along easily with our fellow men, letting them do what they like and be what they like and believe what they like. But this is not Christianity: "the very problem which Christian duty requires us to accomplish is the reconciling in our conduct opposite virtues." We must be kind and charitable, but we must also be zealous in our "custody of the revealed Truths which Christ has left us." This latter is what we are not doing at the present time; we have mistaken Charity for an easy, languid tolerance of things not really Christian, and such is, in the long run, given the judgment awaiting us all, not even charitable. "Now, if by the tolerance of our Church, it be meant that she does not countenance the use of fire and sword against those who separate from her, so far she is truly called a tolerant Church; but she is not tolerant of error, . . . and if she retains within her bosom proud intellects, and cold hearts, and unclean hands, and dispenses her blessings to those who disbelieve or are unworthy of them, this arises from other causes, certainly not from her principles."[26]

Newman thus readily accepts and approves the idea of a tolerant church in the sense that it shall not use fire and sword against "those who separate from her" but rejects the notion of tolerating error within the bosom of the church itself. Such a principle is easily stated in the abstract, but the real problem is to determine what exactly "religious error" is. One reason the Anglican church was so tolerant in Newman's time—too tolerant, as he saw it—was that it did not really know its own doctrine very well, the historically conditioned and rather bizarre mélange of Catholic, Protestant, and Erastian principles mentioned above. Nor did it know church history. It prided itself on being closer to the primitive simplicity of the early church than the Roman church was, but did not really know much about that early church. There was a woeful ignorance in England of ecclesiastical history, and that was part of the present problem. As Newman put it somewhat later (in 1845), "It is melancholy to say it, but the chief, perhaps the only English writer who has any claim to be considered an ecclesiastical historian is the unbeliever Gibbon" (*An Essay on the Development of Christian Doctrine*).[27]

Newman's first published book, *The Arians of the Fourth Century* (1833), may be seen as an effort to improve this situation and, specifically, to explore how that early church, which meant so much to Anglicans, itself dealt with "religious error." The title of Newman's work is an index of the extent of toleration in the early church. That Arianism (which, roughly speaking, denies the divinity of Christ, though it takes many, often extremely subtle, forms) should be a serious issue in a Christian church already advanced three centuries into its history was in itself a startling fact. The reason perhaps lay in the preoccupation of the early church with its own expansion, with spreading the Gospel and making converts, a preoccupation which did not leave much time or energy for settling internal disputes. Newman clearly saw the parallel between the fourth-century church and that of his own time. Both a rapidly expanding church and a church rapidly losing membership to various forms of dissent and to unbelief (the church of Newman's time, as he saw it) tend to be tolerant. How far such toleration can go before the church seems to stand for nothing in particular—and, for that reason, ceases to be attractive—is anybody's guess, but certainly Newman himself felt the Anglican church was in a crisis in the earlier nineteenth century for just that reason.

The answer of the fourth-century church to a growing doctrinal crisis on an important point of its theology (the Trinity itself) was to convene the first universal council of the Christian church, the Council of Nicea, in A.D. 325. The council heard Arius expound and defend his views—Arius was himself a bishop at that time—and listened also to some of his followers and fellow "Arians," then took a vote. This went overwhelmingly against Arius (perhaps 280 to 20; the numbers are difficult to ascertain) and the matter was, in theory, settled. The council promulgated the Nicene Creed, the first statement in writing of the church's position on the divinity of Christ. Some of Arius's followers recanted, but Arius did not; he was posted to a remote parish but was not excommunicated. He continued to preach his now clearly heretical doctrine and, in fact, the number of his adherents grew.[28] The story continued and grew even more complicated, but I shall not pursue it.

The lessons for Newman were several. First, historically, the church has been in fact remarkably tolerant of diverse opinions, especially when the matter at issue is subtle and difficult. Second, toleration ends, or should end, when a consensus is reached—not universal agreement, not the decree of one man, but a recognizable consensus at such a council as the Nicene. Finally, at times the true doctrine of orthodoxy may be preserved not by the clergy but by the laity. This was one of the most striking (and later, controversial) lessons to emerge for Newman from his study of Arianism in the fourth century—the doctrine ultimately found heretical was the creation of priests and bishops. What the lay members of the churches under the domination of Arius and his followers may have believed is perhaps not knowable, but with the removal of Arius from the bishopric of Antioch, worship continued as before, and the lesson seemed clear: the church as a whole is the custodian of truth, not merely its hierarchy.

Those lessons were more fully worked out in *An Essay on the Development of Christian Doctrine* (1845), generally regarded as Newman's richest contribution to theology. Here again the idea of "consensus" (rather than total universality, and certainly as opposed to merely a decree or special revelation to a pope, for example) is at the heart of Newman's vision of the authority of church teaching. In its opening pages he attacks the traditional idea of authority embodied in the ancient formula of St. Vincent ("Quod semper, quod ubique, quod ab omnibus") because, he argues, no doctrine of Christianity whatsoever has in fact been taught or believed "always, everywhere, and by everyone"— not even the doctrine of the Trinity, as the history of the fourth century revealed. The best one could hope for, given the falli- bility of human reason and human institutions (even such an in- stitution as the church), would be a "consensus of doctors."[29] The authority of the church, therefore, and its ability to identify "religious error" are thus collegial and collective in nature. Both the *Arians of the Fourth Century* and the *Essay on the Development of Christian Doctrine* lead to and support this conclusion.

Such a collegial vision of doctrinal authority was at the heart of Newman's thinking about the papal infallibility crisis of 1870, the last major public controversy involving the issue of tolera- tion in which Newman was engaged. That there was and, in a sense, had to be an infallibility lodged in the church Newman never doubted. As he argued so eloquently in the *Apologia*, the bible was not and could not be such an authority: "a book, after all, cannot make a stand against the wild living intellect of man."[30] Books can be and are interpreted in a multitude of con- tradictory ways; there is no real authority in them. Arius himself denied the divinity of Christ after reading the Scriptures selec- tively. Only a "living institution" can represent God in an ever- changing world, that institution being the Catholic church of Christ, founded by God himself and existing in unbroken conti- nuity for eighteen hundred years. The pope was undoubtedly the spokesman, under appropriate conditions, for the infalli- bility lodged in the church, but as Newman argued in his letters to friends at the time of the crisis, any explicit doctrine of Papal Infallibility needed careful formulation, and the ones being sug- gested in the later 1860s had been too abruptly and hastily put forth. He urged a slowing down of the whole process within the church, reminding his friends that it took several centuries to define the Immaculate Conception. In the end Newman was pleased at the moderate tone of the infallibility doctrine of 1870;

it seemed consistent with the collegial vision of church authority which has come to be associated with his name.[31]

On the whole, it seems to me, John Henry Newman can be considered a supporter of the principles of toleration touched on above. It goes almost without saying that, regarding political toleration, Newman in no sense favored the interference of civil power in the religious sphere (certainly not with "fire and sword"); in fact, one of the major themes of his thought and writing emphasized the utter separation of church and state. Such a view, almost too familiar to Americans, had special implications for a priest of the Anglican church, a state church, and its advocacy required courage and subtlety which we Americans may fail to appreciate. On social or civil toleration too it hardly needs saying that Newman favored tolerance and understanding over bigotry and violence, but Newman's fine *Lectures on the Present Position of Catholics in England*—and the events which surrounded and prompted them—are a vivid reminder of how fragile a thing social toleration of religious diversity is, even in comparatively modern times. Finally, on dogmatic toleration, the most complex of the issues treated above (somewhat sketchily, I am afraid), Newman by and large supports toleration of diversity through his collegial rather than centralized idea of church authority, his insistence upon the development of doctrine over time, and his abiding skepticism about the power of human reason to reach anything but premature conclusions (perhaps the chief source of all intolerance). Although Newman unquestionably believed there was and is a final and total truth about life lodged in Christianity, what that truth exactly is only time, deeper reflection, and a measure of tolerance will allow us fully to know.

NOTES

1. Quoted in Edward Norman, *Roman Catholicism in England* (New York: Oxford University Press, 1985), 104.

2. Hugh A. MacDougall, *The Acton-Newman Relations: The Dilemma of Christian Liberalism* (New York: Fordham University Press, 1962), 144–52.

3. Edward Gibbon, *The History of the Decline and Fall of the Roman Empire*, ed. J. B. Bury (London: Methuen, 1909), vol. 2, 350.

4. "Prospects of the Anglican Church," in John Henry Newman, *Es-

says Critical and Historical (London: Basil Montagu Pickering, 1872), vol. 1, 294–95.

5. Quoted in Marvin R. O'Connell, *The Oxford Conspirators* (London: Macmillan, 1969), 15. See also James A. Reynolds, *The Catholic Emancipation Crisis in Ireland, 1823–1829* (New Haven: Yale University Press, 1954), passim.

6. Anne Mozley, ed., *The Letters and Correspondence of John Henry Newman* (London: Longmans, Green, 1890), vol. 1, 174.

7. Ibid., 180.

8. Ibid., 177.

9. Newman, *Essays*, vol. 1, 121.

10. John Henry Cardinal Newman, *Apologia Pro Vita Sua*, ed. Martin J. Svaglic (Oxford: Clarendon Press, 1967), 42.

11. Ibid., 23.

12. Ibid., 24–25.

13. Wilfrid Ward, *The Life of John Henry Cardinal Newman* (London: Longmans, Green, 1912), vol. 1, chap. 2; Meriol Trevor, *Newman: The Pillar of the Cloud* (New York: Doubleday, 1962), 299ff.

14. E. R. Norman, *Anti-Catholicism in Victorian England* (London: George Allen and Unwin, 1968), 55–58.

15. *The Letters and Diaries of John Henry Newman*, ed. Charles Stephen Dessain (London: Thomas Nelson, 1963), vol. 14, 125.

16. Ibid., 126–29.

17. Ibid., 154.

18. Ibid., 122.

19. John Henry Newman, *Lectures on the Present Position of Catholics in England*, ed. Daniel M. O'Connell (Chicago: Loyola University Press, 1925), 38.

20. Ibid., 24–25.

21. Ibid., 32.

22. Ibid., 34.

23. G. K. Chesterton, *The Victorian Age in Literature* (London: Oxford University Press, 1955), 31, first published in 1913; Norman, *Anti-Catholicism*, 20–22.

24. Christopher Hollis, *Newman and the Modern World* (New York: Doubleday, 1968), 10–11, chap. 12, passim.

25. John Henry Newman, *Works*, 39 vols. (London: Longmans, Green, 1898–1903), vol. 2, 286.

26. Ibid., vol. 2, 284–85.

27. Ibid., vol. 14, 8.

28. Ibid., vol. 24, 250–52.

29. Ibid., vol. 14, 15.

30. Newman, *Apologia*, 219.

31. Ward, *Life*, vol. 2, 307.

BRACKENRIDGE'S *MODERN CHIVALRY*: A REASSESSMENT

DARLENE HARBOUR UNRUE

Hugh Henry Brackenridge's *Modern Chivalry* has been given only passing notice by literary critics and perhaps only considered at all because it stands out in an age that, giving little credence to fiction, produced little of it. It was out of print for many years, and any acknowledgment of its existence was predicated on its being an American example of the eighteenth-century picaresque novel and on its author's being a competent imitator of his classical and neoclassical models. M. F. Heiser's assessment in the 1950s of Brackenridge as the "most typical neo-classicist in North America" expressed the long-held attitude toward Brackenridge.[1] Lewis Leary expanded the view of Brackenridge to include his debt to the colonial American experience and to confirm his importance to the development of the American novel. But Leary is careful to avoid overstating Brackenridge's or *Modern Chivalry*'s significance. Rather, he says that modern readers will have to determine "whether this old book deserves to be remembered among native minor classics, and on what shelf it should be placed—whether with books of humor, satire, or honest social commentary, with ordinary fiction, or only set aside as collateral reading for the student of history."[2]

A careful reading of *Modern Chivalry* will show the degree to which the work is important as both history and literature. Daniel Marder has pointed out *Modern Chivalry*'s historical significance in anticipating later nineteenth-century moods and movements,[3] but the work also is a proper index to its time, as it illuminates the American consciousness at that crucial point in

American history when colonials began to think of themselves as nationals and when the American consciousness, after a short history, held not only the seeds of ideologies and aesthetics yet to flower in the American air but also an accumulation of past doctrines and literary conventions. *Modern Chivalry* looks to both America's past and future, and more than any other literary work of its time exhibits the richness of the eighteenth-century American experience that encompassed the confusion and cross-purposes existing at all levels of the emerging nation. Moreover, it is *Modern Chivalry*'s historical validity that underscores its most creditable literary value: it is superbly faithful to the classical standards of satire, which require that a work be firmly grounded in the social reality of its intended audience.

BRACKENRIDGE'S LIFE

Hugh Henry Brackenridge was born Henry Montgomery Brackenridge in 1748 in Kintyre, near Campbells Town, Scotland.[4] He arrived in America in 1753 with his parents, who settled in the "Barrens" of York County, Pennsylvania. As a child Brackenridge endured Indian terrors and the harshness of primitive life, but he was able to teach himself the rudiments of the classics sufficiently well to qualify for a teaching position in a Maryland free school in 1763. In 1768 he entered the College of New Jersey, Princeton, after convincing the admitting officers that what he lacked in background and polish he made up for in brilliance and potential. In 1771 he received from the institution a Bachelor of Arts degree and three years later a Master of Arts degree. Although he had begun to be interested in law, he also had revealed an artistic sensibility harmonious in general with eighteenth-century forms and classical ideals. While an undergraduate he had collaborated with Philip Freneau to produce "Father Bombo's Pilgrimage to Mecca," a piece of epistolary fiction about a confidence man who extricates himself from one scrape after another by his wit and learning. At his own Princeton commencement he recited "The Rising Glory of America," a poem he wrote with Freneau in the style of Virgil and Milton. The poem describes the beginnings of America, the heroic struggle of the people, and a future in which the ideal of freedom is fulfilled.

In 1775 Brackenridge turned to the writing of drama. Upon receiving the news of Bunker Hill, he wrote *The Battle of Bunkers-*

Hill, published the following year when he joined Washington's army as chaplain. In 1777 he published *The Death of General Montgomery at the Siege of Quebec.* Afterward he diverted his artistic impulse into political sermons, which he delivered to the troops and published selectively as *Six Political Discourses founded on the Scriptures.* He established and edited the *United States Magazine* (1774–1779), and in 1780, after the magazine had collapsed, he was admitted to the Philadelphia bar. At this time he was considered a successful Philadelphia man of law and letters.

In 1781 Brackenridge's life seemed to take a dramatic turn, for reasons about which historians can only speculate.[5] He resettled in the frontier village of Pittsburgh, changed his name from Henry Montgomery Brackenridge to Hugh Henry Brackenridge, and resumed his interests in law and letters in a new setting. In 1783 he sent his first report from the frontier to a newspaper back East. It was entitled "Narrative of the Perils and Sufferings of Dr. Knight and John Stover." In 1785 he defended twelve rioters accused of attacking a tax collector, defended an Indian accused of murdering two white men, and married a Miss Montgomery, who bore a son, Hugh Marie, the following year. In 1786 he helped found the first newspaper on the frontier, the *Pittsburgh Gazette,* and was elected to the State Assembly of Pennsylvania. As a legislator he secured a state endowment for the Pittsburgh Academy (the University of Pittsburgh) and fought for the adoption of the new federal constitution. In 1789, after being defeated for reelection, he began writing what would become *Modern Chivalry.* In 1790, already a widower, he married Sofia Wolfe, whom he immediately sent to Philadelphia, according to a contemporary account, to have her manners polished and "to wipe off the rusticities which Mrs. Brackenridge had acquired whilst a Wolfe."[6] In 1791 volumes 1 and 2 of *Modern Chivalry* were published in Philadelphia, and the third volume was published the following year in Pittsburgh. In 1791 Brackenridge also assumed the role of mediator in the notorious whiskey rebellion and wrote a treatise about it. In 1797 volume 4 of *Modern Chivalry* was published, and Brackenridge began to write Scottish dialect poems. He also returned to political activity, becoming a leader of Jefferson's Republican party in western Pennsylvania and accepting an appointment as a judge of the Supreme Court of Pennsylvania. By this time Brackenridge had become socially iconoclastic, and his career as judge became so colorful that Judge Brackenridge absorbed all other public aspects of Hugh Henry Brackenridge. Among the interesting accounts of the legendary Judge Brackenridge is the following:

> He was tall, "bent in the shoulders," with a facetious turn of humor that was often at variance with his judicial functions. Careless in dress, often owning only one suit of clothes and no stockings, he was not above kicking off his boots while on the bench and delivering his charge to the jury with bare feet propped on the bar of justice. Once he was seen riding naked through the rain, with his one suit of clothes folded under the saddle, for, he explained, "the storm, you know, would spoil the clothes, but it couldn't spoil me." Yet this same backwoods political philosophe wrote commentaries on Blackstone, entertained Philip Egalite in his home and was of sufficient stir in the world to have his portrait painted by Gilbert Stuart.[7]

Marder goes so far as to say that this caricature of Brackenridge contributed to the neglect of Brackenridge's literary work and obscured his place in American literary history.[8]

The last decade and a half of Brackenridge's life was spent in less rustic areas of Pennsylvania as he somewhat less vigorously carried out the activities and projects that had interested him most of his life. He successfully defended fellow supreme court judges in impeachment proceedings against them arising out of their contempt-of-court sentence against a Philadelphia merchant. He published *Modern Chivalry*, part 2, collected and published *Gazette Publications* and *The Spirit of the Public Journals: or Beauties of American Newspapers, for 1805*, and began the task of adopting English common law to American society. In 1815 he republished *Modern Chivalry*, with additions. He died at Carlisle, Pennsylvania, June 25, 1816.

Brackenridge's literary output classified itself into periods of development that corresponded to the major phases of his life. His early writings, from 1774 to 1779, are characterized by American revolutionary ideals. The second period is the most significant one, from the literary perspective, because during that time he produced *Modern Chivalry*, his best work. The last period was one of collection and recollection, permeated with a solemn reflectiveness as Brackenridge reviewed his own development as a man of his time.

MODERN CHIVALRY

The form of *Modern Chivalry* is picaresque, a term which denotes that the work focuses on the adventures of a rogue-hero on a journey. Brackenridge's rogue in *Modern Chivalry* is Teague O'Regan, whose name is a generic label for the Irish immigrant in eighteenth-century America. Teague's character was first named by Brackenridge in his and Freneau's "Father Bombo's Pilgrimage," which also foreshadows Brackenridge's later style and which depended in part on dialect and commonplace detail. Brackenridge explained his inspiration for the character of Teague:

> In the winter of 1787, being then of the legislature of Pennsylvania, it was signified to me that I might be put in nomination [for the American Philosophical Society] with several others, that were about to be balloted for, if I thought proper to skin a cat-fish or do something that would save appearances, and justify the society in considering me a man of Philosophic search and resources. Enquiring who these might be, that had been nominated, and put upon the list, and not chusing to be of the *batch*, I thought proper to decline the compliment. It was this which gave rise to my ideas of such a candidate as Teague O'Regan for that honour. Some time after this, when delegates were about to be chosen from the country where I resided to frame a constitution for the United States, after the adoption of the federal government, I offered myself for this, as considering it a special occasion; but to my astonishment, and before I was aware, one of Shakespeare's characters, Snout, the bellows mender, was elected. This led me to introduce Teague as a politician.[9]

Before Brackenridge undertook *Modern Chivalry*, he began a verse satire he called "The Modern Chevalier," in which he developed a knight errant as a foil to an ignorant Irishman named Traddle. When he decided that the verse form of his satire was a deterrent to the message he wanted to convey and thus abandoned it, he changed the chevalier into Captain Farrago, a fifty-three-year-old gentleman, and the Irishman into Teague O'Regan. *Modern Chivalry* comprises the adventures of the captain and Teague, with the comic interest centering on Teague's exploits and mishaps, highlighted by the captain's and the narrator's explanations and moralizations. The captain, a member of the declining American aristocracy who has retained his title presumably from his rank in the Revolution, has decided to travel around the country to learn about the habits and ideas of the citizens, accompanied by his servant, Teague. The pair interact with local characters, and Teague's misadventures are created in the combination of his ambition, the ignorance of his countrymen, and the freedoms available in the new nation. In the course of the long work the pair meet numerous groups who admire Teague and wish to bestow various honors upon him, all of which the captain tries to prevent for the good of the country. In spite of the captain's efforts, however, Teague is a universal success, meets the president, becomes the idol of politicians, beautiful ladies, and scientists, and finally is appointed collector of tax on whiskey, all his predecessors in this office having been tarred and feathered. Teague receives the same treatment and is captured as a strange animal by a philosophic society, which sends him to France. There the tar and feathers wear off, and his only article of clothing being tattered, he is mistaken for a political extremist and borne off in triumph. Each adventure is followed by a passage of moral explanation, and the overt moralizing becomes more aggressive in the succeeding volumes.

In addition to being picaresque, *Modern Chivalry* is a classic satire, a mode favored by neoclassicists. Neoclassicism, a resurrection of classicism tailored to a later age's experience, was grounded on man's relation to his society, particularly an ordered society in which he is allowed to fulfill his greatest potential. It holds that mankind is improvable and that society has an obligation to provide the most amenable atmosphere for that improvability. It is equally structured and rational in matters of literary taste, assuming that literature ought to have a noble purpose of moral instruction or the establishment of models for human behavior. It predated the emotionalism of romantic sensibility and the art-for-art's-sake outgrowth of the literary realism of the late nineteenth century. Literature was regarded as an art which must be perfected through study and practice and required the deliberate adaptation of tested rules to achieve the proper end, an ideal derived especially from Horace's *Ars poetica*. Like the classicist, the neoclassicist believed that truth was absolute rather than subjective. Once discovered and once pointed out, truth was available to all persons through the faculties of the mind. Hence imitation rather than fanciful creation was encouraged. The age is replete with imitations of works of such "ancients" as Homer, Horace, Virgil, and Ovid. The exercise of imagination was controlled by rational restraint and clearly visible didactic goals.

It is no wonder that satire, justified by those who practice it as a corrective of vice and folly, was such a favorite literary mode of the times. Literary critics have classified satire according to its tones: Horatian, which is gentle and sad while disapproving, and Juvenalian, which is contemptuous. The attitude is presented by the satirist's persona in the work, the first-person voice in a direct satire, or the authorial voice implied in the narrative of an indirect satire. By its essential nature, satire has an instructional purpose. The satirist wishes to change the character or the conditions of those he is ridiculing; otherwise his work is gratuitous. Even the most vitriolic satire, like that of Juvenal and on occasion Swift, is linked to an idealism, an implied standard of what life ought to be or what humans ought to aspire to be.

Satire achieves its effectiveness by wearing a mask of humor. The folly and shortcomings of humans are ridiculed as comedy, and the supposition is that while readers are laughing at the foolishness of fictional characters they will see their own mirror selves and mend their ways. Successful satire must appeal to the deepest experiences and habits of its readers; it has to touch the minds and hearts of its intended audience. The degree to which Brackenridge does this in *Modern Chivalry* is reflected in the inordinate popularity of the work during the early nineteenth century, a popularity that stands in stark contrast to its contemporary critical evaluation and its relative obscurity in the twentieth century.

In a recent study Emory Elliott attributes the lack of critical regard for *Modern Chivalry* to eighteenth- and nineteenth-century American critics' favoring works imitative of British social novels.[10] The general readership obviously did not agree with the critical opinion, for the popularity of *Modern Chivalry* was sufficient for Brackenridge to boast in 1815, a year before his death, that five publishers had become wealthy on his book and that a copy existed in every Pennsylvania home. It was said to be a favorite of both the king of France and John Quincy Adams, and the editor of the *Pittsburgh Literary Examiner and Western Monthly Review* claimed that *Modern Chivalry* was to the West what *Don Quixote* was to Europe; that is, a textbook of all classes of society.[11]

It is not completely inaccurate to see *Modern Chivalry* as a neoclassical work. But critics who have dismissed it as only an imitation of classical and neoclassical models have missed Brackenridge's sly humor and failed to see the point of the satire. Early in *Modern Chivalry* Brackenridge declares that his intention was to demonstrate the ideal use for the English language, and he cites his classical and neoclassical models, naming Horace, Homer, Aristotle, and Swift, in particular. The astute reader will discover that Brackenridge's declaration was made with tongue in cheek and is a disguise for his real purpose, which is to warn the new American nation about the pitfalls to which democracy is subject. His noble intention is to save democracy from the dangers anticipated by Crevecoeur and others. The classical and neoclassical elements in the novel are consistently tempered by democratic ideals which sometimes are at odds with classical and neoclassical values. A dramatic example exists in the intended audience of *Modern Chivalry*. Most neoclassic satires were written for the intelligentsia or literati, but Brackenridge's satire was written for, in his own words, "Tom, Dick, and Harry in the woods."[12]

Brackenridge assuredly was steeped in classical philosophy and classical literary style, but his American experience shaded his interpretation of classical theory. For example, it is easy to see in *Modern Chivalry* an advocacy of the classical theory of democratic balances, in which people are naturally divided into the elite and the many, the former notable by its talent, education, and fitness to rule and the latter, without the skills necessary to govern, by its ability to make sound political judgment; in such a theory, if either order fails to fulfill its duties both society and government are weakened by ethical and economic chaos. However, to assume, as one critic has, that Brackenridge was led to develop this theme in *Modern Chivalry* by the influence of British oppositional politics is to ignore Brackenridge's American experience and the obvious purpose of the satire.[13] There are, of course, parallels between Brackenridge's concerns in *Modern Chivalry* and the "country" school of British oppositional thought. But Brackenridge was a man actively involved in the events of his time, not merely a theorist and scholar. The dangers in the new American nation were immediate and threatening, and they, rather than British politics, would have compelled Brackenridge to treat the theory of balances in the satire that he hoped would make Americans see the weaknesses in their new government before it was too late. Brackenridge's dislike of wealthy men and his preference for those of modest means are less likely to have been fostered by a sympathy with a British viewpoint than to have been inspired by his firsthand awareness of the abuses created in the mercantile interests of colonization and in the rise to riches of insensitive entrepreneurs who were becoming the New World aristocracy. Indeed, Brackenridge shared Jefferson's fear that Hamilton's system for strengthening the federal government and moneyed interests at the expense of state government and the farmers would lead to a wealthy and unscrupulous elite that would be the equivalent of a monarchy. Thus, while the theory of balances was classical in origin and had contemporary significance in British politics, the ideal in fact conformed to early American Puritan societies' notions of order and divine plan and reinforced the colonial concepts of natural rights and natural nobility. Rather than its relevance to events in Britain, it was the idea's being tested in frontier politics that made it a proper subject for Brackenridge.

There are other ways in which Brackenridge ties his satire to the society at which it is directed. In particular he circumscribes the American experience by allusion to specific events and attitudes that had special meaning to the American colonial who had become the citizen of the new nation. For literary effect Brackenridge drew upon those elements of the American past that were unusually vivid. Foremost among those elements was religious fervor, with its ancillary interest in devils and witches, an interest that went back to the early Puritan settlements and was renewed in the Great Awakening of the mid-eighteenth century. Brackenridge consistently satirizes all forms of institutional religion through Captain Farrago, who says, "In state affairs, ignorance does very well, and why not the church? I am for having all things of a piece: ignorant statesmen, ignorant philosophers, and ignorant ecclesiastics."[14] The colonial tendency to see the devil's work in all forms of trouble is reflected in the common labeling of Teague as "that red-headed devil." And Brackenridge skillfully elicits the understanding of his readers when he shows the captain exploiting Teague's fear of hell in much the same way that Jonathan Edwards had appealed to his 1740s audiences. He warns Teague, who suddenly aspires to take holy orders, that the disadvantages outweigh the advantages. "This Satan," he says, "is very little of the gentleman. Even where he is well disposed, he will do but little good to one, but a most dangerous creature where he takes a dislike. When you go to hell, as one day you must, you can expect but little quarter, after abusing him in this world. He will make you squeal like a pig; take you by the throat, and kick you like a cat."[15] Teague is sufficiently convinced to think no more of the matter, and Brackenridge has made his satiric point by reversing the hell and brimstone sermon of the past, which was designed to show the power of a wrathful God rather than a wrathful devil.

Brackenridge often alludes to the witchcraft scare of 1692. Captain Farrago declares to Teague that he "knows witches" and once tells him that the prosperous hostess of whom Teague has become enamored is a witch. "She was all night in my room," the captain says, "in the shape of a cat. It is God's mercy, that she had not changed herself into an alligator and eat you up before the morning. When I came into the room I expected to find nothing else but bones, and particles of hair, the remnant of her repast; but it seems she has thought you not fat enough, and has given you a day or two to run, to improve your flesh and take the salt better."[16] Teague of course is instantly up and away without even an adieu to the lady. In one of the many short chapters entitled "Containing Reflections," Brackenridge had set forth the evils of "presumptive testimony," or spectral evidence, which had been allowed in the infamous Salem trials. He wrote, "Invisible things belong to the Omniscient; and it would seem great arrogance in man to take upon him to decide the cases of uncertainty."[17] Brackenridge continually instructs, and he often moralizes on issues that belong to American history.

Teague's problems in the novel usually arise from his failure to see and accept his place in society; he is an ignorant servant and a bog-trotter, not a legislator, a clergyman, an actor, or a sophisticated lover—all of which he aspires to be at one time or another. The captain understands the neoclassic precepts "First

Follow Nature" and "Know Thyself." "Once a Captain always a Captain," he says. But such stasis leads to a social hierarchy which is not consistent with Brackenridge's democratic ideals. In such places as this in the novel the reader is made aware of the differences between the captain and the narrator, differences that have been interpreted by some critics as contradictions or weaknesses in the work but have been properly identified by Elliott as representative of opposing viewpoints.[18] The captain is the kindly aristocrat who practices a Machiavellian philosophy of the ends justifying the means, and he treats Teague with the patronizing concern of his class toward ignorance and ineptness.

Seemingly sincere neoclassic precepts presented in *Modern Chivalry* prove on closer examination to be satiric and to point instead to an opposite view. The captain often recites aphorisms for Teague's benefit such as "Distance and Time are the cure for all passions" and "Hear instruction, refuse it not, and be wise," perfectly legitimate neoclassical guides, but as applied in *Modern Chivalry* they are often ironic and absurd. Distance and Time never cure Teague's passions for the ladies, and the instruction the captain gives Teague is just as likely to be lies as truth. Certainly none of it makes Teague wise.

In order to provide a milieu that would encompass such multiple perspectives and character types, Brackenridge wisely chose the frontier as the primary setting for the novel. It afforded him the opportunity to depict the clash of values that characterized postrevolutionary turn-of-the-century America, and in the course of writing *Modern Chivalry*, if not before, Brackenridge must have grasped the frontier's value as a literary symbol. American writers from Brackenridge on have mined the abstraction of frontier and made it a symbol that is virtually indigenous to American literature; it provided Cooper, Thoreau, Hawthorne, Faulkner, Steinbeck, Kesey, and others with a metaphor that represents the American national consciousness at the same time that it represents both the American dilemma and the American dream. It is the dilemma of choosing between freedom and responsibility, and it is the dream of escaping to an Eden free from the burdens of society. It is that fatal dividing line in the American mind, the demarcation between order and chaos, civilization and nature. Floyd Stovall in fact saw the frontier as the "real America," which was not to be found either in the order of the settled communities or in the disorder of the wilderness. It was found in "that area of dynamic and expanding life which is born out of the union of the two."[19] Thus the frontier setting of *Modern Chivalry* is its most distinctively American element, and consequently it gives Brackenridge's satire its crucial impetus. It explains *Modern Chivalry*'s popularity in its day, for it allowed Brackenridge to touch the deepest experience of his readers.

NOTES

1. See M. F. Heiser, "The Decline of Neo-Classicism, 1801–1848," in Harry Hayden Clark, ed., *Transitions in American Literary History* (Durham, N.C.: Duke University Press, 1953). See also Moses Coit Tyler, *The Literary History of the American Revolution* (New York: G. P. Putnam's Sons, 1897), vol. 2; Vernon Lewis Parrington, *Main Currents of American Thought* (New York: Harcourt, Brace, 1927), vol. 1; Alexander Cowie, *The Rise of the American Novel* (New York: American Book Co., 1948); and Robert E. Spiller et al., eds., *Literary History of the United States* (New York: Macmillan, 1948), vol. 1.

2. See Lewis Leary, editor's introduction to Hugh Henry Brackenridge, *Modern Chivalry* (1792–93, 1797; reprint New Haven, Conn.: College and University Press, 1965). All quotations from the novel are taken from this edition. There does exist the complete *Modern Chivalry*, precisely reproduced, ed. Claude M. Newlin (New York: American Book Co., 1937), but it is not readily available to students except on microfilm.

3. See Daniel Marder, *Hugh Henry Brackenridge*, Twayne's United States Authors Series, ed. Sylvia E. Bowman (New York: Twayne Publishers, 1967).

4. For the facts of Brackenridge's life I am indebted to Claude M. Newlin, *The Life and Writings of Hugh Henry Brackenridge* (Princeton: Princeton University Press, 1932); Henry Adams, *History of the United States of America* (New York: Charles Scribner's Sons, 1889–1901), vol. 1; Leland D. Baldwin, *Pittsburgh: The Story of a City* (Pittsburgh: University of Pittsburgh Press, 1938); Martha Conners, "Hugh Henry Brackenridge at Princeton University, 1767–1771," *Western Pennsylvania Historical Magazine* 10 (July 1927): 146–62; and J. W. F. White, "The Judiciary of Allegheny Court," *Pennsylvania Magazine* 7 (1883): 148–93.

5. Daniel Marder, "Introduction," in *A Hugh Henry Brackenridge Reader* (Pittsburgh: University of Pittsburgh Press, 1970), 6–7.

6. John Pope, *A Tour through the Southern and Western Territories of the United States* (Richmond: J. Dixon, 1792), 15–16; cited by Marder, *Hugh Henry Brackenridge*, 48–49.

7. See William W. Edel, *Bulwark of Liberty* (Carlisle, Penn.: Dickinson College Press, 1950), 124.

8. See Marder, *Hugh Henry Brackenridge*, 62.

9. Hugh Henry Brackenridge, *Modern Chivalry* (Philadelphia, 1815), vol. 4, appendix 1.

10. Emory Elliott, "Hugh Henry Brackenridge: The Regenerative Power of American Humor," *Revolutionary Writers: Literature and Authority in the New Republic, 1725–1810* (New York and Oxford: Oxford University Press, 1986), 181.

11. Cited by Marder, "Introduction," 4.

12. Cited by Elliott, "Hugh Henry Brackenridge," 174.

13. See Michael T. Gilmore, "Eighteenth-Century Oppositional Ideology and Hugh Henry Brackenridge's *Modern Chivalry*," *Early American Literature* 13 (1978): 181–92.

14. Brackenridge, *Modern Chivalry*, vol. 1, book 3, chap. 3, 61.

15. Ibid., 60.

16. Ibid., vol. 2, book 2, chap. 2, 112.

17. Ibid., vol. 1, book 3, chap. 3, 57.

18. Elliott, "Hugh Henry Brackenridge," 177.

19. Floyd Stovall, *American Idealism* (Norman: University of Oklahoma Press, 1943), 20–21.

THE UNIVERSITY IDEAL IN HISTORY; OR, THE AUTHORITY OF THE REBELLIOUS PROFESSOR

JAMES W. HULSE

There is a narcissism within the professoriat that encourages—perhaps even rewards—members of the academic profession in the analysis of the so-called university experience. Histories of individual universities and colleges are legion. All self-respecting institutions that aspire to higher learning have their chroniclers, and the provincialism of their efforts assures that they will never be read, except possibly by others afflicted by the same sort of myopia. Most of the scholars in this category are at some pains to emphasize the glories and achievements of the alma mater. Few of these scholars trouble themselves with looking beyond the boundaries of their own institutions.

There is also another category of books and essays about what ails the contemporary universities and schools in their function as instructors of the young and preservers of the cultural heritage of the civilization. This is not the place to discuss these, but a plenitude of such works has appeared in this country in the past quarter-century.

And there is yet another level of philosophizing (or perhaps rationalizing) about higher education which has also had a large coterie of practitioners. This may be called, for present purposes, the definers of the "university ideal." These we have had in abundance also, and the fate of their writings has been intellectually more satisfying than that of the provincial chroniclers and the diagnosticians. Since I have contributed to the mountain of unread books on a single provincial *studium generale*, the essay that follows may be regarded as a belated experiment in the latter mode and an atonement for past sins.

It is now approximately a hundred years since Hastings Rashdall, the Oxford don, began his landmark history of the medieval universities, one of the most admirable examinations of the university ideal ever written. A half-century has expired since F. M. Powicke and A. B. Emden, Rashdall's successors and revisors, issued their amendment of this opus. Despite its age, Rashdall's work remains an acceptable standard against which histories of the university movement can be measured. It is the Greenwich in its field; a good way to get one's bearings on the landscape of higher education in medieval Europe—or in modern Europe and America, for that matter—is to make reference to Rashdall.[1]

Rashdall's method was "to describe with tolerable fullness the three great archetypal universities—Bologna, Paris, Oxford— and to give short notices of the foundation, constitution, and history of the others, arranged in national groups."[2] He devoted his first volume largely to Bologna and Paris and his third primarily to Oxford and to student life, with only a brief consideration of Cambridge. The second volume treats, in encyclopedic form, more than seventy universities which had been established on the Continent and in Scotland prior to 1500.

Rashdall had many virtues as a scholar, one of which was that he was interested in ideas and the thinkers who propounded them, and he sought to relate the ones who were important intellectually to the universities in which they served. The history of universities for him was not merely the history of the institutions that bore the name, although in some of his briefer surveys he did not get much beyond that level. And he essentially accepted the medieval practice of regarding as a "university" almost any institution that a king, emperor, or pope had recognized as a *studium generale*, entitled to the privilege *ius ubique docendi*; that is, the right to have the degrees which had been awarded to its scholars recognized in other universities. But he recognized that there were many institutions which claimed the name and the privileges of the *studium generale* without having the substance.

Rashdall's work was primarily an encyclopedic survey within which some stimulating intellectual history was introduced. We learn much about the structure, the guilds of professors and students, and the privileges of the universities. We also learn much, if we read selectively, about the struggle of the professoriat for academic autonomy in the Middle Ages.

In this essay, I will restrict my attention to one of the specialized functions of the university—that of service as a forum for intellectual questioning and criticism of the prevailing wisdom. Whatever else the *studium generale* may have done, and whatever else the modern university may be, this is the crucial feature of the "university" as we look at that institution across the past eight centuries. The essential fact is not that it brings teachers and students together (as James Garfield said of Mark Hopkins of Williams College), the professor on one end of the log and the student on the other.[3] In studying essence of the university, we cannot look merely at the phenomenon of a teacher and pupil who have "hit it off" and therefore have produced a wise man or a millionaire at the end of the circuit. The marketplace or the stock exchange can do as much.

A university is a place whose primary business is to create tension, even to stimulate controversy in the minds of its students and the society which it serves. John Henry Newman was at some pains to make the point when he wrote in 1854:

> And such, for the third or fourth time, is a University; I hope I do not weary out the reader by repeating it. It is a place to which a thousand schools make contributions; in which the intellect may safely range and speculate, sure to find its equal in some antagonist activity, and its judge in the tribunal of truth. It is a place where inquiry is pushed forward, and discoveries verified and perfected, and rashness rendered innocuous, and error exposed, by the collision of mind with mind, and knowledge with knowledge.[4]

Nearer to the mark, perhaps, is Karl Jaspers's definition of the university, written soon after World War II when he was trying to build his own shattered alma mater, Heidelberg University, from the ashes of the Third Reich. His lines deserve repetition:

> The university is a community of scholars and students engaged in the task of seeking truth. It is a body which administers its own affairs regardless of whether it derives its means from endowments, ancient property rights or the state; or

whether its original public sanction comes from papal bulls, imperial charters or the acts of provinces or states. In every case its independent existence reflects the express wish or continuing toleration on the part of the founder. Like the church it derives its autonomy—respected even by the state— from an imperishable idea of supranational, world-wide character: academic freedom. This is what the university demands and what it is granted. Academic freedom is a privilege which entails the obligation to teach truth, in defiance of anyone outside or inside the university who wishes to curtail it.[5]

We must emphasize that Jaspers conceived of the university as a *community* of masters and scholars, engaged in the *pursuit of truth* and ready to defy the state or the university itself in that objective if either of them should resist the pursuit.

We need not linger long here over the matter of the origins of the university idea; let me simply assert that Paris has the best claim to the title of mother of the modern university, and Peter Abelard, the controversial son of Normandy, has the best claim to the honor of being the founder of this university ideal expressed by Newman and Jaspers.[6] Although Abelard died in 1142 in disgrace, his technique of asking the most difficult questions and challenging the existing theology was part of the standard repertoire in the schools of the Left Bank a hundred years later, when the *studium generale* there entered its golden age. Rashdall reminds us that the writings of Thomas Aquinas, which emerged a century later at Paris, served the university cause as well as that of the church:

> The work which Aquinas did for the church of his day— the fusion of the highest speculative thought of the time with its profoundest spiritual convictions, the reconciliation of the new truths of the present with the kernel of truth embodied in the traditional creed—is a task which will have to be done again and again as the human mind continues progressive and religion remains a vital force with it.[7]

When his method was rejected by the rigid theologians of the Sorbonne in later centuries, the university itself declined.

Among the characteristics of the modern university are some remnants of the old guild notion, the idea that the community of scholars has the right and the obligation to protect its individual members from interference in the performance of their central duties. There has been, in the world of academia when it was functioning at its best, an unwritten and elementary equivalent of the First Amendment. It does not explicitly forbid Congress or anyone else from censoring the scholar, but an Article One for academia exists nonetheless; as Jaspers said, it is called academic freedom. It assumes that no one—Congress, the legislature, the dean, the chair, or the student—should meddle with the process of learning and teaching, so long as it is done in the Socratic and/or Kantian spirit. It is not foolproof; it has often been violated or abused by those who ought to be most protective of it, but politicians, administrators, students, and professors interfere with it at their peril.

This principle exists in part because neither the academic world nor the political world is a monolith. And because there is a kind of federalism of nations and of learning and of languages, scholars individually and in community have occasionally enjoyed the possibilities of a critical, difficult, creative endeavor. We have tenure, and we need it, to assure that this federalism of learning has a fair chance to survive.

On one level, the history of the university ideal is the record of the gradual expansion of the intellectual options in the traditional fields of learning and beyond those fields into a continually expanding universe of knowledge. When, by fits and starts, the Western world was ready to test new (or to retest old) theories in theology, medicine, law, and the "arts," as the fields of learning were traditionally defined three-quarters of a millennium ago, it was the universities that most often provided the preferred laboratories for such testing. This was not universally true; often new ideas had to fight their way into the academies on the backs of rebels, and often the richer and more famous universities—like Paris—were most resistant to the newer ideas.

Nevertheless, as the values of the high Middle Ages spread outward from their centers in Italy and France in the thirteenth and fourteenth centuries and as the speculations of the Renaissance followed from their Italian base in the fifteenth, it was the universities—when their integrity was highest and their ability to challenge the status quo at its keenest—that proved to be the way stations for the distribution of the new learning. The new alternatives or—to use Thomas Kuhn's widely respected figure—the paradigms usually found their champions among the masters and students at a *studium generale* before they became the common property of the civilization at large. Paris was such a place in the thirteenth century and for part of the fourteenth. Padua and Basle—by some good fortune that needs to be explored in another essay—honored the university idea of inquiry later and for a much longer period than did the "archetypical" *studia* which Rashdall chose to emphasize.

There have been times in the history of Europe when the universities had no arrangement to assure the critical independence of those who were seekers after truth. In the age of Erasmus, for example, when the bitter religious disputes of the Reformation wracked European society, universities became instruments for the suppression of religious and political inquiry, and it was only possible to be a professor in the fullest sense by avoiding the universities. This splendid humanist exercised his academic independence by spending most of his scholarly career on the edge of the universities. Only once did he hold a professorial chair for a couple of years—at Cambridge. But for much of his life he used the resources and the presses and the disputations of Basle (the most tolerant university city of Europe in the early sixteenth century), and thus he did some of his definitive intellectual work, as it were, in a university climate. The seventeenth century was a most unhappy time for the university ideal, and only in the late eighteenth century did a substantial number of European universities begin to recover their medieval autonomy for themselves and their professors.

The best universities have not always been the places that possessed the greatest riches; money does not talk decisively in the university setting, however well it may pay the chancellors or the bishops or presidents who presumably speak for it. Occasionally the great universities have been associated with great wealth, but it is not invariably so. And one certainly cannot measure the quality of a university by the salary of its executives or the prayers of its advocates—whether those prayers are directed toward heaven, the local plutocrats, or the *vox populi*.

Just as the institutions bearing the label of *studium generale* in the medieval and Reformation eras were not invariably dedicated to the advancement of learning, so the universities, so-called, within our own time and region have not been uniformly worthy of the calling that has been outlined here. One need only mention the loyalty oaths in California in 1950, when the board of regents voted to dismiss thirty-two professors who refused to sign a humiliating and meaningless pledge of loyalty as a condition of their employment. The courts eventually interfered with such folly. More recently, regents in Nevada have occasionally tried to tamper with basic academic freedoms, and other offenses against the basic integrity in neighboring states could be cited if supplementary provincial evidence were needed. The history of Western universities is riddled with the efforts of theologians, politicians, and small-minded entrepreneurs who sought to impose their narrow values on the academy. It is also garlanded with the history of its rebels. There are a few principles that need to be reaffirmed from time to time, even though they are the old ones.

First, a university operates best, in its more delicate functions of inquiry and social criticism, when it is either physically or administratively distant from the centers of ecclesiastical and political authority. A controlling king, pope, bishop, or parliamentary body that is too close at hand and that supervises too closely is a potential enemy of learning. A great seat of learning in a national or imperial capital is an anomaly. It is axiomatic that an institution of learning that has doctrine dictated to it by king, pope, or political party is *ipso facto* crippled in its pedagogical and scientific functions. But an ideology and an academic standard can just as readily be imposed by a well-intentioned Republican majority or by social pressure as by a red commissar.

Second, a so-called university functions poorly if its primary function is to grub for money. If its executive officers do so, they may be forgiven so long as they serve the central purpose of the university. If the professoriat does so as its primary goal (if it has as its highest function to seek favor or to "compete for grants"), then it is like a corrupt priesthood that has polluted its calling for the sake of its privileges.

Would that the universities had been more careful of their trust in our own time. It is sad to have to confess that the so-called universities have too often been instruments for suppressing or discouraging new or old paradigms. Some *studia* became notorious for their intolerance of questionable theories and some institutions with long and honorable records in the history of

Western academia are today—as always—threatened with being used as organizations for the suppression, rather than the enhancement, of critical inquiry. There may be inherent prestige in the label "university," but there is no insurance policy to prevent a narrow dogma, or a local commercial imperative, or a totalitarian ideology from stifling the free inquiry that is the fundamental *raison d'être* of a university.

The essential truism is that the university ideal survives because there are professors who do *profess* the ideal of scholarship as intellectual rebellion—an Aquinas in Paris, a Roger Bacon in Oxford and Paris, a Jan Huss in Prague, a Karl Jaspers in Heidelberg, a Pavel Vinogradoff in Moscow, a Miguel de Unomuno in Salamanca, a Robert Paul Wolff at Columbia, and an Allan Bloom at the University of Chicago. Let us conclude these deliberations with reference to these latter two commentators, who have made reaffirmations in our own time of the venerable ideal which repeatedly needs advocates.

One of the most thoughtful essays to emerge from the 1968 crisis in higher education in the United States was that of Wolff, the Columbia University philosopher. Less than a year after the student uprisings in that season of violent protest against the Vietnam War, Wolff was asked to deliver a series of lectures at the University of Wisconsin. He used the occasion to organize his ideas about the role and governance of the modern university.[8]

Wolff's basic assumption about the essential function of the university is rather close to that of Jaspers—the standard idea about the pursuit of truth. But there is a slight Marxist tinge to his thought, and his references were almost entirely to contemporary America, so there were some intentionally provocative variations.

Wolff proposed four models, or "ideal types," for the contemporary university. Each of these models operates in the minds of some professional people associated with the universities, and there are conflicts between them which contribute to internal and external debate about the role of the institution. The university may be perceived as (1) a Sanctuary for Scholarship; (2) a Training Camp for the Professions; (3) a Social Service Station; and (4) an Assembly Line for Establishment Men.

The first is the traditional, humanistic model based upon the long tradition of the university as ivory tower, preserver of culture, and place for conducting the various quests for truth. Such a model has few advocates outside the academy in the waning years of the twentieth century. Wolff was sympathetic with this tradition and eloquently insisted upon a place for it in the contemporary university.

But he recognized that the traditional sanctuary role had serious competition from the other models. To the extent that a university was a Training Camp for the Professions, it represented a "centrifugal dispersion of energies": "In countless ways, the activities of the professors and students of the professional schools reach out beyond the university, and inevitably loyalties are divided. The professional faculties cannot commit themselves or their energies to the university unconditionally, as professors in the arts and sciences regularly do."[9] The existence of this catbird in the nest of academia and the requirement for professional certification created an awkward situation for the university. So far, the turf is familiar.

Wolff's radical streak becomes more apparent when he discusses the university as a Social Service Station and challenges the arguments of Clark Kerr, former chancellor of the University of California System, and his concept of the "multiversity." In this model, the university emerges as a place which is immediately responsive to the perceived needs of anybody and everybody in society. It is therefore also a place of chaos, because it surrenders its standards and expectations to the demands of the marketplace. In the interest of serving the so-called needs of society, it makes little or no distinction between legitimate social requirements and current market fads. Wolff says of Kerr, "Instead of calling his essay *The Uses of the University*, he could more appropriately have titled it *University for Hire*."[10] For Wolff, it was essential that the university not become merely an *instrument* of the prevailing national purpose—even if that can be defined by a president or Congress. The university must maintain its right to serve as a *critic* of such purpose. It must be a place for the evaluation of the political purposes of the current regime; it must become an arena for "teach-ins" when the governing establishment stumbles into irresponsible folly, as in the case of the Vietnam War. Wolff saw little room for this in Kerr's "multiversity" concept, so he rejected it—with eloquent rhetoric.

Wolff finds the fourth model even more offensive. It assumes that the university exists to produce the Establishment Man for the existing society. Bright students are funneled from their earliest years of schooling into those social roles that are perceived to be most desirable. He rejects this model, which was accepted in the 1960s by many radicals who attacked the entire structure of higher education.

For all its flaws and faults, Wolff believed the American universities to be

> the only major viable institutional centers of opposition to the dominant values and policies of the society. The churches are weak, the unions have long since made their peace with the established order, the poor and the Black are as yet not organized, and little can be expected from the corporate world or the agricultural sector. It is in the universities that opposition to the Vietnamese war started and flourished. There, if anywhere, new and deeper attacks on the evils of American society will be mounted. *Here again, the opposition role of the university flows from its very nature as a center of free inquiry.* Against all the pressures from the larger society, colleges and universities in the United States have for half a century been in the van of progressive social reform and social criticism.[11]

After dismissing several "myths" about the university (that its work can be judged by some standards of objectivity, productivity, or numerical data), Wolff returns to discuss the heart of the university. At the core of the true university, distinctive relationships exist between scholars and those who want to become scholars in the search for social and ethical truths. There also, the maturing young man and woman has an opportunity to examine his or her life in the Socratic manner—sometimes alone, sometimes with other scholars or potential scholars.

When we consider the essential role of the university, the activities of administrators, politicians, and budget makers are of little consequence. In which of these educational relationships, Wolff asks, is there an appropriate exercise of "authority"? He responds, "To put my case as simply and forcefully as possible, the answer is: *None. Claims to authority, the exercise of authority, and submission to authority have no place whatsoever in any of the characteristic educational relationships of a university.*"[12] Boards of trustees, administrators, recruiters, faculty senates, secret research, certification procedures, and the like are not central to the university's work, yet it is in these forums and on the issues that arise there—separate from the basic searching, teaching, and critical responsibilities of the university—that most of the institutional energies are expended.

The most provocative contemporary example of professorial narcissism for the benefit of the larger society is *The Closing of the American Mind*, by Professor Allan Bloom of the University of Chicago. This book was the surprise of 1987 in academia and perhaps in all of the book-publishing world, because a formidable tome dedicated to intellectual history rose to the top of the best-seller lists and remained in that nonacademic marketplace for several weeks.

This work is of course much more than yet another examination of the university ideal. It is that, but it gained its notoriety, presumably, because it is a devastating indictment of American civilization and a chronicle of the collapse of the Judeo-Christian, Greco-Roman ethic in this country. Bloom's message is that American culture has lost its bearings, that a kind of neofascism has become predominant, and that the higher educational establishment is both accessory to and victim of the process.[13]

In one superficial reading of Bloom's book, one might conclude that American universities were in their golden age in the 1950s (when Bloom and some others among us were going to school) but that the disaster occurred in the 1960s, when the sexual revolution, the student rebellions, the professorial abdication, and the rage for "relevance" dominated the academic scene. If this is the only fragment that survives the scanning that we must all, perforce, do in these days, more's the pity. Bloom will then be perceived to be a human trapped in his own time and experience. After all, this can happen even to a philosopher, and Bloom's own venerable discipline is one of those most severely abused and neglected in the contemporary age. But he knows his way out of that trap, and that is not the essence of his book. This is a magnificent effort by a dedicated university man to use his university calling and the free press for a statement about the state of contemporary learning.

This is certainly one of the most important books of our time, probably of this century. I predict that it will someday be ranked up there with Emerson's essay on *The American Scholar*, with de

Tocqueville's *Democracy in America*, and with *The Education of Henry Adams* as a classic statement on the American condition. But this will only be so if Bloom's thesis is largely wrong. If the decline of literacy and morality continues at the pace that he has described, nobody will be reading books or thinking about them at all a generation or two from now.

So this is indeed a good book, a necessary slap in the face of American culture and—more specifically—the academic community in the best tradition of that community. It is a profoundly pessimistic book; the humanities, the Great Books, the biblical heritage, the belief in democracy and the principles of the Founding Fathers have all disappeared, Bloom says repeatedly. Near the end, one finds this poignant sentence about the possibility of revitalizing the university: "The matter is still present in the university; it is the form that has vanished. One cannot and should not hope for a general reform. The hope is that the embers do not die out." [14]

Bloom's argument that higher education has abandoned its responsibility for providing the moral and social adhesiveness to the society is disturbing, but he is mostly right on this score. The academy has badly shirked its duty to raise the large questions of life and death, ultimate meaning, and social responsibility. Most of us who regard ourselves as humanists, I think, would plead guilty on this score.

But there is another charge which he levels at higher education that is much more troubling, and Bloom made some of these points in a lecture at the University of Nevada, Reno, a couple of years ago. It is the accusation that we have surrendered to a kind of neo-Nazi "nihilism" similar to the one that inspired the Third Reich in the 1930s. He argues this most cogently in a middle chapter entitled "The German Connection." [15]

Most of the book is written in this tone; the battle is lost, the barbarians have won, and the affliction is more or less universal. He talks as though all academics, except perhaps a small "saving remnant" of humanists, have gone over to the enemy. He is categorical in his testimonials to the ignorance and lack of concern for ethics in the contemporary student population.

Here I believe he is wrong, and the success of his book is an argument against his own thesis. There are more students familiar with and dedicated to the old values, and there are more who are eager to tackle the big questions and the classics than Bloom admits. And there are even more professors bucking the tide—and there is no question that the tide has been against them these past several years—than he allows.

The protesting professoriat is alive and well in America. Bloom's book and the reactions to it are sound proof of this fact. It is appropriate that that should be so, because the species that he represents is much older than institutions in which he has lectured.

One of the most engaging reactions to *The Closing of the American Mind* is the commentary which was thrown into the fan by Robert Paul Wolff. A casual thought about the works of these two rebellious professors might lead one to expect that they would stand together in their assault upon the academic structure which they have both served and challenged for so many years. But it would be folly to linger over such a misconception.

Wolff has written a sarcastic, satirical review of Bloom's book, pretending that Bloom is a fictional character created by Saul Bellow (who wrote the preface to *The Closing*).[16] Wolff swings right and left, with mock seriousness, at Bloom's assumptions, at the University of Chicago "Great Books" tradition from which they flow, and at Bloom himself. The critical attitude is more hostile than comical, although there is no doubt that he means to be both; Wolff dislikes Bloom's Platonism and his affection for the Judeo-Christian and Greco-Roman values—in short, his liberalism. One suspects that he dislikes Bloom because the Chicago professor stands for a "Sanctuary for Scholarship."

It is not merely that Bloom is coming from "the right" in academia and Wolff from "the left"—if such terms make any sense in this arena. More important is the fact that each is a totally autonomous authority, responsible to no one except peers, who happily can do little more in this society than challenge the arguments and the egos of their rivals. There may be institutional dead ends, but so far we have no gulags.

In this short review, Wolff reminds us of one of the basic features of the community of rebellious professors. They are at least as demanding and as critical of one another as they are of the public and the institutions whom they torment. Their guild is magnificently eclectic and anarchistic, and they regularly keep their colleagues, as well as the state and the academy, slightly off balance. That has been and is the most important achievement of the rebellious professors.

Bloom has lectured in a hundred places, from Rashdall's paradigmatic universities in Europe to the University of Nevada in Reno. That he is welcome, both in person and in his writings, in such diverse places is an encouraging testimonial to the health of the university ideal in our time. There are hundreds of wolves out there to circle and seek to savage his ideas, and that is one of the strengths of contemporary university life.

NOTES

1. Hastings Rashdall, *The Universities of Europe in the Middle Ages,* a new edition by F. M. Powicke and A. B. Emden (London: Oxford University Press, 1895; new edition 1936), vii.

2. Ibid.

3. Frederick Rudolph, *The American College and University: A History* (New York: Alfred A. Knopf, 1962), 243.

4. John Henry Newman, "What Is a University," originally published in the Dublin *Catholic University Gazette* in 1854 and subsequently reprinted in his *The Rise and Progress of Universities.*

5. Karl Jaspers, *The Idea of the University,* ed. Karl Deutsch (London: Peter Owen, 1960), 19.

6. An excellent study of the twelfth-century beginnings of the university is Stephen C. Ferruolo, *The Origins of the University: The Schools of Paris and Their Critics, 1100–1215* (Stanford, Calif.: Stanford University Press, 1985).

7. Rashdall, *Universities of Europe,* vol. 1, 368.

8. Robert Paul Wolff, *The Ideal of the University* (Boston: Beacon Press, 1969).

9. Ibid., 13.

10. Ibid., 40.

11. Ibid., 56, emphasis in original.

12. Ibid., 100.

13. Allan Bloom, *The Closing of the American Mind: How Higher Education Has Failed Democracy and Impoverished the Souls of Today's Students* (New York: Simon and Schuster, 1987).

14. Ibid., 380.

15. Ibid., 141–56.

16. Robert Paul Wolff, "Review of *The Closing of the American Mind,*" *Academe* 73 (September–October 1987): 64–65.

COMPANY FOR A *LONESOME DOVE*

ANN RONALD

The dust jacket proclaims that Larry McMurtry's *Lonesome Dove* "is his long-awaited masterpiece, the major novel at last of the American West as it really was." A second paragraph sounds almost as sweeping in its pronouncement. "A love story, an adventure, an American epic, *Lonesome Dove* embraces *all* the West—legend and fact, heroes and outlaws, whores and ladies, Indians and settlers—in a novel that recreates the central American experience, the most enduring of our national myths."

Such purple prose ought to stir the curiosity of all of us who read and love western American literature. Can it be that someone finally has written the definitive western novel? Has a Faulkner finally emerged beyond the hundredth meridian? Do we at last have a book against which we can measure *Angle of Repose, The Big Sky, The Ox-bow Incident, Shane, The Virginian* (to name a few of my particular candidates for greatness), a writer against whom we can project Zane Grey or Louis L'Amour, Vardis Fisher or Frank Waters, William Eastlake or Edward Abbey? Is *Lonesome Dove* indeed "the major novel" of the American West?

The Pulitzer Prize people were willing to give it a lot of credit. My local public library says its waiting list of readers is a long one, while its paperback edition highlights supermarket shelves across the country. And quite frankly, I liked it so well that I haven't been able to shake it loose from my imagination. If it isn't "the major novel" of the American West, it's certainly among the top ten.

That generalization leads directly to a second (and even more debatable) issue. Just what *is* a "major novel" of the American

West? What kind of story line, characters, and thematic complexities appear? What kind of ambience pervades? And how are we to judge? That is, even as we contemplate measuring a variety of novels against *Lonesome Dove*, we must also discern those touchstones alongside which *Lonesome Dove* must stand.

The problem is compounded by the fact that our touchstones for the great western novel have been generated inappropriately. Whereas William Faulkner defined a literature of the South by writing a series of superior novels, a formula defines the literature of the West. We measure greatness not by analyzing the achievements of a master but by examining the intelligence with which a given author treats a list of expected ingredients. Focusing on such elements as the chronological and geographical settings, a somewhat specialized group of human beings, and the essential themes of the frontier experience, we simply decide whether or not a novelist treats them seriously enough. Until the West generates an author who transcends the genre, we have no other option. Witness my assessment of *Lonesome Dove*.

Many readers insist first on a historical perspective, with action set a hundred years ago and characters involved in events that conceivably might have taken place. Although most aficionados accept tales of mountain men, of explorers, of forty-niners, or of pioneers as appropriate to the genre, some purists even go so far as to require the presence of cowboys. *Lonesome Dove* would satisfy them. Set in the latter part of the nineteenth century—after the Civil War and before the closing of the frontier—*Lonesome Dove* not only exudes history but also takes place in the Great Plains West. A dimension of history shapes every page, as cowboys who once were Texas Rangers embark on a cattle drive typical of—though longer than—a thousand other such ventures in the 1870s.

Andy Adams's *Log of a Cowboy*, a 1903 narrative that compresses one such cowhand's experiences, reveals that those real-life adventures were not as romantic as Zane Grey would have us believe. Trail driving actually was dusty, lonely, unpleasant work. Storms, stampedes, dry treks, and river crossings provided dangers to make any man uneasy, while the distances involved made a long drive feel interminable. Even the infrequent pockets of civilization—Abilene, Dodge, Ogallala—were anything but glamorous. In a word, the trail was a harsh one, testing character, ingenuity, and endurance at every bend.

Adams's and McMurtry's cowboys faced strikingly similar obstacles. Some were relatively benign irritants ("swarms of mosquitoes, which attacked horses and men alike, settling on them so thickly that they could be wiped off like stains" [LD, 273]); others were fatal ("a scream cut the air, so terrible it almost made him faint . . . Sean was barely clinging to his horse . . . a lot of brown things were wiggling around him and over him . . . they seemed like giant worms . . . the giant worms were snakes—water moccasins" [LD, 277]). When Sean's companions finally dragged the victim from the river and cut his shirt off, they found "eight sets of fang marks, including one on his neck. 'That don't count the legs,' Augustus said. 'There ain't no point in counting the legs'" (LD, 278). The horror of that crossing is only one such instance of pain in Lonesome Dove. Like Sam Peckinpah's, McMurtry's West is a place where romantic possibilities too often are destroyed by violence and degradation.

In his 1902 novel The Virginian, Owen Wister outlined the formula of romanticized adventures and pseudoviolence that Zane Grey was content to borrow and that early twentieth-century readers soon came to expect. In most cases, the harsh realities of the frontier were tinted by the colors of the rainbow, Grey's so-called rainbow trail. After the 1950s, however, technicolor no longer beautified the path. Where Shane and the Virginian once had ridden, the Wild Bunch and Clint Eastwood's gunslingers followed, and now the men of the Hat Creek Cattle Company find the brutal track.

When a renegade Indian kidnaps a Lonesome Dove heroine, "it wasn't death she got—just the four men" (LD, 385). Later she is forced to witness scenes perhaps gratuitously savage.

> One Kiowa cut his belt and two more pulled his pants off. Before Lorena could even turn her head, they castrated him. Another slashed a knife across his forehead and began to rip off his hair. Dog Face screamed again, but it was soon muffled as the Kiowas held his head and stuffed his own bloody organs into his mouth, shoving them down his throat with the handle of a knife. His hair was soon ripped off and the Kiowa took the scalp and tied it to his lance. Dog Face struggled for breath, a pool of blood beneath his legs. Yet he wasn't dead.

> Lorena had her face in her arms, but she could still hear him
> moan and gurgle for breath. She wished he would die—it
> shouldn't take so long just to die. (*LD*, 450)

If that episode isn't grotesque enough, even her rescue turns
bitter when her kidnapper methodically axes three innocent
people while escaping unhurt. So *Lonesome Dove* differs significantly from earlier predecessors in that its genuine atrocities upset a reader's formulaic expectations. Just when one least ex-
pects it, the romance of the Old West gives way to an onslaught
of naturalistic detail.

The characters, as well as the scenes in this novel, are disarm-
ingly different. Content to enjoy an afternoon jug and gabble
away his remaining years, Augustus McCrae at first seems wholly
unheroic. Yet when heroics become necessary, when the renegade Blue Duck needs tracking or when a swarm of Indians
needs dispersing ("He then proceeded to shoot six times, rapidly. Five of the Indians [*sic*] horses dropped, and a sixth ran
squealing over the prairie—it fell several hundred yards away"
[*LD*, 753]), Gus McCrae's verbosity gives way to amazingly competent action. Reminiscent of John Wayne's Rooster Cogburn,
Gus oscillates between antihero and hero, idling away page after
page with "pokes" and poker, then executing courageous deeds
without hesitation. In either guise he is likable. Thoughtful, rea-
sonably considerate of women and other men, sensitive, he belies the stereotype of the macho western male even as he functions just as potently.

His partner, Capt. Woodrow F. Call, is equally valorous, as
effective in a tense situation and just as unique. A superb com-
mander of men, he displays his leadership without aggression.
He would rather give his orders and then ride alone, rally his
cowhands by day and simply disappear at night. Provocation,
however, may make him explode. "Call had destruction in him
and would go on killing when there was no need. Once his
blood heated, it was slow to cool" (*LD*, 440). More like a bad guy
than good, he may charge beyond the bounds of conventional
civilized behavior. His strong, silent reluctance to express his
feelings overstates a stereotype, too. Both Call and Gus, then,
are viewed somewhat askew, conventional western heroes portrayed finally as genuinely multifaceted human beings. "As
a team, the two of them were perfectly balanced" (*LD*, 167).

A study in contrasts (one taciturn, the other loquacious), the two leaders counterpoint each other in ways that confound our formulaic expectations.

Their troops are presented stereotypically and then behave in unusual ways, too. The most surprising is the handsome but balding cowboy Jake Spoon. "There was no more likable man in the west, and no better rider, either; but riding wasn't everything, and neither was likableness. Something in Jake didn't quite stick," McMurtry explains when the man first rides into the novel. "Something wasn't quite consistent" (*LD*, 65). That inconsistency drives Jake to abandon Lorena and finally to follow the unsavory Suggs brothers. By then, "life had slipped out of line. It was unfair, it was too bad, but he couldn't find the energy to fight it any longer" (*LD*, 574). Blessed by so many of the characteristics that comprise a cowboy hero, Jake fails instead.

Jake's admirer, young Newt, is another character who initially reminds the reader of someone from a Zane Grey western. A boy becoming a man, he watches the action around him, develops his own skills, and grows to maturity in the process. Yet his behavior—whether riding in the heart of a stampede, discovering the suddenness of death, or learning about sex for the first time—isn't trite. "He trotted the last two hundred yards to where he had tied Mouse. But the horse wasn't there! He had used a boulder as a landmark, and the boulder was where it should be—but not the horse. Newt knew the stampede might have scared him and caused him to break the rein, but there was no broken rein hanging from the tree where Mouse had been tied. Before he could stop himself, Newt began to cry" (*LD*, 364). In the western novels that preceded *Lonesome Dove*, few young protagonists were seen in tears. But Newt unabashedly sobs at least ten different times during the course of his maturation. Learning of Gus's death, "He cried all afternoon, riding as far back on the drags as he could get. For once he was grateful for the dust the herd raised" (*LD*, 792).

On the distaff side, the characterizations are just as surprising. Clara, the earth mother, and her opposite, Elmira Johnson, exemplify a real polarity of female behavior. Where the one sacrifices self for family, the other sacrifices family for self. More interesting, though, is the woman whom the dust jacket calls "the whore with the proverbial heart of gold." Damaged first by her life-style and then by her kidnapping, Lorena retreats into a childlike state from which she never quite emerges. The subtleties of her personality—her responses to the individual men, her reactions to episodes on the trail, her inscrutable silence at the novel's end—take her well beyond the confines of caricature or even formula.

One of my friends complains that the people in *Lonesome Dove* are somewhat hastily drawn and too quickly discarded. He sees Lorena, for example, as a character with enormous possibilities, arguing that to deposit her with Clara is to give up on her potential. While I agree that a lot of men and women come and go rather precipitously, I dispute my colleague's conclusion because I view *Lonesome Dove* as a panorama of types. Its artistic goal is the creation of a broad-swept canvas rather than the portraiture of psychological cameos.

Certainly Lorena could have been developed further. McMurtry emotionally drops her just as, when the catalytic result suits him, he more permanently disposes of other people, too. Sean, Deets, Jake, Elmira, and even Gus are expendable in time. "Though he had seen hundreds of surprising things in battle, this was the most shocking. An Indian boy who probably hadn't been fifteen years old had run up to Deets and killed him" (*LD*, 718). Ignominiously eliminating Deets, the seasoned fighter and the leaders' right-hand man, McMurtry makes his point clear. *Lonesome Dove* is not the story of any one cliché.

Rather, *Lonesome Dove* is all the stories of the Old West, 843 pages of neophytes and heroes, horses and longhorns, mothers and whores, good guys and bad. The book judges those people and their lives from a perspective designed to elicit surprise.

McMurtry sets the pattern at the beginning. Unlike an adventure yarn, not much happens at first. The first quarter of this novel occurs before the cattle drive even begins, with slow delicious moments on the Hat Creek Cattle Company and Livery Emporium property and at the nearby Dry Bean Saloon. The leisurely pace—perhaps more typical of the rural West than most novelists care to admit—belies the conventional rhythm of formula fiction. "As was his custom, Augustus drank a fair amount of whiskey as he sat and watched the sun ease out of the day" (*LD*, 16). His partner, on the other hand, just looks busier. "Call walked the river for an hour, though he knew there was no real need. It was just an old habit he had, left over from wilder times" (*LD*, 26). So the days—and two hundred pages—pass, without incident.

Highlighting the two men's lives are infrequent forays into Mexico when, reversing their earlier Texas Ranger roles, the cowboys rustle available horses and cattle. Even that turns out to be a joke, though. Pedro Flores, their nemesis, is dead. "We might as well go on to Montana," Call says quietly. "The fun's over around here" (*LD*, 170). The fun isn't over in McMurtry's imagination, however, as he delimits life off the range. "The piano was the pride of the saloon, and, for that matter, of the town. The church folks even borrowed it on Sundays. Luckily the church house was right next to the saloon and the piano had wheels. Some of the deacons had built a ramp out at the back of the saloon, and a board track across to the church, so that all they had to do was push the piano right across to the church. Even so, the arrangement was a threat to the sobriety of the deacons, some of whom considered it their duty to spend their evenings in the saloon, safeguarding the piano" (*LD*, 30–31).

Trailing away from Lonesome Dove leads to more sobering experiences, but a lightheartedness makes the tension easier to bear. Like *Little Big Man* and *The Monkey-Wrench Gang* before it, this novel disguises serious themes in comic dress. Not surprisingly, those themes are appropriate to the frontier.

The first of these I call the "jackpot mentality"—the idealistic notion that the grass will be greener on the other side. What should be the energy of the American dream but instead is the impetus of boredom sends Call north to Montana. Once there, he turns back to Texas again, a cyclical movement that highlights the futility of the quest in the first place. Macabre, hollow, even silly, his final adventure ends almost pathetically. One might say that Augustus McCrae's last moments are just as counterproductive.

In fact, most of *Lonesome Dove's* adventures are ultimately counterproductive. Elmira runs away from her husband because she wants to go back to her ex-lover and live free again. She finds Dee Boot in jail. "He seemed scared, and his hair had little pieces of cotton ticking in it from a tear in the thin mattress he slept on. The scruffy growth of whiskers made him seem a lot older than she had remembered him" (*LD*, 606). Running away one more time, she finds a cruel death at the hands of a band of marauding Indians—another dream dashed.

Another theme is dashed, too. Experience regularly replaces

innocence in many western novels. Sometimes that innocence is painfully apparent, as we see in the narrator of *The Virginian* or of *Shane;* sometimes it's trite, as we discover in a Zane Grey formulaic rendition of learning the "Code of the West"; sometimes it's less obtrusive but no less significant. Neither Elmira nor her husband, July Johnson, knows anything about survival in the West, yet they're decisively educated McMurtry-style. July, for example, joins Gus in a bloody confrontation with the Kiowas. "I didn't shoot a one," he moans after the last man falls. "You shot the whole bunch" (*LD,* 451). The lesson he learns an hour later is even more painful. "For a long time, July did not go into the camp. He couldn't. He stood and listened to the flies buzz over them. He didn't want to see what had been done" (*LD,* 456). Education, in this case, embraces violence and pain. It isn't the least bit romantic or technicolorful.

Newt's learning process takes painful form, too. Dusty trail rides, lonely nights with the herd, violent weather, and blind stampedes shape his physical development. Deaths like Sean's and Deet's and Jake's age him psychologically. "'Have we got to hang Jake too?' he asked. 'He was my ma's friend'" (*LD,* 572). Newt's question elicits no comment from the men of the Hat Creek Cattle Company.

Good and evil are as clear-cut in *Lonesome Dove* as they are in most western novels, but they well may be mixed in a single human being. That is to say, a strong ethical code informs the novel, though not everyone wears a white hat or a black hat and not every character receives his just desserts. Jake, of course, deserves punishment because he silently allowed the Suggs brothers to perpetrate mayhem. That he spurs his horse from under the noose—"He died fine," says Gus (*LD,* 576)—reminds us of his good qualities; that he must be hung iterates the bad. So, too, do we see other mixed indications of frontier justice. Innocents like Roscoe, Joe, and Janey, for example, are brutally dismembered, while their murderer, Blue Duck, escapes. About to be hung a year later, the renegade dies instead by leaping, in chains, through a third-story courthouse window. Once again McMurtry raises expectations and then dashes them to the prairie sod.

This, then, is *Lonesome Dove*'s pattern. Not a theme exists that hasn't, in one form or another, appeared in another western novel, just as no character or setting occurs that the reader hasn't seen before. But McMurtry, rather than simply revisiting the past, turns it topsy-turvy. Familiar river crossings, familiar faces, familiar formulas emerge and fade in twisted fashion.

For readers who take their cowboys seriously, the reversals and dispersals may prove unsettling; the black humor and the inhuman violence unpleasant. For the iconoclast who finds George Washington Hayduke a welcome antidote, however, the one who would like to see the high plains drifter ride into Dallas, *Lonesome Dove's* heroes are perfectly fine. As a matter of fact, the iconoclast would approve of the entire ambience of the book. While not taking the formulas too seriously, it takes the Old West very seriously indeed.

On a level we haven't touched yet, *Lonesome Dove* is profound. A penetrating examination of historical forces and the passage of time, it explores what happens when generations permute and dreams fail to materialize. This particular theme I believe dominates the best of western fiction. *The Big Sky* and *Angle of Repose*, to choose two outstanding examples, both turn on fulcrums of change—Boone Caudill's West disappears in the irony of his own actions, Susan and Oliver Ward's is transmuted through the years. In both cases, and in *Lonesome Dove*, change and perpetuity weave together as one generation gives way to the next and as the ever-present American dream reasserts itself in different guise.

In a scene reminiscent of Shane's final heroic departure, Woodrow Call leaves his horse, his rifle, and his father's pocket watch to Newt, newly dubbed range boss of the Montana spread. Much could be made, I suppose, of the symbolism, but in actuality the entire scene takes place in almost utter silence. The painfully inarticulate Call can transfer the artifacts, not the wisdom, the strength, the heart. Later Call defends himself by saying, "'I gave him my horse.'" Clara counters, "'Your horse but not your name? . . . You haven't even given him your name?' 'I put more value on the horse,'" Call rightly replies (*LD*, 831). Penetrating the stereotypes with an almost painful irony, McMurtry successfully warps the formula one more time.

When I finished *Lonesome Dove*, I was struck not only by how thoroughly the old formulas had been dispersed but also by how completely the Hat Creek Cattle Company and Livery Emporium had disappeared. Call hears a dinner bell that "made him feel that he rode through a land of ghosts. He felt lost in his mind and wondered if all the boys would be there when he got home" (*LD*, 841). They aren't, of course. The novel ends two pages after that, but not before exposing one more instance of fraudulent idealism—the Dry Bean Saloon, burned to the ground because its owner "missed that whore" (*LD*, 843). So the reader closes the book with inadvertent thoughts of Dish Boggett, another cowboy pursuing the same futility into an unknown future.

In scenes like the preceding, *Lonesome Dove* addresses what Wallace Stegner calls the crucial issue of western fiction. Time passes, generations come and go, the same mistakes are made again—variations on a theme. Like the author of *Angle of Repose*, McMurtry discerns the sweep of history as cyclical, then points to its transitory ironies.

> "Imagine getting killed by an arrow in this day and age," Augustus said. "It's ridiculous, especially since they shot at us fifty times with modern weapons and did no harm."
>
> "You always was careless," Call said. "Pea said you rode over a hill and right into them. I've warned you about that very thing a thousand times. There's better ways to approach a hill."
>
> "Yes, but I like being free on the earth," Augustus said. "I'll cross the hills where I please." (*LD*, 784–85)

So will the author of *Lonesome Dove*.

McMurtry rides in the company of the Stegners and the Abbeys and the Clarks and all the first-rate western novelists who ever described a cowboy without quite keeping to the trail. The characters are all there in his book, the setting, the themes, the social and psychological milieus—all combined in a panoramic vista of the Old West. But just when the reader thinks a cliché will materialize, McMurtry stands the formula on its head. Just when the expected turns up, the unexpected turns it upside down. Sometimes comically, sometimes violently, often with emotions mixed, the world of *Lonesome Dove* moves south to north and back again via a route signed by reversals of what should be familiar. "'Why in the hell would anybody think they wanted to take cattle to Montana?'" someone asks. "'We thought it would be a good place to sit back and watch 'em shit,'" comes the irreverent answer (*LD*, 649).

That McMurtry's imagination sees a landscape beyond the rainbow trail is what makes *Lonesome Dove* first-rate. That he crafts a panorama which makes all the old expectations seem fresh and new is a measure of his talent. That he addresses significant themes in a fresh way is obviously a mark of excellence. *A* major novel of the American West? Absolutely. *The* major novel? No.

The very characteristic that makes this book great is also the one that keeps it from being the greatest. Rather than challenging the formulas and clichés from the past, the greatest literature makes its own. McMurtry, content to warp the pattern, finally has done nothing more. *Lonesome Dove* is the best epic western of the last ten years, but it wasn't made by a man imagining a masterpiece. Its author isn't the Faulkner of the West; its dust jacket is wrong. On the other hand, I like the book enormously. So maybe that dust jacket, when it labels *Lonesome Dove* "the novel about the West that [we have] long been waiting for," isn't out of line after all. I was indeed waiting for *Lonesome Dove*, though I continue to fancy a Faulkner wearing spurs.

NOTE

1. All citations included in the text are from Larry McMurtry, *Lonesome Dove* (New York: Simon and Schuster, 1985).

PUBLICATIONS BY WILBUR S. SHEPPERSON

COMPILED BY JOHN G. FOLKES

BOOKS AND MONOGRAPHS

The Promotion of British Emigration by Agents for American Lands, 1840–1860 (Reno: University of Nevada Press, 1954).

British Emigration to North America (Oxford: Basil Blackwell Press, 1957). Republished in the United States by the University of Minnesota Press, 1957.

Six Who Returned: America Viewed by British Repatriates (Reno: University of Nevada Press, 1961).

Samuel Roberts: A Welsh Colonizer in Civil War Tennessee (Knoxville: University of Tennessee Press, 1961).

In the Trek of the Immigrants, ed. F. Ander (Rock Island, Ill.: Augustana College Library, 1964).

The Disenchanted: Portraits of Englishmen Repatriated from the United States (Norman: University of Oklahoma Press, 1965).

Retreat to Nevada: A Socialist Colony of World War I (Reno: University of Nevada Press, 1966).

Restless Strangers: Nevada's Immigrants and Their Interpreters (Reno: University of Nevada Press, 1970).

Questions from the Past (Reno: University of Nevada Press, 1973).

Land and the Pursuit of Happiness (Los Angeles: University of California Extension Publication, 1975).

Hardscrabble: A Narrative of the California Hill Country (Reno: University of Nevada Press, 1975).

ARTICLES

"The Place of the Mormons in the Religious Emigration of Britain, 1840–1860," *Utah Historical Quarterly* 20, no. 3 (July 1952): 207–18.

"Aspects of Early Victorian Emigration to North America," *Canadian Historical Review* 33, no. 3 (September 1952): 254–64.

"Industrial Emigration in Early Victorian Britain," *Journal of Economic History* 13, no. 2 (Spring 1953): 179–92.

"Thomas Rawlings and David Hoffman: European Salesmen of Western Virginia Lands," *West Virginia History* 15, no. 4 (July 1954): 311–20.

"A Survey of British Emigration to American Lands," attached as appendix to *Journals of Senate and Assembly of State of Nevada* (1955).

"A Welsh Settlement in Scott County, Tennessee," *Tennessee Historical Quarterly* 18, no. 2 (July 1959): 162–68.

"The First Welsh Family to Cross the Wisconsin River," *Wisconsin Magazine of History* 43, no. 2 (Winter 1959–60): 129–32.

"Some Plans for British Immigration to Texas in 1849 and 1850," *Southwestern Historical Quarterly* 63, no. 3 (January 1960): 439–49.

"Sir Charles Wentworth Dilke: A Republican Baronet in Nevada," *Nevada Historical Society Quarterly* 3, no. 4 (Fall 1960): 13–29.

"William Bullock: An American Failure," *Bulletin of the Historical and Philosophical Society of Ohio* 19, no. 2 (April 1961): 144–52.

"Biographical Notes on Sir John Oldmixon," *Notes and Queries* 9, no. 1 (January 1962).

"Socialist Pacifism in the American West During W.W.I.: A Case Study," *Historian* (August 1967).

"Immigrant Themes in Nevada Newspapers," *Nevada Historical Society Quarterly* (Summer 1969):3–46.

"The Foreign-Born Response to Nevada," *Pacific Historical Review* 39 (1970):1–18.

"The Immigrant in Nevada's Short Stories and Biographical Essays," *Nevada Historical Society Quarterly* (Fall 1970):3–15.

"The Foreign Born in Nevada," *Nichibei Forum (Japan-American Forum)* 17 (1971):66–84.

"The Humanities and Rural Nevada," *Proceedings of the Nevada Humanities Development Conference* (1975):8–10.

"An Essay on Amerikanuak," *Nevada Historical Society Quarterly* (Summer 1976):139–44.

"Teaching the Constitution," *Nevada Historical Society Quarterly* (Winter 1977):252–59.

"Humanities: On a Fault Line," *Halcyon: A Journal of the Humanities* (Spring 1979). Republished by the National Endowment for the Humanities, September 1979. Republished by the *American Historical Association Quarterly Newsletter* (December 1980).

"Portraits from an Antique West," *Nevada Historical Society Quarterly* (Fall 1980).

"A Modest Harangue to the National Endowment," *Halcyon: A Journal of the Humanities* (Spring 1982).
"The Maverick and the Cowboy," *Nevada State Historical Society Quarterly* (Spring 1983).
"Cowboy Poetry: The New Folk Art," *Nevada Historical Society Quarterly* (Winter 1986–87).

REVIEWS

The Germans in Texas: A Study in Immigration, by Gilbert Benjamin. For *American Historical Review* (October 1976).
Amerikanuak: Basques in the New World, by William Douglass and Jon Bilbao. For *Pacific Historical Review* (November 1976).
A Trace of Desert Waters: The Great Basin Story, by Samuel Houghton. For *Nevada Historical Society Quarterly* (Fall 1976).
Condemned to the Mines: The Life of Eugene O'Connell, by Thomas Dwyer. For *Nevada Historical Society Quarterly* (Summer 1977).
Nevada: Land of Discovery, by David and Robert Beatty. For *Western Historical Quarterly* (October 1977).
Nevada: A History, by Robert Laxalt. For *Western Historical Quarterly* (July 1978).
Western Carpetbagger: The Extraordinary Memoirs of "Senator" Thomas Fitch, ed. Eric Moody. For *Nevada Historical Society Quarterly* (Fall 1980).
Beltran: Basque Sheepman of the American West, ed. William A. Douglass. For *Nevada Historical Society Quarterly* (Spring 1981).
The British and Irish in Oklahoma, by Patrick J. Blessing. For *Great Plains Quarterly* (Summer 1981).
Sikhs in England: The Development of a Migrant Community, by A. W. Helweg. For *International Migration Review* (Winter 1981–82).
The Mexicans in Oklahoma, by Michael M. Smith. For *New Mexico Historical Review* (Summer 1982).
Quicksand and Cactus: A Memoir of the Southern Mormon Frontier, by Juanita Brooks. For *Pacific Historian* (Spring 1983).
Swedes in Wisconsin, by Frederick Hale. For *Illinois Historical Journal* (Autumn 1984).
Tahoe: An Environmental History, by Douglas H. Strong. For *Montana Magazine of History* (Winter 1985–86).
The Pioneer Swedish Settlements and Swedish Lutheran Churches in America, 1845–1860, by Erick Norelius, trans. Conrad Bergendoff. For *Illinois State Historical Journal* (Spring 1986).

MISCELLANEOUS PUBLICATIONS

Commentary on "A Survey of British Emigration to America's

Lands," attached as appendix to *Journals of Senate and Assembly of State of Nevada* (Carson City, 1955).

Sound Recording: *"Nevada,"* a program of interviews about Nevada, past and present, with M. Wheat, R. R. Elliott, W. S. Shepperson, M. O'Callaghan, and others for broadcast nationally over Public Service Radio (Reno, 1976).

One chapter in *Land and the Pursuit of Happiness* (Los Angeles: University of California Press, 1975).

Commentary on a history of the North Wales slate industry by Jean Lindsay. Published in *Eighteenth Century* (1976).

Commentary on "British Backtrailers: Working-Class Immigrants Return," a chapter in *Immigration Essays* (Rock Island, Ill.: Augustana Press).

Introduction to "The Virginia," Published in *Halcyon: A Journal of the Humanities* (1983).

Commentary on "English Radicals and Reformers 1760–1840," by Edward Royle. Published in *Eighteenth Century* (1984).

Commentary on "Frontiers." Published in *Pacific Historian* 27, no. 2 (1983).

Introduction to *Forty Years in the Wilderness*, by James Hulse (Reno: University of Nevada Press, 1986).

CONTRIBUTORS TO THIS VOLUME

BOARDMAN

As associate professor of English and as a member of the Nevada Humanities Committee, *Phillip C. Boardman* has devoted many years to the humanities. His scholarly interests include Chaucer and King Arthur. The current article arises from his interest in Chaucer and humanism. His most recent publication is *The Legacy of Language: A Tribute to Charlton Laird*, which he edited. He is a member of the faculty at the University of Nevada-Reno.

BRODHEAD

Michael J. Brodhead, who is known for his study of North American naturalists, is professor of history at the University of Nevada-Reno. He co-authored with Paul Russell Cutright *Elliott Coues: Naturalist and Frontier Historian*. Recently Brodhead completed a book-length manuscript on contributions to natural history by army engineers in the nineteenth century. The work presented here is part of a larger research project on the overall contribution of the army to natural history; it was originally delivered as a paper at the annual meeting of the American Military Institute in 1986.

CHUNG

Sue Fawn Chung is associate professor of history at the University of Nevada-Las Vegas. In addition to her historical work she has also served the university as director of international programs. Her scholarly interests include China and the Chinese in the United States. She has published on the Empress Dowager Tz'u-hsi and her present work is part of her research on the Chinese in Nevada.

CLARK

Thomas L. Clark, professor of English at the University of Nevada-Las Vegas, has served as head of the Nevada Language Survey and as president of the American Dialect Society. The study of language has been paramount in his career and he has published studies of the various dialects found in the Midwest and on the use of language in Nevada. His publications include the *Dictionary of Gambling and Gaming.* In this article he discusses language in Nevada as it relates to gambling and the law.

CORAY

Michael S. Coray, associate professor of history at the University of Nevada-Reno, teaches African, Afro-American, and American history. He is working on a book-length comparative study, "Blacks in White Man's Country: Land and Labor in the 'New South' and Colonial Kenya." The present essay is a product of a long-standing interest in the role of racialist thought in nineteenth-century British imperialism. It was influenced by a 1986 Summer Seminar for College Teachers sponsored by the National Endowment for the Humanities at Duke University.

EARL

Phillip I. Earl is Curator of History at the Nevada Historical Society and a well-known historian of Nevada. For over thirteen years he has published a historical column which is currently syndicated in some thirty newspapers. A collection of his articles was published as *This Was Nevada,* and other collections of his articles are forthcoming. His most recent publication is a study of Nevada's miscegenation law.

FOLKES

John Gregg Folkes is lecturer in history at the University of Nevada-Reno. In addition to compiling the bibliography in this book, he has published *Nevada's Newspapers, A Bibliography: A Compilation of Nevada History, 1854–1964.* Folkes teaches American history and U.S. Constitutional history to foreign students.

HARTIGAN

Francis X. Hartigan is professor of history and director of the Honors Program at the University of Nevada-Reno. Among his major publications are *Questions From the Past* (1973), which he co-authored with Wilbur S. Shepperson and Neal Ferguson, and *The Accounts of Alphonse of Poitiers, 1243–1248* (1984). He also is editor and contributor to *MX in Nevada: A Humanistic Perspective* (1980). His major field of interest is medieval Europe and his current research concerns the fears of the end of the world in the year 1000. Hartigan was president of the Rocky Mountain Medieval and Renaissance Association in 1985–86.

HAZEN

James F. Hazen is director of graduate studies and professor of English at the University of Nevada-Las Vegas, where he teaches Victorian and modern literature. He wrote the account of John Henry Newman for the *Dictionary of Literary Biography*. The current article reflects his continuing interest in Newman.

HILDRETH

A specialist in French history and the history of medicine, *Martha L. Hildreth* is author of *Doctors, Bureaucrats and Public Health in France, 1888–1902*. In addition to medicine she is also interested in women in history and the use of computers in historical research. She is a member of the faculty at the University of Nevada-Reno, where she is associate professor of history.

HULSE

Distinguished for his work in European revolutionary movements and Nevada history, *James W. Hulse* is a member of the history department at the University of Nevada-Reno. In recent years his interests have turned to the concept and history of the university. Among his many publications is *The University of Nevada: A Centennial History*. The present article continues his interest in universities, faculties, and academic freedom.

MOEHRING

A specialist in American urban history, *Eugene P. Moehring* is associate professor of history and chairman of the department at the University of Nevada-Las Vegas. His publications include *Public Works and the Patterns of Urban Real Estate Growth in Manhattan, 1835–1894* and the multivolume series *Foreign Travelers in America, 1810–1935*, which he co-edited with Arthur M.

Schlesinger, Jr. The present work is the product of his current interest—the history of Las Vegas.

MORAN

Bruce T. Moran is associate professor of history at the University of Nevada-Reno, where he teaches the history of science and early modern European history. He is author of numerous articles on science and the European court that have appeared in German, Austrian, British, and American journals. His major study of mystical philosophies in Renaissance northern Europe, entitled *The Hermetic World of the German Court*, is now complete and will appear shortly.

RAYMOND

Elizabeth Raymond is assistant professor of history at the University of Nevada-Reno, where she teaches American cultural history. As a student of the history and perception of landscape she has written separately about the nuances of regional identity in both the Prairie Midwest and the Great Basin West. The present article grew out of the logical attempt to compare the two. Its preparation was assisted by a 1986 Summer Seminar for College Teachers sponsored by the National Endowment for the Humanities at Notre Dame University.

RONALD

With a long-standing interest in western literature, *Ann Ronald* has developed a particular interest in the environment and those who write about it. She has published *The New West of Edward Abbey* and *Words for the Wild*. The present article reflects these interests. She is professor of English and acting dean of the Graduate School at the University of Nevada-Reno.

TITUS

A. Costandina Titus is associate professor of political science and director of the Institute for the Study of Ethnic Politics at the University of Nevada-Las Vegas. In addition to other interests, she has become an expert on the significance of atomic testing in Nevada. Her present contribution flows from this interest. She is the author of *Bombs in the Backyard: Atomic Testing and American*

Politics and she has also published on federal-state conflict in Nevada.

UNRUE

Darlene H. Unrue is professor of English at the University of Nevada-Las Vegas. Her wide-ranging interests in literature have led her to study such figures as Poe, Thoreau, D. H. Lawrence, and Katherine Anne Porter. Her recent publications include *Truth and Vision in Katherine Anne Porter's Fiction* and *Understanding Katherine Anne Porter*. In the present article she recalls from neglect an important work of American neoclassical satire.